How to Master CCNP SWITCH

René Molenaar

Copyright © 2015 René Molenaar
All rights reserved.
ISBN: 1492113093
ISBN-13: 978-1492113096
All contents copyright C 2002-2015 by René Molenaar. All rights reserved. No part of this document or the related files may be reproduced or transmitted in

any form, by any means (electronic, photocopying, recording, or otherwise) without the prior written permission of the publisher.

Limit of Liability and Disclaimer of Warranty: The publisher has used its best efforts in preparing this book, and the information provided herein is provided "as is." René Molenaar makes no representation or warranties with respect to the accuracy or completeness of the contents of this book and specifically disclaims any implied warranties of merchantability or fitness for any particular purpose and shall in no event be liable for any loss of profit or any other commercial damage, including but not limited to special, incidental, consequential, or other damages.

Trademarks: This book identifies product names and services known to be trademarks, registered trademarks, or service marks of their respective holders. They are used throughout this book in an editorial fashion only. In addition, terms suspected of being trademarks, registered trademarks, or service marks have been appropriately capitalized, although René Molenaar cannot attest to the accuracy of this information. Use of a term in this book should not be regarded as affecting the validity of any trademark, registered trademark, or service mark. René Molenaar is not associated with any product or vendor mentioned in this book.

Introduction

One of the things I do in life is work as a Cisco Instructor and after teaching CCNP for a few years I've learned which topics people find difficult to understand. This is the reason I created http://gns3vault.com where I offer free Cisco labs and videos to help people learn networking. The problem with networking is that you need to know what you are doing before you can configure anything. Even if you have all the commands you still need to understand *what* and *why* you are typing these commands. I created this book to give you a compact guide which will provide you the answer to *what* and *why* to help you master the CCNP exam.

CCNP is one of the well-known certifications you can get in the world of IT. Cisco is the largest supplier of networking equipment but also famous for its CCNA, CCNP and CCIE certifications. Whether you are new to networking or already in the field for some time, getting a certification is the best way to prove your knowledge on paper! Having said that, I also love routing & switching because it's one of those fields in IT that doesn't change much…some of the protocols you are about to learn are 10 or 20 years old and still alive and kicking!

I have tried to put all the important keywords in **bold**. If you see a **term or concept** in **bold** it's something you should remember / write down and make sure you understand it since its core knowledge for your CCNP!

One last thing before we get started. When I'm teaching I always advise students to create mindmaps instead of notes. Notes are just lists with random information while mindmaps show the relationship between the different items. If you are reading this book on your computer I highly suggest you download "Xmind" which you can get for free here:

http://www.xmind.net/

If you are new to mindmapping, check out "Appendix A – How to create mindmaps" at the end of this book where I show you how I do it.

Enjoy reading my book and good luck getting your CCNP certification!

René Molenaar

P.S. If you have any questions or comments about this book, please let me know:

E-mail: info@gns3vault.com
Website: gns3vault.com
Facebook: facebook.com/gns3vault
Twitter: twitter.com/gns3vault
Youtube: youtube.com/gns3vault

Index

Introduction 4
1. Lab Equipment... 7
2. Campus Network Design 13
3. VLANs (Virtual LANs) 27
4. VTP (VLAN Trunking Protocol) 51
5. Private VLANs... 75
6. STP (Spanning Tree Protocol).. 93
7. Rapid Spanning Tree..159
8. MST (Multiple Spanning Tree) 197
9. Spanning Tree Toolkit 219
10. Etherchannel (Link Aggregation) 241
11. InterVLAN routing..253
12. CEF (Cisco Express Forwarding)...267
13. SPAN and RSPAN...285
14. High Availability / Switch Virtualization 291
15. Gateway Redundancy (VRRP, GLBP, HSRP) 305
16. Switch Security 337
17. Final Thoughts 377
Appendix A – How to create mindmaps 379

1. Lab Equipment

Before we are going to start on our switching journey we are going to take a look at the lab equipment you will need. GNS3 is a very useful tool but it only supports the emulation of routers using Dynamips. You are unable to emulate a switch in GNS3 like a Cisco Catalyst 2950, 2960, 3550, 3560 or 3750.

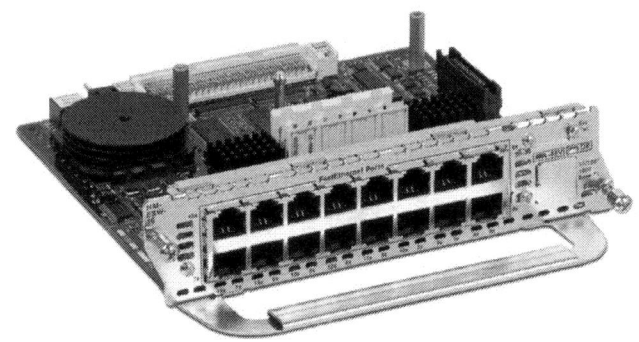

Courtesy of Cisco Systems, Inc. Unauthorized use not permitted.

The closest you can get to emulate a switch in GNS3 is inserting this NM16-ESW Etherswitch module in your virtual router.

It adds 16 switch ports to your virtual router and supports basic trunking and spanning-tree features. Unfortunately this module is very limited and it doesn't cut it for CCNP SWITCH labs.

Since GNS3 1.x support has been added for IOU (IOS on Unix) but the switching images that are required are not freely available to the public.

Cisco released their own emulator that supports IOS, IOS XE, IOS XR and NX-OS. It's called VIRL and it's up for purchase right here:

http://virl.cisco.com/

The personal edition costs $199 and to be honest, but at time of writing it doesn't support switching. You might want to check it though, see if a future version has added support for it.

So what is the best option? My advice is to buy some **real physical switches**. Don't be scared...I'm not going to advise you to buy ultra-high tech brand new switches! We are going to buy used Cisco switches that are easy to find and they won't burn a hole in your wallet...

"If I had eight hours to chop down a tree, I'd spend six hours sharpening my ax"
~Abraham Lincoln

How to Master CCNP SWITCH

Without further ado...here are our candidates:

Courtesy of Cisco Systems, Inc. Unauthorized use not permitted.

Cisco Catalyst 2950: This is a layer 2 switch that can do all the vlan, trunking and spanning-tree stuff we need for CCNP SWITCH.

Courtesy of Cisco Systems, Inc. Unauthorized use not permitted.

Cisco Catalyst 3550: This is a layer 3 switch. It offers pretty much the same features as the 2950 but it also supports routing.

If you look at eBay you can find the Cisco Catalyst 2950 for around $50, the Cisco Catalyst 3550 is around $100. It doesn't matter if you buy the 8, 24 or 48 port model. Not too bad right? Keep in mind you can sell them once you are done with CCNP without losing (much) money.

1. Lab Equipment

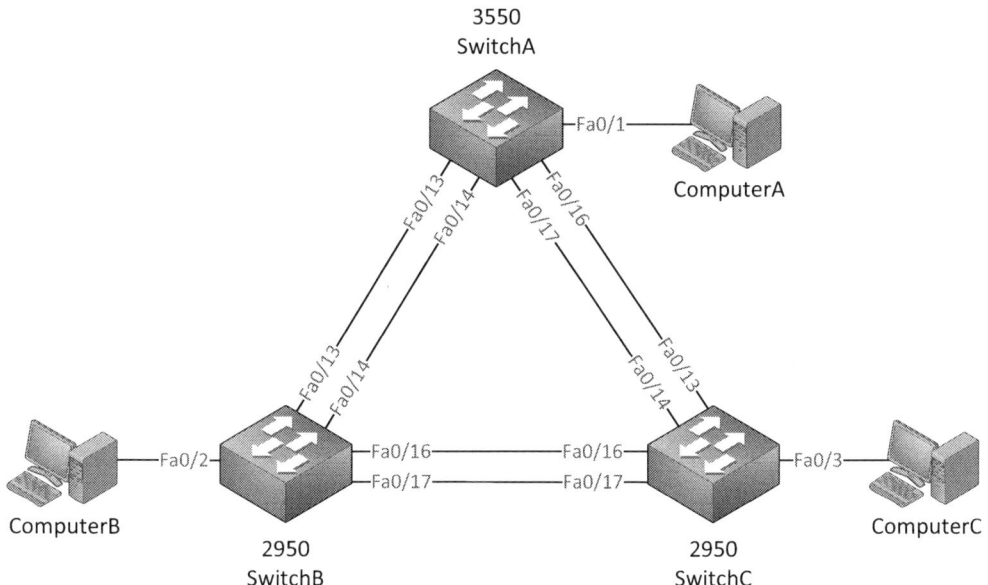

This is the topology I will be using throughout (most of) the book and I advise you to build it so you can do all the labs in this book by yourself. I did my best so you don't have to re-cable that often. We need one Cisco Catalyst 3550 because it can do routing; the other two Cisco Catalyst 2950 switches are sufficient for all the other stuff.

What about other switch models? Anything else we can use? Sure!
- The Cisco Catalyst 2960 is the successor of the Cisco Catalyst 2950, it's a great layer 2 switch but more expensive.
- The Cisco Catalyst 3560 is the successor of the Cisco Catalyst 3550, it also offers layer 3 features and it's quite more expensive…around $300 on eBay.
- The Cisco Catalyst 3750 is a layer 3 switch that is suitable for CCNP SWITCH.

I don't recommend buying the Cisco Catalyst 2960 because it doesn't offer anything extra compared to the Cisco Catalyst 2950 that'll help you beat the exam.

The Cisco Catalyst 3560 does offer two features that might justify buying it:

- It can do **private vlans** which is a CCNP SWITCH topic. It's impossible to configure it on a Cisco Catalyst 3550! It's a small topic though and personally I don't think it's worth the additional $200 just to configure private vlans.
- **QoS (Quality of Service)** is different on the Cisco Catalyst 3560 compared to the Cisco Catalyst 3550. If you intend to study QoS in the future I would recommend buying this switch. You won't need it for the CCNP SWITCH exam.

How to Master CCNP SWITCH

The Cisco catalyst 3750 switch supports Stackwise which is a (minor) topic on the CCNP SWITCH exam now. You will need two 3750 switches to test it but I don't think it's worth the extra money just for this feature.

Are there any switches that you should NOT buy?

- Don't buy the Cisco Catalyst 2900XL switch; you'll need at least the Cisco Catalyst 2950 switch. Many features are not supported on the Cisco Catalyst 2900XL switch.
- Don't buy the Cisco Catalyst 3500XL switch, same problem as the one above.

If you studied CCNA you probably know the difference between straight-through and crossover cables. Modern switches and network cards support auto-sensing so it really doesn't matter what kind of cable you use.

If you are going to connect these older switches to each other make sure you **buy crossover cables** since they don't support auto-sensing!

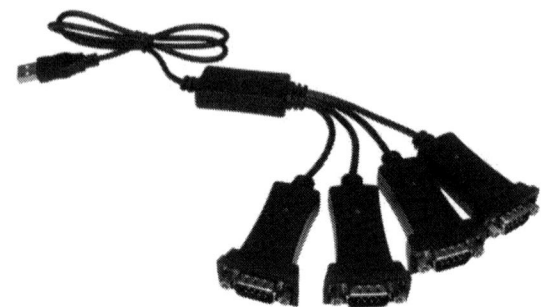

I also like to use one of these. It's a USB connector with 4x RS-232 serial connectors you can use for your blue Cisco console cables to connect to your switches.

It saves the hassle of plugging and unplugging your console cable between your switches.

The one I'm using is from KÖNIG and costs around $30. Google for "USB 4x RS-232" and you should be able to find something similar.

In my topology picture you saw that I have three computers connected to my switches. For most of the labs I'm only using those computers to generate some traffic or send some pings so don't worry if you only have one computer, you can also use a cisco router if you have one.

1. Lab Equipment

2. Campus Network Design

In this chapter we will take a look at the "building blocks" of a well designed campus network. What is a "campus" network anyway?

A campus network is an enterprise network (hundreds or thousands of users) where we have one or more LANs in one or multiple buildings. Everything is geographically close to each other so we typically use Ethernet (and Wireless) for connectivity. Typically the company owns everything on the campus...hardware, cabling, etc.

To support this many users we require a lot of switchports which means a lot of switches. We need a physical design to connect these switches to each other and also a good logical design to make it work.

Let's take a look at some networks to see how they "grow" and some design issues that we will face. Let's start with a simple example:

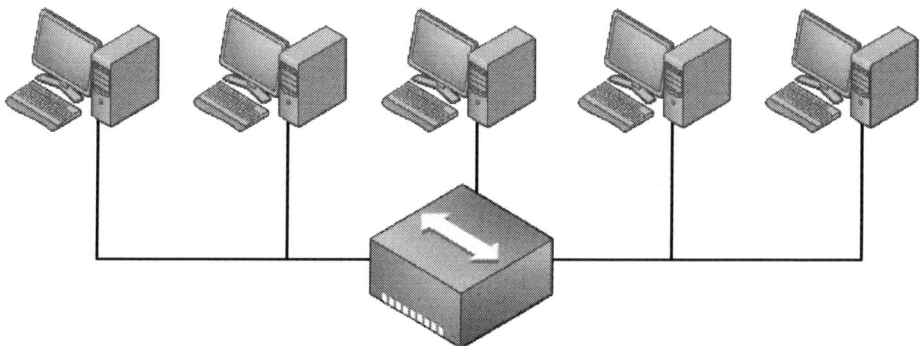

Back in the old days we used to have hubs so we had half-duplex networks. When one host would transmit something, the others had to wait. When two hosts would send at the same time we'd get a collision and we used the CSMA/CD algorithm to deal with these collisions. Everything that is connected to the hub is a **single collision domain**. Also, whenever a host sends a broadcast everyone will receive it. There's only one **broadcast domain**.

In this example there are only 5 hosts so it's no problem but when you have hundreds of hosts the collisions and broadcasts will have a serious impact on the available bandwidth. To reduce the size of the collision domain we started using bridges and then switches. The broadcast domains can be reduced by using VLANs. Here's an example:

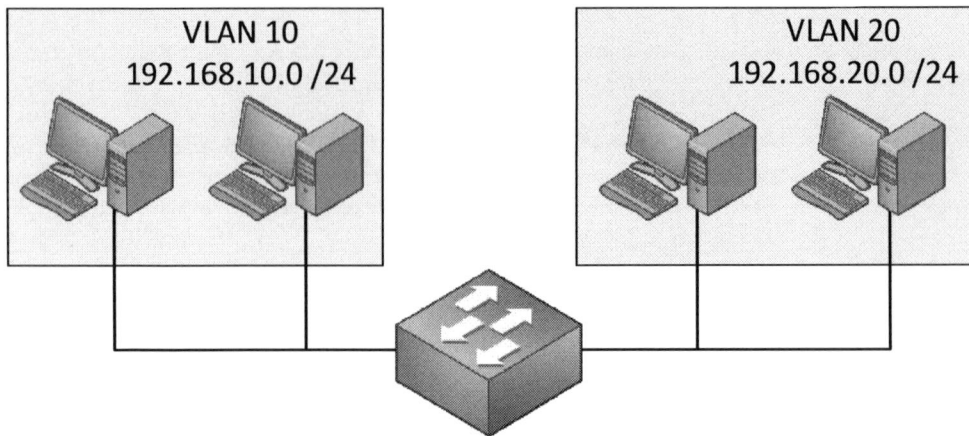

Now we have a single switch and some hosts that are in different VLANs. Each port on the switch is a collision domain and each VLAN is a separate broadcast domain. If we use a multilayer switch, the VLANs will be able to communicate with each other (more on this in the InterVLAN routing chapter).

Once this network starts growing we might now have enough switchports anymore on a single switch. You could add a second switch and connect it to the first one but what if we add a third of fourth switch? How are we going to connect them to each other?

If you don't think about your design beforehand, you might end up with something like this:

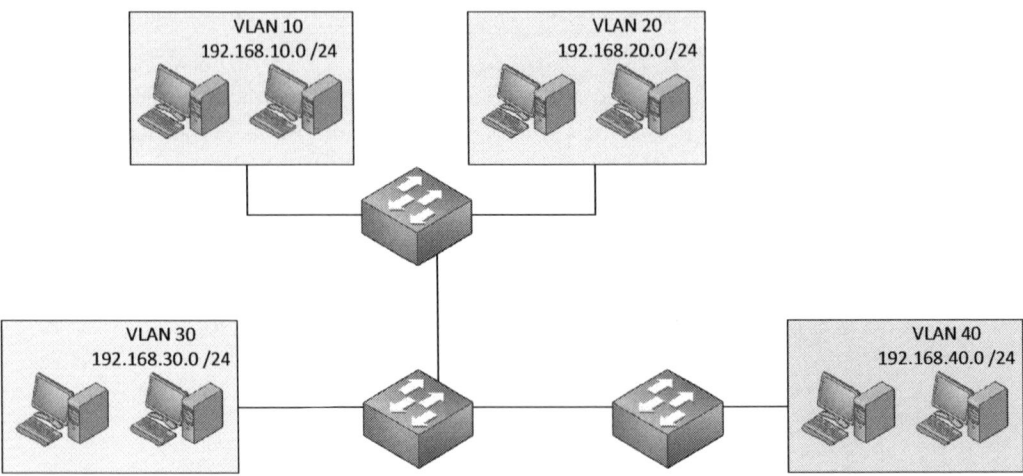

Switches, hosts, cables and VLANs everywhere. Before we know it, the network is one big spaghetti.

We need a network that is easy to maintain, offers high availability, scalability and is able to quickly respond to changes in the topology. To achieve all of

2. Campus Network Design

this, Cisco has a **hierarchical approach to network design** where we have **multiple layers** in the network. Here's an example:

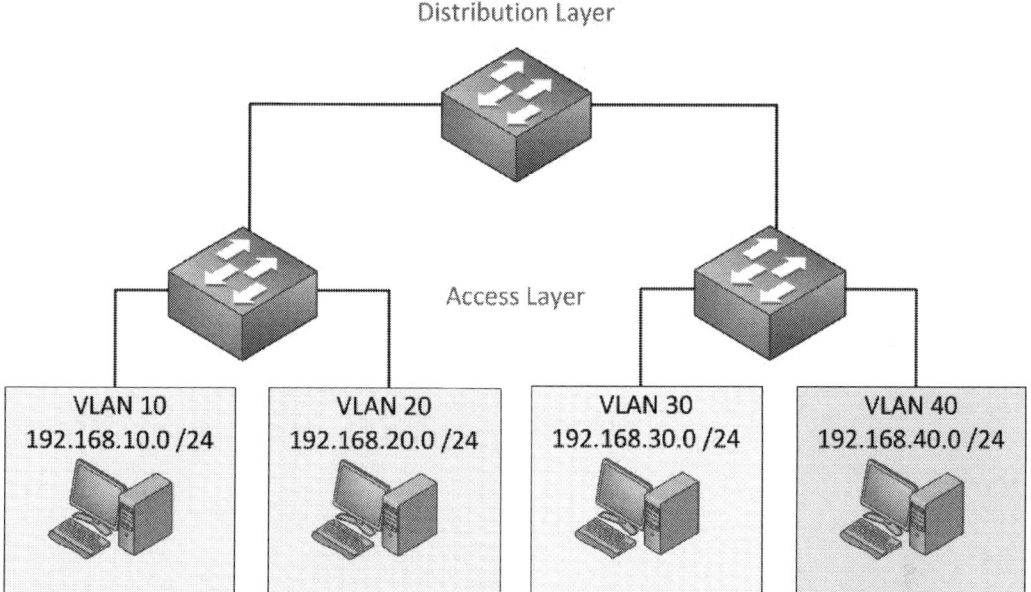

In this design we have an access layer and distribution layer. The access layer is close to the end users, these are switches that we use to connect computers, laptops, access points and more. The distribution layer is used to aggregate all the different access layer switches.

The advantage of this hierarchical network design is that it's scalable. When the campus grows and we get more users, building and floors then we can add multiple distribution layers.

When this happens, we'll add another layer:

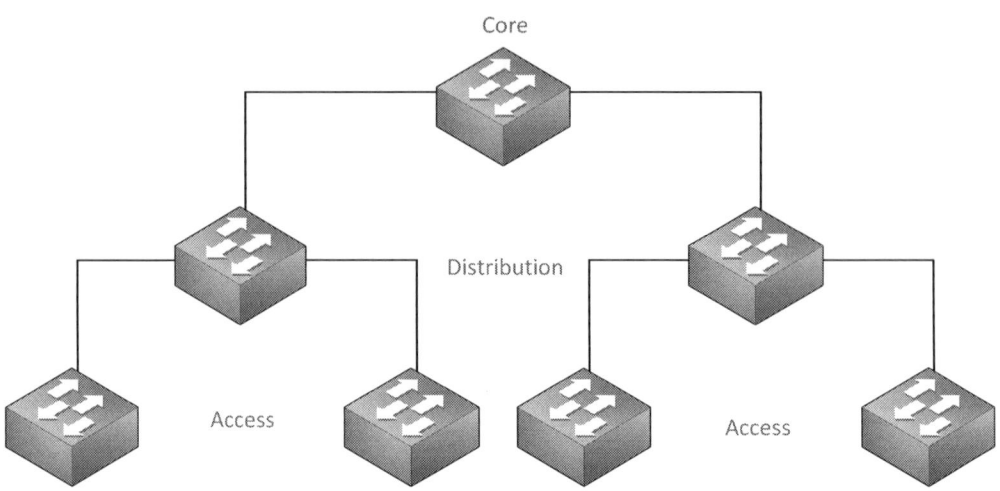

The core layer aggregates all the different distribution layer switches. This design also makes our traffic paths predictable and easy to visualize. Basically there are three different traffic flows:

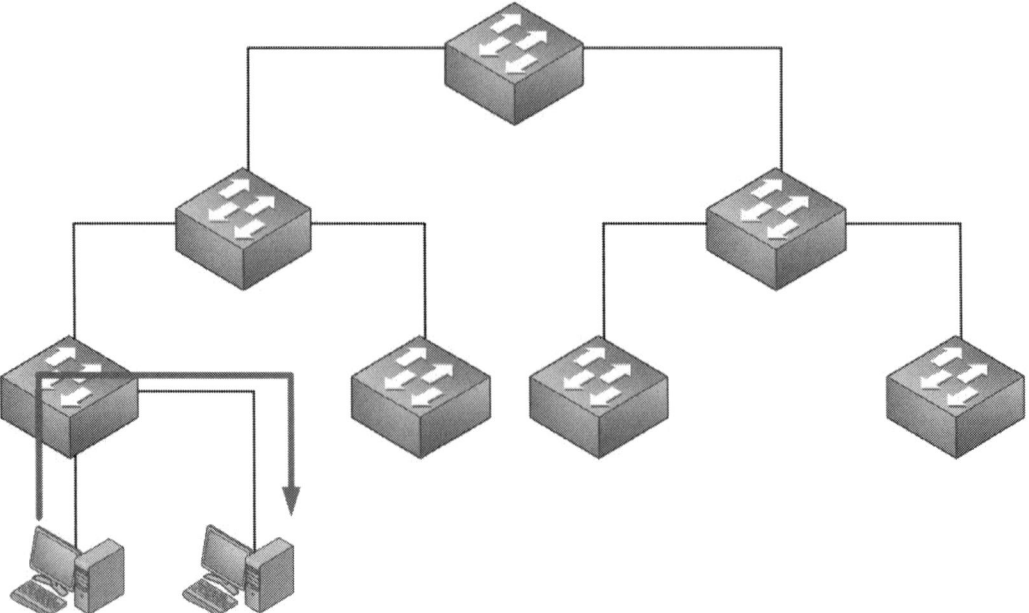

All traffic **starts at the access layer** and if needed it will move up the distribution and core layer. In this example the traffic is **local**; it doesn't leave the access layer switch. This could be traffic between two hosts within the same VLAN. Here's another example:

2. Campus Network Design

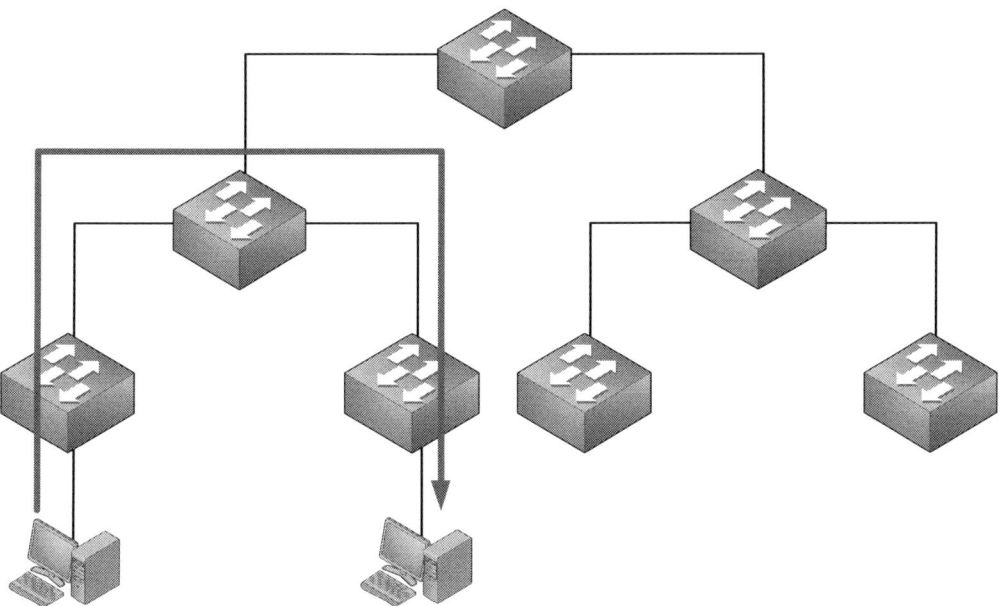

Traffic between hosts that are on different access layer switches has to cross the distribution layer switch. Finally, sometimes we have to cross the core layer:

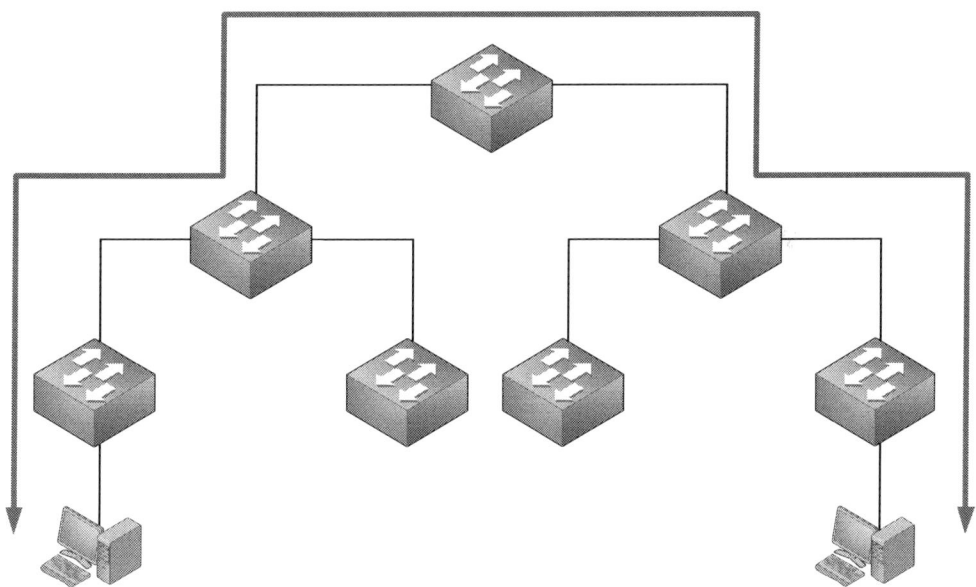

Each of the layers has a different function and requirements.

Let's discuss each layer:

Access Layer:

The main function of the access layer is to connect all end devices like computers, laptops, access points, IP phones, printers, etc.

- We require a lot of switchports to connect all these end devices. This means the price per switchport should be low, for this reason we typically use layer 2 switches on the access layer.
- Depending on our traffic flows, traffic from the access layer has to go towards the distribution layer so we might require multiple uplinks.
- POE (Power over Ethernet): if you have IP phones or wireless access points then we'll need POE on the access layer.
- QoS features: If we use VoIP then we might need switches that support QoS to give precedence to VoIP traffic.
- Security: The access layer is the "entry" of our network. You might want to protect DHCP, ARP and spanning-tree from malicious devices that are connected to the access layer.

Distribution Layer:

The distribution layer connects the access and core layer together. Since this is where we aggregate the access layer, we need sufficient bandwidth up to the core layer. Typically the distribution layer is where we use routing, this is where we terminate the VLANs from the access layer.

- We use routing on the distribution layer so we need switches that are capable of high throughput routing performance.
- Multiple redundant uplinks to the access and core layer. If a distribution layer switch fails, multiple access layer switches might lose connectivity.
- QoS features: just like the access layer, we might need QoS to give preference to certain traffic like VoIP.
- Security: we use access-lists on the distribution layer to filter certain inter-VLAN traffic.

2. Campus Network Design

Core Layer:

The core aggregates all the different distribution layer switches, this is the backbone of our network. This means the switches in the core layer should be able to handle all traffic from the distribution layer switches. Also, if the core fails all connectivity between distribution layers will be impossible.

- High bandwidth / throughput required.
- High availability / redundancy required. Think about multiple links, redundant power supplies, and redundant supervisors (CPU).
- QoS features: Qos is end-to-end in the campus so we also need support in the core.
- No packet manipulation: We don't configure access-lists or make changes to packets in the core.

Sometimes the size of the network is too small to justify a separate core layer. In this case we the function of the core and distribution layer is combined into a single layer. This is also called the **collapsed core**.

The three layer model is pretty straight forward but we haven't talked about real redundancy yet. In all of the models I showed you so far we only had one link between the switches. Let's look at redundancy between the access and distribution layer first:

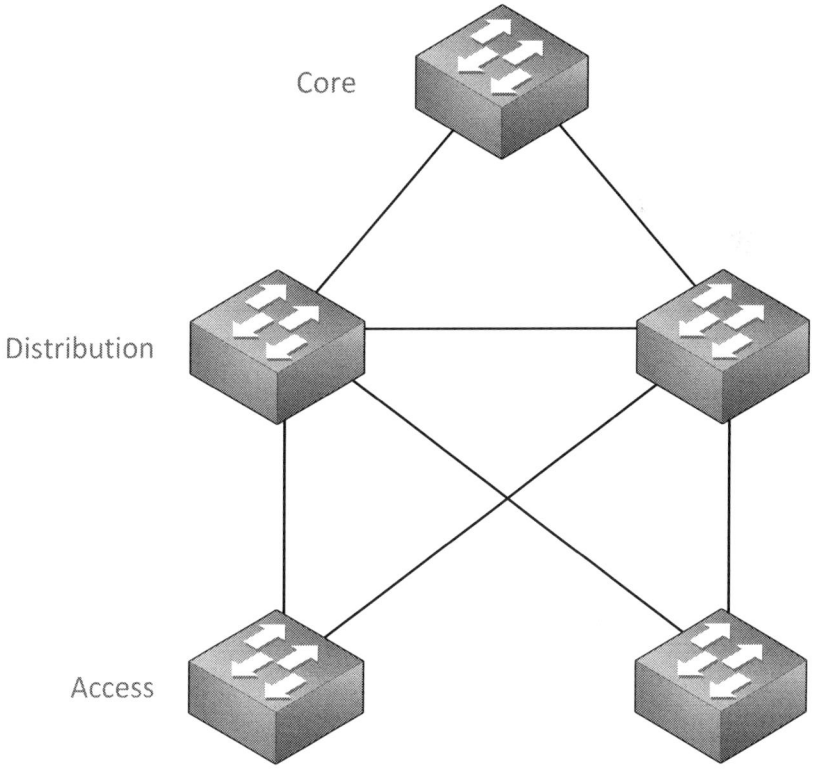

19

In this example we added some redundancy. Instead of a single distribution layer switch we now have two switches and each access layer switch is connected to both distribution layer switches. The link in between the distribution layer switches is required so that they can reach each other directly (needed for routing protocols). We still have one problem...there's no redundancy in the core yet. Let's add it:

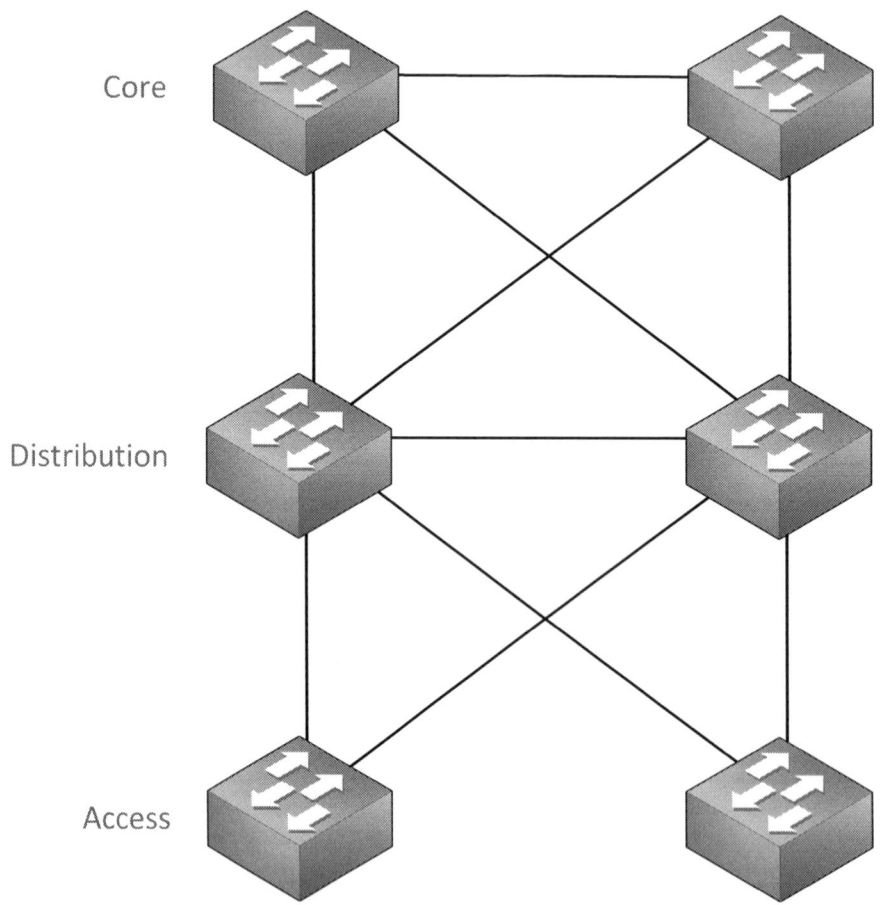

The core is the backbone and the most important part of the network so we need redundancy here. We'll add another switch and redundant links to our distribution layer switches.

The design above is still pretty simple with only a few switches. What if we add more distribution layers and multiple access layers? Should we connect all distribution layer switches to the others? What about the access layer switches? Should we connect them to all distribution layer switches?

When the network grows, we create so-called **switch blocks**. A switch block are two distribution layer switches with access layer switches beneath them.

2. Campus Network Design

Each switch block is then connected to the core layer:

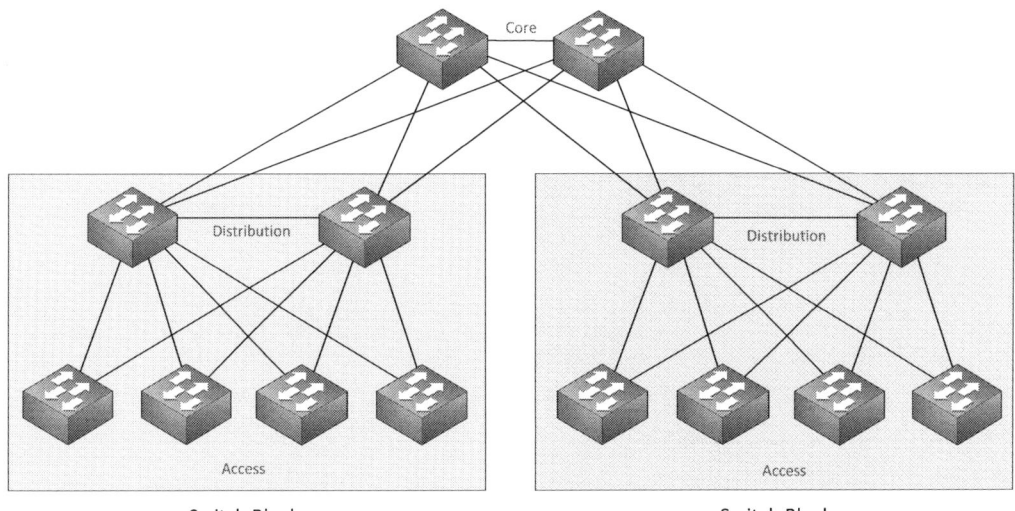

This is a nice and tidy hierarchical network diagram. You can see two switch blocks, each switch block has two distribution layer switches and there are multiple access layer switches. There is no connectivity between the different switch blocks, only with the core layer. Switch blocks are also used to connect (large) server farms to the core layer.

The size of a switch block really depends on the number of users and the applications / traffic types. Network analysis is required to see what traffic patterns there are on the network and what kind of bandwidth requirements we have.

So far we mostly talked about physical topologies, what about logical topologies? I explained earlier that we typically use layer 2 on the access layer and layer 3 (routing) on the distribution layer but there's more to this story. Let's look at some examples:

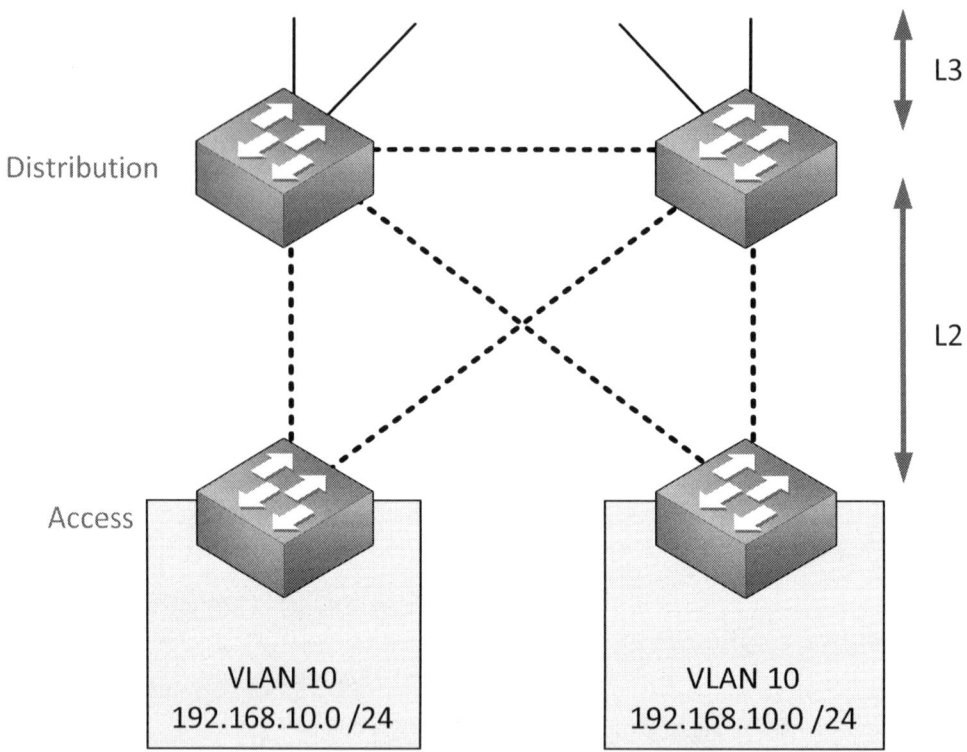

In this example we have a switch block with two distribution layer switches and two access layer switches. There's one VLAN that is used on both access layer switches.

Between the distribution and access layer switches we use layer 2, from the distribution to the core layer we use layer 3. The distribution layer switches are used as the routers for the devices behind the access layer switches.

Because VLAN 10 is used on both access layer switches, the link between the two distribution layer switches HAS to be a layer 2 link as well. There are two reasons for this:

- If one of the uplinks from the access to the distribution layer fails, VLAN 10 could become isolated.
- The switches on the distribution layer will use a protocol to create a virtual gateway IP address. We need layer two connectivity for this (you'll learn about this in the gateway redundancy chapter).

The dashed lines indicate where we need VLAN 10 which is on every link...this will work but it's not optimal. We will require spanning-tree to create a loop-free topology and the entire switch block becomes a single point of failure. If a host starts sending a lot of broadcast frames then the entire switch block is affected.

2. Campus Network Design

A better solution would be this:

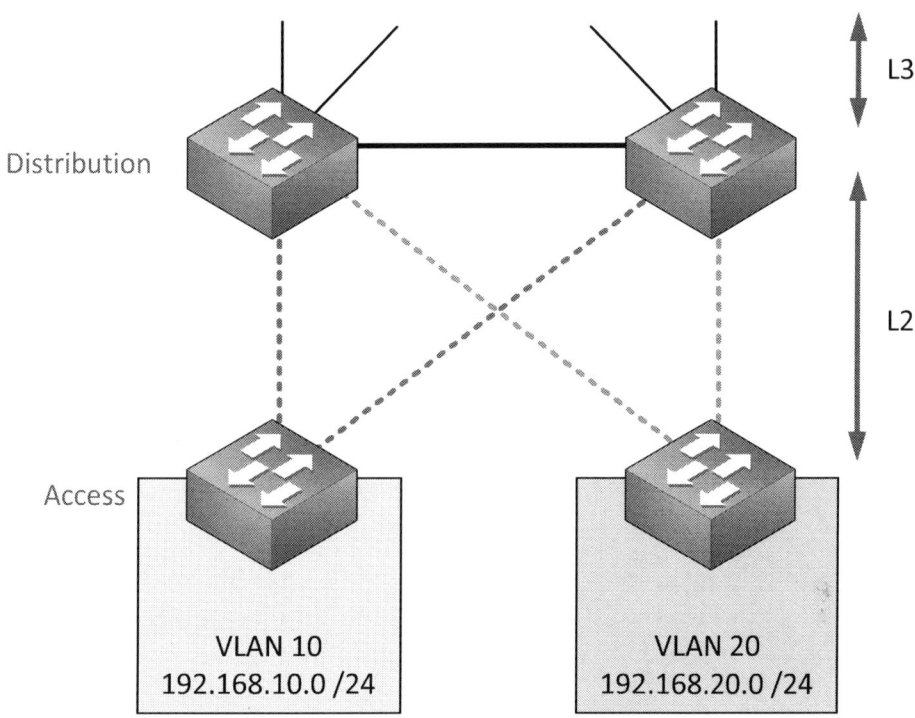

Each access layer switch now has a single VLAN, this has a number of advantages. First of all, there is no redundant topology within VLAN 10 or 20 now so we don't have to rely on spanning-tree to create a loop-free topology...this makes the switch block more stable.

Also each VLAN can use both uplinks which allow load balancing. The link between the two distribution layer switches is now a layer 3 link.

The third option is to use routing everywhere:

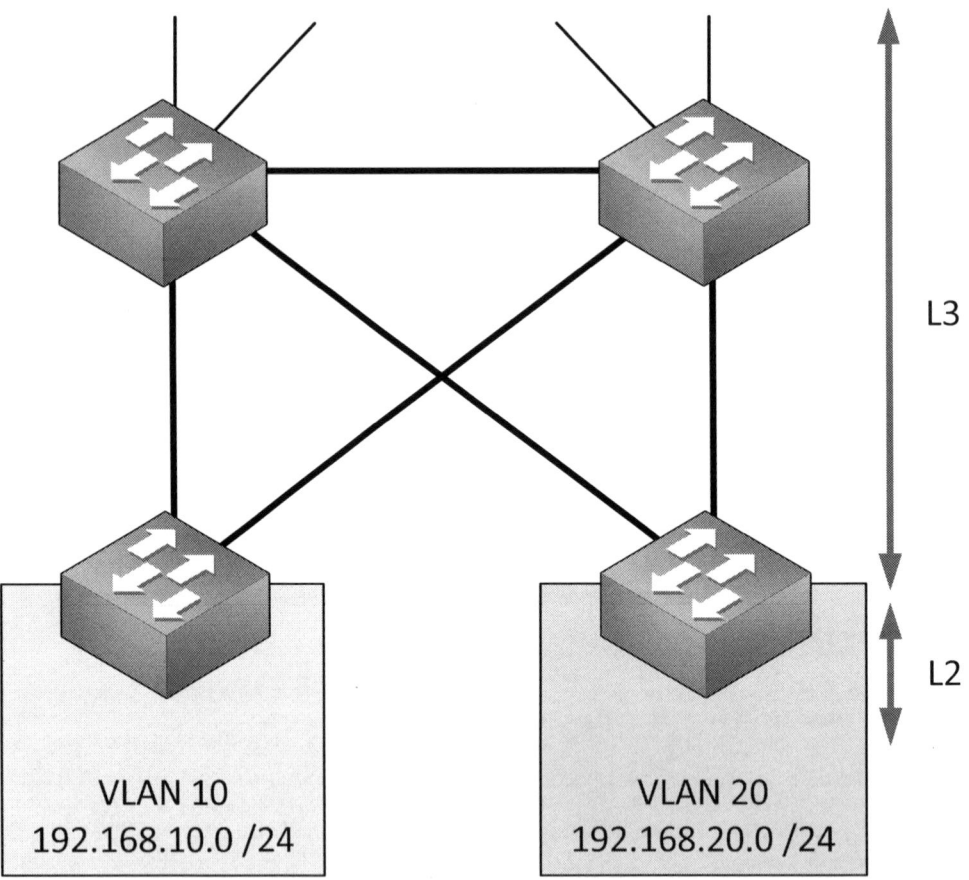

We can push layer 3 even to the access layer if the switches support it. The advantage is that routing protocols typically have a fast(er) convergence time and you can use all available links. OSPF and EIGRP allow load balancing.

You have now seen the different layers and the options we have for layer 2 / 3 in the campus. Here are some of the key points that you should remember from this story:

- Each layer should have a pair of switches for redundancy.
- Each switch should be connected to the upper layer with two links for redundancy.
- Connect each pair of distribution layer switches together with a link, this is needed for some (routing) protocols.
- Don't connect the access layer switches to each other.
- Don't extend VLANs above the distribution layer, this is our boundary. From the distribution layer up to the core layer we only use routing.
- If possible, don't span VLANs over multiple access layer switches.
- The core layer is simple...we don't do any packet manipulation but we require high bandwidth, availability and scalability since it aggregates all the distribution layers.

2. Campus Network Design

This should give you an idea about the different layers and what a (large) campus network design looks like. What about the switches? What models should we use in each layer? Here's an overview with switches that are commonly used in the access layer:

Model	Port Density	Uplinks	Backplane	Features
2960-X	384 (8x 48-port switches stacked)	2x 10GE or 4x GE	80 Gbps	RIP, OSPF, POE+
3650	432 (9x 48-port switches stacked)	4x 10GE or 2x GE	160 Gbps	All routing protocols, POE+, wireless controller
3850	432 (9x 48-port switches stacked)	4x 10GE or 4x GE	480 Gbps	All routing protocols, POE+, wireless controller integrated
4500E	384 (8x 48-port modules in chassis)	Up to 12x 10GE per module	928 Gbps	Dual supervisors, all routing protocols, integrated wireless controller.

And here are some commonly used switches used in the distribution and/or core layer:

Model	Port Density	Backplane	Features
4500-X	80x 10GE	1.6 Tbps	Dual chassis VSS redundancy
4500-E	96x 10GE or 384x GE	928 Gbps	Dual supervisors
6807-XL	40x 40Gbps, 160x GE and 480x GE	22.8 Tbps	Dual supervisors, dual chassis VSS redundancy

If you want to see the actual specifications then I would recommend to take a look at the Cisco.com website. Later in the book we will discuss some of the redundancy features of these switches.

This is the end of the chapter and now you should have an idea what the building blocks of a campus network look like. Cisco has an entire track for design so this really is just an overview of a campus network design.

3. VLANs (Virtual LANs)

In this chapter we will take a look at the configuration of VLANs, Trunks, Etherchannels and Private VLANs. If you studied CCNA then the first part of this chapter should be familiar to you.

Let's start off by looking at a picture of a network:

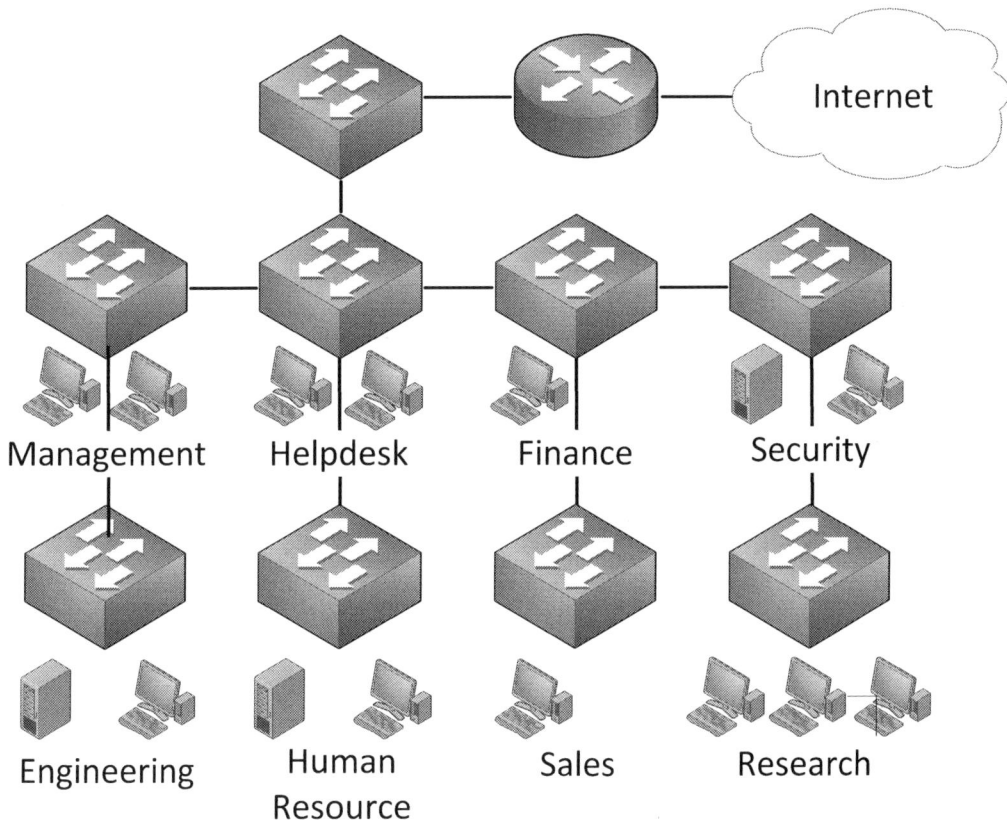

Look at this picture for a minute, we have many departments and each department has its own switch. Users are grouped physically together and are connected to their switch. What do you think of it? Does this look like a good network design? If you are unsure let me ask you some questions to think about:

- What happens when a computer connected to the Research switch sends a broadcast like an ARP request?
- What happens when the Helpdesk switch fails?
- Will our users at the Human Resource switch have fast network connectivity?
- How can we implement security in this network?

Now let me explain why this is a bad network design. If any of our computers sends a broadcast what will our switches do? They flood it! This means that a single broadcast frame will be flooded on this entire network. This also happens when a switch hasn't learned about a certain MAC address, the frame will be flooded.

If our helpdesk switch would fail this means that users from Human Resource are "isolated" from the rest and unable to access other departments or the internet, this applies to other switches as well. Everyone has to go through the Helpdesk switch in order to reach the Internet which means we are sharing bandwidth, probably not a very good idea performance-wise.

Last but not least, what about security? We could implement port-security and filter on MAC addresses but that's not a very secure method since MAC addresses are very easy to spoof. VLANs are one way to solve our problems.

Two more questions I'd like to ask you to refresh your knowledge:

- How many collision domains do we have here?
- How many broadcast domains do we have here?

Each port on a switch is a separate collision domain so in this picture we have a LOT of collision domains...more than 20.

What about broadcast domains? If a computer from the Sales switch would send a broadcast frame we know that all other switches will forward it.

Routers don't forward broadcast frames so they effectively "limit" our broadcast domain. Of course on the right side of our router where we have an Internet connection this would be another broadcast domain...so we have 2 broadcast domains here.

3. VLANs (Virtual LANs)

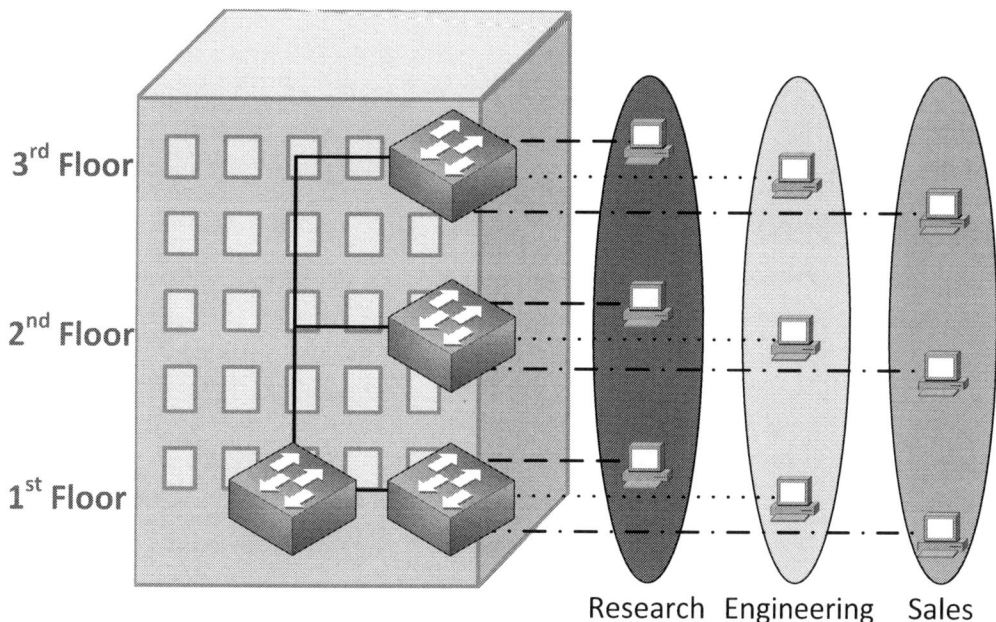

When you work with switches you have to keep in mind there's a big difference between physical and logical topology. Physical is just the way our cables are connected while logical is how we have configure things 'virtually'. In the example above we have 4 switches and I have created 3 VLANs called Research, Engineering and Sales. A VLAN is a Virtual LAN so it's like having a "switch inside a switch".

What are the advantages of using vlans?

- A VLAN is a single broadcast domain which means that if a user in the research VLAN sends a broadcast frame only users in the same VLAN will receive it.
- Users are only able to communicate within the same VLAN (unless you use a router).
- Users don't have to be grouped physically together, as you can see we have users in the Engineering vlan sitting on the 1st, 2nd and 3rd floor.

In my example I grouped different users in different VLANs but you can also use VLANs to separate different traffic types. Perhaps you want to have all printers in one VLAN, all servers in a VLAN and all the computers in another. What about VoIP? Put all your Voice over IP phones in a separate Vlan so its traffic is separated from other data (more on VoIP later!)

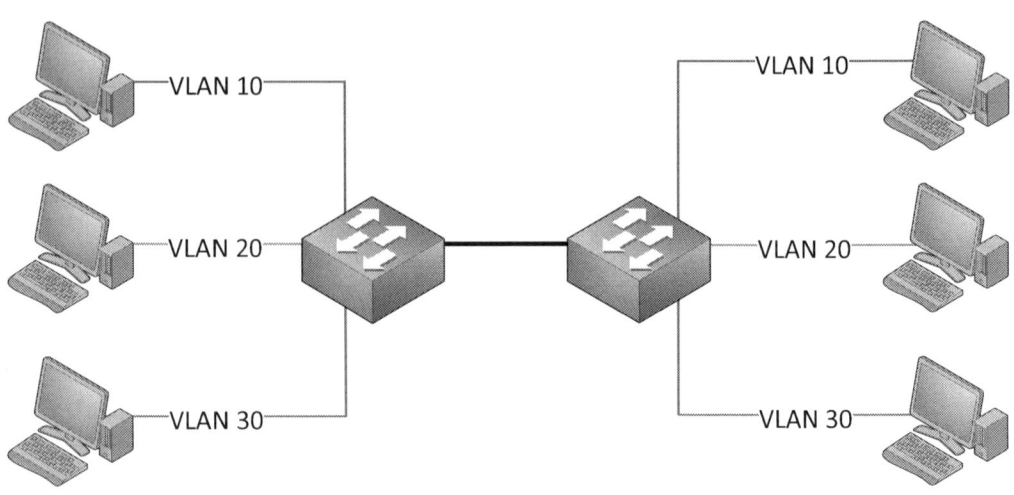

Let's take a look at the example above. There are three computers on each side belonging to three different VLANs. VLAN 10,20 and 30. There are two switches connecting these computers to each other.

Our switches will forward traffic but how do they know to which vlan our traffic belongs?

Let's take a look at an Ethernet frame:

| Preamble | SOF | Dest | Source | Length | 802.2 Header/Data | FCS |

Do you see any field where we can specify to which vlan our Ethernet frame belongs? Well there isn't! That's why we need a **trunking protocol** to help us.

Between switches we are going to create a **trunk.** A trunk connection is simply said an interface that carries multiple VLANs.

3. VLANs (Virtual LANs)

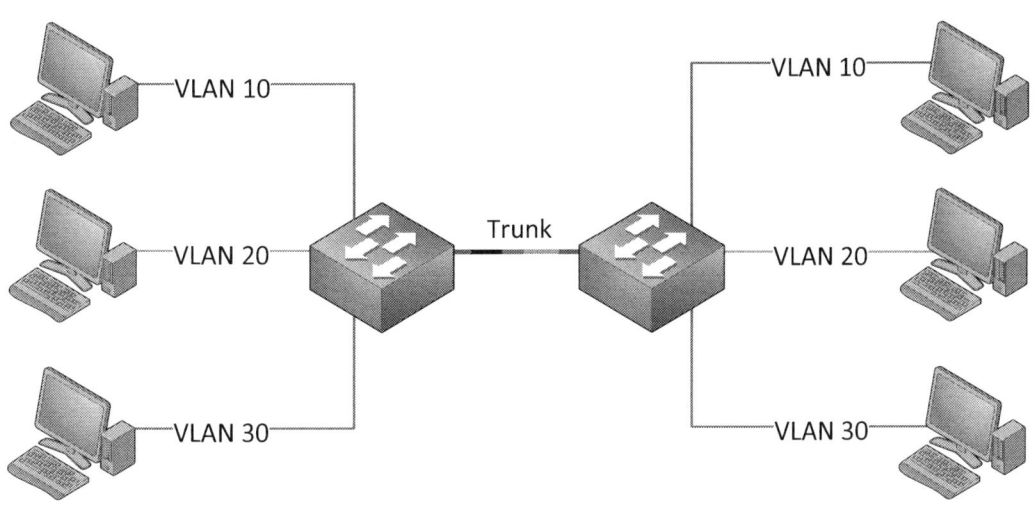

There are **two trunking protocols** we can use:

- **IEEE 802.1Q**: An open standard that is supported on switches from many vendors and most NICs.
- **Cisco ISL (Inter-Switch Link)**: An old Cisco proprietary protocol that is only supported on some Cisco switches. If you bought some old Cisco catalyst 2950 switches you'll notice they only support 802.1Q.

802.1Q FRAME

Let's start by looking at 802.1Q. In the picture you see an example of an 802.1Q Ethernet frame. As you can see it's the same as a normal Ethernet frame but we have added a **tag** in the middle (that's the blue field). In our tag you will find a "**VLAN identifier**" which is the VLAN to which this Ethernet frame belongs.

This is how switches know to which VLAN our traffic belongs. There's also a field called "**Priority**" which is used for QoS (Quality of Service). Keep in mind 802.1Q is a **standard** and supported on switches from many different vendors. You can also use 802.1Q on many NICs.

31

How to Master CCNP SWITCH

ISL FRAME

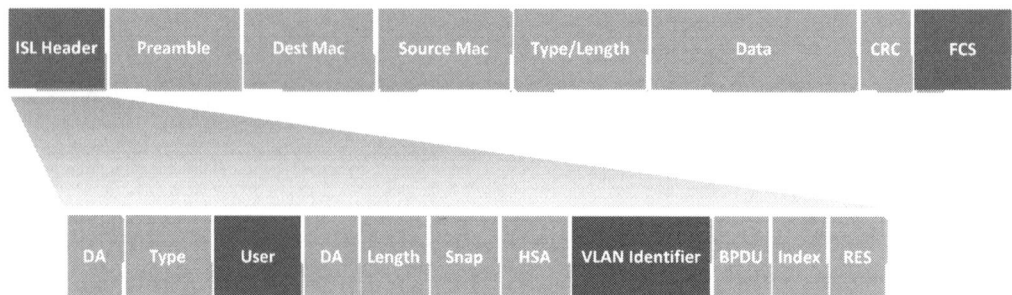

This is an example of an ISL Frame. The difference between 802.1Q and ISL is that 802.1 **tags** the Ethernet frame while ISL **encapsulates** the Ethernet Frame. You can see in the picture that ISL adds a new header in front of the Ethernet Frame and it adds a FCS (Frame Check Sequence). The header contains the "VLAN identifier" so we know to which VLAN this Ethernet Frame belongs. The **user** field is used for QoS (Quality of Service).

*If you studied CCNA you might recall the "native VLAN". On a Cisco switch this is VLAN 1 by default. The difference between 802.1Q and ISL concerning the native VLAN is that 802.1Q will **not tag** the native VLAN while ISL **does tag** the native VLAN.*

Enough theory for now, let's take a look at the configuration of VLANs and trunks.

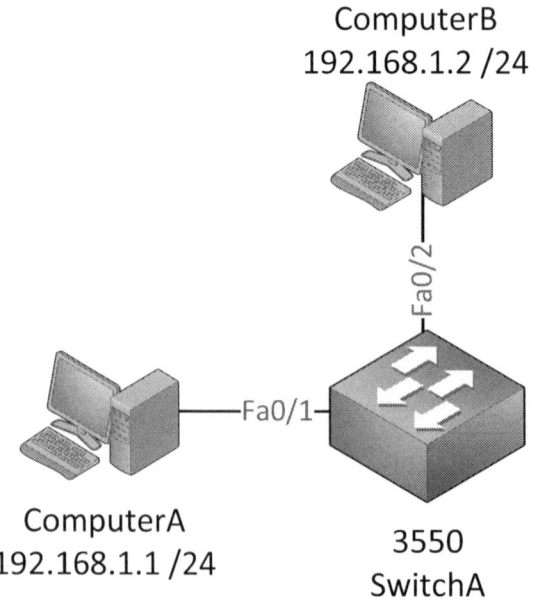

Let's start with a simple example. ComputerA and ComputerB are connected to SwitchA.

32

3. VLANs (Virtual LANs)

First we will look at the default VLAN configuration on SwitchA:

```
SwitchA#show vlan

VLAN Name                             Status    Ports
---- -------------------------------- --------- -------------------
1    default                          active    Fa0/1, Fa0/2,
Fa0/3, Fa0/4
                                                Fa0/5, Fa0/6,
Fa0/7, Fa0/8
                                                Fa0/9, Fa0/10,
Fa0/11, Fa0/12
                                                Fa0/13, Fa0/14,
Fa0/15, Fa0/22
                                                Fa0/23, Fa0/24,
Gi0/1, Gi0/2
1002 fddi-default                     act/unsup
1003 token-ring-default               act/unsup
1004 fddinet-default                  act/unsup
1005 trnet-default                    act/unsup
```

Interesting...VLAN 1 is the default VLAN and you can see that all interfaces are parked in VLAN 1.

*VLAN information is not saved in the running-config or startup-config but in a separate file called **vlan.dat** on your flash memory. If you want to delete the VLAN information you should delete this file by typing **delete flash:vlan.dat**.*

I configured an IP address on ComputerA and ComputerB so they are in the same subnet.

```
C:\Documents and Settings\ComputerA>ping 192.168.1.2

Pinging 192.168.1.2 with 32 bytes of data:

Reply from 192.168.1.2: bytes=32 time<1ms TTL=128
Reply from 192.168.1.2: bytes=32 time<1ms TTL=128
Reply from 192.168.1.2: bytes=32 time<1ms TTL=128
Reply from 192.168.1.2: bytes=32 time<1ms TTL=128

Ping statistics for 192.168.1.2:
    Packets: Sent = 4, Received = 4, Lost = 0 (0% loss),
Approximate round trip times in milli-seconds:
    Minimum = 0ms, Maximum = 0ms, Average = 0ms
```

Even with the default switch configuration ComputerA is able to reach ComputerB. Let's see if I can create a new VLAN for ComputerA and ComputerB:

33

```
SwitchA(config)#vlan 50
SwitchA(config-vlan)#name Computers
SwitchA(config-vlan)#exit
```

This is how you create a new VLAN. If you want you can give it a name but this is optional. I'm calling my VLAN "Computers".

```
SwitchA#show vlan

VLAN Name                             Status    Ports
---- -------------------------------- --------- -------------------
1    default                          active    Fa0/1, Fa0/2,
Fa0/3, Fa0/4
                                                Fa0/5, Fa0/6,
Fa0/7, Fa0/8
                                                Fa0/9, Fa0/10,
Fa0/11, Fa0/12
                                                Fa0/13, Fa0/14,
Fa0/15,
                                                Fa0/23, Fa0/24,
Gi0/1, Gi0/2
50   Computers                        active
```

VLAN 50 was created on SwitchA and you can see that it's active. However no ports are currently in VLAN 50. Let's see if we can change this...

```
SwitchA(config)interface fa0/1
SwitchA(config-if)#switchport mode access
SwitchA(config-if)#switchport access vlan 50
```

```
SwitchA(config)interface fa0/2
SwitchA(config-if)#switchport mode access
SwitchA(config-if)#switchport access vlan 50
```

First I will configure the switchport in **access mode** with the **"switchport mode access" command.**

3. VLANs (Virtual LANs)

By using the "**switchport access vlan**" command we can move our interfaces to another VLAN.

```
SwitchA#show vlan

VLAN Name                            Status     Ports
---- -------------------------------- --------- -------------------
1    default                          active    Fa0/3, Fa0/4
                                                Fa0/5, Fa0/6,
Fa0/7, Fa0/8
                                                Fa0/9, Fa0/10,
Fa0/11, Fa0/12
                                                Fa0/13, Fa0/14,
Fa0/15,
                                                Fa0/23, Fa0/24,
Gi0/1, Gi0/2
50   Computers                        active    Fa0/1, Fa0/2
```

Excellent! Both computers are now in VLAN 50. Let's verify our configuration by checking if they can ping each other:

```
C:\Documents and Settings\ComputerA>ping 192.168.1.2

Pinging 192.168.1.2 with 32 bytes of data:

Reply from 192.168.1.2: bytes=32 time<1ms TTL=128
Reply from 192.168.1.2: bytes=32 time<1ms TTL=128
Reply from 192.168.1.2: bytes=32 time<1ms TTL=128
Reply from 192.168.1.2: bytes=32 time<1ms TTL=128

Ping statistics for 192.168.1.2:
    Packets: Sent = 4, Received = 4, Lost = 0 (0% loss),
Approximate round trip times in milli-seconds:
    Minimum = 0ms, Maximum = 0ms, Average = 0ms
```

Our computers are able to reach each other within VLAN 50.

Besides pinging each other we can also use another show command to verify our configuration:

```
SwitchA#show interfaces fa0/1 switchport
Name: Fa0/1
Switchport: Enabled
Administrative Mode: static access
Operational Mode: static access
Administrative Trunking Encapsulation: negotiate
Operational Trunking Encapsulation: native
Negotiation of Trunking: Off
Access Mode VLAN: 50 (Computers)
Trunking Native Mode VLAN: 1 (default)
```

```
SwitchA#show interfaces fa0/2 switchport
Name: Fa0/1
Switchport: Enabled
Administrative Mode: static access
Operational Mode: static access
Administrative Trunking Encapsulation: negotiate
Operational Trunking Encapsulation: native
Negotiation of Trunking: Off
Access Mode VLAN: 50 (Computers)
Trunking Native Mode VLAN: 1 (default)
```

By using the "show interfaces switchport" command we can see that the **operational mode** is "static access" which means it's in access mode. We can also verify that the interface is assigned to VLAN 50.

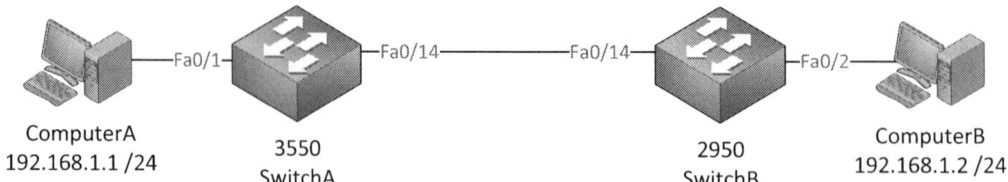

ComputerA
192.168.1.1 /24

3550
SwitchA

2950
SwitchB

ComputerB
192.168.1.2 /24

Let's continue our VLAN adventure by adding SwitchB to the topology. I also moved ComputerB from SwitchA to SwitchB.

```
SwitchB(config)#vlan 50
SwitchB(config-vlan)#name Computers
SwitchB(config-vlan)#exit
```

```
SwitchB(config)#interface fa0/2
SwitchB(config-if)#switchport access vlan 50
```

I just created VLAN 50 on SwitchB and the interface connected to ComputerB is assigned to VLAN 50.

Next step is to create a trunk between SwitchA and SwitchB:

3. VLANs (Virtual LANs)

```
SwitchA(config)#interface fa0/14
SwitchA(config-if)#switchport mode trunk
Command rejected: An interface whose trunk encapsulation is
"Auto" can not be configured to "trunk" mode.
```

```
SwitchB(config)#interface fa0/14
SwitchB(config-if)#switchport mode trunk
Command rejected: An interface whose trunk encapsulation is
"Auto" can not be configured to "trunk" mode.
```

I try to change the interface to trunk mode with the **"switchport mode trunk"** command. Depending on the switch model you might see the same error as me. If we want to change the interface to trunk mode we need to change the trunk encapsulation type. Let's see what options we have:

```
SwitchA(config-if)#switchport trunk encapsulation ?
  dot1q      Interface uses only 802.1q trunking encapsulation
when trunking
  isl        Interface uses only ISL trunking encapsulation when
trunking
  negotiate  Device will negotiate trunking encapsulation with
peer on
             interface
```

Aha...so this is where you can choose between 802.1Q and ISL. By default our switch will negotiate about the trunk encapsulation type.

```
SwitchA(config-if)#switchport trunk encapsulation dot1q
```

```
SwitchB(config-if)#switchport trunk encapsulation dot1q
```

Let's change it to 802.1Q by using the **"switchport trunk encapsulation"** command.

```
SwitchA#show interfaces fa0/14 switchport
Name: Fa0/14
Switchport: Enabled
Administrative Mode: dynamic auto
Operational Mode: static access
Administrative Trunking Encapsulation: dot1q
```

```
SwitchB#show interfaces fa0/14 switchport
Name: Fa0/14
Switchport: Enabled
Administrative Mode: dynamic auto
Operational Mode: static access
Administrative Trunking Encapsulation: dot1q
```

As you can see the trunk encapsulation is now 802.1Q.

```
SwitchA(config)#interface fa0/14
SwitchA(config-if)#switchport mode trunk
```

```
SwitchB(config)#interface fa0/14
SwitchB(config-if)#switchport mode trunk
```

Now I can successfully change the switchport mode to trunk.

```
SwitchA#show interfaces fa0/14 switchport
Name: Fa0/14
Switchport: Enabled
Administrative Mode: trunk
Operational Mode: trunk
Administrative Trunking Encapsulation: dot1q
Operational Trunking Encapsulation: dot1q
```

```
SwitchB#show interfaces fa0/14 switchport
Name: Fa0/14
Switchport: Enabled
Administrative Mode: trunk
Operational Mode: trunk
Administrative Trunking Encapsulation: dot1q
Operational Trunking Encapsulation: dot1q
```

We can confirm we have a trunk because the operational mode is "dot1q". Let's try if ComputerA and ComputerB can reach each other:

```
C:\Documents and Settings\ComputerA>ping 192.168.1.2

Pinging 192.168.1.2 with 32 bytes of data:

Reply from 192.168.1.2: bytes=32 time<1ms TTL=128
Reply from 192.168.1.2: bytes=32 time<1ms TTL=128
Reply from 192.168.1.2: bytes=32 time<1ms TTL=128
Reply from 192.168.1.2: bytes=32 time<1ms TTL=128

Ping statistics for 192.168.1.2:
    Packets: Sent = 4, Received = 4, Lost = 0 (0% loss),
Approximate round trip times in milli-seconds:
    Minimum = 0ms, Maximum = 0ms, Average = 0ms
```

Excellent! ComputerA and ComputerB can reach each other! Does this mean we are done?

3. VLANs (Virtual LANs)

Not quite yet...there's more I want to show to you:

```
SwitchB#show vlan

VLAN Name                            Status      Ports
---- -------------------------------- --------- ----------------
1    default                          active     Fa0/1, Fa0/3,
Fa0/4, Fa0/5
                                                 Fa0/6, Fa0/7,
Fa0/8, Fa0/9
                                                 Fa0/10, Fa0/11,
Fa0/12, Fa0/13
                                                 Fa0/15, Fa0/22,
Fa0/23, Fa0/24
                                                 Gi0/1, Gi0/2
50   Computers                        active     Fa0/2
```

First of all, if we use the show vlan command we don't see the Fa0/14 interface.

This is completely normal because the show vlan command **only shows interfaces in access mode** and **no trunk interfaces**.

```
SwitchB#show interface fa0/14 trunk

Port        Mode          Encapsulation  Status        Native vlan
Fa0/14      on            802.1q         trunking      1

Port        Vlans allowed on trunk
Fa0/14      1-4094

Port        Vlans allowed and active in management domain
Fa0/14      1,50

Port        Vlans in spanning tree forwarding state and not pruned
Fa0/14      50
```

The **show interface trunk** is very useful. You can see if an interface is in trunk mode, which trunk encapsulation protocol it is using (802.1Q or ISL) and what the native VLAN is. We can also see that VLAN 1 – 4094 are allowed on this trunk.

We can also see that currently only VLAN 1 (native VLAN) and VLAN 50 are active.

Last but not least you can see something which VLANs are in the forwarding state for spanning-tree (more on spanning-tree later!).

```
SwitchB(config-if)#switchport trunk allowed vlan ?
  WORD    VLAN IDs of the allowed VLANs when this port is in trunking mode
  add     add VLANs to the current list
  all     all VLANs
  except  all VLANs except the following
  none    no VLANs
  remove  remove VLANs from the current list
```

For security reasons it might be a good idea not to allow all VLANs on your trunk link. We can change this by using the **switchport trunk allowed vlan** command.

```
SwitchB(config-if)#switchport trunk allowed vlan remove 1-4094
SwitchB(config-if)#switchport trunk allowed vlan add 1-50
```

I just removed all allowed VLANs from the trunk and now only VLAN 1 – 50 are allowed.

```
SwitchB#show interface fa0/14 trunk

Port      Mode       Encapsulation   Status      Native vlan
Fa0/14    on         802.1q          trunking    1

Port      Vlans allowed on trunk
Fa0/14    1-50
```

Verify this by using the show interface trunk command.

3. VLANs (Virtual LANs)

```
SwitchB#show interfaces trunk

Port         Mode              Encapsulation      Status            Native
vlan
Fa0/14       on                802.1q             trunking          1
Fa0/16       auto              n-isl              trunking          1

Port         Vlans allowed on trunk
Fa0/14       1-50
Fa0/16       1-4094

Port         Vlans allowed and active in management domain
Fa0/14       1,50
Fa0/16       1,50

Port         Vlans allowed and active in management domain
Fa0/20       1,50
Fa0/21       1,50

Port         Vlans in spanning tree forwarding state and not
pruned
Fa0/14       50
Fa0/16       50
```

You can also use the **show interfaces trunk** command to get an overview of all your trunk interfaces. Besides our Fa0/14 interface you can see I got a couple of other interfaces that are in trunk mode.

Besides "access" and "trunk" mode we also have two "dynamic" methods.

Let me show you what I mean:

```
SwitchB#show interface fa0/2 switchport
Name: Fa0/2
Switchport: Enabled
Administrative Mode: static access
Operational Mode: static access
```

An interface can be in access mode or in trunk mode. The interface above is connected to ComputerB and you can see that the operational mode is "static access" which means it's in access mode.

```
SwitchB#show interfaces fa0/14 switchport
Name: Fa0/14
Switchport: Enabled
Administrative Mode: trunk
Operational Mode: trunk
```

This is our trunk interface which is connected to SwitchA. You can see the operational mode is trunk mode.

41

```
SwitchB(config-if)#switchport mode ?
  access        Set trunking mode to ACCESS unconditionally
  dot1q-tunnel  set trunking mode to TUNNEL unconditionally
  dynamic       Set trunking mode to dynamically negotiate
access or trunk
  private-vlan  Set private-vlan mode
  trunk         Set trunking mode to TRUNK unconditionally
```

If I go to the interface configuration to change the switchport mode you can see I have more options than access or trunk mode. There is also a **dynamic** method. Don't worry about the other options for now.

```
SwitchB(config-if)#switchport mode dynamic ?
  auto       Set trunking mode dynamic negotiation parameter to AUTO
  desirable  Set trunking mode dynamic negotiation parameter to DESIRABLE
```

We can choose between **dynamic auto** and **dynamic desirable.** Our switch will automatically find out if the interface should become an access or trunk port. So what's the difference between dynamic auto and dynamic desirable? Let's find out!

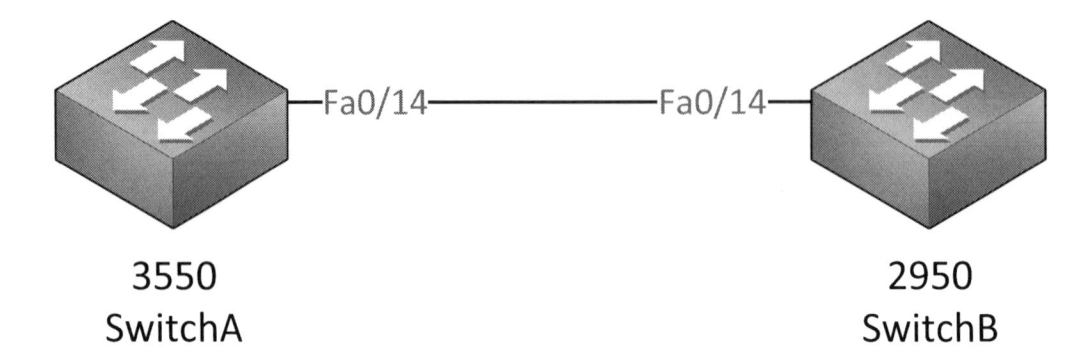

```
                    ──Fa0/14────────Fa0/14──

         3550                                    2950
        SwitchA                                 SwitchB
```

I'm going to play with the switchport mode on SwitchA and SwitchB and we'll see what the result will be.

```
SwitchA(config)#interface fa0/14
SwitchA(config-if)#switchport mode dynamic auto
```

```
SwitchA(config)#interface fa0/14
SwitchB(config-if)#switchport mode dynamic auto
```

First I'll change both interfaces to dynamic auto.

3. VLANs (Virtual LANs)

Let's check this:

```
SwitchA(config-if)#do show interface f0/14 switchport
Name: Fa0/14
Switchport: Enabled
Administrative Mode: dynamic auto
Operational Mode: static access
```

```
SwitchB(config-if)#do show interface f0/14 switchport
Name: Fa0/14
Switchport: Enabled
Administrative Mode: dynamic auto
Operational Mode: static access
```

Our administrative mode is dynamic auto and as a result we now have an access port.

```
SwitchA(config)#interface fa0/14
SwitchA(config-if)#switchport mode dynamic desirable
```

```
SwitchB(config)#interface fa0/14
SwitchB(config-if)#switchport mode dynamic desirable
```

```
SwitchA#show interfaces fa0/14 switchport
Name: Fa0/14
Switchport: Enabled
Administrative Mode: dynamic desirable
Operational Mode: trunk
SwitchB#show interfaces fa0/14 switchport
Name: Fa0/14
Switchport: Enabled
Administrative Mode: dynamic desirable
Operational Mode: trunk
```

Once we change both interfaces to dynamic desirable we end up with a trunk link. What do you think will happen if we mix the switchport types? Maybe dynamic auto on one side and dynamic desirable on the other side?

How to Master CCNP SWITCH

Let's find out!

```
SwitchA(config)#interface fa0/14
SwitchA(config-if)#switchport mode dynamic desirable
```

```
SwitchB(config)#interface fa0/14
SwitchB(config-if)#switchport mode dynamic auto
```

```
SwitchA#show interfaces f0/14 switchport
Name: Fa0/14
Switchport: Enabled
Administrative Mode: dynamic desirable
Operational Mode: trunk
```

```
SwitchB#show interfaces fa0/14 switchport
Name: Fa0/14
Switchport: Enabled
Administrative Mode: dynamic auto
Operational Mode: trunk
```

It seems our switch has a strong desire to become a trunk. Let's see what happens with other combinations!

```
SwitchA(config)#interface fa0/14
SwitchA(config-if)#switchport mode dynamic auto
```

```
SwitchB(config)#interface fa0/14
SwitchB(config-if)#switchport mode trunk
```

```
SwitchA#show interfaces f0/14 switchport
Name: Fa0/14
Switchport: Enabled
Administrative Mode: dynamic auto
Operational Mode: trunk
```

```
SwitchB#show interfaces fa0/14 switchport
Name: Fa0/14
Switchport: Enabled
Administrative Mode: trunk
Operational Mode: trunk
```

Dynamic auto will prefer to become an access port but if the other interface has been configured as trunk we will end up with a trunk.

```
SwitchA(config)#interface fa0/14
SwitchA(config-if)#switchport mode dynamic auto
```

```
SwitchB(config)#interface fa0/14
SwitchB(config-if)#switchport mode access
```

3. VLANs (Virtual LANs)

```
SwitchA#show interfaces f0/14 switchport
Name: Fa0/14
Switchport: Enabled
Administrative Mode: dynamic auto
Operational Mode: static access
```

```
SwitchB#show interfaces fa0/14 switchport
Name: Fa0/14
Switchport: Enabled
Administrative Mode: static access
Operational Mode: static access
```

Configuring one side as dynamic auto and the other one as access and the result will be an access port.

```
SwitchA(config)#interface fa0/14
SwitchA(config-if)#switchport mode dynamic desirable
```

```
SwitchB(config)#interface fa0/14
SwitchB(config-if)#switchport mode trunk
```

```
SwitchA#show interfaces f0/14 switchport
Name: Fa0/14
Switchport: Enabled
Administrative Mode: dynamic desirable
Operational Mode: trunk
```

```
SwitchB#show interfaces fa0/14 switchport
Name: Fa0/14
Switchport: Enabled
Administrative Mode: trunk
Operational Mode: trunk
```

Dynamic desirable and trunk mode offers us a working trunk.

What do you think will happen if I set one interface in access mode and the other one as trunk? Doesn't sound like a good idea but let's push our luck:

```
SwitchA(config)#interface fa0/14
SwitchA(config-if)#switchport mode access
SwitchB(config)#interface fa0/14
SwitchB(config-if)#switchport mode trunk
```

```
SwitchA#show interfaces f0/14 switchport
Name: Fa0/14
Switchport: Enabled
Administrative Mode: static access
Operational Mode: trunk
```

```
SwitchB#show interfaces fa0/14 switchport
Name: Fa0/14
Switchport: Enabled
Administrative Mode: trunk
Operational Mode: trunk
```

```
SwitchA#
%SPANTREE-7-RECV_1Q_NON_TRUNK: Received 802.1Q BPDU on non trunk
FastEthernet0/14 VLAN1.
%SPANTREE-7-BLOCK_PORT_TYPE: Blocking FastEthernet0/14 on
VLAN0001. Inconsistent port type.
%SPANTREE-2-UNBLOCK_CONSIST_PORT: Unblocking FastEthernet0/14 on
VLAN0001. Port consistency restored.
```

As soon as I change the switchport mode I see these spanning-tree error messages on SwitchA. Spanning-tree receives an 802.1Q BPDU on an access port and doesn't like it. The interface goes into blocking mode for VLAN 1 and only 14 seconds later its unblocking VLAN 1 again. Does this mean we have connectivity even though this smells fishy?

```
SwitchA#show interfaces fa0/14 switchport
Name: Fa0/14
Switchport: Enabled
Administrative Mode: static access
Operational Mode: static access
```

```
SwitchB#show interfaces fa0/14 switchport
Name: Fa0/14
Switchport: Enabled
Administrative Mode: trunk
Operational Mode: trunk
```

This doesn't look good; let's continue by looking at the trunk…

```
SwitchA#show interfaces fa0/14 trunk

Port          Mode              Encapsulation  Status        Native
vlan
Fa0/14        off               802.1q         not-trunking  1

Port          Vlans allowed on trunk
Fa0/14        1

Port          Vlans allowed and active in management domain
Fa0/14        1

Port          Vlans in spanning tree forwarding state and not
pruned
Fa0/14        1
```

3. VLANs (Virtual LANs)

```
SwitchB#show interfaces fa0/14 trunk

Port         Mode              Encapsulation  Status      Native
vlan
Fa0/14       on                802.1q         trunking    1

Port         Vlans allowed on trunk
Fa0/14       1-50

Port         Vlans allowed and active in management domain
Fa0/14       1,50

Port         Vlans in spanning tree forwarding state and not
pruned
Fa0/14       50
```

Now this looks interesting. It seems SwitchA only allows VLAN 1 and SwitchB allows VLAN 1-50.

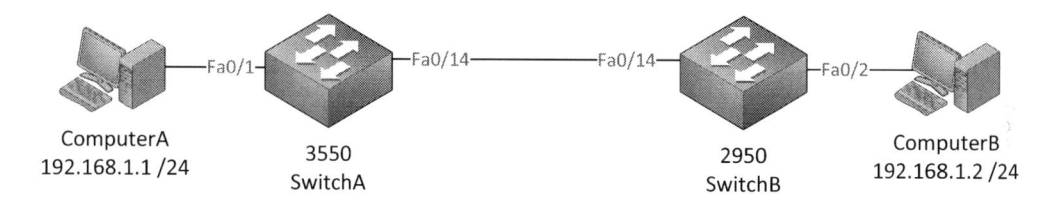

ComputerA 192.168.1.1 /24 —Fa0/1— 3550 SwitchA —Fa0/14— —Fa0/14— 2950 SwitchB —Fa0/2— ComputerB 192.168.1.2 /24

ComputerA and ComputerB are still in VLAN 50. Let's see if they can still reach each other:

```
C:\Documents and Settings\ComputerA>ping 192.168.1.2

Pinging 192.168.1.2 with 32 bytes of data:

Request timed out.
Request timed out.
Request timed out.
Request timed out.

Ping statistics for 192.168.1.2:
    Packets: Sent = 4, Received = 0, Lost = 4 (100% loss),
```

No luck here...ComputerA and ComputerB are unable to reach each other. What if I move them to VLAN 1?

```
SwitchA(config)#interface fa0/1
SwitchA(config-if)#switchport access vlan 1
```

```
SwitchB(config)#interface fa0/2
SwitchB(config-if)#switchport access vlan 1
```

```
C:\Documents and Settings\ComputerA>ping 192.168.1.2

Pinging 192.168.1.2 with 32 bytes of data:

Reply from 192.168.1.2: bytes=32 time<1ms TTL=128
Reply from 192.168.1.2: bytes=32 time<1ms TTL=128
Reply from 192.168.1.2: bytes=32 time<1ms TTL=128
Reply from 192.168.1.2: bytes=32 time<1ms TTL=128

Ping statistics for 192.168.1.2:
    Packets: Sent = 4, Received = 4, Lost = 0 (0% loss),
Approximate round trip times in milli-seconds:
```

Excellent now it is working! So even though we have a mismatch between the switchport types we still have **limited connectivity** because **only VLAN 1 is allowed**.

Let me give you an overview of the different switchport modes and the result:

	Trunk	Access	Dynamic Auto	Dynamic Desirable
Trunk	Trunk	Limited	Trunk	Trunk
Access	Limited	Access	Access	Access
Dynamic Auto	Trunk	Access	Access	Trunk
Dynamic Desirable	Trunk	Access	Trunk	Trunk

Make sure you know the result of these combinations if you plan to do the CCNP SWITCH exam. I always like to think that the switch has a strong "desire" to become a trunk. Its wish will always be granted unless the other side has been configured as access port. The "A" in dynamic auto stands for "Access", it would like to become an access port but only if the other side also is configured as dynamic auto or access mode.

I recommend **never to use** the "dynamic" types. I want my interfaces to be in trunk OR access mode and I like to make the decision myself. Keep in mind that dynamic auto is the **default** on most modern switches which means it's possible to form a trunk with any interface on your switch automatically. Some of the older switches use dynamic desirable as the default. This is a security issue you should deal with! If I walk into your company building I could connect my laptop to any wall jack, boot up GNS3, form a trunk to your switch and I'll have access to all your VLANs…doesn't sound like a good idea right?

This is what I recommend for <u>trunk</u> interfaces:

```
Switch(config-if)#switchport mode trunk
Switch(config-if)#switchport nonegotiate
```

The negotiation of the switchport status by using dynamic auto or dynamic

3. VLANs (Virtual LANs)

desirable is called **DTP (Dynamic Trunking Protocol).** You can disable it completely by using the **switchport nonegotiate** command.

One more thing about VLANs and trunks before we continue with the next chapter. I recommend changing the native VLAN to something else:

```
SwitchB#show interfaces fa0/14 trunk

Port        Mode            Encapsulation    Status       Native vlan
Fa0/14      on              802.1q           trunking     1
```

You can see that VLAN 1 is the default native VLAN on Cisco switches. Management protocols like CDP, DTP and LACP/PagP (Etherchannels...more on this later!) use the native VLAN so for security reasons it might be a good idea to change it to something else:

```
SwitchA(config)#interface fa0/14
SwitchA(config-if)#switchport trunk native vlan 100
```

```
SwitchB(config)#interface fa0/14
SwitchB(config-if)#switchport trunk native vlan 100
```

This is how we change the native VLAN.

```
SwitchB#show interfaces fa0/14 trunk

Port        Mode            Encapsulation    Status       Native vlan
Fa0/14      on              802.1q           trunking     100
```

You can see the native VLAN is now VLAN 100.

By default the native VLAN is untagged when we use 802.1Q trunks. This can cause a security vulnerability (double tagging attack or "VLAN hopping") where we send double-tagged frames from one VLAN to another. One way of preventing this is by making sure that the native VLAN is tagged:

```
SwitchA(config)#vlan dot1q tag native
```

```
SwitchB(config)#vlan dot1q tag native
```

The **vlan dot1q tag native** command above will ensure that the native VLAN will be tagged on all trunks.

This is all that I have for you about VLANs and trunking. In the next chapter we will look at VTP (VLAN Trunking Protocol) which can help you to synchronize VLANS between switches.

you want to get some practice I recommend you to take a look at the following labs:

http://gns3vault.com/Switching/vlans-and-trunks.html

http://gns3vault.com/Switching/vtp-vlan-trunking-protocol.html

4. VTP (VLAN Trunking Protocol)

Let's say you have a network with 20 switches and 50 VLANs. Normally you have to configure each switch separately and create those VLANs on each and every switch. That's a time consuming task so there is something to help us called VTP (Vlan Trunking Protocol). VTP will let you create VLANs on one switch and all the other switches will synchronize themselves.

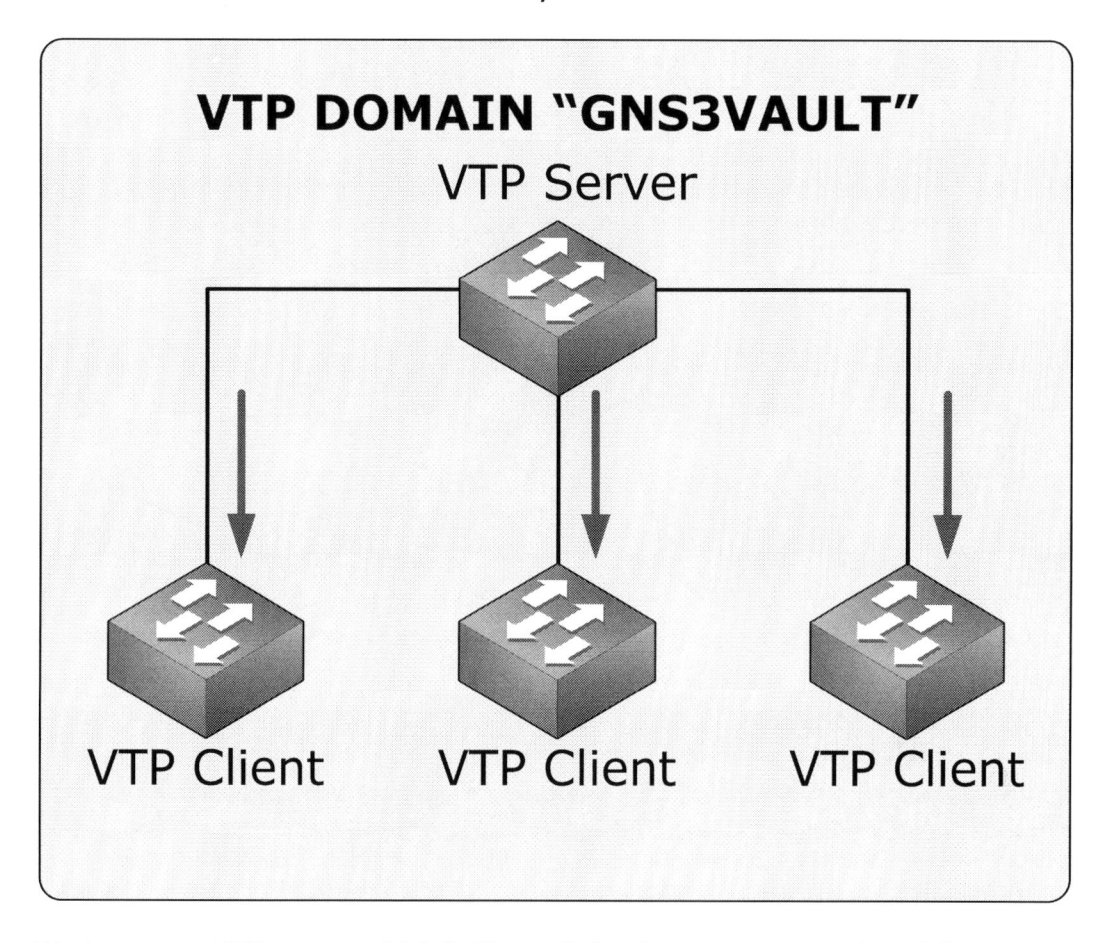

VTP DOMAIN "GNS3VAULT"
VTP Server

VTP Client   VTP Client   VTP Client

We have one VTP server which is the switch where you create / modify or delete vlans. The other switches are VTP clients. The VTP configuration has a revision number which will increase when you make a change. Every time you make a change on the VTP server this will be synchronized to the VTP clients. Oh and by the way you can have multiple VTP servers since it also functions as a VTP client so you can make changes on multiple switches in your network. In order to make VTP work you need to setup a VTP domain name which is something you can just make up, as long as you configure it to be the same on all your switches.

This is the short version of what I just described:

1. VTP adds / modifies / deletes vlans.
2. For every change the revision number will increase.
3. The latest advertisement will be sent to all VTP clients.
4. VTP clients will synchronize themselves with the latest information.

Besides the VTP server and VTP client there's also a VTP transparent which is a bit different, let me show you an example:

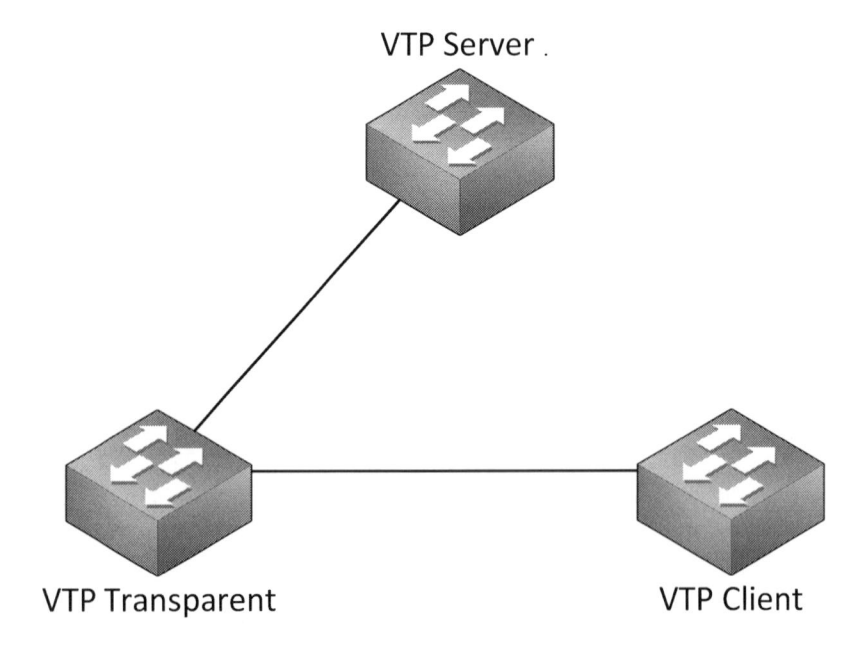

VTP Server

VTP Transparent   VTP Client

Our VTP Transparent will forward advertisements but will **not synchronize** itself. You can create vlans locally though which is impossible on the VTP client. Let's say you create vlan 20 on our VTP server, this is what will happen:

1. You create VLAN 20 on the VTP server.
2. The revision number will increase.
3. The VTP server will forward the latest advertisement which will reach the VTP transparent switch.
4. The VTP transparent will not synchronize itself but will forward the advertisement to the VTP client.
5. The VTP client will synchronize itself with the latest information

4. VTP (VLAN Trunking Protocol)

Here's an overview of the 3 VTP modes:

	VTP Server	**VTP Client**	**VTP Transparent**
Create/Modify/Delete Vlans	Yes	No	Only local
Synchronizes itself	Yes	Yes	No
Forwards advertisements	Yes	Yes	Yes

If you don't want to use VTP, you can also set it to "off". Should you use VTP? It might sound useful but VTP has a **huge security risk**...the problem with VTP is that a VTP server is also a VTP Client and any VTP client will synchronize itself with the highest revision number.

The following situation can happen with VTP:

You have a network with a single VTP server and a couple of VTP client switches, everything is working fine but one day you want to test some stuff and decide to take one of the VTP clients out of the network and put it in a lab environment.

1. You take the VTP client switch out of the network.
2. You configure it so it's no longer a VTP Client but a VTP server.
3. You play around with VTP, create some vlans, and modify some.
4. Every time you make a change the revision number increases.
5. You are done playing...you delete all vlans.
6. You configure the switch from VTP Server to VTP Client.
7. You connect your switch to your production network.

What do you think the result will be? The revision number of VTP on the switch we played with is higher than the revision number on the switches of our production network. The VTP client will advertise its information to the other switches, they synchronize to the latest information and POOF all your vlans are gone! A VTP client can **overwrite** a VTP server if the revision number is higher because a VTP server is also a VTP client.

Yes I know this sounds silly but this is the way it works...very dangerous since you'll lose all your VLAN information. Your interfaces won't go back to VLAN 1 by default but will float around in no man's land...

Back in the days networks were typically "flat" and we used VLANs end-to-end. As you learned in the campus design chapter, it's recommended to keep VLANs on the access and distribution layer so we don't use them everywhere anymore. Because of this reason, Cisco also recommends to use VTP transparent mode or to disable it.

VTP has three versions...1,2 and 3. The different versions are **incompatible** so make sure you use the same version. Version 1 is the default. VTP version 2 offers a number of additional features:

- **Version dependent transparent mode**: When using VTP transparent mode, VTP version 1 matches the VTP version and domain name before it forwards VTP messages to other VTP switches. Version 2 forwards VTP messages without checking the version number.
- **Consistency checks**: VTP version 2 does consistency checks when you enter VTP or VLAN information. This is done to ensure no incorrect VLAN names or numbers are sent to other VTP switches. These checks don't apply on incoming VTP messages.
- **Token ring support**: You probably won't see it anymore but VTP version 2 supports token ring, VTP version 1 does not.
- **Unrecognized TLV support**: VTP version 2 will forward received VTP configuration change messages even if it doesn't understand some fields in the VTP message. VTP version 1 will drop VTP messages that it doesn't understand.

Version 3 also has some new features:

- **Extended VLAN range**: all VLANs are supported, 1 – 4094.
- **Authentication**: Switches are able to authenticate each other with a hidden key that is not visibile in the config.
- **Private VLAN support**: we'll talk about private VLANs in the next chapter.
- **Supports multiple databases**: Besides VTP information, VTPv3 can also synchronize the MST database (Multiple Spanning Tree). We'll cover MST in another chapter.
- **Primary and secondary servers**: the primary VTP server updates the database information, all other VTP devices will use this information. The VTP secondary server is only able to backup the VTP information to its NVRAM.
- **Per-port VTP**: You can now run VTP only on selected trunks instead of running it on the entire switch.

Let's take a look at the configuration of VTP:

4. VTP (VLAN Trunking Protocol)

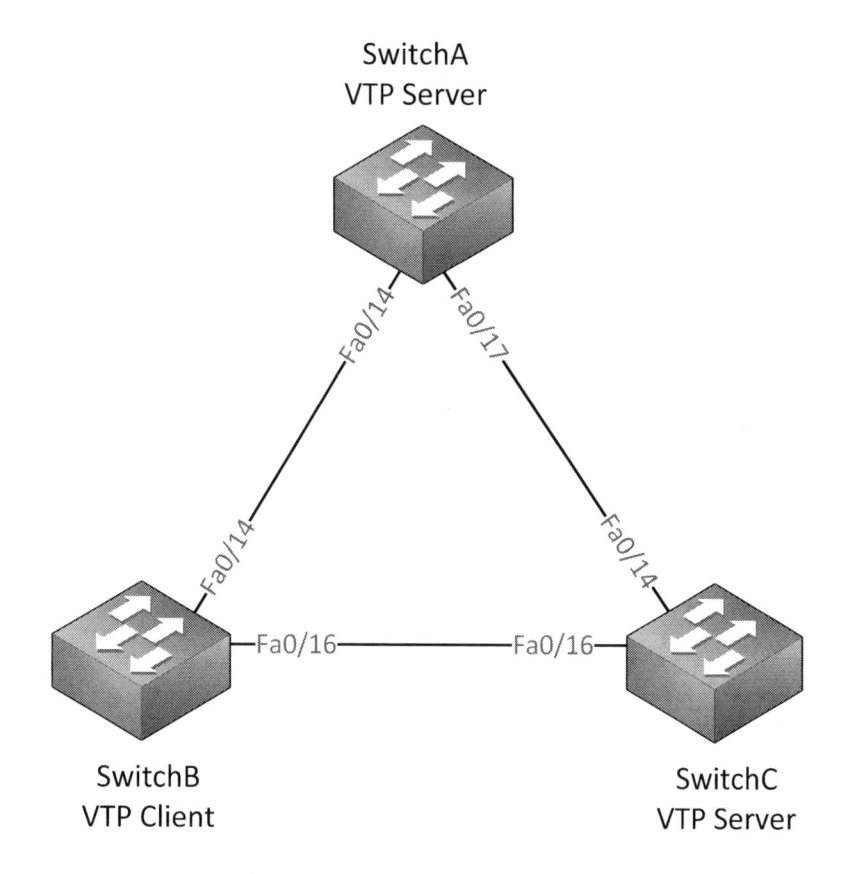

SwitchA
VTP Server

SwitchB
VTP Client

SwitchC
VTP Server

I will be using three switches for this task.

55

I erased the VLAN database and the startup-configuration on all switches.

```
SwitchA#show vtp status
VTP Version                     : running VTP1 (VTP2 capable)
Configuration Revision          : 0
Maximum VLANs supported locally : 1005
Number of existing VLANs        : 5
VTP Operating Mode              : Server
VTP Domain Name                 :
VTP Pruning Mode                : Disabled
VTP V2 Mode                     : Disabled
VTP Traps Generation            : Disabled
MD5 digest                      : 0x57 0xCD 0x40 0x65 0x63 0x59 0x47 0xBD
Configuration last modified by 0.0.0.0 at 0-0-00 00:00:00
Local updater ID is 0.0.0.0 (no valid interface found)
```

```
SwitchB#show vtp status
VTP Version                     : running VTP1 (VTP2 capable)
Configuration Revision          : 0
Maximum VLANs supported locally : 1005
Number of existing VLANs        : 5
VTP Operating Mode              : Server
VTP Domain Name                 :
VTP Pruning Mode                : Disabled
VTP V2 Mode                     : Disabled
VTP Traps Generation            : Disabled
MD5 digest                      : 0x57 0xCD 0x40 0x65 0x63 0x59 0x47 0xBD
Configuration last modified by 0.0.0.0 at 0-0-00 00:00:00
Local updater ID is 0.0.0.0 (no valid interface found)
```

```
SwitchC#show vtp status
VTP Version                     : 2
Configuration Revision          : 0
Maximum VLANs supported locally : 1005
Number of existing VLANs        : 5
VTP Operating Mode              : Server
VTP Domain Name                 :
VTP Pruning Mode                : Disabled
VTP V2 Mode                     : Disabled
VTP Traps Generation            : Disabled
MD5 digest                      : 0x57 0xCD 0x40 0x65 0x63 0x59 0x47 0xBD
Configuration last modified by 0.0.0.0 at 0-0-00 00:00:00
Local updater ID is 0.0.0.0 (no valid interface found)
```

Depending on the switch model you will see a similar output if you use the **show vtp status** command.

4. VTP (VLAN Trunking Protocol)

There's a couple of interesting things to see here:

- Configuration revision 0: Each time we add or remove VLANs this number will change. It's 0 at the moment since I haven't created or removed any VLANs.
- VTP Operating mode: the default is VTP server.
- VTP Pruning: this will help to prevent unnecessary traffic on your trunk links, more in this later.
- VTP V2 Mode: The switch is capable of running VTP version 2 but it's currently running VTP version 1.

```
SwitchA(config)#vlan 10
SwitchA(config-vlan)#name Printers
```

Let's create a VLAN on SwitchA and we'll see if anything changes...

```
SwitchA#show vlan

VLAN Name                             Status      Ports
---- -------------------------------- ---------   -------------------
1    default                          active      Fa0/1, Fa0/2,
Fa0/3, Fa0/4
                                                  Fa0/5, Fa0/6,
Fa0/7, Fa0/8
                                                  Fa0/9, Fa0/10,
Fa0/11, Fa0/12
                                                  Fa0/13, Fa0/14,
Fa0/15, Fa0/22
                                                  Fa0/23, Fa0/24,
Gi0/1, Gi0/2
10   Printers                         active
```

My new VLAN shows up in the VLAN database, so far so good...

```
SwitchA#show vtp status
VTP Version              : running VTP1 (VTP2 capable)
Configuration Revision   : 1
```

You can see that the configuration revision has increased by one.

```
SwitchB#show vtp status
VTP Version              : running VTP1 (VTP2 capable)
Configuration Revision   : 0
```

```
SwitchC#show vtp status
VTP Version              : 2
Configuration Revision   : 0
```

57

Unfortunately nothing has changed on SwitchB and SwitchC. This is because we need to configure a **VTP domain-name** before it starts working.

```
SwitchB#debug sw-vlan vtp events
vtp events debugging is on
```

```
SwitchC#debug sw-vlan vtp events
vtp events debugging is on
```

Before I change the domain-name I'm going to enable a debug using the **debug sw-vlan vtp events** command. This way we can see in real-time what is going on.

```
SwitchA(config)#vtp domain GNS3VAULT
Changing VTP domain name from NULL to GNS3VAULT
```

```
SwitchB#
VTP LOG RUNTIME: Summary packet received in NULL domain state
VTP LOG RUNTIME: Summary packet received, domain = GNS3VAULT,
rev = 1, followers = 1, length 77, trunk Fa0/16
VTP LOG RUNTIME: Transitioning from NULL to GNS3VAULT domain
VTP LOG RUNTIME: Summary packet rev 1 greater than domain
GNS3VAULT rev 0
```

You will see the following debug information on SwitchB and SwitchC; there are two interesting things we can see here:

- The switch receives a VTP packet from domain "GNS3VAULT" and decides to change its own domain-name from "NULL" (nothing) to "GNS3VAULT". It will only change the domain-name if it doesn't have a domain-name.
- The switch sees that the VTP packet has a higher revision number (1) than what it currently has (0) and as a result it will synchronize itself.

```
SwitchB#no debug all
All possible debugging has been turned off
```

```
SwitchC#no debug all
All possible debugging has been turned off
```

Make sure to disable the debug output before you get flooded with information.

```
SwitchB#show vtp status
VTP Version                     : running VTP1 (VTP2 capable)
Configuration Revision          : 1
```

```
SwitchC#show vtp status
VTP Version                     : 2
Configuration Revision          : 1
```

4. VTP (VLAN Trunking Protocol)

The revision number on SwitchB and SwitchC is now "1".

```
SwitchB#show vlan

VLAN Name                              Status     Ports
---- ------------------------------    ---------  -------------------
1    default                           active     Fa0/1, Fa0/2,
Fa0/3, Fa0/4
                                                  Fa0/5, Fa0/6,
Fa0/7, Fa0/8
                                                  Fa0/9, Fa0/10,
Fa0/11, Fa0/12
                                                  Fa0/13, Fa0/14,
Fa0/15,
                                                  Fa0/23, Fa0/24,
Gi0/1, Gi0/2
10   Printers                          active
```

```
SwitchC#show vlan

VLAN Name                              Status     Ports
---- ------------------------------    ---------  -------------------
1    default                           active     Fa0/1, Fa0/2,
Fa0/3, Fa0/4
                                                  Fa0/5, Fa0/6,
Fa0/7, Fa0/8
                                                  Fa0/9, Fa0/10,
Fa0/11, Fa0/12
                                                  Fa0/20, Fa0/22,
Fa0/23,
                                                  Gi0/1, Gi0/2
10   Printers                          active
```

The show vlan command tells us that SwitchB and SwitchC have learned VLAN 10 through VTP.
Since all switches are in VTP Server mode I can create VLANs on any switch and they should all synchronize:

```
SwitchB(config)#vlan 20
SwitchB(config-vlan)#name Servers
```

```
SwitchC(config)#vlan 30
SwitchC(config-vlan)#name Management
```

59

Let's create VLAN 20 on SwitchB and VLAN 30 on SwitchC.

```
SwitchA#show vlan

VLAN  Name                             Status     Ports
----  -------------------------------- ---------  --------------
10    Printers                         active
20    Servers                          active
30    Management                       active
```

```
SwitchB#show vlan

VLAN  Name                             Status     Ports
----  -------------------------------- ---------  --------------
10    Printers                         active
20    Servers                          active
30    Management                       active
```

```
SwitchC#show vlan

VLAN  Name                             Status     Ports
----  -------------------------------- ---------  --------------
10    Printers                         active
20    Servers                          active
30    Management                       active
```

As you can see all switches know about the VLANs. What about the revision number? Did it change?

```
SwitchA#show vtp status
VTP Version                   : running VTP1 (VTP2 capable)
Configuration Revision        : 3
```

```
SwitchB#show vtp status
VTP Version                   : running VTP1 (VTP2 capable)
Configuration Revision        : 3
```

```
SwitchC#show vtp status
VTP Version                   : 2
Configuration Revision        : 3
```

Each time I create another VLAN the revision number increases by one. Let's change the VTP mode on SwitchB to see what it does.

```
SwitchB(config)#vtp mode client
Setting device to VTP CLIENT mode.
```

4. VTP (VLAN Trunking Protocol)

```
SwitchB#show vtp status
VTP Version                       : running VTP1 (VTP2 capable)
Configuration Revision            : 3
Maximum VLANs supported locally   : 1005
Number of existing VLANs          : 7
VTP Operating Mode                : Client
```

It's now running in VTP Client mode.

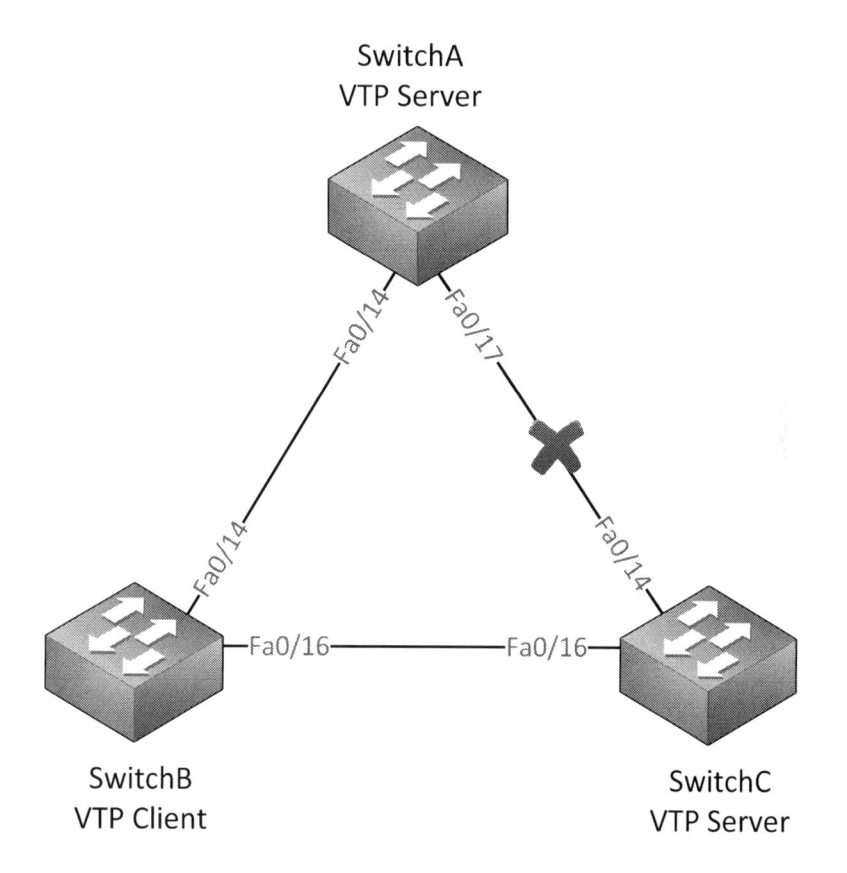

```
                    SwitchA
                   VTP Server



    SwitchB                           SwitchC
   VTP Client                        VTP Server
```

Right now SwitchA and SwitchC are in VTP Server mode. SwitchB is running VTP Client mode. I have disconnected the link between SwitchA and SwitchC so there is no direct connection between them.

```
SwitchA(config)#vlan 40
SwitchA(config-vlan)#name Engineering
```

I'll create another VLAN on SwitchA so we can see if SwitchB and SwitchC will learn it.

```
SwitchB#show vlan

VLAN  Name                             Status     Ports
----  -------------------------------- ---------  ----------------
----------------
10    Printers                         active
20    Servers                          active
30    Management                       active
40    Engineering                      active
```

SwitchB learns about VLAN 40 through SwitchA.

```
SwitchC#show vlan

VLAN  Name                             Status     Ports
----  -------------------------------- ---------  ----------------
----------------
10    Printers                         active
20    Servers                          active
30    Management                       active
40    Engineering                      active
```

SwitchC learns about VLAN 40 through SwitchB. SwitchB as a VTP client will synchronize itself but it will also forward VTP advertisements.

```
SwitchB(config)#vlan 50
%VTP VLAN configuration not allowed when device is in CLIENT mode.
```

A switch running in VTP Client mode is unable to create VLANs so that's why I get this error if I try to create one.

What about the VTP Transparent mode? That's the last one we have to try...

4. VTP (VLAN Trunking Protocol)

SwitchA
VTP Server

SwitchB
VTP Transparent

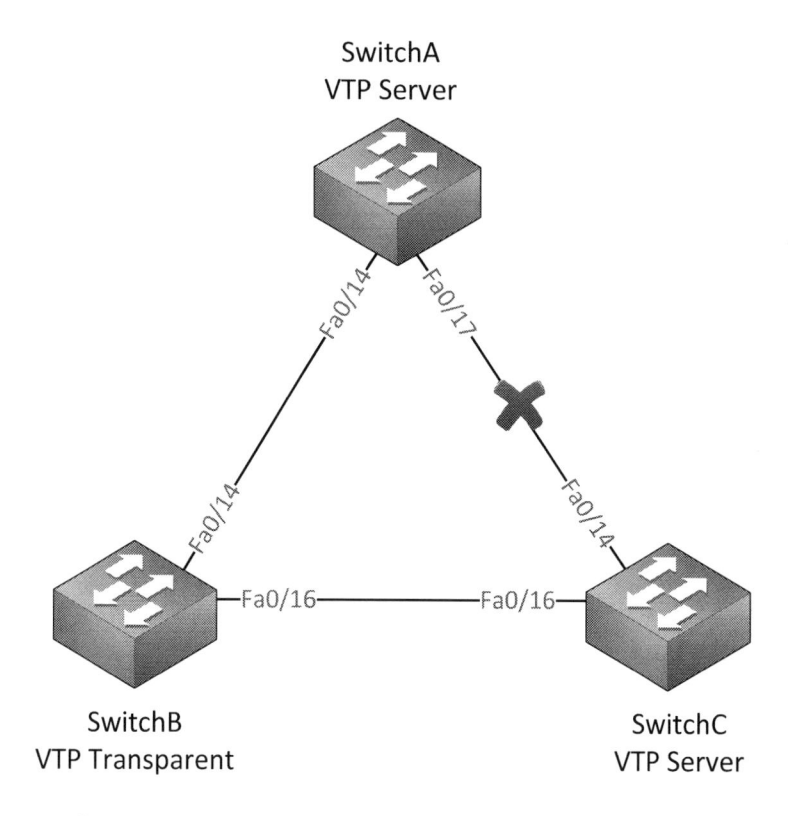

SwitchC
VTP Server

I'll change SwitchB to VTP Transparent mode and the link between SwitchA and SwitchC is still disconnected.

```
SwitchB(config)#vtp mode transparent
Setting device to VTP TRANSPARENT mode.
```

This is how we change SwitchB to VTP Transparent mode.

```
SwitchA(config)#vlan 50
SwitchA(config-vlan)#name Research
```

Let's create VLAN 50 for this experiment on SwitchA.

```
SwitchA#show vlan

VLAN Name                             Status    Ports
---- -------------------------------- --------- -------------------
10   Printers                         active
20   Servers                          active
30   Management                       active
40   Engineering                      active
50   Research                         active
```

It shows up on SwitchA as expected.

63

```
SwitchB#show vlan

VLAN Name                              Status      Ports
---- ------------------------------   ---------   ----------------
10   Printers                          active
20   Servers                           active
30   Management                        active
40   Engineering                       active
```

It doesn't show up on SwitchB because it's in VTP transparent mode and doesn't synchronize itself.

```
SwitchC#show vlan

VLAN Name                              Status      Ports
---- ------------------------------   ---------   ----------------
10   Printers                          active
20   Servers                           active
30   Management                        active
40   Engineering                       active
50   Research                          active
```

It does show up on SwitchC! A switch in VTP Transparent mode will **not synchronize itself** but it will **forward VTP advertisements** to other switches so they can synchronize themselves.

What will happen if I create a VLAN on SwitchB? Let's find out!

```
SwitchB(config)#vlan 60
SwitchB(config-vlan)#name Cameras
```

```
SwitchB#show vlan

VLAN Name                              Status      Ports
---- ------------------------------   ---------   ----------------
10   Printers                          active
20   Servers                           active
30   Management                        active
40   Engineering                       active
60   Cameras                           active
```

We can create this new VLAN on SwitchB without any trouble.

4. VTP (VLAN Trunking Protocol)

It's in VTP Transparent mode so we can do this.

```
SwitchA#show vlan

VLAN  Name                              Status     Ports
----  --------------------------------  ---------  ----------------
10    Printers                          active
20    Servers                           active
30    Management                        active
40    Engineering                       active
50    Research                          active
```

```
SwitchC#show vlan

VLAN  Name                              Status     Ports
----  --------------------------------  ---------  ----------------
10    Printers                          active
20    Servers                           active
30    Management                        active
40    Engineering                       active
50    Research                          active
```

VLAN 60 doesn't show up on SwitchA and SwitchC because SwitchB is in VTP Transparent mode. SwitchB will not advertise its VLANs because they are only **known locally.**

Is there anything else you need to know about VTP Transparent mode?

```
SwitchB#show running-config
Building configuration...

vlan 10
 name Printers
!
vlan 20
 name Servers
!
vlan 30
 name Management
!
vlan 40
 name Engineering
!
vlan 60
 name Cameras
```

There's a difference between VTP Transparent mode VS Server/Client mode. If you look at the running-config you will see that VTP Transparent stores all VLAN information in the running-config. VTP Server and Client mode store their information in the VLAN database (vlan.dat on your flash memory).

I haven't showed you yet how to change the VTP version, for the configurations you just witnessed it doesn't matter what version you use. Here's how to do it:

```
SwitchA(config)#vtp version 2
```

```
SwitchB(config)#vtp version 2
```

```
SwitchC(config)#vtp version 2
```

Use the **vtp version** command to change the VTP version. Normally you only have to configure this on the VTP server, the VTP clients will sync themselves and change their version. You can verify our configuration like this:

```
SwitchA#show vtp status | include Version
VTP Version                     : running VTP2
```

If you understand the difference between VTP Server, Client and Transparent mode...good! There's one more thing I want to show to you about VTP.

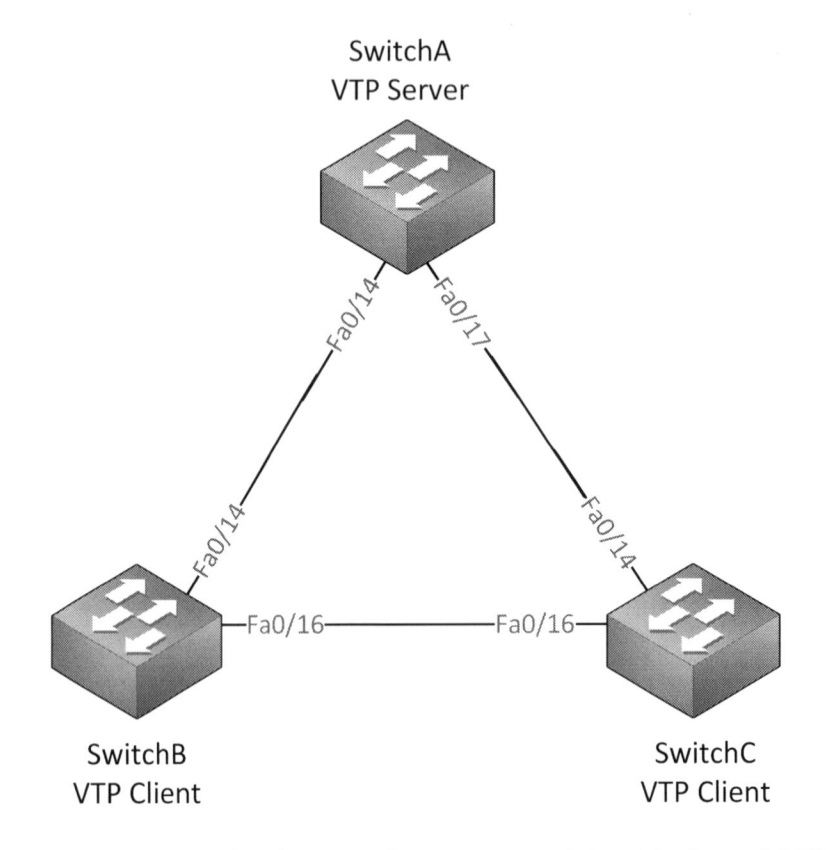

SwitchA
VTP Server

Fa0/14   Fa0/17

Fa0/14   Fa0/14

SwitchB ——Fa0/16————Fa0/16—— SwitchC

SwitchB
VTP Client

SwitchC
VTP Client

I'm going to demonstrate the danger of VTP as I explained before. A VTP client

4. VTP (VLAN Trunking Protocol)

can overwrite a VTP server if the revision number of the VTP client is higher. I'm using the same topology but this time SwitchA is the VTP Server and SwitchB and SwitchC are VTP Clients.

```
SwitchA(config)#vtp mode server
Device mode already VTP SERVER.
SwitchA(config)#vtp domain GNS3VAULT
Changing VTP domain name from NULL to GNS3VAULT
```

```
SwitchB(config)#vtp mode client
Setting device to VTP CLIENT mode.
```

```
SwitchC(config)#vtp mode client
Setting device to VTP CLIENT mode.
```

First I change the domain-name and configure the correct VTP modes.

```
SwitchA(config)#vlan 10
SwitchA(config-vlan)#name Printers
SwitchA(config)#vlan 20
SwitchA(config-vlan)#name Servers
SwitchA(config)#vlan 30
SwitchA(config-vlan)#name Management
```

Next step is to create a couple of VLANS.

```
SwitchA(config)#interface fa0/1
SwitchA(config-if)#switchport mode access
SwitchA(config-if)#switchport access vlan 10
```

I will configure one (random) interface so it's in VLAN 10.

```
SwitchA#show vtp status
VTP Version                  : running VTP2
Configuration Revision       : 4
```

```
SwitchB#show vtp status
VTP Version                  : running VTP2
Configuration Revision       : 4
```

```
SwitchC#show vtp status
VTP Version                  : 2
Configuration Revision       : 4
```

All switches currently have the same revision number.

```
SwitchA#show vlan

VLAN Name                              Status     Ports
---- -------------------------------- --------- ----------------
1    default                           active     Fa0/2, Fa0/3,
Fa0/4, Fa0/5
10   Printers                          active     Fa0/1
20   Servers                           active
30   Management                        active
```

```
SwitchB#show vlan

VLAN Name                              Status     Ports
---- -------------------------------- --------- ----------------
1    default                           active     Fa0/2, Fa0/3,
Fa0/4, Fa0/5
10   Printers                          active
20   Servers                           active
30   Management                        active
```

```
SwitchC#show vlan

VLAN Name                              Status     Ports
---- -------------------------------- --------- ----------------
1    default                           active     Fa0/2, Fa0/3,
Fa0/4, Fa0/5
10   Printers                          active
20   Servers                           active
30   Management                        active
```

All switches are up-to-date with the latest VLAN information. Note that Fa0/1 on SwitchA is in VLAN 10 at this moment.

4. VTP (VLAN Trunking Protocol)

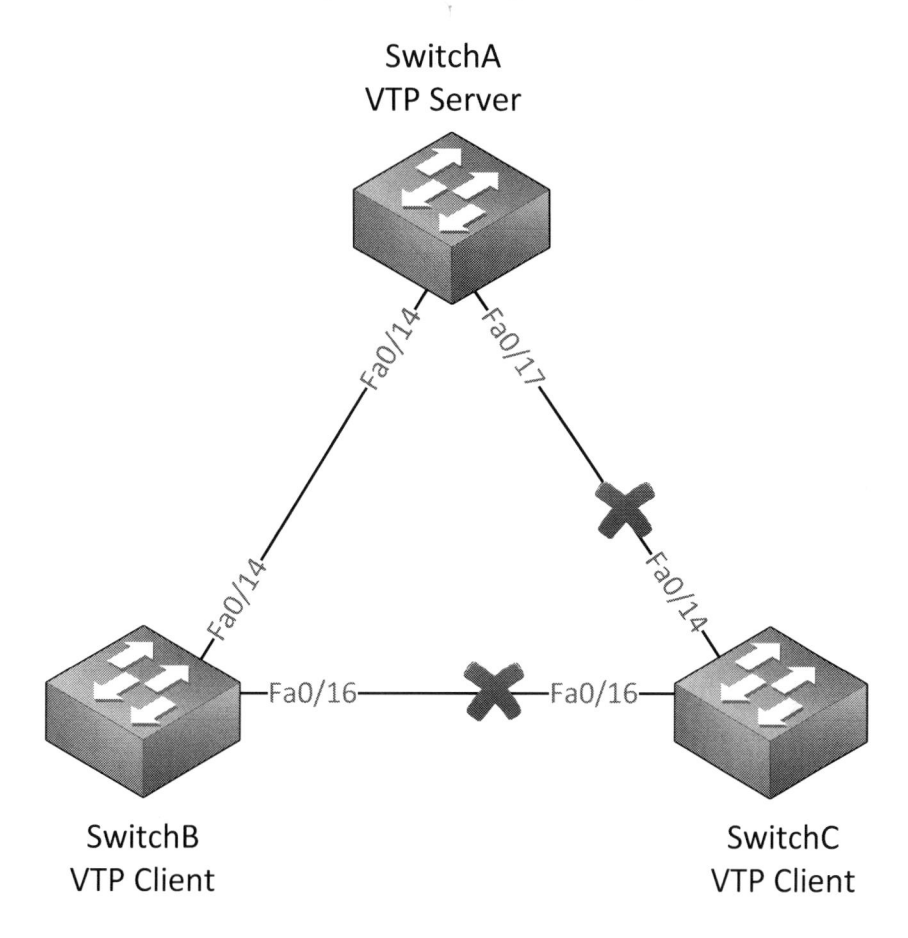

SwitchA
VTP Server

SwitchB
VTP Client

SwitchC
VTP Client

Now I'm going to shut down the interfaces on SwitchC connecting SwitchA and SwitchB. This could happen if you want to remove a switch from your production network and temporarily use it in a lab.

```
SwitchC(config)#interface fa0/14
SwitchC(config-if)#shutdown
SwitchC(config)#interface fa0/16
SwitchC(config-if)#shutdown
```

I will change SwitchC from VTP Client mode to VTP Server mode:

```
SwitchC(config)#vtp mode server
Setting device to VTP SERVER mode
```

Easy enough! Let's add some VLANs:

```
SwitchC(config)#vlan 70
SwitchC(config-vlan)#name Lab
SwitchC(config)#vlan 80
SwitchC(config-vlan)#name Experiment
```

```
SwitchC#show vtp status
VTP Version                    : 2
Configuration Revision         : 6
```

After adding the VLANs you can see that the VTP revision number has increased.

```
SwitchC(config)#no vlan 10
SwitchC(config)#no vlan 20
SwitchC(config)#no vlan 30
SwitchC(config)#no vlan 70
SwitchC(config)#no vlan 80
```

```
SwitchC(config)#vtp mode client
Setting device to VTP CLIENT mode.
```

After playing with my lab I'm going to erase the VLANs and change the switch back to VTP Client mode so we can return it to the production network.

```
SwitchC#show vtp status
VTP Version                    : 2
Configuration Revision         : 11
```

Note that after deleting the VLANs the VTP revision number increased even more.

```
SwitchC(config)#interface fa0/14
SwitchC(config-if)#no shutdown
SwitchC(config)#interface fa0/16
SwitchC(config-if)#no shutdown
```

Let's do a "no shutdown" on the interfaces and return SwitchC to the production network.

```
SwitchA#show vtp status
VTP Version                    : running VTP2
Configuration Revision         : 11
```

```
SwitchB#show vtp status
VTP Version                    : running VTP2
Configuration Revision         : 11
```

Ugh...this doesn't look good. SwitchA and SwitchB now have the same revision number as SwitchC.

4. VTP (VLAN Trunking Protocol)

This is the moment where you start to get nervous before you type in the next command...

```
SwitchA#show vlan

VLAN Name                              Status      Ports
---- ------------------------------    ---------   ---------------
1    default                           active      Fa0/2, Fa0/3,
Fa0/4, Fa0/5
```

```
SwitchB#show vlan

VLAN Name                              Status      Ports
---- ------------------------------    ---------   ---------------
1    default                           active      Fa0/1, Fa0/2,
Fa0/3, Fa0/4
```

OUCH! All VLAN information is lost since SwitchA and SwitchB are synchronized to the latest information from SwitchC.

This is the moment where your relaxing Monday morning turns into a horrible day...if you are lucky the support ticket system doesn't work anymore...if you are using VoIP than there's a chance your phones don't work anymore and you just have to wait till a mob of angry users will ram your door because they blame you for not being able to reach Facebook anymore...

Ok maybe I'm exaggerating a bit but you get the idea. If you have a big flat network with lots of switches and VLANs than this would be a disaster. I would advise to use VTP Transparent mode on all your switches and create VLANs locally!

If you do want to use VTP Server / Client mode you need to make sure you

reset the revision number:

- Changing the **domain-name** will reset the revision number.
- Deleting the vlan.dat file on your flash memory will reset the revision number.

What happens to interfaces when you delete a VLAN? Take a close look at the show vlan command on SwitchA on the previous page. When you delete a VLAN all interfaces are in 'no-man's land'. They don't return to VLAN 1…you'll have to re-assign them yourself!

This is the end of the VTP chapter, if you want to give this a try yourself then check out the following lab:

http://gns3vault.com/switching/vtp-vlan-trunking-protocol/

4. VTP (VLAN Trunking Protocol)

5. Private VLANs

If you studied CCNA then the previous chapter about VLANs, trunks and VTP was probably very familiar to you. In this chapter we will take a look at the **protected port** and **private VLANs.**

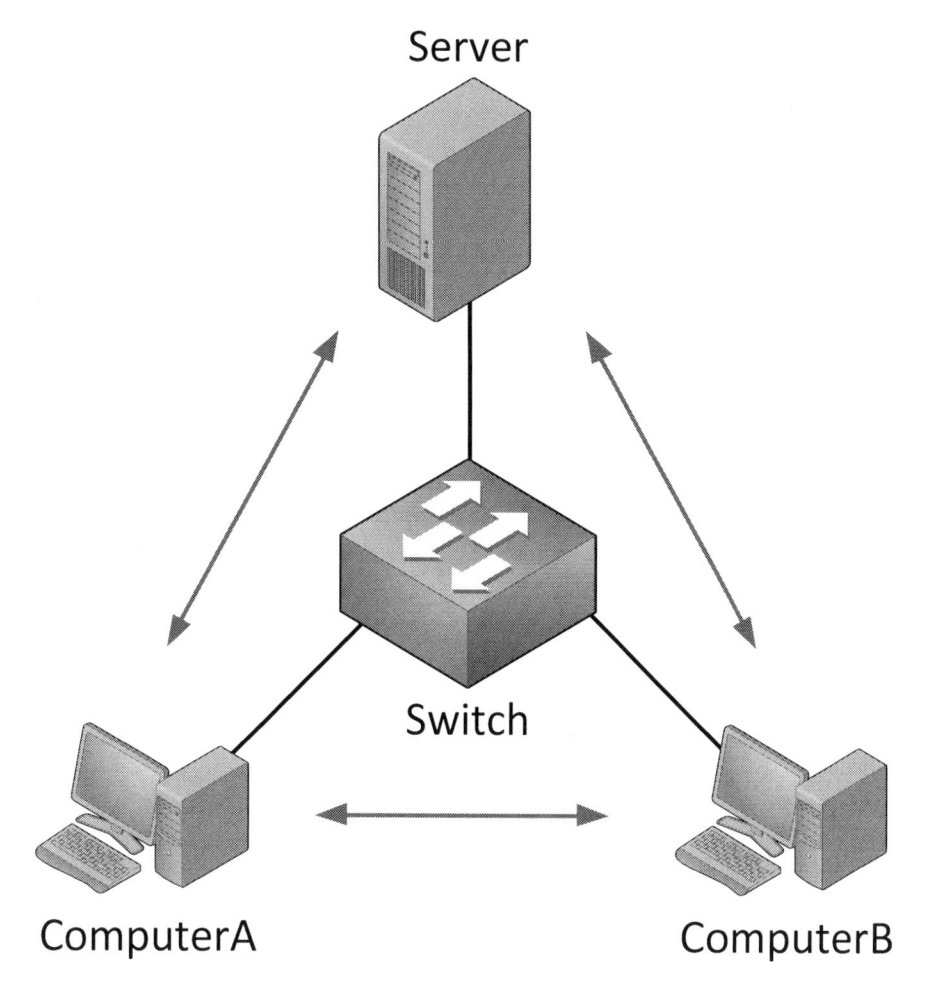

Take a look at the picture above. We have two computers, one switch and one server. Nothing fancy here...everything is in one VLAN and the two computers and server can communicate with each other.

What if I want to enhance security and ensure that ComputerA and ComputerB can only reach the server but not each other? This makes perfect sense in a client-server network. Normally there is no need for computers to connect to each other (unless Bob and Jane are secretly using shared folders on their computers without permission from the windows administrator).

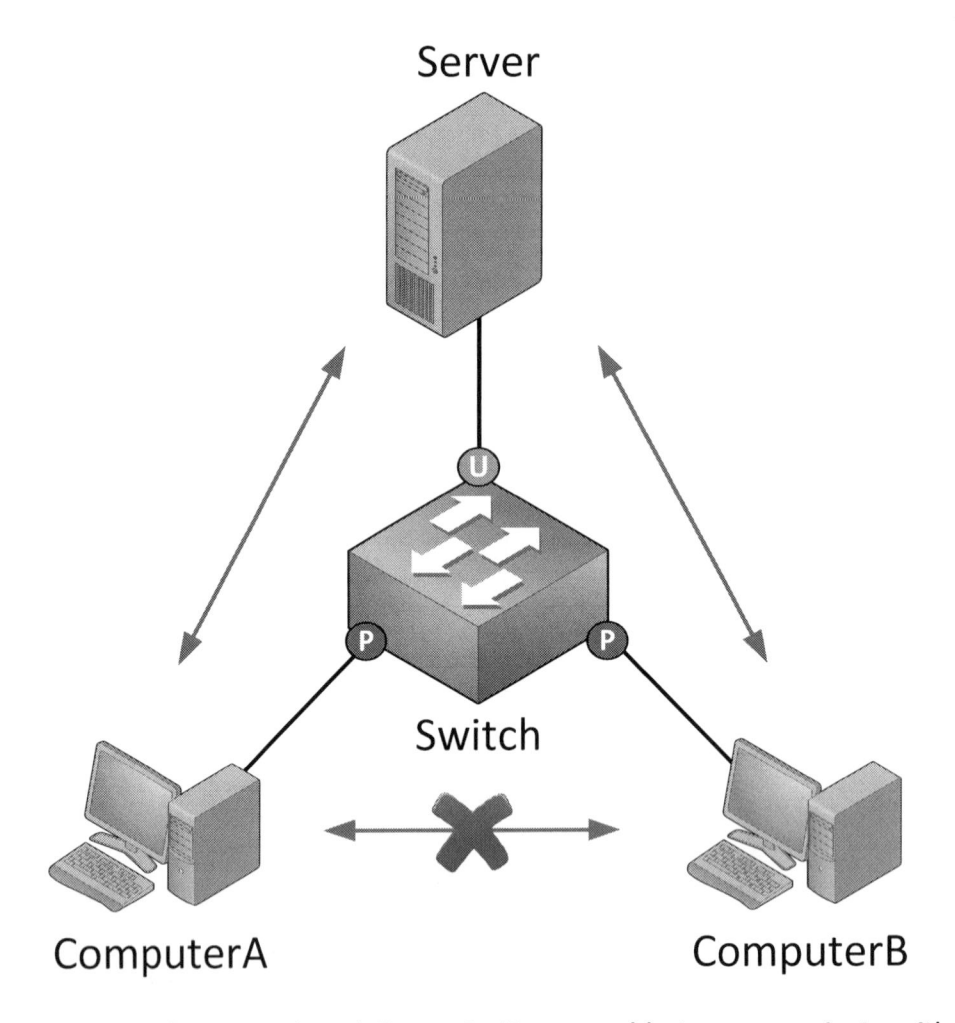

We can ensure ComputerA and ComputerB are unable to communicate with each other by using **protected ports**. By default all switch ports are unprotected.

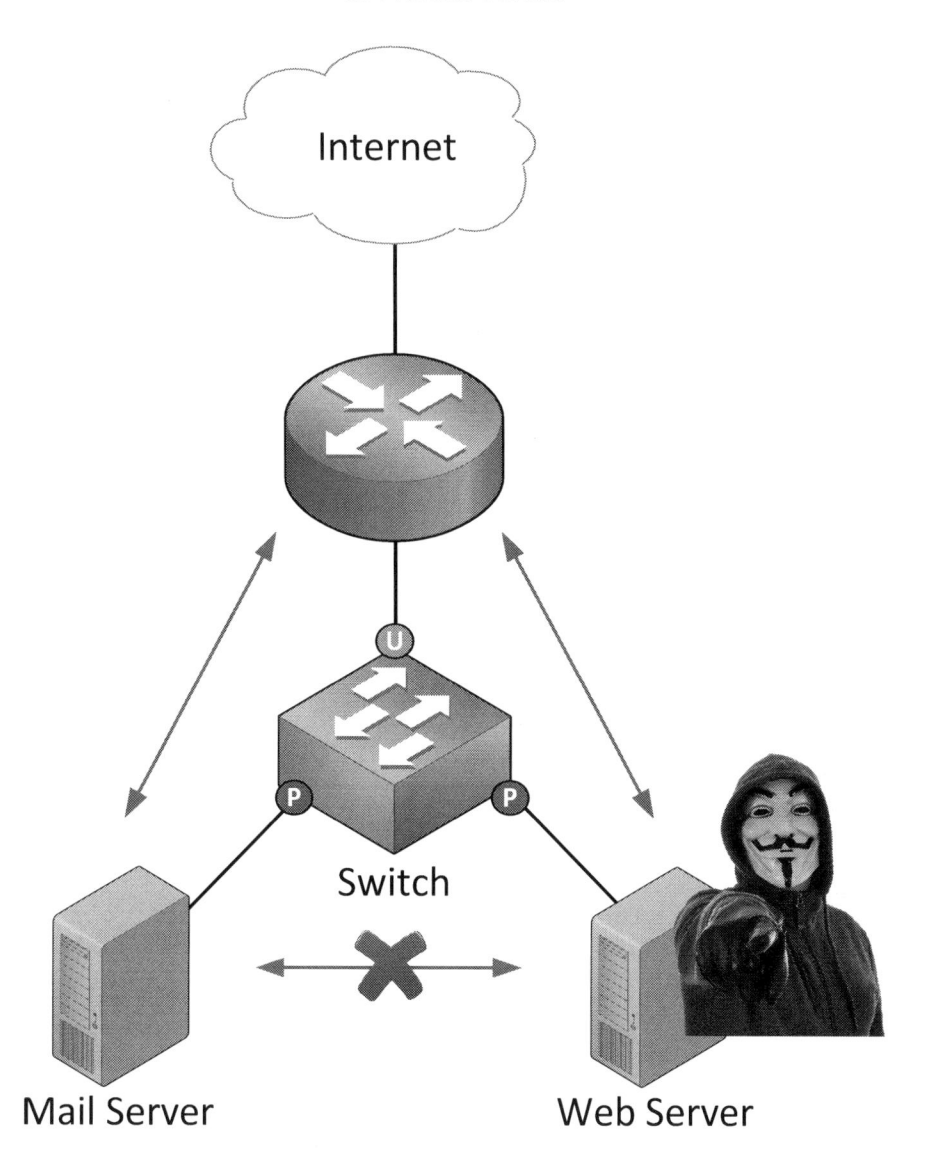

You might also want to use it for servers in your network. If a ~~hacker~~ freedom fighter takes over your web server you can reduce the attack surface by preventing them from connecting to other servers in your network.

Let's take a switch and configure some protected ports!

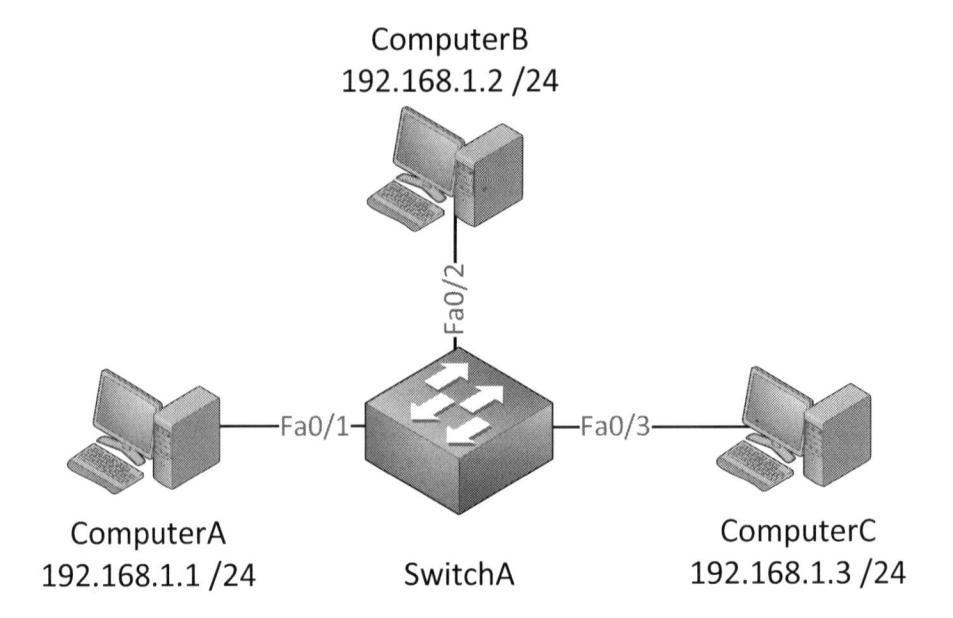

ComputerB
192.168.1.2 /24

ComputerA   ComputerC
192.168.1.1 /24   SwitchA   192.168.1.3 /24

This is the topology:

- Three computers in one subnet (192.168.1.0 /24)
- All computers are in the same VLAN (VLAN 1 by default).
- Default configuration on the switch.

```
C:\Documents and Settings\ComputerA>ping 192.168.1.2

Pinging 192.168.1.2 with 32 bytes of data:

Reply from 192.168.1.2: bytes=32 time<1ms TTL=128
```

```
C:\Documents and Settings\ComputerA>ping 192.168.1.3

Pinging 192.168.1.2 with 32 bytes of data:

Reply from 192.168.1.3: bytes=32 time<1ms TTL=128
```

```
C:\Documents and Settings\ComputerC>ping 192.168.1.2

Pinging 192.168.1.2 with 32 bytes of data:

Reply from 192.168.1.2: bytes=32 time<1ms TTL=128
```

By sending a couple of pings between the computers we can verify that we have full reachability at this moment.

5. Private VLANs

```
SwitchA(config)#interface fa0/1
SwitchA(config-if)#switchport protected
```

```
SwitchA(config)#interface fa0/3
SwitchA(config-if)#switchport protected
```

The interfaces connected to ComputerA and ComputerC are now protected. Interface fa0/2 to ComputerB is still unprotected.

```
SwitchB#show interfaces fa0/1 switchport
Name: Fa0/1
Switchport: Enabled
Administrative Mode: dynamic auto
Operational Mode: down
Administrative Trunking Encapsulation: negotiate
Negotiation of Trunking: On
Access Mode VLAN: 1 (default)
Trunking Native Mode VLAN: 1 (default)
Administrative Native VLAN tagging: enabled
Voice VLAN: none
Administrative private-vlan host-association: none
Administrative private-vlan mapping: none
Administrative private-vlan trunk native VLAN: none
Administrative private-vlan trunk Native VLAN tagging: enabled
Administrative private-vlan trunk encapsulation: dot1q
Administrative private-vlan trunk normal VLANs: none
Administrative private-vlan trunk associations: none
Administrative private-vlan trunk mappings: none
Operational private-vlan: none
Trunking VLANs Enabled: ALL
Pruning VLANs Enabled: 2-1001
Capture Mode Disabled
Capture VLANs Allowed: ALL
Protected: true
```

We can verify our configuration by using the show interfaces switchport command. Close to the bottom of the output you will find:

Protected: true

```
SwitchB#show interfaces fa0/1 switchport | include Protected
Protected: true
```

If you know what you are looking for in the output it's easier to use the "include" command.

This saves you hammering on the enter or space button of your keyboard...

```
C:\Documents and Settings\ComputerA>ping 192.168.1.2

Pinging 192.168.1.2 with 32 bytes of data:

Reply from 192.168.1.2: bytes=32 time<1ms TTL=128
```

```
C:\Documents and Settings\ComputerC>ping 192.168.1.2

Pinging 192.168.1.2 with 32 bytes of data:

Reply from 192.168.1.2: bytes=32 time<1ms TTL=128
```

ComputerA and ComputerC are still able to reach ComputerB.

```
C:\Documents and Settings\ComputerA>ping 192.168.1.3

Pinging 192.168.1.2 with 32 bytes of data:

Request timed out.

Ping statistics for 192.168.1.2:
    Packets: Sent = 1, Received = 0, Lost = 1 (100% loss),
```

```
C:\Documents and Settings\ComputerC>ping 192.168.1.1

Pinging 192.168.1.2 with 32 bytes of data:

Request timed out.

Ping statistics for 192.168.1.2:
    Packets: Sent = 1, Received = 0, Lost = 1 (100% loss),
```

ComputerA and ComputerC are unable to reach each other now.

Protected port ←→ Unprotected = **working**
Protected port ←→ Protected port = **not working**

The protected port is pretty neat and as you have seen very easy to configure however it is very limited. In the last part of this chapter we'll take a look at **private VLANs.** Private VLANs are like protected ports on steroids!

5. Private VLANs

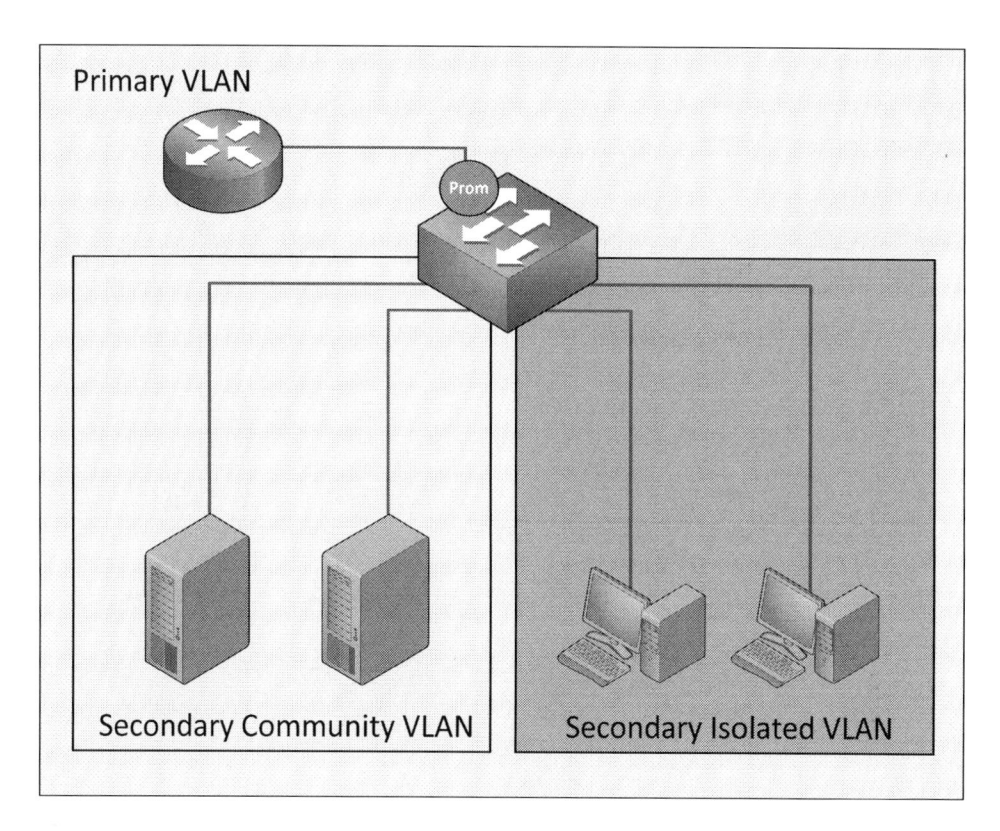

Many network students believe private VLANs are very complex when they see this for the first time. I'm going to break it down and explain to you how it works.

The private VLAN always has one **primary VLAN.** Within the primary VLAN you will find the **promiscuous port**. In my picture above you can see that there's a router connected to a promiscuous port. **All other ports are able to communicate** with the promiscuous port.

Within the primary VLAN you will encounter one or more **secondary VLANs**, there are two types:

- **Community VLAN:** All ports within the community VLAN are **able** to communicate with each other and the promiscuous port.
- **Isolated VLAN:** All ports within the isolated VLAN are **unable** to communicate with each other but they can communicate with the promiscuous port.

The names for these secondary VLANs are well chosen if you ask me. In a *community* everyone is able to talk to each other. When you are *isolated* you can only talk to yourself or in case of our private VLANs...the *promiscuous port*

Secondary VLANS can always communicate with the promiscuous port but they can never communicate with **other secondary VLANs!**

Are you following me so far? If so...good! If you are still a little fuzzy, don't worry. I'm going to show you the configuration and demonstrate you how this works.

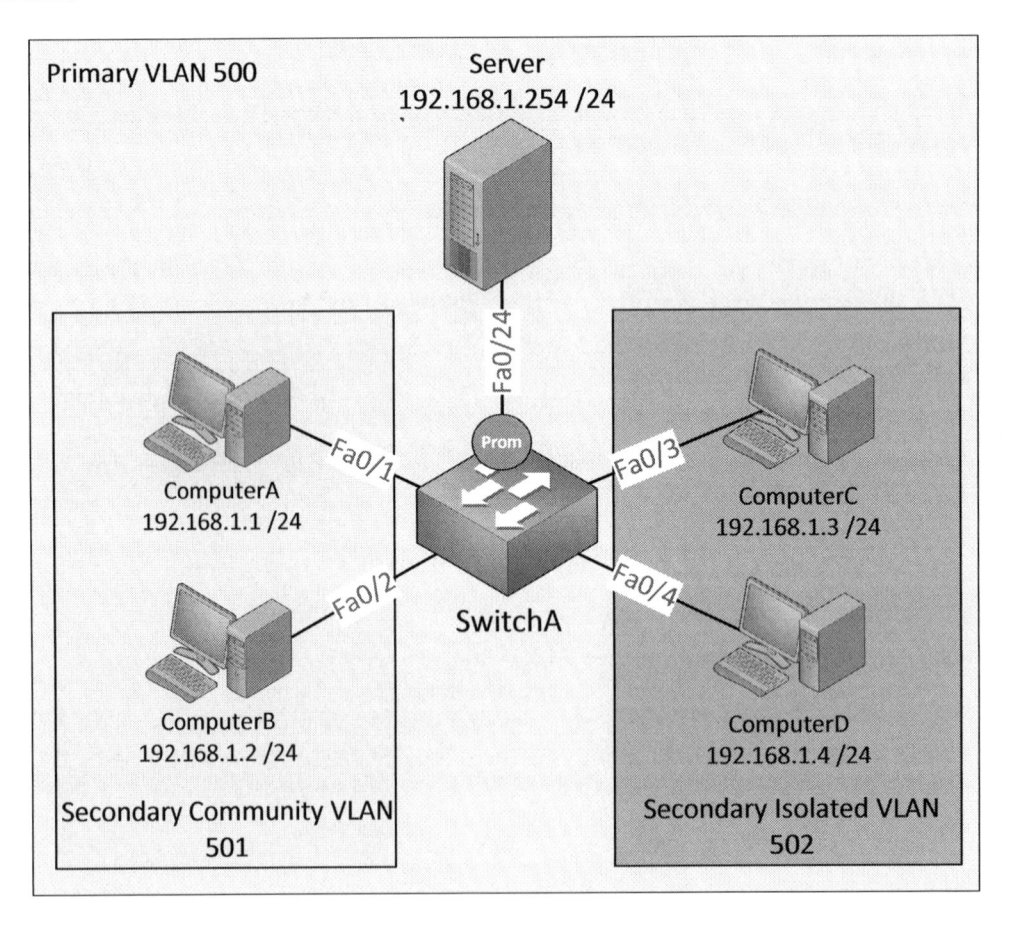

Primary VLAN 500

Server
192.168.1.254 /24

ComputerA
192.168.1.1 /24

ComputerB
192.168.1.2 /24

Secondary Community VLAN
501

SwitchA

ComputerC
192.168.1.3 /24

ComputerD
192.168.1.4 /24

Secondary Isolated VLAN
502

5. Private VLANs

Let me sum up what we have here:

- The primary VLAN has number 500.
- The secondary community VLAN has number 501.
- The secondary isolated VLAN has number 502.
- I just made up these VLAN numbers; you can use whatever you like.
- ComputerA and ComputerB in the community VLAN should be able to reach each other and also the server connected to the promiscuous port.
- ComputerC and ComputerD in the isolated VLAN can only communicate with the server on the promiscuous port.
- The server should be able to reach all ports.

```
SwitchA(config)#vtp mode transparent
Setting device to VTP TRANSPARENT mode.
```

Configuring private VLANs requires us to **change the VTP mode to Transparent**.

```
SwitchA(config)#vlan 501
SwitchA(config-vlan)#private-vlan community
SwitchA(config-vlan)#vlan 500
SwitchA(config-vlan)#private-vlan primary
SwitchA(config-vlan)#private-vlan association add 501
```

Let's start with the configuration of the community VLAN. First I create VLAN 501 and tell the switch that this is a community VLAN by typing the **private-vlan community** command. Secondly I am creating VLAN 500 and configuring it as the primary VLAN with the **private-vlan primary** command. Last but not least I need to tell the switch that VLAN 501 is a secondary VLAN by using the **private-vlan association** command.

```
SwitchA(config)#interface range fa0/1 - 2
SwitchA(config-if-range)#switchport mode private-vlan host
SwitchA(config-if-range)#switchport private-vlan host-association 500 501
```

Interface fa0/1 and fa0/2 are connected to ComputerA and ComputerB and belong to the community VLAN 501. On the interface level I need to tell the switch that these are host ports by issuing the **switchport mode private-vlan host** command. I also have to use the **switchport private-vlan host-association** command to tell the switch that VLAN 500 is the primary VLAN and 501 is the secondary VLAN.

```
SwitchA(config)#interface fa0/24
SwitchA(config-if)#switchport mode private-vlan promiscuous
SwitchA(config-if)#switchport private-vlan mapping 500 501
```

This is how I configure the promiscuous port. First I have to tell the switch that fa0/24 is a promiscuous port by typing the **switchport mode private-vlan promiscuous** command. I also have to map the VLANs by using the **switchport private-vlan mapping** command.

```
SwitchA#show interfaces fastEthernet 0/1 switchport
Name: Fa0/1
Switchport: Enabled
Administrative Mode: private-vlan host
Operational Mode: down
Administrative Trunking Encapsulation: negotiate
Negotiation of Trunking: Off
Access Mode VLAN: 1 (default)
Trunking Native Mode VLAN: 1 (default)
Administrative Native VLAN tagging: enabled
Voice VLAN: none
Administrative private-vlan host-association: 500 (VLAN0500) 501 (VLAN0501)
Administrative private-vlan mapping: none
```

We can verify our configuration by looking at the switchport information. Here is the output for fa0/1.

```
SwitchA#show interfaces fastEthernet 0/2 switchport | include host-as
Administrative private-vlan host-association: 500 (VLAN0500) 501 (VLAN0501)
```

Interface fa0/2 has the same configuration as fa0/1.

```
SwitchA#show interface fa0/24 switchport
Name: Fa0/24
Switchport: Enabled
Administrative Mode: private-vlan promiscuous
Operational Mode: private-vlan promiscuous
Administrative Trunking Encapsulation: negotiate
Operational Trunking Encapsulation: native
Negotiation of Trunking: Off
Access Mode VLAN: 1 (default)
Trunking Native Mode VLAN: 1 (default)
Administrative Native VLAN tagging: enabled
Voice VLAN: none
Administrative private-vlan host-association: none
Administrative private-vlan mapping: 500 (VLAN0500) 501 (VLAN0501)
```

Here is the switchport information for fa0/24 (our promiscuous port). You can see the mapping information.

5. Private VLANs

```
SwitchA#show vlan private-vlan

Primary  Secondary  Type               Ports
-------  ---------  -----------------  ---------------------------
---------------
500      501        community          Fa0/1, Fa0/2, Fa0/24
```

The **show vlan private-vlan** command gives us valuable information. You can see that VLAN 500 is the primary VLAN and 501 is the secondary VLAN. It also tells us whether the VLAN is a community or isolated VLAN the ports.

```
SwitchA#show vlan private-vlan type

Vlan Type
---- -----------------
500  primary
501  community
```

I also like the **show vlan private-vlan type** command because it gives us a quick overview of the private VLANs.

So what's the result of this configuration? If everything is OK we should now have a working community VLAN...let's find out!

```
C:\Documents and Settings\ComputerA>ping 192.168.1.2

Pinging 192.168.1.2 with 32 bytes of data:

Reply from 192.168.1.2: bytes=32 time<1ms TTL=128
```

ComputerA is able to reach ComputerB.

```
C:\Documents and Settings\ComputerA>ping 192.168.1.254

Pinging 192.168.1.254 with 32 bytes of data:

Reply from 192.168.1.254: bytes=32 time<1ms TTL=128
```

ComputerA can also reach the server behind the promiscuous port.

```
C:\Documents and Settings\Server>ping 192.168.1.2

Pinging 192.168.1.2 with 32 bytes of data:

Reply from 192.168.1.2: bytes=32 time<1ms TTL=128
```

The server is able to reach ComputerB. Great! Our community VLAN seems to be up and running. Let's continue with the configuration of the isolated VLAN.

```
SwitchA(config)#vlan 502
SwitchA(config-vlan)#private-vlan isolated
SwitchA(config-vlan)#vlan 500
SwitchA(config-vlan)#private-vlan primary
SwitchA(config-vlan)#private-vlan association add 502
```

The configuration is the same as the community VLAN but this time I'm using the **private-vlan isolated** command. Don't forget to **add the association between the primary and secondary VLAN using the private-vlan association add command**. The private-vlan primary command is obsolete because I already did this before, I'm just showing it to keep the configuration complete.

```
SwitchA(config)#interface range fa0/3 - 4
SwitchA(config-if-range)#switchport mode private-vlan host
SwitchA(config-if-range)#switchport private-vlan host-association 500 502
```

This part is exactly the same as the configuration for the community VLAN but I'm configuring interface fa0/3 and fa0/4 which are connected to ComputerC and ComputerD.

```
SwitchA(config)#interface fa0/24
SwitchA(config-if)#switchport mode private-vlan promiscuous
SwitchA(config-if)#switchport private-vlan mapping 500 502
```

I already configured fa0/24 as a promiscuous port but I'm showing it here as well to keep the configuration complete. I do need to create an additional mapping between VLAN 500 (primary) and VLAN 502 (secondary).

Let's verify our work!

```
SwitchA#show interfaces fa0/3 switchport
Name: Fa0/3
Switchport: Enabled
Administrative Mode: private-vlan host
Operational Mode: down
Administrative Trunking Encapsulation: negotiate
Negotiation of Trunking: Off
Access Mode VLAN: 1 (default)
Trunking Native Mode VLAN: 1 (default)
Administrative Native VLAN tagging: enabled
Voice VLAN: none
Administrative private-vlan host-association: 500 (VLAN0500) 502
(VLAN0502)
Administrative private-vlan mapping: none
```

Looking good...we can see the host-association between VLAN 500 and 502.

5. Private VLANs

```
SwitchA#show interfaces fastEthernet 0/4 switchport | include
host-as
Administrative private-vlan host-association: 500 (VLAN0500) 502
(VLAN0502)
```

A quick look at fa0/4 shows me the same output as fa0/3.

```
SwitchA#show interfaces fa0/24 switchport
Name: Fa0/24
Switchport: Enabled
Administrative Mode: private-vlan promiscuous
Operational Mode: private-vlan promiscuous
Administrative Trunking Encapsulation: negotiate
Operational Trunking Encapsulation: native
Negotiation of Trunking: Off
Access Mode VLAN: 1 (default)
Trunking Native Mode VLAN: 1 (default)
Administrative Native VLAN tagging: enabled
Voice VLAN: none
Administrative private-vlan host-association: none
Administrative private-vlan mapping: 500 (VLAN0500) 501
(VLAN0501) 502 (VLAN0502)
```

We can now see that VLAN 501 and VLAN 502 are mapped to primary VLAN 500.

```
SwitchA#show vlan private-vlan

Primary Secondary Type              Ports
------- --------- ----------------- ----------------------------
500     501       community         Fa0/1, Fa0/2, Fa0/24
500     502       isolated          Fa0/3, Fa0/4, Fa0/24
```

Here's a nice clean overview which shows us all the VLANs, the mappings and the interfaces.

```
SwitchA#show vlan private-vlan type

Vlan Type
---- -----------------
500  primary
501  community
502  isolated
```

Or if you only care about the VLAN numbers and the VLAN type this is what you need.

What will the result be of our hard labor?

```
C:\Documents and Settings\ComputerC>ping 192.168.1.254

Pinging 192.168.1.254 with 32 bytes of data:

Reply from 192.168.1.254: bytes=32 time<1ms TTL=128
```

ComputerC can reach the server behind the promiscuous port.

```
C:\Documents and Settings\ComputerD>ping 192.168.1.254

Pinging 192.168.1.254 with 32 bytes of data:

Reply from 192.168.1.254: bytes=32 time<1ms TTL=128
```

ComputerD can also reach the server behind the promiscuous port.

```
C:\Documents and Settings\ComputerC>ping 192.168.1.4

Pinging 192.168.1.4 with 32 bytes of data:

Request timed out.

Ping statistics for 192.168.1.4:
    Packets: Sent = 1, Received = 0, Lost = 1 (100% loss),
```

There is no reachability between ComputerC and ComputerD because they are in the isolated VLAN.

What about reachability between VLAN 501 and VLAN 502? Let's give it a try:

```
C:\Documents and Settings\ComputerA>ping 192.168.1.4

Pinging 192.168.1.4 with 32 bytes of data:

Request timed out.

Ping statistics for 192.168.1.4:
    Packets: Sent = 1, Received = 0, Lost = 1 (100% loss),
```

This is ComputerA in VLAN 501 trying to reach ComputerD in VLAN 502. As you can see this isn't possible. You are unable to communicate between different secondary VLANs.

Anything else you need to know about private VLANs?

5. Private VLANs

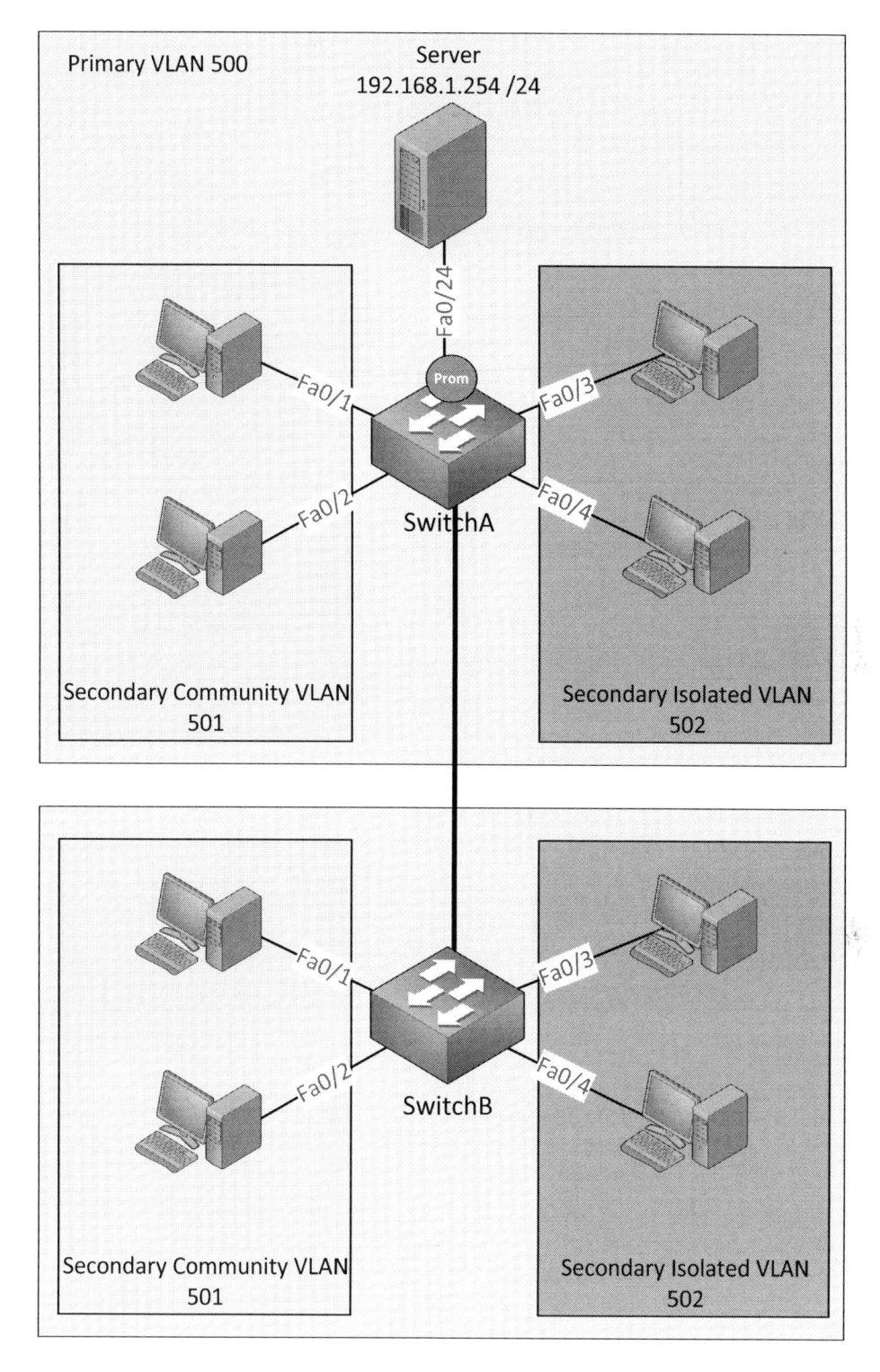

Private VLANs can be carried over 802.1Q links so it's possible to span your configuration over multiple switches. In the picture above I expanded our configuration to SwitchB. The configuration on SwitchB will be the same as

89

SwitchA. You just need to make sure that VLAN 500, 501 and 502 can be carried over the trunk between SwitchA and SwitchB. Don't forget that because of VTP transparent mode, VLAN information is not synchronized between the two switches. You'll have to create the VLANS yourself on the other switches.

Let me give you a short overview of what we have seen now:

- Devices within a community VLAN can communicate with each other AND the promiscuous port.
- Devices within an isolated VLAN cannot communicate with each other and can ONLY communicate with the promiscuous port.
- The promiscuous port can communicate with any other port.
- Secondary VLANs are unable to communicate with other secondary VLANs.
- Private VLANs can be spanned across multiple switches if you use trunks.

That's all I have for you about private VLANs! What do you think? I hope this all makes sense to you. There are a bunch of different commands you need to use in order to configure this and it may be difficult to remember them all. If you want to try the configuration yourself you can try the following lab:

http://gns3vault.com/Switching/private-vlan.html

Keep in mind that you **need at least** a Cisco Catalyst 3560 switch to configure private VLANs. If you try this on a Cisco Catalyst 3550 you will notice that some of the commands are accepted but it won't work.

5. Private VLANs

6. STP (Spanning Tree Protocol)

If you studied CCNA you will have a basic understanding of spanning-tree. If you haven't studied CCNA and are still new to switching...don't worry, in the first part of this chapter I will start with the basics of spanning-tree and we'll dive deeper into the material as we move along.

In short, spanning-tree helps you to **create a loop-free topology** in your switched network. The question we should ask ourselves is:

- What causes a loop in a switched network?

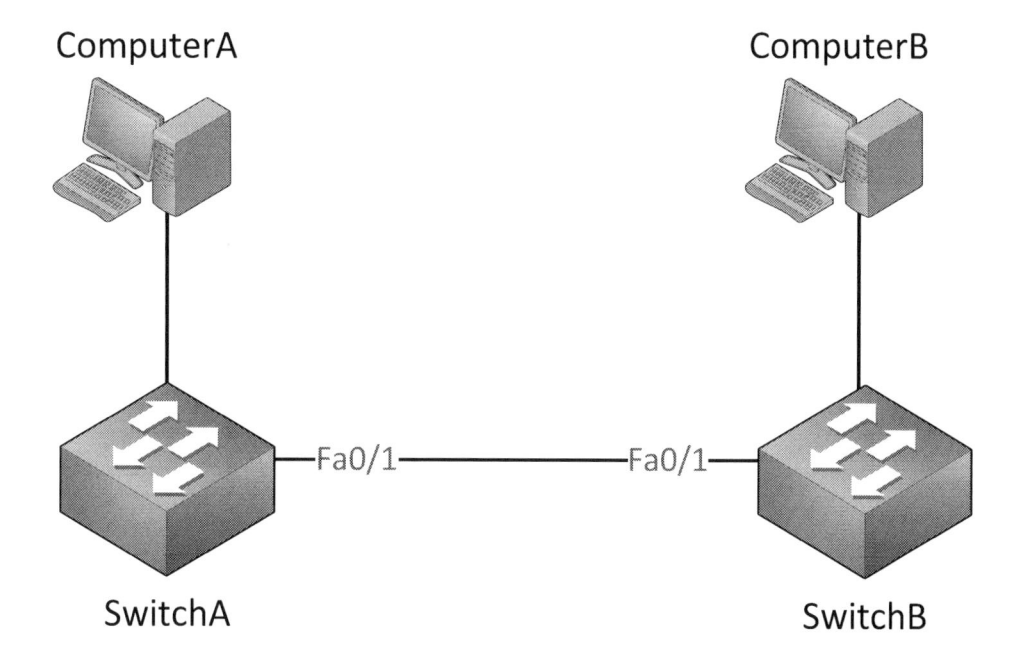

We add **loops in our network by adding redundancy** in our switched network. In our picture above we have two switches and only a single link between them. Having a single point of failure isn't something we like to see so to add redundancy we will add another cable.

ComputerA　　　　　　　　　ComputerB

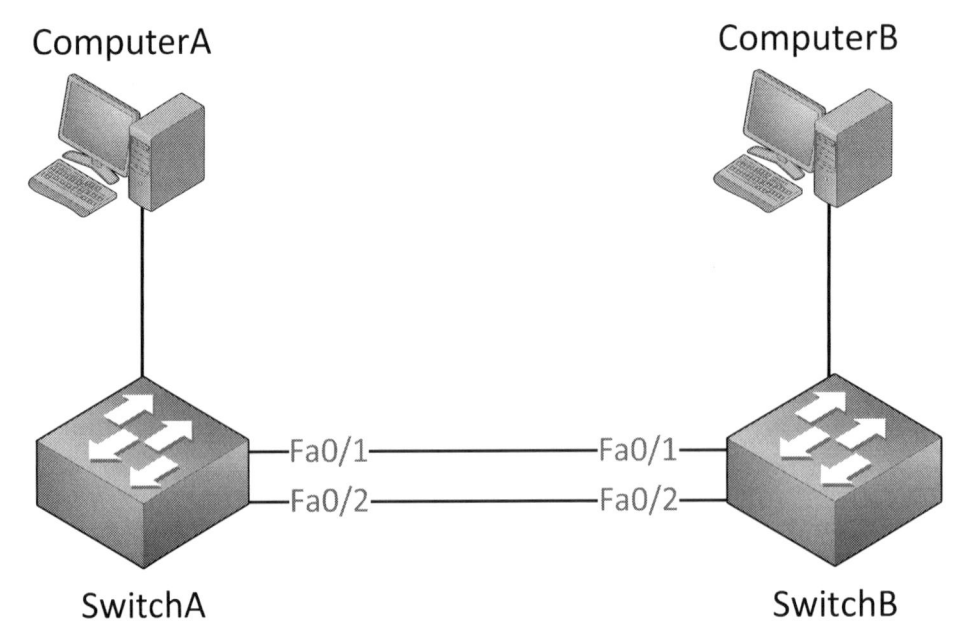

```
     —Fa0/1———————Fa0/1—
     —Fa0/2———————Fa0/2—
```

SwitchA　　　　　　　　　　SwitchB

Very nice...another cable adds redundancy to our network, our single point of failure is gone. However we now have a loop in our network! So why do we have a loop? Let's take a look at the following situation:

1. Computer A sends an ARP request because it's looking for the MAC address of computer B. An ARP request is a broadcast frame.
2. Switch A will forward this broadcast frame on all it interfaces, except the link where the frame originated from.
3. Switch B will receive both broadcast frames.

Now what does switch B do with those broadcast frames?

4. It will forward it out of every link except the interface where it originated from.
5. This means that the frame that was received on Interface fa0/1 will be forwarded on Interface fa0/2.
6. The frame that was received on Interface fa0/2 will be forwarded on Interface fa0/1.

Do you see where this is going? We have a loop! Both switches will keep forwarding over and over until this will happen:

- You fix the loop by disconnecting one of the cables.
- Your switches will crash because they are overburdened with traffic (not good!)
- Ethernet frames don't have a TTL (Time to Live) field so frames will loop forever.

The same thing will occur with "unknown unicast traffic". If your switch doesn't know on which interface it can reach a MAC address the frame will be flooded

6. STP (Spanning Tree Protocol)

on all interfaces except the one where it originated from.

Having a loop in our switched network doesn't sound like a good idea; let's take a look at how spanning-tree works!

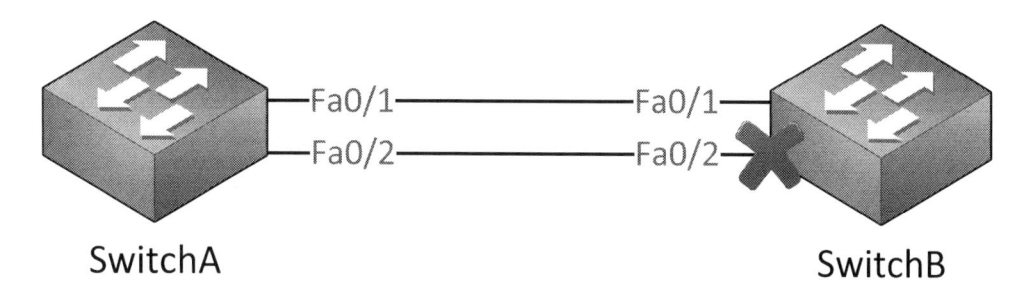

Here is the short answer: spanning-tree will block one or more interfaces in your switched network so the result is a **loop-free topology**.

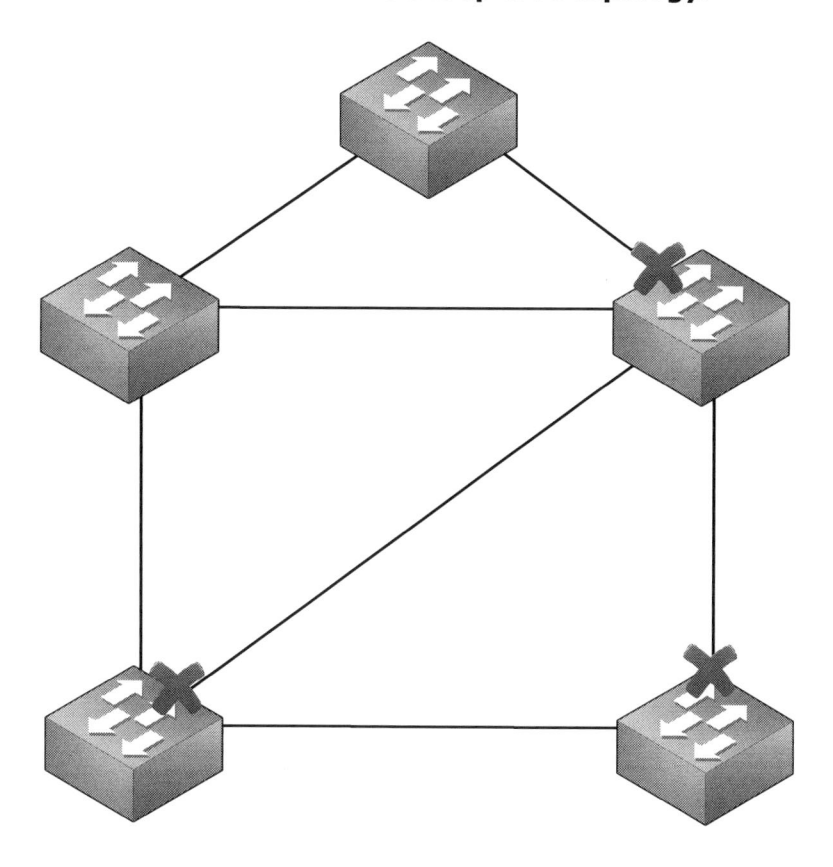

If you have a (larger) network like the one in the picture above you will see that spanning-tree will block multiple interfaces so that we end up with a loop-free topology.

Now you have an idea how spanning-tree works, let's have a more detailed look to see how it operates.

SwitchA
Priority 32768
MAC: AAA

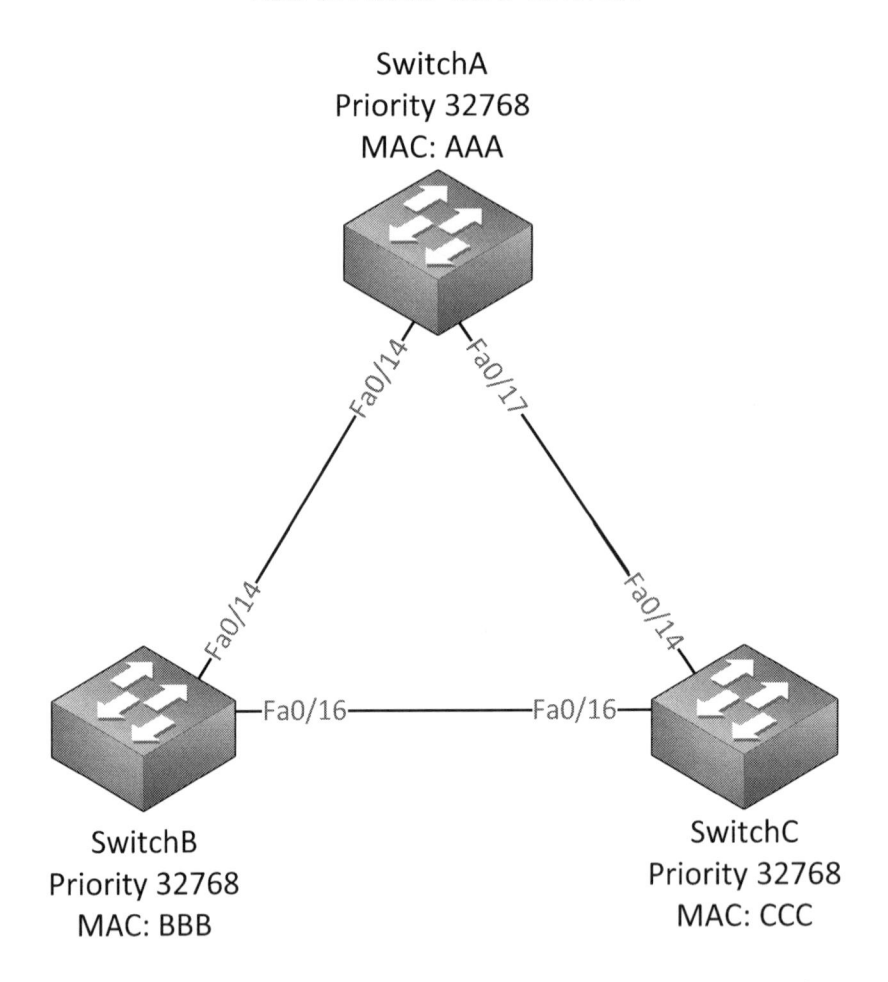

Fa0/14   Fa0/17

Fa0/14   Fa0/14

SwitchB —Fa0/16————Fa0/16— SwitchC

SwitchB
Priority 32768
MAC: BBB

SwitchC
Priority 32768
MAC: CCC

This is the topology I will be using to demonstrate spanning-tree. The switches are connected in a triangle which means that we have redundancy and thus a loop. In the picture you will find the MAC address for each switch but I have simplified them for this example:

- SwitchA: MAC address AAA
- SwitchB: MAC address BBB
- SwitchC: MAC address CCC

In our picture you can also see a **priority** field which has value 32768 on all switches. This is a default value that we can change if we want, I'll show you later why and how we can do this.

Switches running spanning-tree exchange information with a special message called the **(BPDU) bridge protocol data unit.** All the information in the BPDU is needed to create and maintain the spanning-tree topology.

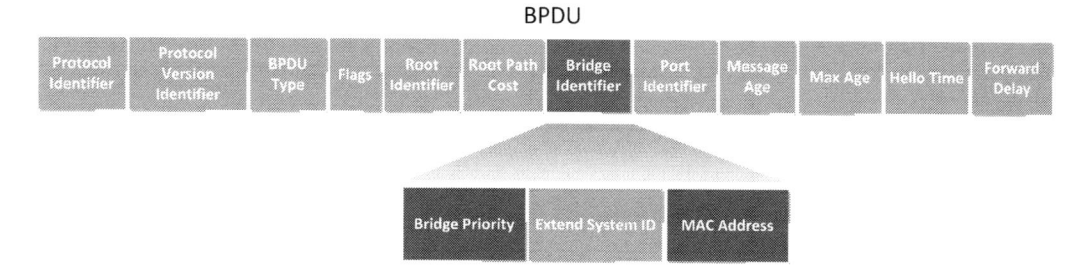

6. STP (Spanning Tree Protocol)

BPDU

| Protocol Identifier | Protocol Version Identifier | BPDU Type | Flags | Root Identifier | Root Path Cost | Bridge Identifier | Port Identifier | Message Age | Max Age | Hello Time | Forward Delay |

Bridge Identifier breakdown: Bridge Priority | Extend System ID | MAC Address

You can see the BPDU in the picture above and the only field that is important right now is the **bridge identifier**. It contains the **bridge priority** and the **MAC address**. It also has a extend system ID field but that's of no concern to us at this moment.

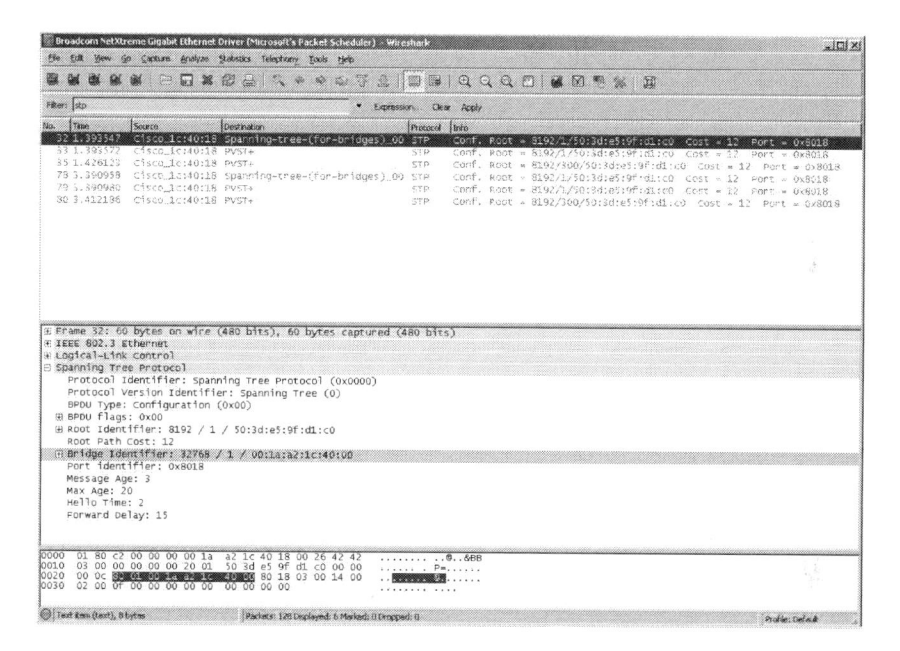

If you run Wireshark on a device that is connected to a Cisco switch you can capture a BPDU and see its contents.

Let me give you a demonstration of how spanning-tree operates and how it uses the information in the bridge identifier:

97

SwitchA
Priority 32768
MAC: AAA

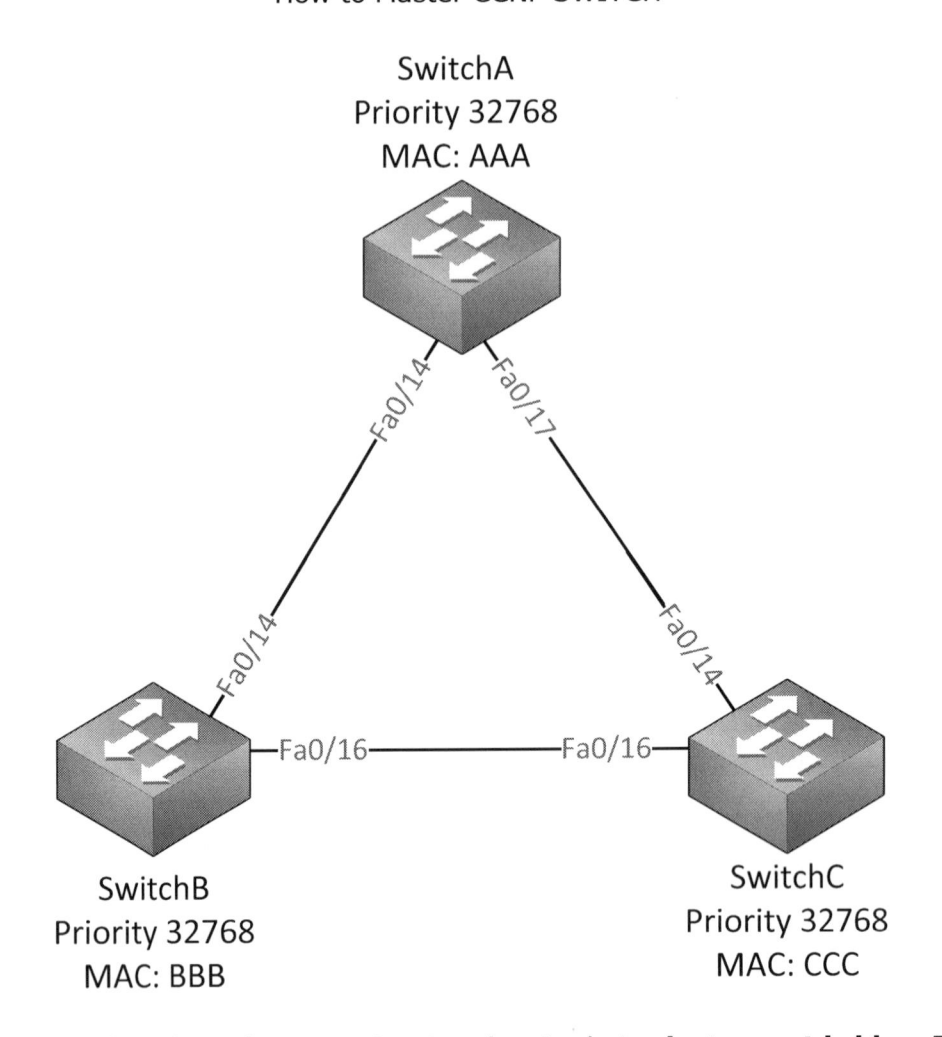

Fa0/14   Fa0/17

Fa0/14   Fa0/14

SwitchB —Fa0/16————Fa0/16— SwitchC

SwitchB
Priority 32768
MAC: BBB

SwitchC
Priority 32768
MAC: CCC

1. The first thing that spanning-tree has to do is **elect a root bridge**. The root bridge is the switch with the lowest **bridge identifier.** The bridge identifier as I just explained consists of the priority plus MAC address. In our example SwitchA will become the root bridge. The priority is the same on all switches so the MAC address will be the tiebreaker!

6. STP (Spanning Tree Protocol)

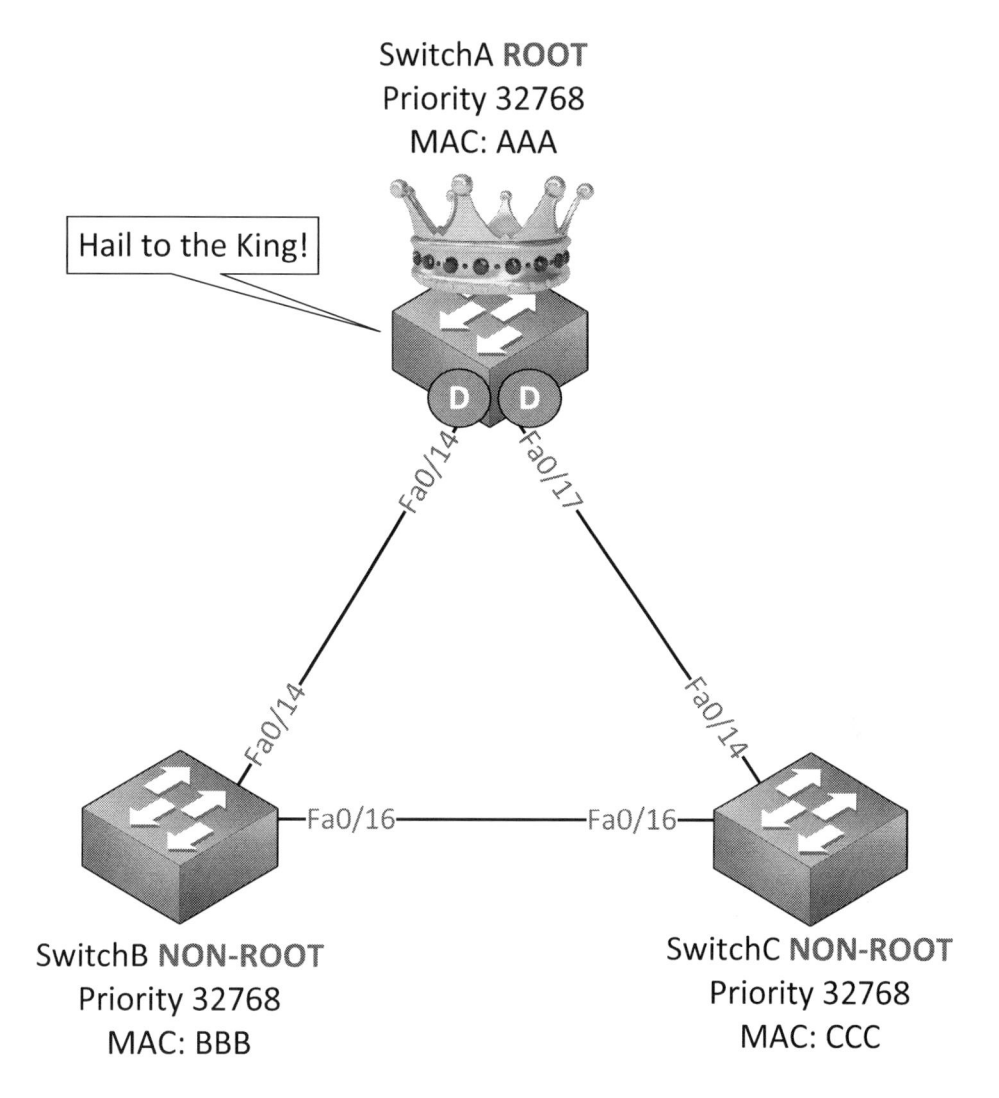

SwitchA **ROOT**
Priority 32768
MAC: AAA

Hail to the King!

D   D
Fa0/14   Fa0/17

Fa0/14   Fa0/14

—Fa0/16————Fa0/16—

SwitchB **NON-ROOT**   SwitchC **NON-ROOT**
Priority 32768   Priority 32768
MAC: BBB   MAC: CCC

2. SwitchA is now the root bridge because it has the best bridge identifier. All the other switches are called **non-root**. Interfaces that forward traffic are called **designated ports** in spanning-tree. On a root bridge the interfaces are always in forwarding mode because the non-root switches will need to find the root bridge. In the picture above I added the "D" to show that the fa0/14 and fa0/17 interfaces on SwitchA are designated and forwarding traffic.

SwitchA **ROOT**
Priority 32768
MAC: AAA

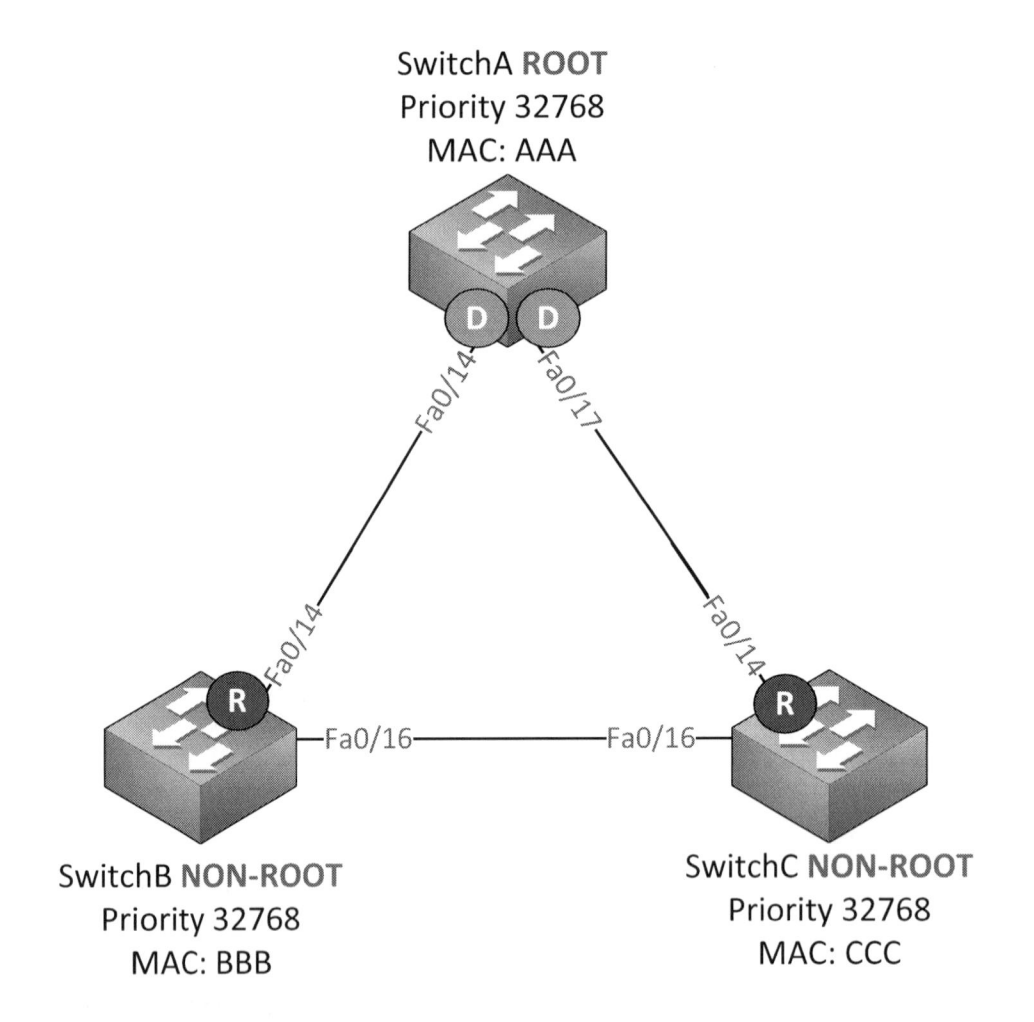

SwitchB **NON-ROOT**
Priority 32768
MAC: BBB

SwitchC **NON-ROOT**
Priority 32768
MAC: CCC

3. All the non-root switches have to find the **shortest path to the root bridge**. So what is the shortest path? Spanning-tree is smart enough to decide that a Gigabit interface is a better choice than a FastEthernet link. To keep things simple at this stage I am using FastEthernet links between all switches. SwitchB its fa0/14 interface is the shortest path to get to the root bridge. SwitchC its fa0/14 is also the shortest path to get to the root bridge. The interface that leads us to the root bridge is called the **root port** and is forwarding traffic.

6. STP (Spanning Tree Protocol)

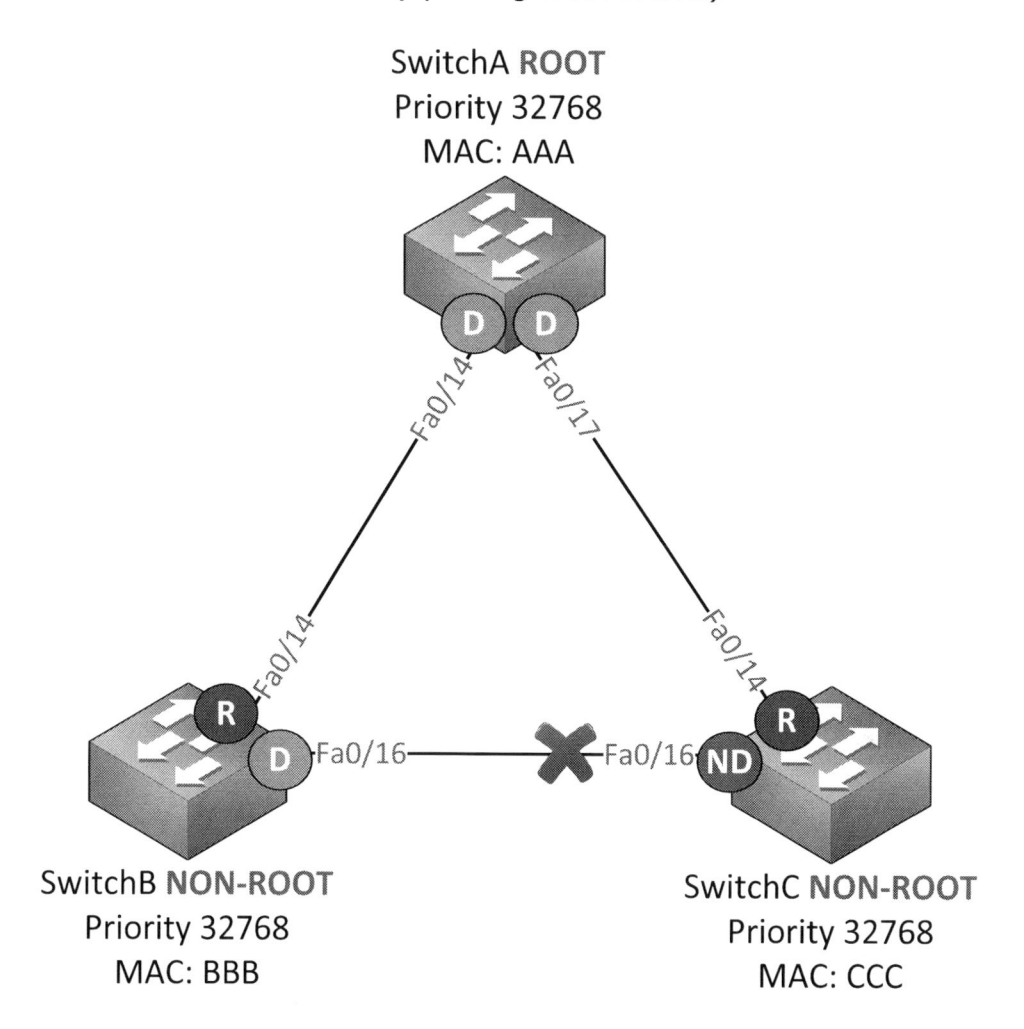

SwitchA ROOT
Priority 32768
MAC: AAA

SwitchB NON-ROOT
Priority 32768
MAC: BBB

SwitchC NON-ROOT
Priority 32768
MAC: CCC

4. In order to break the loop we have to block an interface between SwitchB and SwitchC. So which one are we going to block? SwitchB and SwitchC will duke it out by comparing their bridge identifier. Keep in mind the bridge identifier consists of the priority and MAC address. The lowest bridge identifier is the best one, SwitchB and SwitchC have the same priority but SwitchB has a lower MAC address. SwitchB will win this battle and as a result the fa0/16 of SwitchC will be blocked. A port that is **blocking** traffic is called a **non-designated** port. The fa0/16 interface of SwitchB will become a designated port.

Because the priority is 32768 by default the MAC address is the tie-breaker for the root bridge election. Which switch do you think will become the root bridge?

Your brand-spanking-brand-new-just-out-of-the-box switch or that old dust collector that has been in the datacenter for 10 years? The old switch probably has a lower MAC address and will become the root bridge...not a good idea right? I'll show you how to change the priority so the MAC address is no longer

101

the tie-breaker!

Are you following me so far? Good! You just learned the basics of spanning-tree. Let's add some more detail to this story...

Non-root bridges need to find the **shortest path to the root bridge**. In our previous example this was easy because all the interfaces are FastEthernet. What will happen if we have a mix of different interface types like Ethernet, FastEthernet and Gigabit? Let's find out!

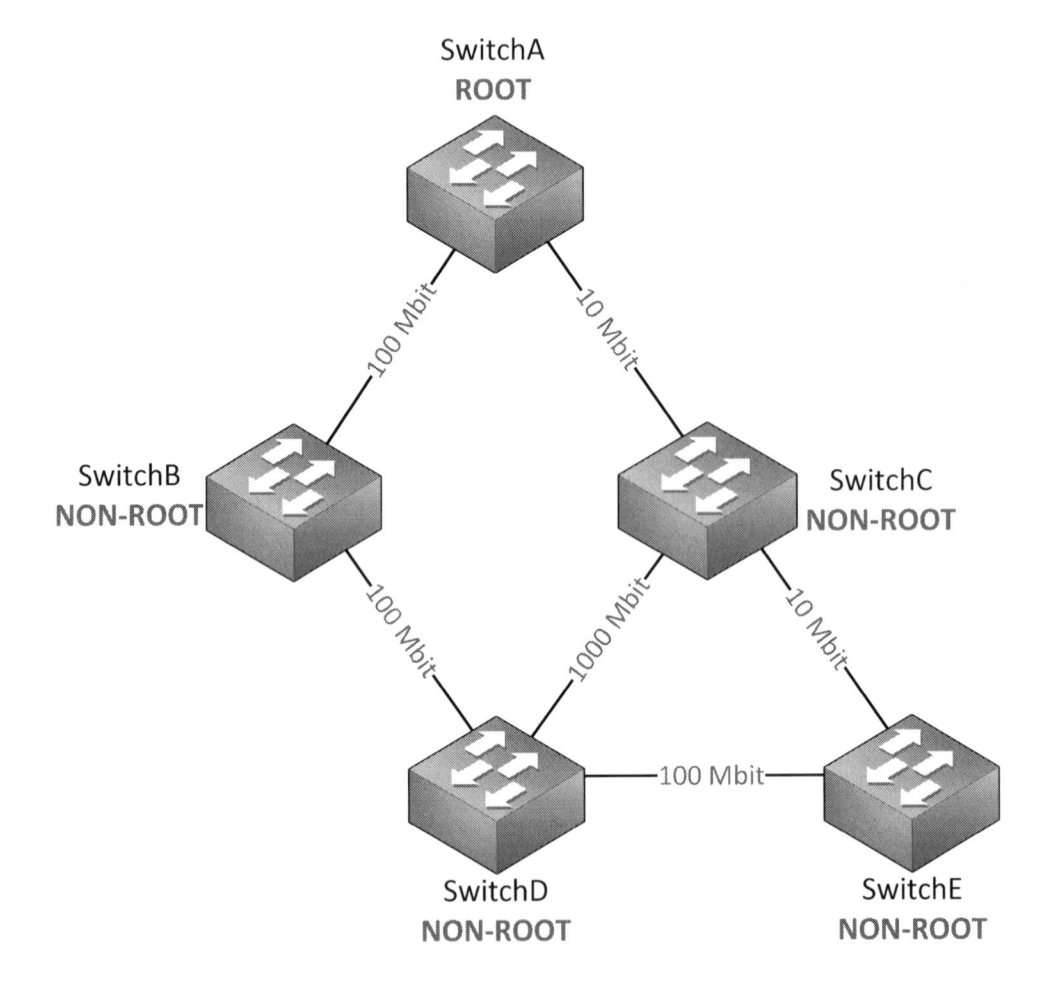

SwitchA
ROOT

100 Mbit
10 Mbit

SwitchB
NON-ROOT

SwitchC
NON-ROOT

100 Mbit
1000 Mbit
10 Mbit

100 Mbit

SwitchD
NON-ROOT

SwitchE
NON-ROOT

In the picture above we have a larger network with multiple switches. You can also see that there are different interface types, we have Ethernet (10 Mbit), FastEthernet (100Mbit) and Gigabit (1000Mbit). SwitchA on top is the root bridge so all other switches are non-root and need to find the shortest path to the root bridge.

6. STP (Spanning Tree Protocol)

	Cost
10 Mbit	100
100 Mbit	19
1000 Mbit	4

Spanning-tree uses **cost** to determine the shortest path to the root bridge. The slower the interface, the higher the cost is. The path with the lowest cost will be used to reach the root bridge.

BPDU

| Protocol Identifier | Protocol Version Identifier | BPDU Type | Flags | Root Identifier | Root Path Cost | Bridge Identifier | Port Identifier | Message Age | Max Age | Hello Time | Forward Delay |

In the BPDU you can see a field called **root path cost**. This is where each switch will insert the **cost of its shortest path** to the root bridge. Once the switches found out which switch is declared as root bridge they will look for the shortest path to get there. **BPDUs will flow from the root bridge downwards to all switches**.

If you studied CCNA or CCNP ROUTE then this story about spanning-tree cost might sound familiar. OSPF (Open Shortest Path First) also uses cost to calculate the shortest path to its destination. Both spanning-tree and OSPF use cost to find the shortest path but there is one big difference. OSPF builds a topology database (LSDB) so all routers know exactly what the network looks like. Spanning-tree is "dumb"...switches have no idea what the topology looks like. BPDUs flow from the root bridge downwards to all switches, switches will make a decision based on the BPDUs that they receive!

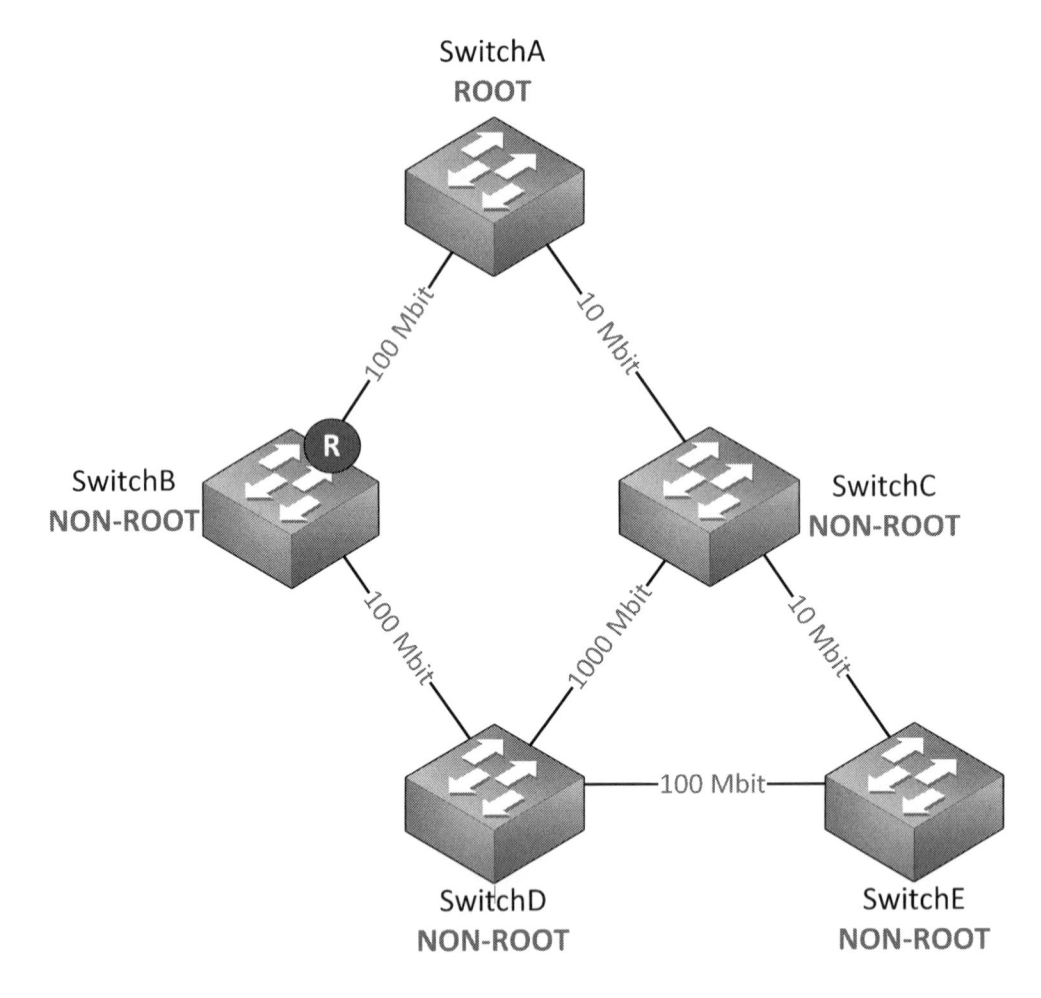

SwitchB will use the direct link to SwitchA as its root port since this is a 100 Mbit interface and has a cost of 19. It will forward BPDUs towards SwitchD; in the root path cost field of the BPDU you will find a cost of 19.

6. STP (Spanning Tree Protocol)

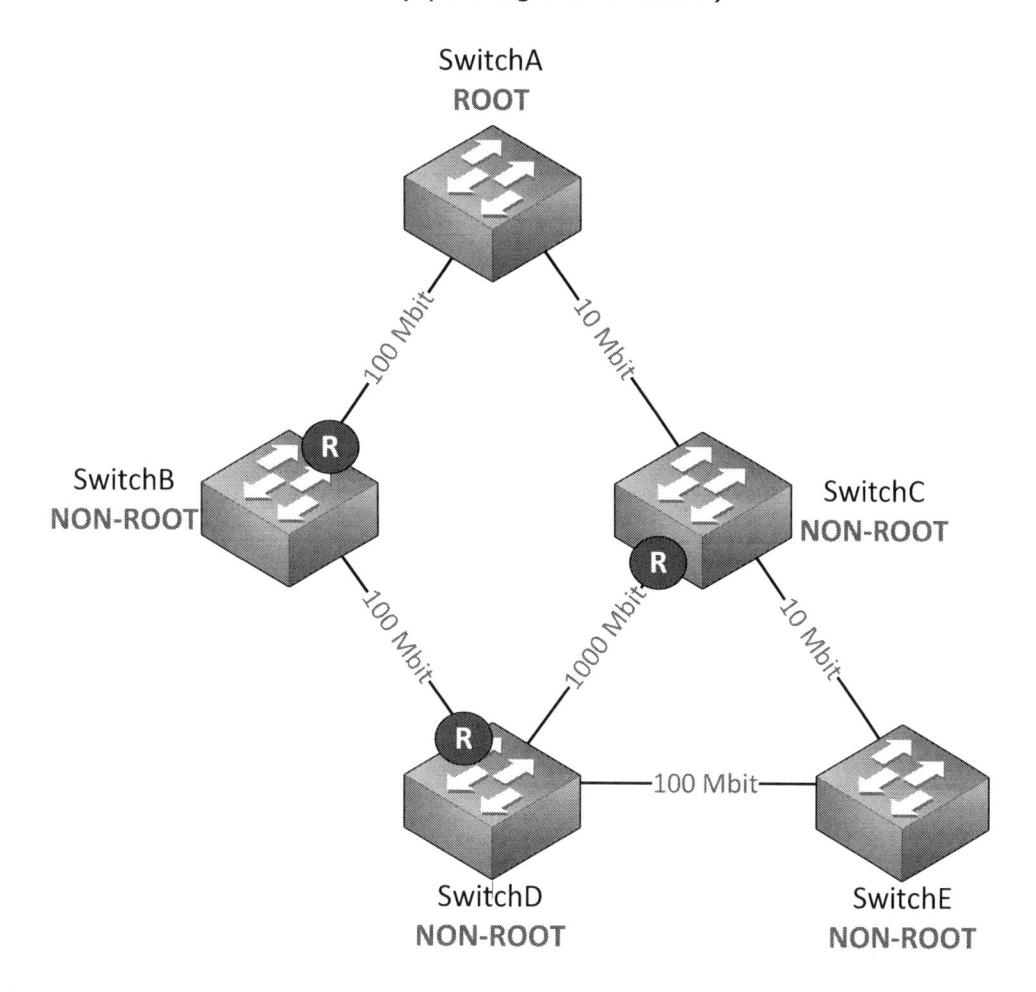

SwitchA
ROOT

100 Mbit
10 Mbit

SwitchB
NON-ROOT

SwitchC
NON-ROOT

100 Mbit
1000 Mbit
10 Mbit

100 Mbit

SwitchD
NON-ROOT

SwitchE
NON-ROOT

This picture needs some more explanation so let me break it down:

- SwitchC will receive BPDUs on its 10 Mbit interface (cost 100) and on its 1000 Mbit interface (cost 4). It will use its 1000 Mbit interface as its root port.
- SwitchC will forward BPDUs to SwitchD. The root path cost field will be 100.
- SwitchD receives a BPDU from SwitchB with a root path cost of 19.
- SwitchD receives a BPDU from SwitchC with a root path cost of 100.
- The path through SwitchB is shorter so this will become the root port for SwitchD.
- SwitchD will forward BPDUs towards SwitchC and SwitchE. In the root path cost field of the BPDU we will find a cost of 38 (its root path cost of 19 + its own interface cost of 19).
- SwitchC will forward BPDUs towards SwitchE and inserts a cost of 42 in the root path cost field (19 + 19 + 4).

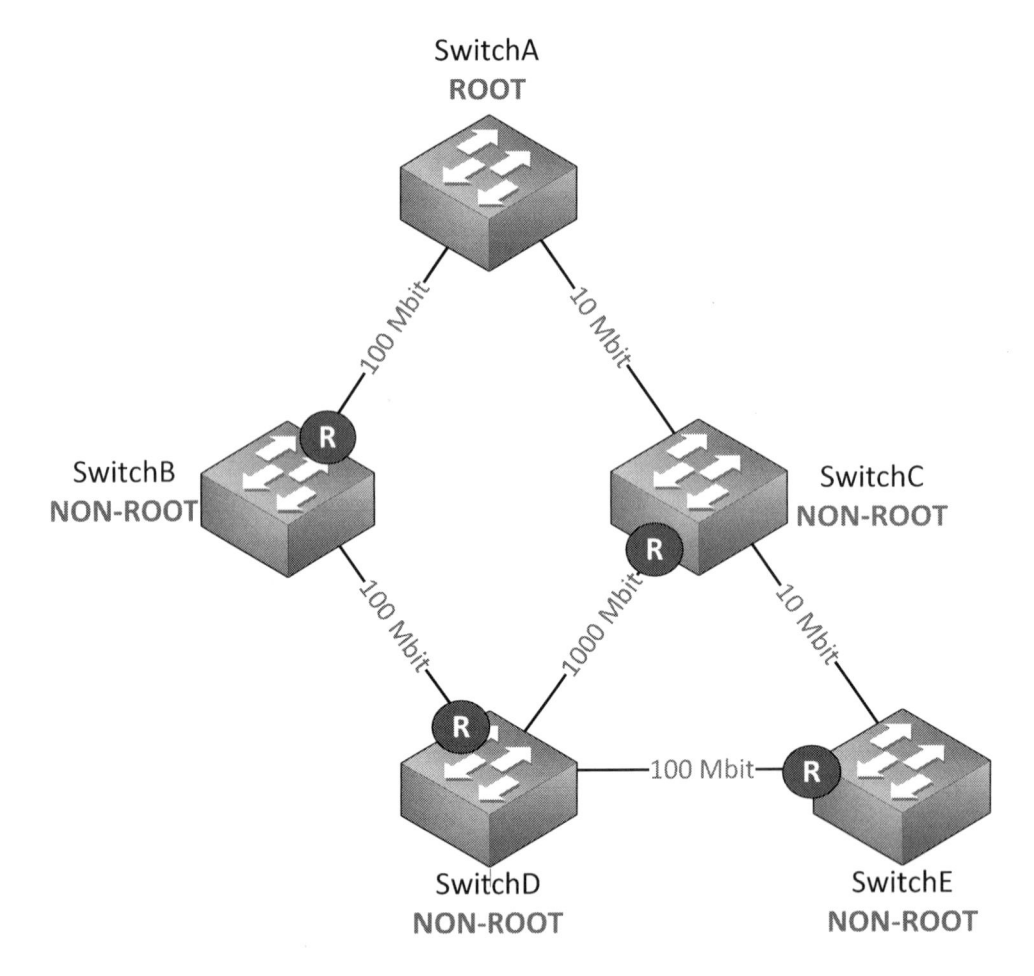

SwitchE receives BPDUs from SwitchC and SwitchD. In the BPDU we will look at the root path cost field and we'll see the following information:

- BPDU from SwitchC: cost 42
- BPDU from SwitchD: cost 38

SwitchE will add the cost of its own interface towards SwitchD so the total cost to reach the root bridge through SwitchD is 38 + 19 (cost of 100 Mbit interface) = 57. The total cost to reach the root bridge through SwitchC is 42 + 100 (10 Mbit interface) = 142. As result it will select the interface towards SwitchD as its root port.

Are you following me so far? Keep in mind that switches only make decisions on the BPDUs that they receive! They have no idea what the topology looks like. The only thing they do know is on which interface they received the **best BPDU.** The best BPDU is the one with the shortest path to the root bridge!

6. STP (Spanning Tree Protocol)

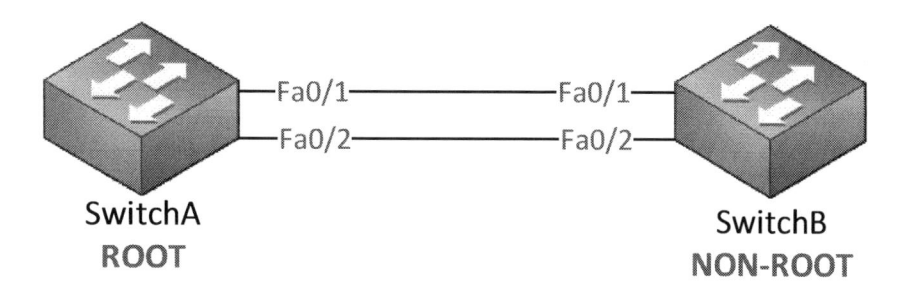

SwitchA — Fa0/1 — Fa0/1 — **SwitchB**
ROOT — Fa0/2 — Fa0/2 — **NON-ROOT**

What if the cost is equal? Take a look at the picture above. SwitchA is the root bridge and SwitchB is non-root. We have two links between these switches so that we have redundancy. Redundancy means loops so spanning-tree is going to block one the interfaces on SwitchB.

SwitchB will receive BPDUs on both interfaces but the root path cost field will be the same! Which one are we going to block? Fa0/1 or fa0/2?

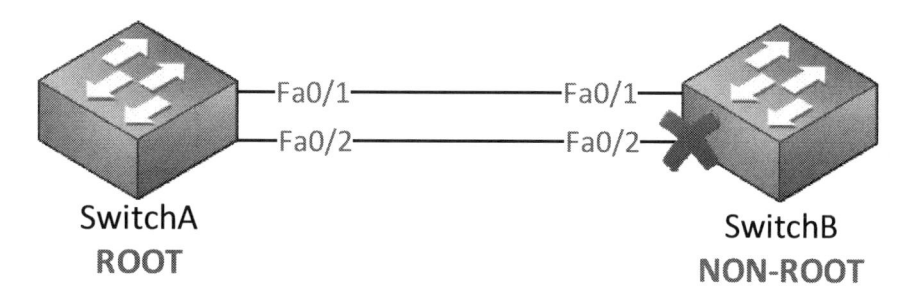

SwitchA — Fa0/1 — Fa0/1 — **SwitchB**
ROOT — Fa0/2 — Fa0/2✗ — **NON-ROOT**

When the cost is equal spanning-tree will look at the **port priority.** By default the port priority is the **same for all interfaces** which means that the **interface number will be the tie-breaker.** The lowest interface number will be chosen so fa0/2 will be blocked here. Of course port priority is a value that we can change so we can choose which interface will be blocked, I'll show you later how to do this!

Whenever spanning-tree has to make a decision, this is the list that it will use. This is something to write down and remember:

1) **Lowest bridge ID**: the switch with the lowest bridge ID becomes the root bridge.
2) **Lowest path cost to root bridge**: when the switch receives multiple BPDUs it will select the interface that has the lowest cost to reach the root bridge as the root port.
3) **Lowest sender bridge ID**: when a switch is connected to two switches that it can use to reach the root bridge and the cost to reach the root bridge is the same, it will select the interface connecting to the switch with the lowest bridge ID as the root port.
4) **Lowest sender port ID**: when the switch has two interfaces connecting to the same switch, and the cost to reach the root bridge is

the same it will use the interface with the lowest number as the root port.

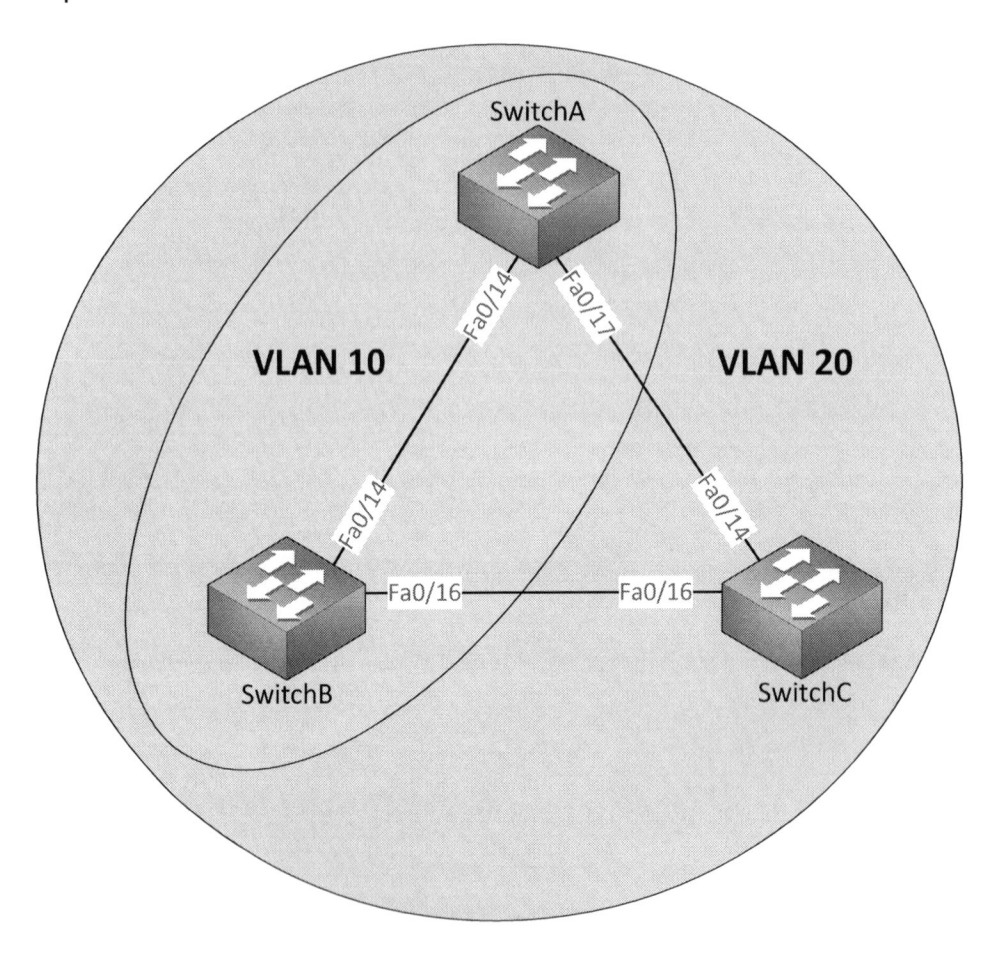

There's more to spanning-tree! Take a look at the picture above:

- VLAN 10 is configured on SwitchA and SwitchB.
- VLAN 20 is configured on SwitchA, SwitchB and SwitchC.

Question for you: do we have a loop in VLAN 10? What about VLAN 20?

There's a big difference between our **physical** and **logical** topology. We don't have a loop in VLAN 10 because it only runs on the link between SwitchA and SwitchB. We DO have a loop within VLAN 20 however.

How does spanning-tree deal with this? Simple...we'll just calculate a different spanning-tree for each VLAN! The oldest version of spanning-tree is called **CST (Common Spanning-Tree)** and is defined in the 802.1D standard. It only calculates a **single spanning-tree for all VLANs.**

Another version of spanning-tree is able to calculate a topology for **each**

6. STP (Spanning Tree Protocol)

VLAN. This version is called **PVST (Per VLAN Spanning-Tree)** and it's the **default on Cisco switches.**

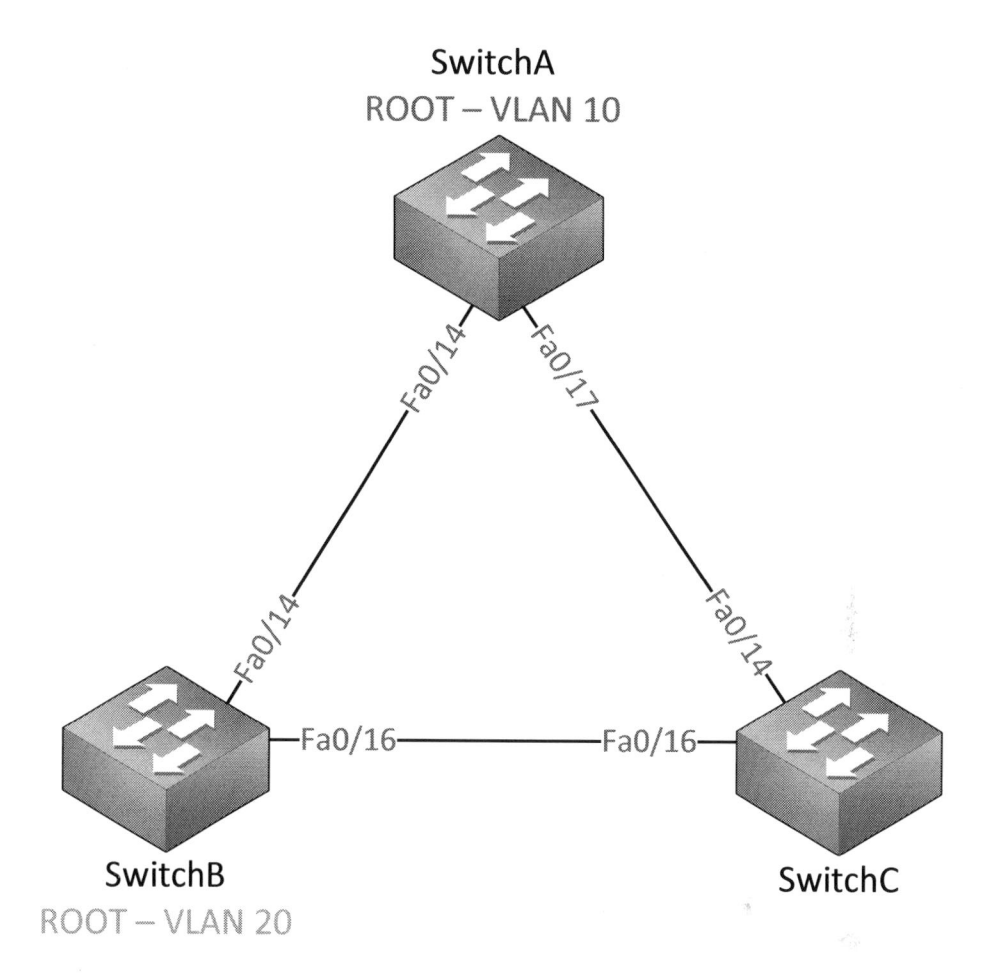

SwitchA
ROOT – VLAN 10

Fa0/14
Fa0/17
Fa0/14
Fa0/14
Fa0/16 ─────── Fa0/16

SwitchB
ROOT – VLAN 20

SwitchC

If we use PVST we can create a different root bridge for each VLAN if we want. SwitchA could be the root bridge for VLAN 10 and SwitchB could be the root bridge for VLAN 20. Why would you want to do this?

SwitchA
ROOT – VLAN 10
ROOT – VLAN 20

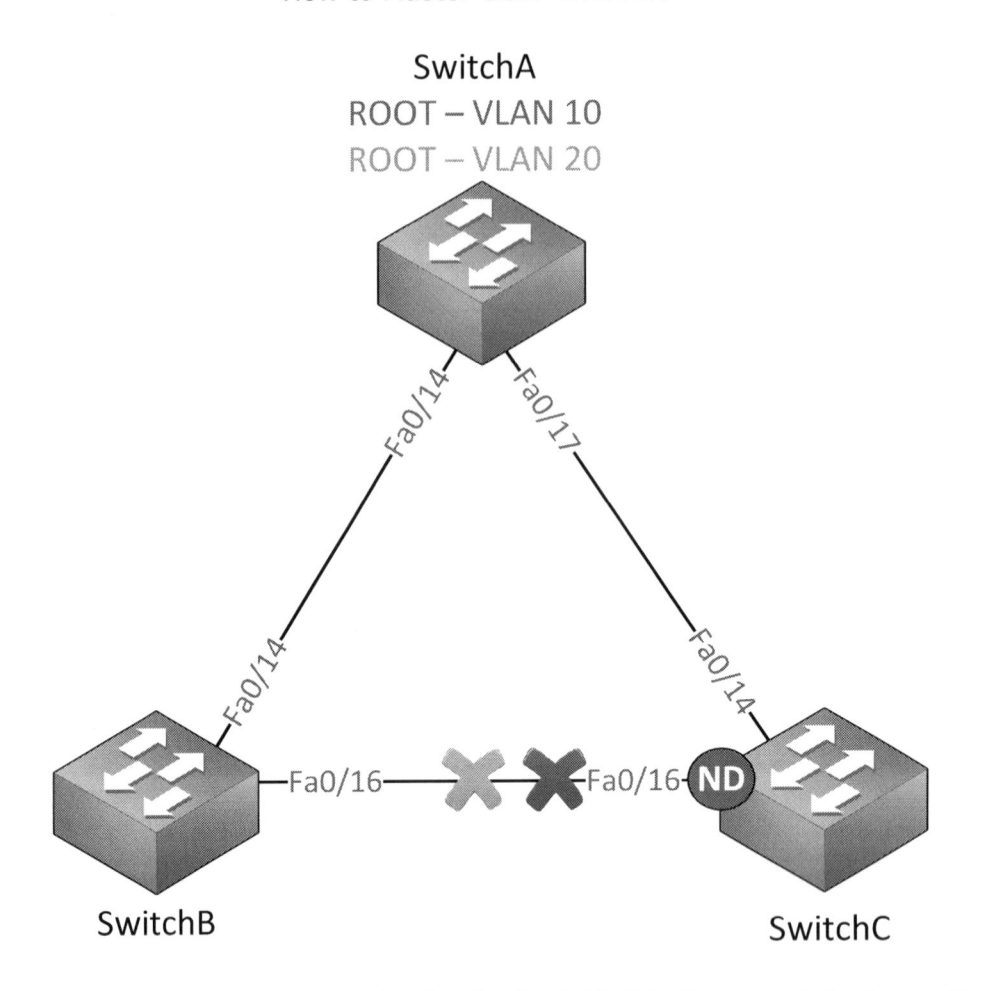

If I would make one switch root bridge for both VLANs then one interface will be blocked for both VLANs. In my example above SwitchA is the root bridge for VLAN 10 and 20 and as a result the fa0/16 interface on SwitchC is blocked for **both VLANs.** No traffic will be forwarded on the fa0/16 interface at all. Imagine these were 10 Gigabit interfaces. It would be a shame if one of those expensive interfaces wasn't doing anything right?

6. STP (Spanning Tree Protocol)

SwitchA
ROOT – VLAN 10

SwitchB
ROOT – VLAN 20

SwitchC

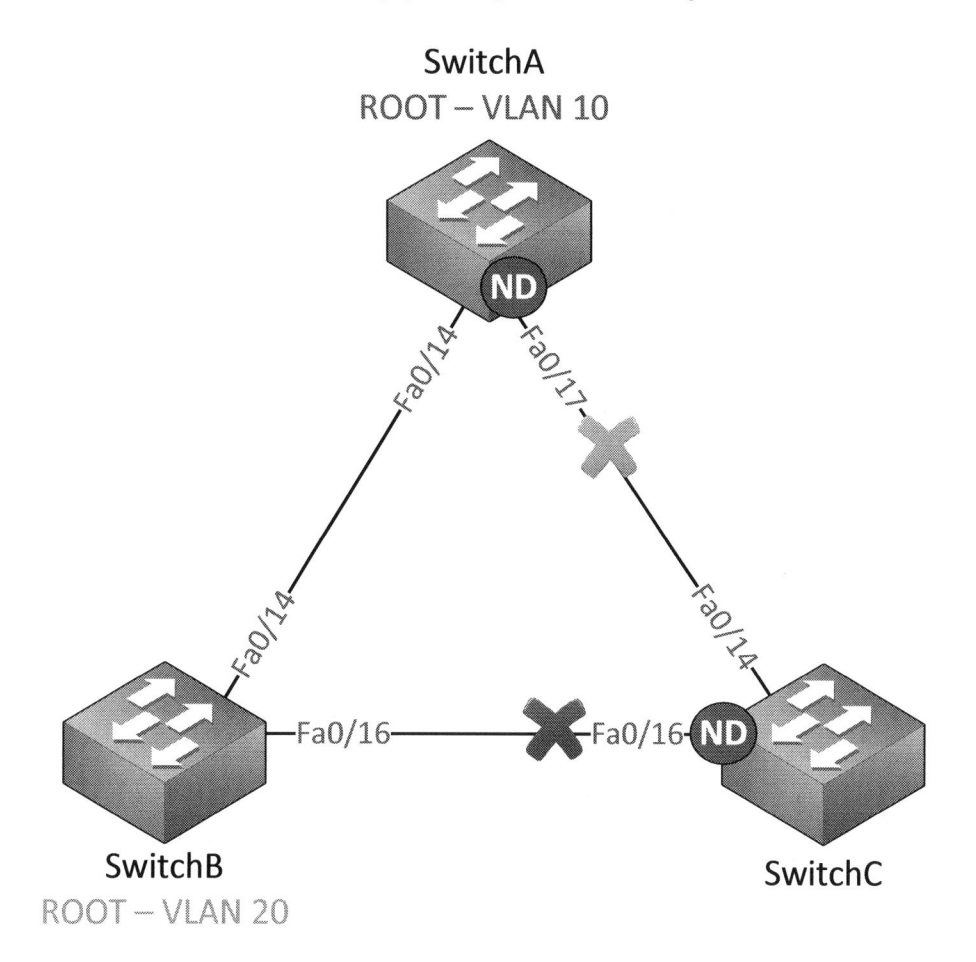

If I choose another switch as the root bridge for VLAN 20 we will see different results. In my example I made SwitchB the root bridge for VLAN 20. As you can see the fa0/17 interface on SwitchA is blocked for VLAN 10 while the fa0/17 interface on SwitchA is blocked for VLAN 20. The advantage of having multiple root bridges is that I can do some **load sharing/balancing.**

How are we doing so far? There's one more topic I want to discuss before we dive into the configuration of spanning-tree. We'll take a look at the timers of spanning-tree.

If you have played with some Cisco switches before you might have noticed that every time you plug in a cable the led above the interface was orange and after a while became green. What is happening at this moment is that spanning tree is determining the state of the interface.

This is what happens as soon as you plug in a cable:

- **Listening state**: Only a root or designated port will move to the listening state. The non-designated port will stay in the blocking state. No data transmission occurs at this state for 15 seconds just to make sure the topology doesn't change in the meantime. After the listening state we move to the learning state.

- **Learning state:** At this moment the interface will process Ethernet frames by looking at the source MAC address to fill the mac-address-table. Ethernet frames however are not forwarded to the destination. It takes 15 seconds to move to the next state called the forwarding state.

- **Forwarding state:** This is the final state of the interface and finally the interface will forward Ethernet frames so that we have data transmission!

When a port is not a designated or root port it will be in **blocking mode**.

This means it takes 30 seconds in total to move from listening to forwarding...that's not really fast right? This will happen on **all interfaces** on the switch.

When an interface is in blocking mode and the topology changes, it's possible that an interface that is currently in blocking mode has to move to the forwarding state. When this is the case, the blocking mode will last for 20 seconds before it moves to the listening state. This means that it takes 20 (blocking) + 15 (listening) + 15 (learning) = 50 seconds before the interface is in the forwarding state.

Any modern PC boots much faster than 30 seconds. Here's an overview of the port states:

State	Forward Frames	Learn MAC addresses	Duration
Blocking	No	No	20 seconds
Listening	No	No	15 seconds
Learning	No	Yes	15 seconds
Forwarding	Yes	Yes	-

There is a way to speed up this process; I'll show you how to do this later.

What do you think of spanning-tree so far? In the next part of this chapter I'm going to look at some real switches and walk you through the configuration.

6. STP (Spanning Tree Protocol)

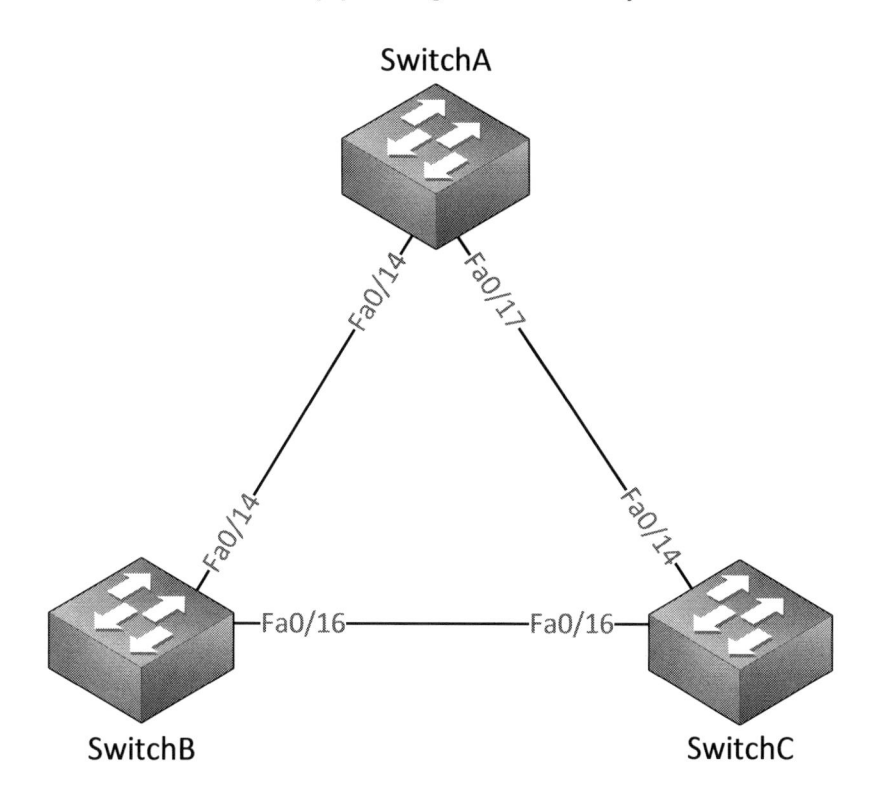

[Topology diagram: SwitchA at top connects via Fa0/14 to SwitchB's Fa0/14 and via Fa0/17 to SwitchC's Fa0/14. SwitchB's Fa0/16 connects to SwitchC's Fa0/16.]

This is the topology we will use. Spanning-tree is enabled by default; let's start by checking some show commands.

```
SwitchA#show spanning-tree

VLAN0001
  Spanning tree enabled protocol ieee
  Root ID    Priority    32769
             Address     000f.34ca.1000
             Cost        19
             Port        19 (FastEthernet0/17)
             Hello Time  2 sec  Max Age 20 sec  Forward Delay 15 sec

  Bridge ID  Priority    32769  (priority 32768 sys-id-ext 1)
             Address     0011.bb0b.3600
             Hello Time  2 sec  Max Age 20 sec  Forward Delay 15 sec
             Aging Time 300

Interface           Role Sts Cost      Prio.Nbr Type
------------------- ---- --- --------- -------- --------------------
Fa0/14              Desg FWD 19        128.16   P2p
Fa0/17              Root FWD 19        128.19   P2p
```

113

The **show spanning-tree** command is the most important show command to remember. There's quite some stuff here so I'm going to break it down for you!

```
VLAN0001
  Spanning tree enabled protocol ieee
```

We are looking at the spanning-tree information for VLAN 1. Spanning-tree has multiple versions and the default version on Cisco switches is PVST (Per VLAN spanning-tree). This is the spanning-tree for VLAN 1.

```
Root ID    Priority    32769
           Address     000f.34ca.1000
           Cost        19
           Port        19 (FastEthernet0/17)
```

Here you see the **information of the root bridge**. You can see that it has a priority of 32769 and its MAC address is 000f.34ca.1000. From the perspective of SwitchA it has a cost of 19 to reach the root bridge. The port that leads to the root bridge is called the root port and for SwitchA this is fa0/17.

```
Bridge ID  Priority    32769  (priority 32768 sys-id-ext 1)
           Address     0011.bb0b.3600
```

This part shows us the **information about the local switch**, SwitchA in our case. There's something funny about the priority here....you can see it show two things:

- Priority 32769
- Priority 32768 sys-id-ext 1

The **sys-id-ext** value that you see is the VLAN number. The priority is 32768 but spanning-tree will add the VLAN number so we end up with priority value 32769. Last but not least we can see the MAC address of SwitchA which is 0011.bb0b.3600.

```
Hello Time   2 sec   Max Age 20 sec   Forward Delay 15 sec
```

Here's some information on the different times that spanning-tree uses:

- **Hello time:** every 2 seconds a BPDU is sent.
- **Max Age:** If we don't receive BPDUs for 20 seconds we know something has changed in the network and we need to re-check the topology.
- **Forward Delay:** This is the time spent in the "listening" and "learning" states. By default it's 15 seconds.

6. STP (Spanning Tree Protocol)

```
Interface              Role Sts Cost      Prio.Nbr Type
-------------------    ---- --- --------- -------- ----------------
Fa0/14                 Desg FWD 19        128.16   P2p
Fa0/17                 Root FWD 19        128.19   P2p
```

The last part of the show spanning-tree commands shows us the interfaces and their status. SwitchA has two interfaces:

- Fa0/14 is a **designated** port and in **(FWD) forwarding mode**.
- Fa0/17 is a **root** port and in **(FWD) forwarding mode.**

The **prio.nbr** you see here is the **port priority** that I explained earlier. We'll play with this in a bit.

Because only non-root switches have a root-port I can conclude that SwitchA is a non-root switch. I know that fa0/17 on SwitchA leads to the root bridge.

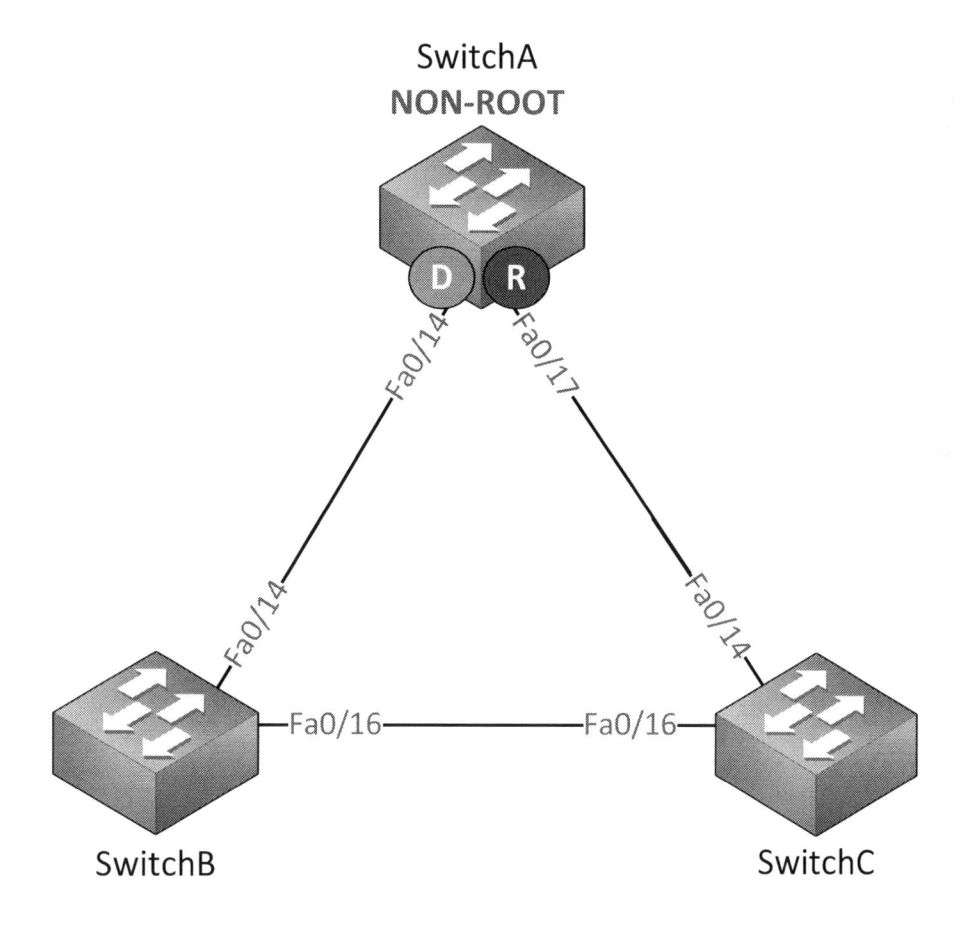

For the sake of having a good overview I just added what we saw in the show spanning-tree command in the picture above. We know that SwitchA is a non-root, fa0/14 is a designated port and fa0/17 is a root port.

115

```
SwitchB#show spanning-tree

VLAN0001
  Spanning tree enabled protocol ieee
  Root ID    Priority    32769
             Address     000f.34ca.1000
             Cost        19
             Port        18 (FastEthernet0/16)
             Hello Time  2 sec  Max Age 20 sec  Forward Delay
15 sec

  Bridge ID  Priority    32769  (priority 32768 sys-id-ext 1)
             Address     0019.569d.5700
             Hello Time  2 sec  Max Age 20 sec  Forward Delay
15 sec
             Aging Time 300

Interface           Role Sts Cost      Prio.Nbr Type
------------------- ---- --- --------- -------- ----------------
-----------------
Fa0/14              Altn BLK 19        128.16   P2p
Fa0/16              Root FWD 19        128.18   P2p
```

Let's take a look at SwitchB...what do we have here?

```
  Root ID    Priority    32769
             Address     000f.34ca.1000
             Cost        19
             Port        18 (FastEthernet0/16)
```

Here we see information about the root bridge. This information is similar to what we saw on SwitchA. The root port for SwitchB seems to be fa0/16.

```
  Bridge ID  Priority    32769  (priority 32768 sys-id-ext 1)
             Address     0019.569d.5700
```

This is the information about SwitchB. The priority is the same as on SwitchA, only the MAC address (0019.569d.5700) is different.

```
Interface           Role Sts Cost      Prio.Nbr Type
------------------- ---- --- --------- -------- ----------------
-----------------
Fa0/14              Altn BLK 19        128.16   P2p
Fa0/16              Root FWD 19        128.18   P2p
```

This part looks interesting; there are two things we see here:

- Interface fa0/14 is an **non-designated** port and in **(BLK) blocking** mode. Cisco IOS switches will show the role as ALTN (Alternate port)

6. STP (Spanning Tree Protocol)

but in reality this is a non-designated port. We'll talk about the alternate port later when we discuss rapid spanning-tree.
- Interface fa0/16 is a **root** port and in **(FWD) forwarding** mode.

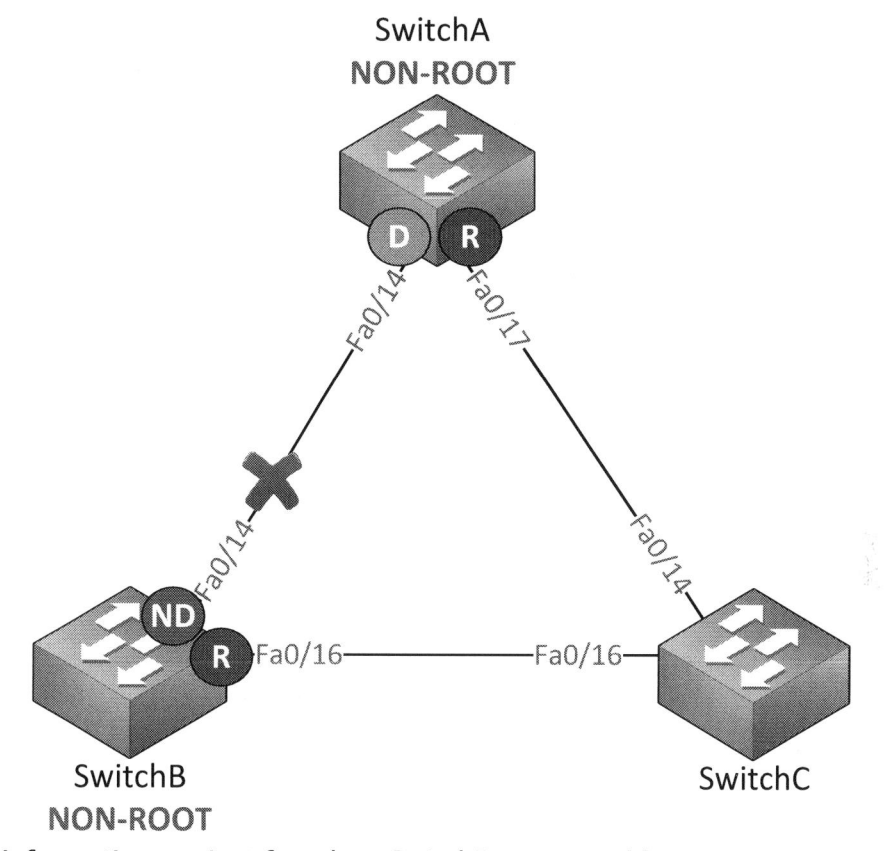

SwitchA
NON-ROOT

SwitchB
NON-ROOT

SwitchC

With the information we just found on SwitchB we can add more items to our topology picture.

How to Master CCNP SWITCH

We are almost finished!

```
SwitchC#show spanning-tree

VLAN0001
  Spanning tree enabled protocol ieee
  Root ID    Priority    32769
             Address     000f.34ca.1000
             This bridge is the root
             Hello Time   2 sec  Max Age 20 sec  Forward Delay
15 sec

  Bridge ID  Priority    32769  (priority 32768 sys-id-ext 1)
             Address     000f.34ca.1000
             Hello Time   2 sec  Max Age 20 sec  Forward Delay
15 sec
             Aging Time 300

Interface        Role Sts Cost      Prio.Nbr Type
---------------- ---- --- --------- -------- --------------------
Fa0/14           Desg FWD 19        128.14   P2p
Fa0/16           Desg FWD 19        128.16   P2p
```

Let's break down what we have here:

```
  Root ID    Priority    32769
             Address     000f.34ca.1000
             This bridge is the root
```

Bingo...SwitchC is the root bridge in this network. We already knew that because SwitchA and SwitchB are both non-root but this is how we verify it by looking at SwitchC.

```
  Bridge ID  Priority    32769  (priority 32768 sys-id-ext 1)
             Address     000f.34ca.1000
```

We can also see the MAC address of SwitchC.

```
Interface        Role Sts Cost      Prio.Nbr Type
---------------- ---- --- --------- -------- --------------------
Fa0/14           Desg FWD 19        128.14   P2p
Fa0/16           Desg FWD 19        128.16   P2p
```

Both interfaces on SwitchC are **designated ports** and in **(FWD) forwarding** mode.

118

6. STP (Spanning Tree Protocol)

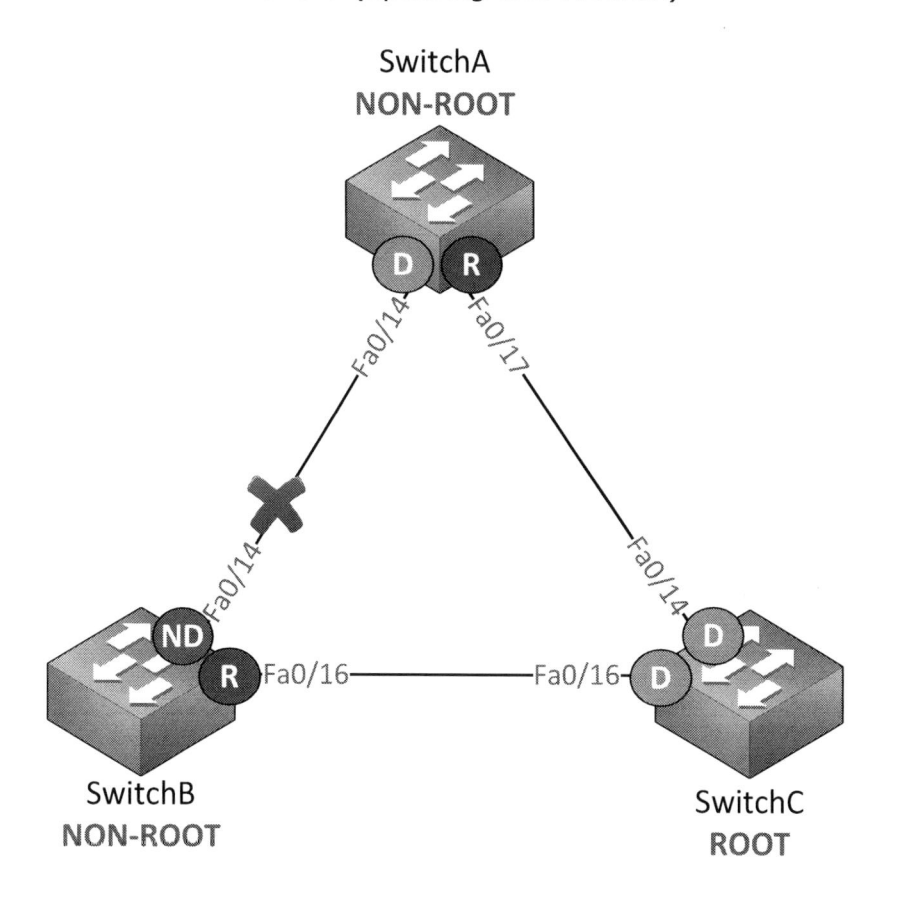

```
        SwitchA
       NON-ROOT
         (D)(R)
        Fa0/14  Fa0/17
       /            \
      /              \
   Fa0/14           Fa0/14
    X                  \
   /                    \
 (ND)                   (D)
  (R)─Fa0/16────Fa0/16─(D)
  SwitchB              SwitchC
  NON-ROOT              ROOT
```

Our picture is now complete. We successfully found out what the spanning-tree topology looks like by using the show spanning-tree command! Why was SwitchC chosen as the root bridge? We have to look at the bridge identifier for the answer:

```
SwitchA#show spanning-tree | begin Bridge ID
  Bridge ID  Priority    32769  (priority 32768 sys-id-ext 1)
             Address     0011.bb0b.3600
```

```
SwitchB#show spanning-tree | begin Bridge ID
  Bridge ID  Priority    32769  (priority 32768 sys-id-ext 1)
             Address     0019.569d.5700
```

```
SwitchC#show spanning-tree | begin Bridge ID
  Bridge ID  Priority    32769  (priority 32768 sys-id-ext 1)
             Address     000f.34ca.1000
```

The priority is the same on all switches (32768) so we have to look at the MAC addresses:

- SwitchA: 0011.bb0b.3600
- SwitchB: 0019.569d.5700
- SwitchC: 000f.34ca.1000

SwitchC has the lowest MAC address so that's why it became root bridge. Why was the fa0/14 interface on SwitchB blocked and not the fa0/14 interface on SwitchA? Once again we have to look at the bridge identifier. The priority is 32768 on both switches so we have to compare the MAC address:

- SwitchA: 0011.bb0b.3600
- SwitchB: 0019.569d.5700

SwitchA has a lower MAC address and thus a better bridge identifier. That's why SwitchB lost this battle and has to shut down its fa0/14 interface.

What if I want another switch to become root bridge? For example SwitchA:

```
SwitchA(config)#spanning-tree vlan 1 root primary
```

There are two methods so I can change the root bridge. The **spanning-tree vlan root primary** command is the first one. This is a **macro that runs only once and** that looks at the current priority of the root bridge and changes your running-config to lower your own priority. Because we use PVST (Per VLAN Spanning-Tree) we can change this for each VLAN.

```
SwitchA#show spanning-tree

VLAN0001
  Spanning tree enabled protocol ieee
  Root ID    Priority    24577
             Address     0011.bb0b.3600
             This bridge is the root
             Hello Time  2 sec  Max Age 20 sec  Forward Delay
15 sec

  Bridge ID  Priority    24577    (priority 24576 sys-id-ext 1)
```

You can see that SwitchA is now the root bridge because its priority has been changed to 24576. It has decreased its priority by 4096 to become the root bridge.

```
SwitchA#show run | include priority
spanning-tree vlan 1 priority 24576
```

If you look at the running-config you can see that that the spanning-tree vlan

6. STP (Spanning Tree Protocol)

root primary command/macro changed the priority for us.

```
SwitchA(config)#spanning-tree vlan 1 priority ?
  <0-61440>  bridge priority in increments of 4096

SwitchA(config)#spanning-tree vlan 1 priority 4096
```

Changing the priority manually is the second method.

Just type in the **spanning-tree vlan priority** command and set it to whatever value you like.

```
SwitchA#show spanning-tree

VLAN0001
  Spanning tree enabled protocol ieee
  Root ID    Priority    4097
             Address     0011.bb0b.3600
             This bridge is the root
             Hello Time   2 sec  Max Age 20 sec  Forward Delay 15 sec

  Bridge ID  Priority    4097      (priority 4096 sys-id-ext 1)
             Address     0011.bb0b.3600
```

We can verify this by checking the show spanning-tree command once again.

Because SwitchA is now the root bridge our spanning-tree topology looks different:

```
SwitchA#show spanning-tree | begin Interface
Interface           Role Sts Cost      Prio.Nbr Type
------------------- ---- --- --------- -------- --------------------

Fa0/14              Desg FWD 19        128.16   P2p
Fa0/17              Desg FWD 19        128.19   P2p
```

```
SwitchB#show spanning-tree | begin Interface
Interface           Role Sts Cost      Prio.Nbr Type
------------------- ---- --- --------- -------- --------------------

Fa0/14              Root FWD 19        128.16   P2p
Fa0/16              Altn BLK 19        128.18   P2p
```

```
SwitchC#show spanning-tree | begin Interface
Interface           Role Sts Cost      Prio.Nbr Type
------------------- ---- --- --------- -------- --------------------

Fa0/14              Root FWD 19        128.14   P2p
Fa0/16              Desg FWD 19        128.16   P2p
```

This is all the information we need. Let's update our topology picture...

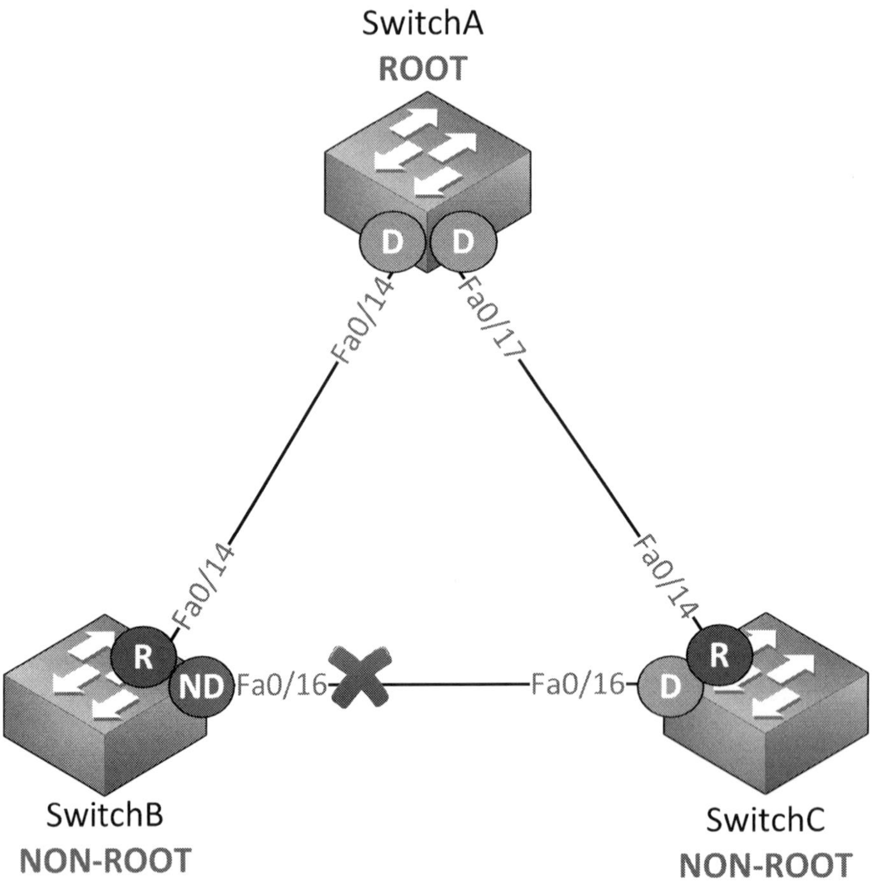
SwitchA
ROOT
D
D
Fa0/14
Fa0/17
Fa0/14
Fa0/14
R
ND
Fa0/16
Fa0/16
D
R
SwitchB
NON-ROOT
SwitchC
NON-ROOT

Let's play some more with spanning-tree! What if I want to change the root port on SwitchB so it reaches the root bridge through SwitchC? From SwitchB's perspective it can reach the root bridge through fa0/14 (cost 19) or by going through fa0/16 (cost 19+19 = 38). Let's change the cost and see what happens.

```
SwitchB(config)#interface fa0/14
SwitchB(config-if)#spanning-tree cost 500
```

Let's change the cost of the fa0/14 interface by using the **spanning-tree cost** command.

```
SwitchB#show spanning-tree | begin Interface
Interface           Role Sts Cost      Prio.Nbr Type
------------------- ---- --- --------- -------- ----------------
----------------
Fa0/14              Altn BLK 500       128.16   P2p
Fa0/16              Root FWD 19        128.18   P2p
```

6. STP (Spanning Tree Protocol)

You can see that the fa0/14 now has a cost of 500 and it has been blocked. Fa0/16 is now the root port.

```
SwitchB#show spanning-tree

VLAN0001
  Spanning tree enabled protocol ieee
  Root ID    Priority    4097
             Address     0011.bb0b.3600
             Cost        38
```

To reach the root the total cost is now 38.

```
SwitchB(config)#interface fa0/14
SwitchB(config-if)#no spanning-tree cost 500
```

Let's get rid of the higher cost before we continue.

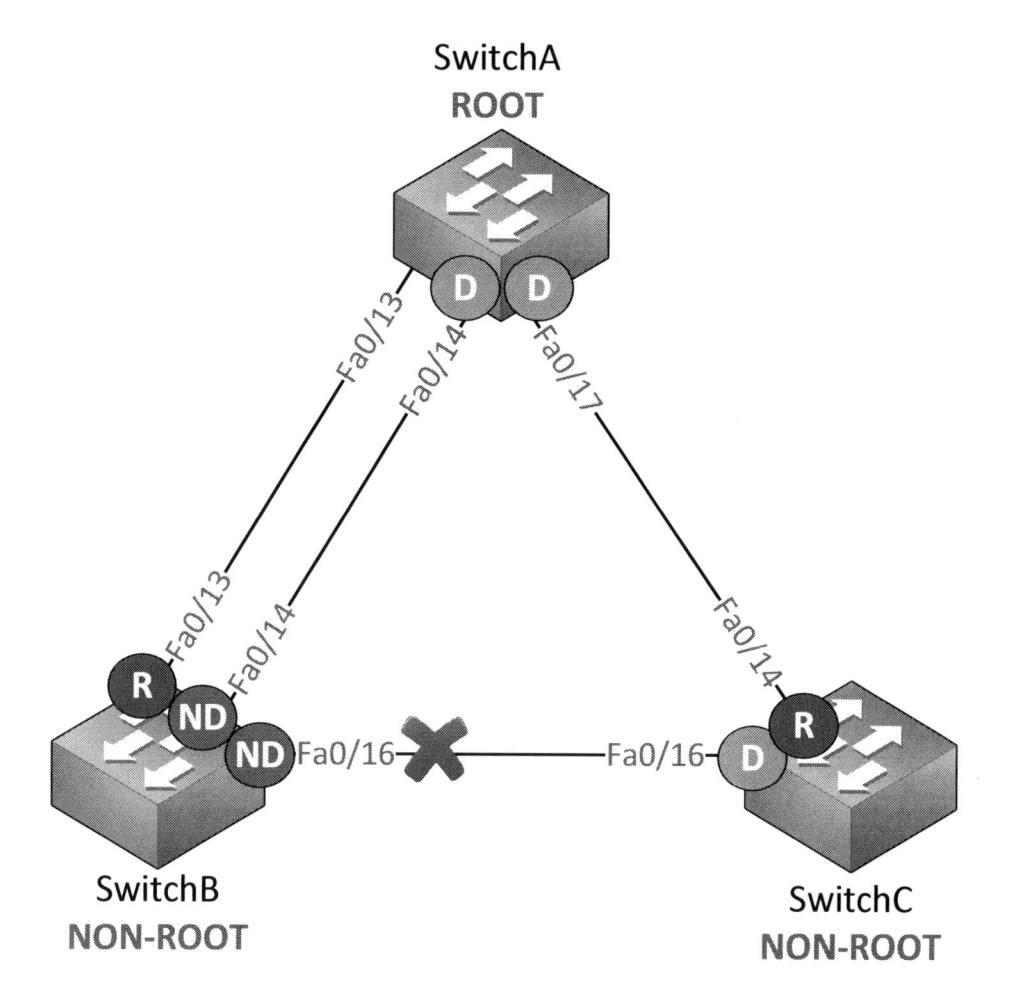

I have added another cable between SwitchA and SwitchB. In the picture

123

above you can see that fa0/13 is now the root port. Fa0/14 has been blocked.

```
SwitchB#show spanning-tree | begin Interface
Interface            Role Sts Cost      Prio.Nbr Type
-------------------- ---- --- --------- -------- ----------------
----------------
Fa0/13               Root FWD 19        128.15   P2p
Fa0/14               Altn BLK 19        128.16   P2p
Fa0/16               Altn BLK 19        128.18   P2p
```

Why did fa0/13 become the root port instead of fa0/14? The cost to reach the root bridge is the same on both interfaces. The answer lies in the port priority:

- Fa0/13: port priority 128.15
- Fa0/14: port priority 128.16

The "128" is a default value which we can change. 15 and 16 are the port numbers, each interface is assigned a port number. Fa0/13 has a lower port priority so that's why it was chosen.

Let's change the port priority and see what happens:

```
SwitchA(config)#interface fa0/14
SwitchA(config-if)#spanning-tree port-priority 16
```

Note that I'm changing the port priority on SwitchA, not on SwitchB. At the moment SwitchB is receiving a BPDU on its fa0/13 and fa0/14 interfaces. Both BPDUs are the same. By changing the port priority on SwitchA, SwitchB will receive a BPDU with a better port priority on its fa0/14 interface.

```
SwitchA#show spanning-tree | begin Interface
Interface            Role Sts Cost      Prio.Nbr Type
-------------------- ---- --- --------- -------- ----------------
----------------
Fa0/13               Desg FWD 19        128.15   P2p
Fa0/14               Desg FWD 19        16.16    P2p
```

You can see the port priority has been changed on SwitchA.

```
SwitchB#show spanning-tree | begin Interface
Interface            Role Sts Cost      Prio.Nbr Type
-------------------- ---- --- --------- -------- ----------------
----------------
Fa0/13               Altn BLK 19        128.15   P2p
Fa0/14               Root FWD 19        128.16   P2p
Fa0/16               Altn BLK 19        128.18   P2p
```

Interface fa0/14 on SwitchB is now the root port!

6. STP (Spanning Tree Protocol)

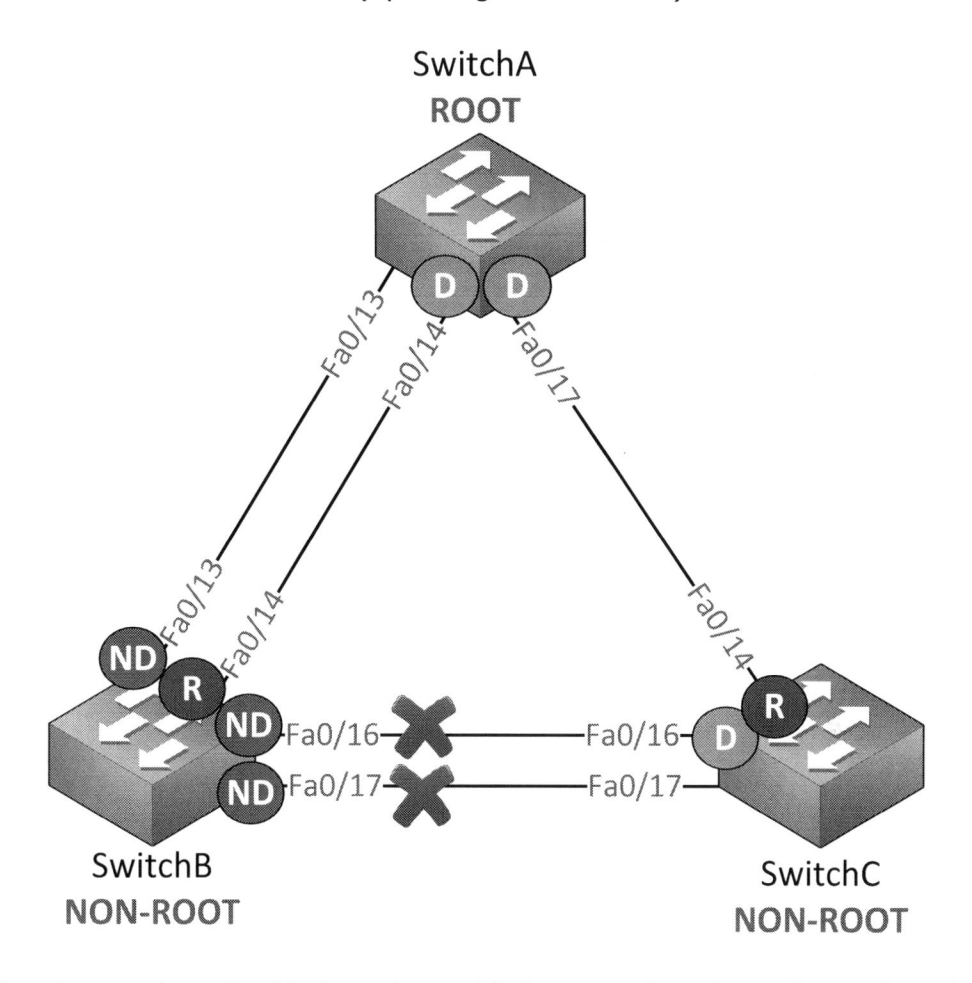

SwitchA
ROOT

SwitchB
NON-ROOT

SwitchC
NON-ROOT

In the picture above I added another cable between SwitchB and SwitchC. This interface will also become a non-designated port and it will be blocked.

```
SwitchB#show spanning-tree | begin Interface
Interface           Role Sts Cost      Prio.Nbr Type
------------------- ---- --- --------- -------- --------------------

Fa0/13              Altn BLK 19        128.15   P2p
Fa0/14              Root FWD 19        128.16   P2p
Fa0/16              Altn BLK 19        128.18   P2p
Fa0/17              Altn BLK 19        128.19   P2p
```

We can verify our configuration here. Just another blocked port...

Are you following me so far? I hope so! If you are having trouble understanding the different spanning-tree commands I recommend you to build the same topology as the one I'm using above and to take a look at your own spanning-tree topology. Play with the priority, cost and port priority to see what the result will be.

125

                              SwitchA
                          ROOT – VLAN 10

SwitchB   SwitchC
ROOT – VLAN 20   ROOT – VLAN 30

Let's get back to the basics. I have resetted all switches back to factory default settings because I want to show you how spanning-tree works with multiple VLANs. In the previous example we were only using VLAN 1. Now I'm going to add VLAN 10, 20 and 30 and each switch will become root bridge for a VLAN.

```
SwitchA(config)#vlan 10
SwitchA(config-vlan)#vlan 20
SwitchA(config-vlan)#vlan 30
```

```
SwitchB(config)#vlan 10
SwitchB(config-vlan)#vlan 20
SwitchB(config-vlan)#vlan 30
```

```
SwitchC(config)#vlan 10
SwitchC(config-vlan)#vlan 20
SwitchC(config-vlan)#vlan 30
```

6. STP (Spanning Tree Protocol)

First I'm going to create all VLANs. If you are running VTP server/client mode you only have to do this on one switch.

```
SwitchA(config)#interface fa0/14
SwitchA(config-if)#switchport trunk encapsulation dot1q
SwitchA(config-if)#switchport mode trunk
SwitchA(config)#interface fa0/17
SwitchA(config-if)#switchport trunk encapsulation dot1q
SwitchA(config-if)#switchport mode trunk
```

```
SwitchB(config)#interface fa0/14
SwitchB(config-if)#switchport trunk encapsulation dot1q
SwitchB(config-if)#switchport mode trunk
SwitchB(config)#interface fa0/16
SwitchB(config-if)#switchport trunk encapsulation dot1q
SwitchB(config-if)#switchport mode trunk
```

```
SwitchC(config)#interface fa0/14
SwitchC(config-if)#switchport trunk encapsulation dot1q
SwitchC(config-if)#switchport mode trunk
SwitchC(config)#interface fa0/16
SwitchC(config-if)#switchport trunk encapsulation dot1q
SwitchC(config-if)#switchport mode trunk
```

Make sure the interfaces between the switches are trunks. Mine were access interfaces so I changed them to trunk mode myself.

```
SwitchA#show spanning-tree summary | begin Name
Name                    Blocking Listening Learning Forwarding STP Active
---------------------- -------- --------- -------- ---------- ----------
VLAN0001                    0         0         0         2         2
VLAN0010                    0         0         0         2         2
VLAN0020                    0         0         0         2         2
VLAN0030                    0         0         0         2         2
---------------------- -------- --------- -------- ---------- ----------
4 vlans                     0         0         0         8         8
```

127

```
SwitchB#show spanning-tree summary | begin Name
Name                          Blocking  Listening  Learning  Forwarding
STP Active
---------------------------   --------  ---------  --------  ----------  --
--------
VLAN0001                          1          0         0          1
2
VLAN0010                          1          0         0          1
2
VLAN0020                          1          0         0          1
2
VLAN0030                          1          0         0          1
2
---------------------------   --------  ---------  --------  ----------  --
--------
4 vlans                           4          0         0          4
8
```

```
SwitchC#show spanning-tree summary | begin Name
Name                          Blocking  Listening  Learning  Forwarding
STP Active
---------------------------   --------  ---------  --------  ----------  --
--------
VLAN0001                          0          0         0          2
2
VLAN0010                          0          0         0          2
2
VLAN0020                          0          0         0          2
2
VLAN0030                          0          0         0          2
2
---------------------------   --------  ---------  --------  ----------  --
--------
4 vlans                           0          0         0          8
8
```

You can use the **show spanning-tree summary** command for a quick overview of the spanning-tree topologies. You can also just use the show spanning-tree command and you will get information on all the VLANs. As you can see my switches have created a spanning-tree topology for each VLAN.

```
SwitchC#show spanning-tree vlan 10

VLAN0010
  Spanning tree enabled protocol ieee
  Root ID     Priority     32778
              Address      000f.34ca.1000
              This bridge is the root
```

6. STP (Spanning Tree Protocol)

```
SwitchC#show spanning-tree vlan 20

VLAN0020
  Spanning tree enabled protocol ieee
  Root ID    Priority    32788
             Address     000f.34ca.1000
             This bridge is the root
```

```
SwitchC#show spanning-tree vlan 30

VLAN0030
  Spanning tree enabled protocol ieee
  Root ID    Priority    32798
             Address     000f.34ca.1000
             This bridge is the root
```

Some show commands reveal to us that SwitchC is the root bridge for VLAN 10, 20 and 30.

```
SwitchA(config)#spanning-tree vlan 10 priority 4096
```

Let's lower the priority on SwitchA for VLAN 10 to 4096 so it will become the root bridge.

```
SwitchA#show spanning-tree vlan 10 | include root
         This bridge is the root
```

Here's a quick way to verify our configuration.

```
SwitchB(config)#spanning-tree vlan 20 priority 4096
```

```
SwitchB#show spanning-tree vlan 20 | include root
         This bridge is the root
```

SwitchB is the root for VLAN 20.

```
SwitchC(config)#spanning-tree vlan 30 priority 4096
SwitchC#show spanning-tree vlan 30 | include root
         This bridge is the root
```

And last but not least here is SwitchC as the root bridge for VLAN 30.

That's all there is to it! Of course different interfaces will be blocked because we have a different root bridge for each VLAN. I'm not going to try to create a picture that shows all the designated/non-designated/root ports for all VLANs because we'll end up with a Picasso-style picture!

We can change the configuration of our spanning-tree configuration per VLAN. For example I can tune the timers if I want to speed up the spanning-tree process:

```
SwitchA#show spanning-tree vlan 10 | begin Root ID
  Root ID    Priority    4106
             Address     0011.bb0b.3600
             This bridge is the root
             Hello Time   2 sec  Max Age 20 sec  Forward Delay
15 sec
```

Let's change these default timers.

```
SwitchA(config)#spanning-tree vlan 10 hello-time 1
```

The hello time specifies how often a BPDU is sent. The default is 2 seconds but I changed it to 1 second.

```
SwitchA#show spanning-tree vlan 10 | begin Root ID
  Root ID    Priority    4106
             Address     0011.bb0b.3600
             This bridge is the root
             Hello Time   1 sec  Max Age 20 sec  Forward Delay
15 sec
```

Our configuration is successful! These changes are only applied to VLAN 10.

```
SwitchB(config)#spanning-tree vlan 20 max-age 6
```

We can also change the max-age timer. When a switch no longer receives periodic BPDUs on a switch it will wait for the max-age timer before it decides to re-check the spanning-tree topology. The default is 20 seconds but we can change it to 6 seconds.

```
SwitchB#show spanning-tree vlan 20 | begin Root ID
  Root ID    Priority    4116
             Address     0019.569d.5700
             This bridge is the root
             Hello Time   2 sec  Max Age 6 sec  Forward Delay
15 sec
```

Verify it by looking at the show spanning VLAN 20 command.

6. STP (Spanning Tree Protocol)

```
SwitchC#show spanning-tree vlan 30

VLAN0030
  Spanning tree enabled protocol ieee
  Root ID    Priority    4126
             Address     000f.34ca.1000
             This bridge is the root
             Hello Time   2 sec  Max Age 20 sec  Forward Delay
15 sec
```

While we're at it...why not change the forward delay timer too.
The default is 15 seconds.

```
SwitchC(config)#spanning-tree vlan 30 forward-time 4
```

```
SwitchC#show spanning-tree vlan 30 | begin Root ID
  Root ID    Priority    4126
             Address     000f.34ca.1000
             This bridge is the root
             Hello Time   2 sec  Max Age 20 sec  Forward Delay
4 sec
```

Easy enough to change and this is how we verify it.

> *The show spanning-tree command is excellent and gives you all the information you need to know. If you want to see in real-time what is going on you should try the **debug spanning-tree** command.*

How does spanning-tree deal with topology changes? This is a topic that isn't (heavily) tested on the CCNP SWITCH exam but it's very important to understand if you deal with a network with a lot of switches.

How to Master CCNP SWITCH

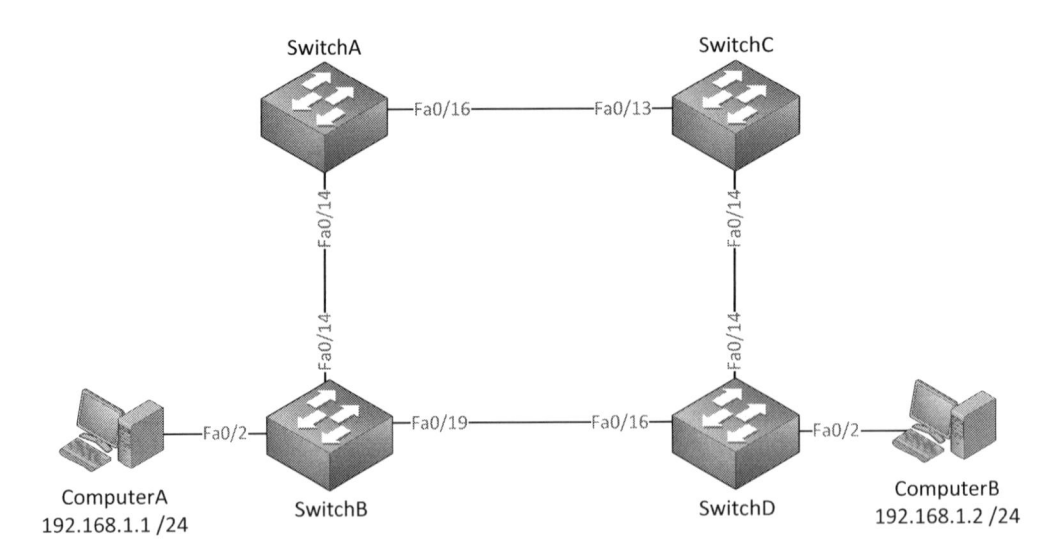

[Network diagram: SwitchA connects to SwitchC via Fa0/16—Fa0/13. SwitchA Fa0/14 connects to SwitchB Fa0/14. SwitchC Fa0/14 connects to SwitchD Fa0/14. SwitchB Fa0/19 connects to SwitchD Fa0/16. ComputerA (192.168.1.1/24) connects to SwitchB Fa0/2. ComputerB (192.168.1.2/24) connects to SwitchD Fa0/2.]

Let's take a look at the picture above. We have two computers because I need something to fill the MAC address tables of these switches. All switches have the default configuration.

```
SwitchC(config)#spanning-tree vlan 1 priority 4096
```

```
SwitchB(config)#interface fa0/19
SwitchB(config-if)#spanning-tree cost 50
```

I want SwitchC to be the root bridge and the fa0/19 interface of SwitchB should be blocked. I'll show you why in a minute.

```
SwitchA#show spanning-tree | begin Interface
Interface           Role Sts Cost      Prio.Nbr Type
------------------- ---- --- --------- -------- ----------------
Fa0/14              Desg FWD 19        128.16   P2p
Fa0/16              Root FWD 19        128.18   P2p
```

```
SwitchB#show spanning-tree | begin Interface
Interface           Role Sts Cost      Prio.Nbr Type
------------------- ---- --- --------- -------- ----------------
Fa0/2               Desg FWD 19        128.4    P2p
Fa0/14              Root FWD 19        128.16   P2p
Fa0/19              Altn BLK 50        128.21   P2p
```

6. STP (Spanning Tree Protocol)

```
SwitchC#show spanning-tree | begin Interface
Interface           Role Sts Cost      Prio.Nbr Type
------------------- ---- --- --------- -------- -----------------
---------------
Fa0/13              Desg FWD 19        128.13   P2p
Fa0/19              Desg FWD 19        128.19   P2p
```

```
SwitchD#show spanning-tree | begin Interface
Interface           Role Sts Cost      Prio.Nbr Type
------------------- ---- --- --------- -------- -----------------
---------------
Fa0/4               Desg FWD 19        128.4    P2p
Fa0/16              Desg FWD 19        128.16   P2p
Fa0/19              Root FWD 19        128.19   P2p
```

So here we have all the different interfaces, time to draw a nice picture!

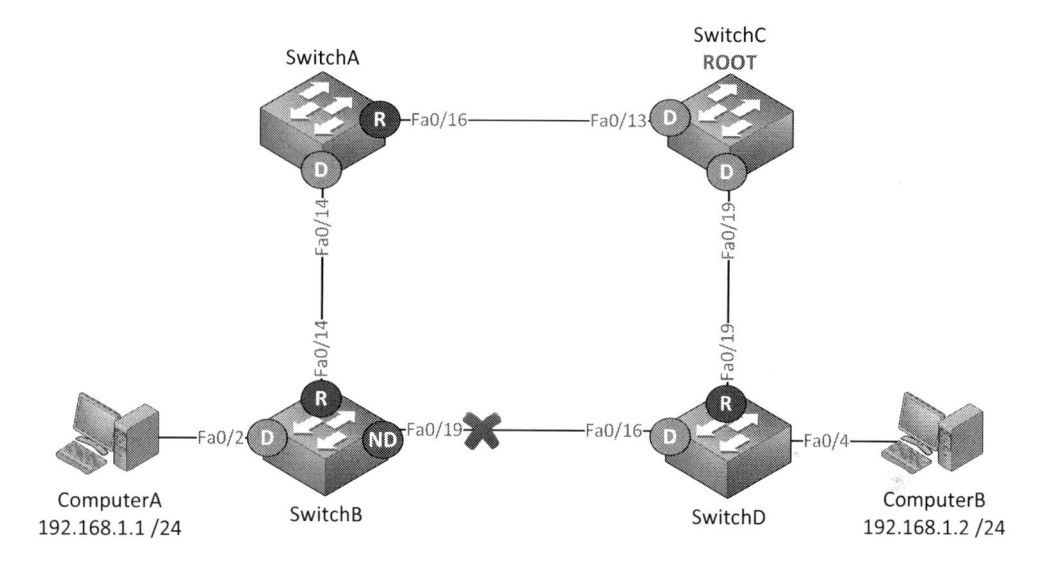

Traffic between ComputerA and ComputerB will flow from SwitchB to SwitchA, SwitchC and then towards SwitchD. Interface fa0/19 on SwitchB has been blocked.

```
C:\Documents and Settings\ComputerA>ping 192.168.1.2

Pinging 192.168.1.2 with 32 bytes of data:

Reply from 192.168.1.2: bytes=32 time<1ms TTL=128
Reply from 192.168.1.2: bytes=32 time<1ms TTL=128
Reply from 192.168.1.2: bytes=32 time<1ms TTL=128
Reply from 192.168.1.2: bytes=32 time<1ms TTL=128

Ping statistics for 192.168.1.2:
    Packets: Sent = 4, Received = 4, Lost = 0 (0% loss),
Approximate round trip times in milli-seconds:
    Minimum = 0ms, Maximum = 0ms, Average = 0ms
```

I'm sending a ping from ComputerA to ComputerB to fill the MAC address tables of our switches.

In my case these are the MAC addresses for the computers:

- ComputerA: 000c.2928.5c6c
- ComputerB: 000c.29e2.03ba

```
SwitchA#show mac address-table dynamic
        Mac Address Table
-------------------------------------------

Vlan    Mac Address       Type        Ports
----    -----------       --------    -----
   1    000c.2928.5c6c    DYNAMIC     Fa0/14
   1    000c.29e2.03ba    DYNAMIC     Fa0/16
```

```
SwitchB#show mac address-table dynamic
        Mac Address Table
-------------------------------------------

Vlan    Mac Address       Type        Ports
----    -----------       --------    -----
   1    000c.2928.5c6c    DYNAMIC     Fa0/2
   1    000c.29e2.03ba    DYNAMIC     Fa0/14
```

```
SwitchC#show mac address-table dynamic
        Mac Address Table
-------------------------------------------

Vlan    Mac Address       Type        Ports
----    -----------       --------    -----
   1    000c.2928.5c6c    DYNAMIC     Fa0/13
   1    000c.29e2.03ba    DYNAMIC     Fa0/19
```

6. STP (Spanning Tree Protocol)

```
SwitchD#show mac address-table dynamic
          Mac Address Table
-------------------------------------------

Vlan      Mac Address       Type        Ports
----      -----------       --------    -----
   1      000c.2928.5c6c    DYNAMIC     Fa0/19
   1      000c.29e2.03ba    DYNAMIC     Fa0/4
```

We can confirm the traffic path by looking at the MAC address table. I like to use the **show mac address-table dynamic** command so we don't have to browse through a list of static MAC addresses.

```
SwitchA#show mac address-table aging-time
Global Aging Time:   300
```

If we look at one of the switches we can check the **default aging time** of the MAC address table. As you can see this is **300 seconds** (5 minutes by default). If a host has been silent for 5 minutes its MAC address will be **removed** from the table.

Why do we care about aging time? I'll show you why!

```
C:\Documents and Settings\ComputerA>ping 192.168.1.2 -t
```

First I'm going to get some traffic going from ComputerA to ComputerB. By using ping –t it will run forever.

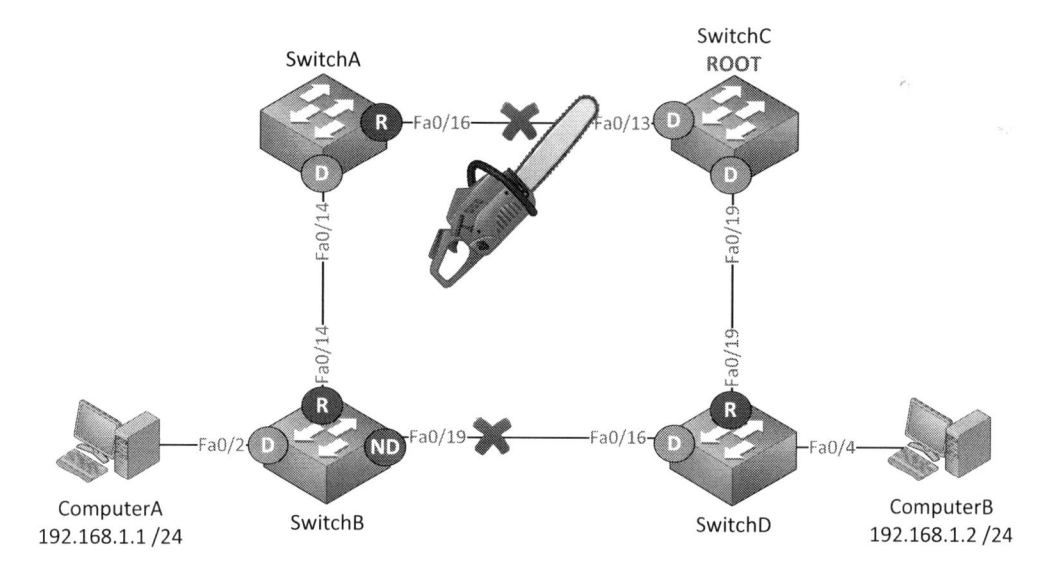

Assume the link between SwitchA and SwitchC fails. ComputerA and ComputerB will be unable to communicate with each other until the fa0/19 interface of SwitchB goes into forwarding.

135

It will take a maximum of 50 seconds for SwitchB to move the fa0/19 interface from blocking to listening, learning and finally the forwarding state.

Meanwhile SwitchB still has the MAC address of ComputerB in its MAC address table and will keep forwarding it to SwitchA where it will be **dropped**. It will be impossible for our computers to communicate with each other **for 300 seconds** until the MAC address tables age out.

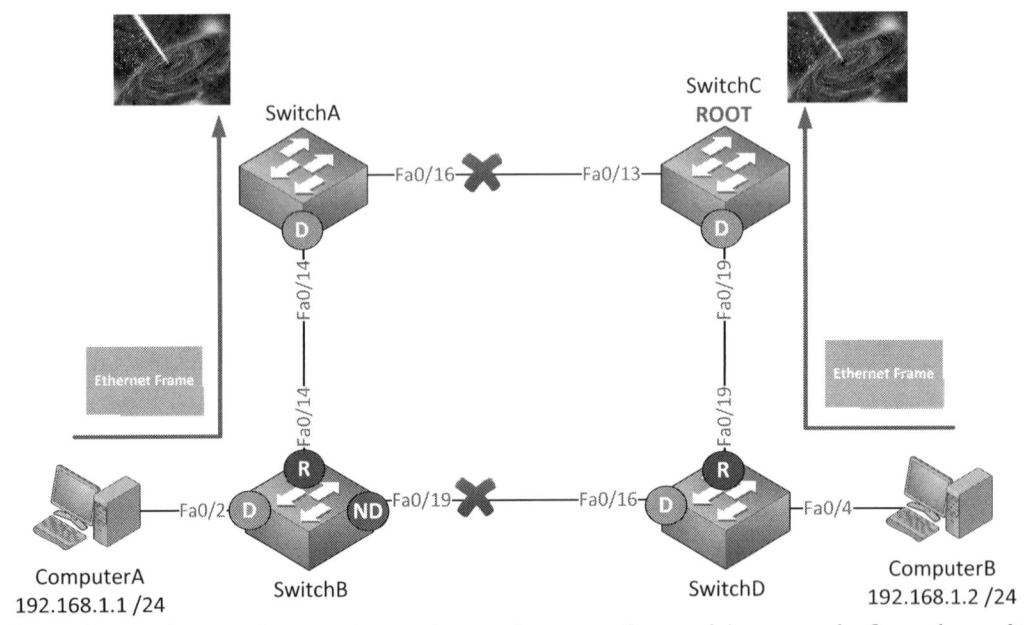

"Sending Ethernet frames to a place where no frame has gone before doesn't sound like a good idea if you want to keep your users happy..."

The idea of MAC address tables that age out after 300 seconds works perfectly fine in a **stable network** but not when the topology changes. Of course there's a solution to every problem and that's why spanning-tree has a **topology change mechanism.**

When a switch detects a **change in the network (interface going down or into forwarding state)** it will advertise this event to the **whole switched network**.

When the switches receive this message they will reduce the aging time of the MAC address table from 300 seconds to 15 seconds (this is the forward delay timer). This message is called the **TCN (Topology Change Notification).**

```
SwitchA#debug spanning-tree events
Spanning Tree event debugging is on
```

```
SwitchB#debug spanning-tree events
Spanning Tree event debugging is on
```

6. STP (Spanning Tree Protocol)

```
SwitchC#debug spanning-tree events
Spanning Tree event debugging is on
```

```
SwitchD#debug spanning-tree events
Spanning Tree event debugging is on
```

I'm going to enable **debug spanning-tree events** on all switches so you can see this process in action.

```
SwitchA(config)#interface fa0/16
SwitchA(config-if)#shut
```

Now we will shut interface fa0/16 on SwitchA to simulate an interface failure.

```
SwitchA#STP: VLAN0001 sent Topology Change Notice on Fa0/14
```

You will see quite some debug information but somewhere along the lines you'll see that SwitchA is generating a topology change notification and sends it on its fa0/14 interface to SwitchB.

```
SwitchB#STP: VLAN0001 Topology Change rcvd on Fa0/14
```

SwitchB will throw quite some debug stuff in your face but this is what I was looking for. You can see that it received the topology change notification from SwitchA. Upon arrival of this topology change notification SwitchB will age out its MAC address table in 15 seconds.

```
SwitchB#STP: VLAN0001 new root port Fa0/19, cost 69
SwitchB#STP: VLAN0001 Fa0/19 -> listening
SwitchB#STP: VLAN0001 Topology Change rcvd on Fa0/14
SwitchB#STP: VLAN0001 sent Topology Change Notice on Fa0/19
SwitchB#STP: VLAN0001 Fa0/19 -> learning
SwitchB#STP: VLAN0001 sent Topology Change Notice on Fa0/19
SwitchB#STP: VLAN0001 Fa0/19 -> forwarding
```

SwitchB decides that fa0/19 is now the new root port and you can see the transition from listening to learning and forwarding mode. It's also sending a topology change notification towards SwitchD.

```
SwitchC#STP: VLAN0001 Topology Change rcvd on Fa0/19
```

SwitchC receives a topology change notification on its fa0/19 interface and will reduce its age out timer of the MAC address table to 15 seconds.

```
SwitchD#STP: VLAN0001 Topology Change rcvd on Fa0/16
SwitchD#STP: VLAN0001 sent Topology Change Notice on Fa0/19
```

Here we see that SwitchD receives the topology change notification from SwitchB and as a result it will reduce its age out timer of the MAC address table to 15 seconds. It's also sending a topology change notification to SwitchC.

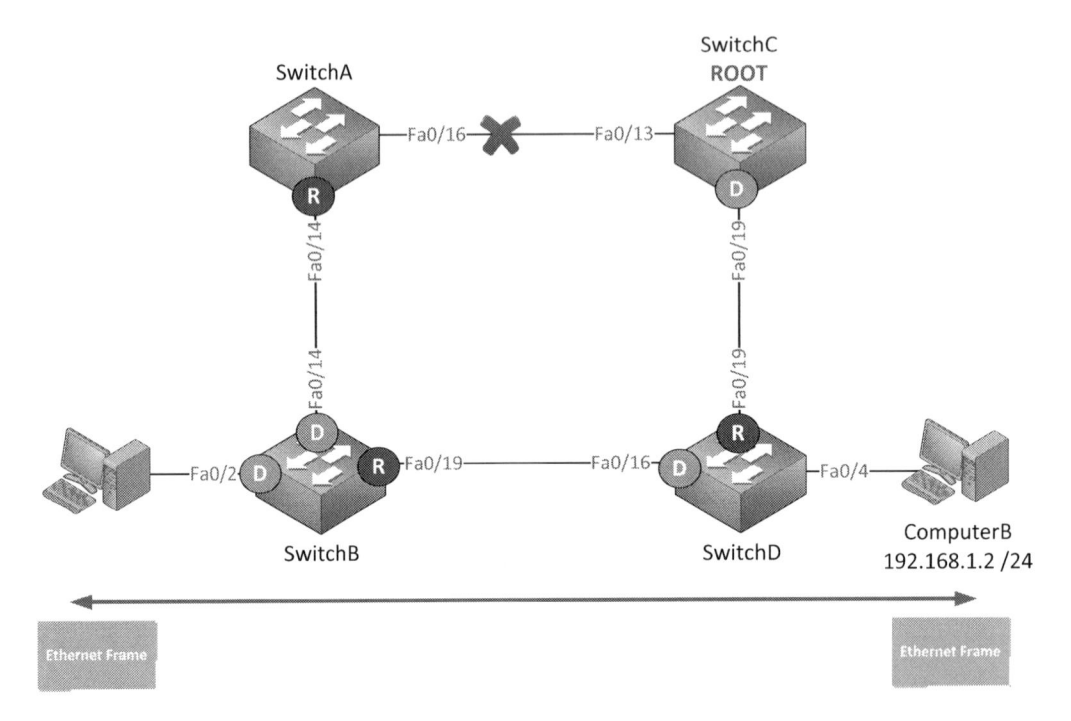

All switches received the topology change notification and set their age out timer to 15 seconds. SwitchB doesn't receive any Ethernet Frames with the MAC address of ComputerB as the source on its fa0/14 interface and will remove this entry from the MAC address table. Meanwhile the fa0/19 interface on SwitchB changed from blocking to listening, learning and forwarding state (50 seconds total). SwitchB will now learn the MAC address of ComputerB on its fa0/19 interface and life is good!

Of course the same thing will happen for the MAC address of ComputerA on SwitchD.

Are you following me so far? To keep a long story short...we need the topology change notification to reduce the MAC address table aging timer from 300 seconds to 15 seconds to prevent blackholing traffic in a situation like I just explained to you.

So which switches will send and forward the topology change notifications? In our previous debug you saw a couple of messages but where do we send them and why? Is it flooded to all switches? Let's check it out!

6. STP (Spanning Tree Protocol)

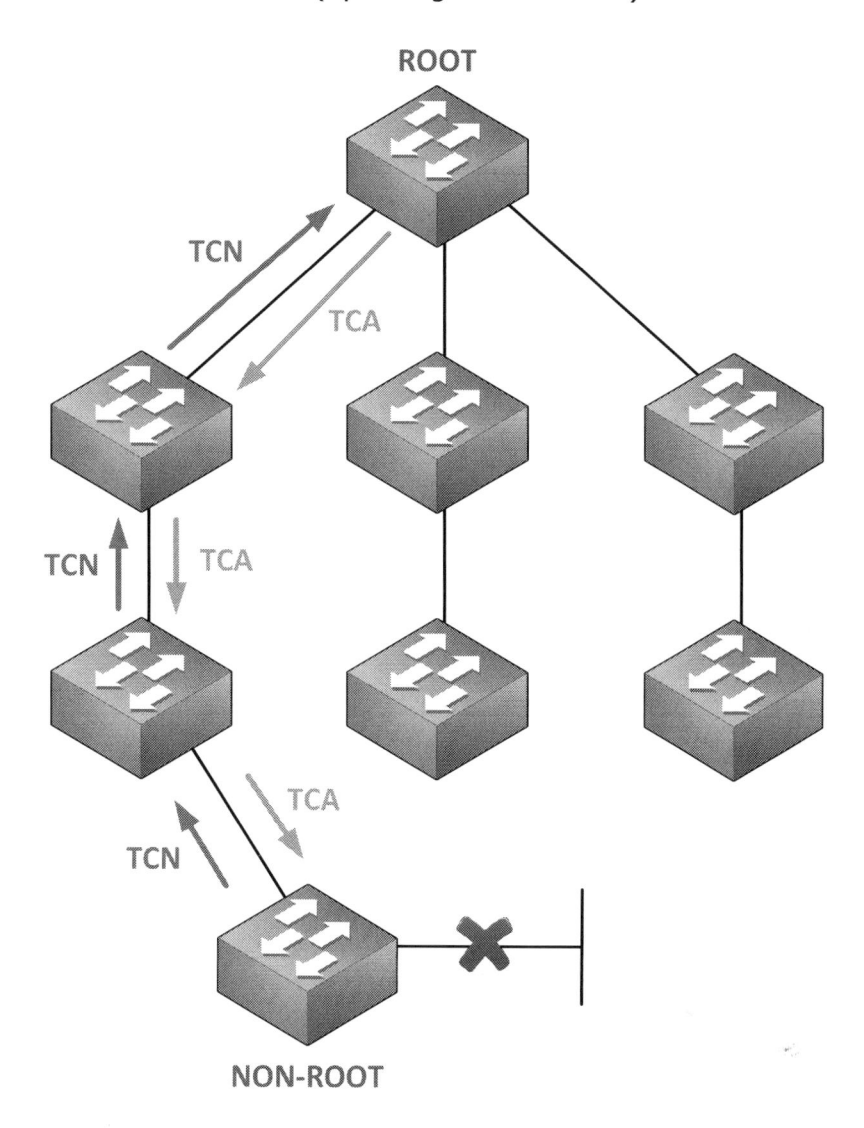

In a normal situation a non-root switch will receive BPDUs on its root port but will **never** send any BPDUs to the root bridge. When a non-root switch detects a topology change it will generate a topology change notification and send it on its root port towards the root bridge. When a switch receives the topology change notification it will send a **(TCA) topology change acknowledgement** on its designated port towards the downstream switch. It will create a topology change notification itself and send it on its root port as well...we will work our way up the tree until we reach the root bridge.

TCN

| Protocol Identifier | Protocol Version Identifier | BPDU Type | Flags | Root Identifier | Root Path Cost | Bridge Identifier | Port Identifier | Message Age | Max Age | Hello Time | Forward Delay |

Here's the BPDU again. You can see it has a field called **BPDU type**. This value will change to indicate it's a topology change notification.

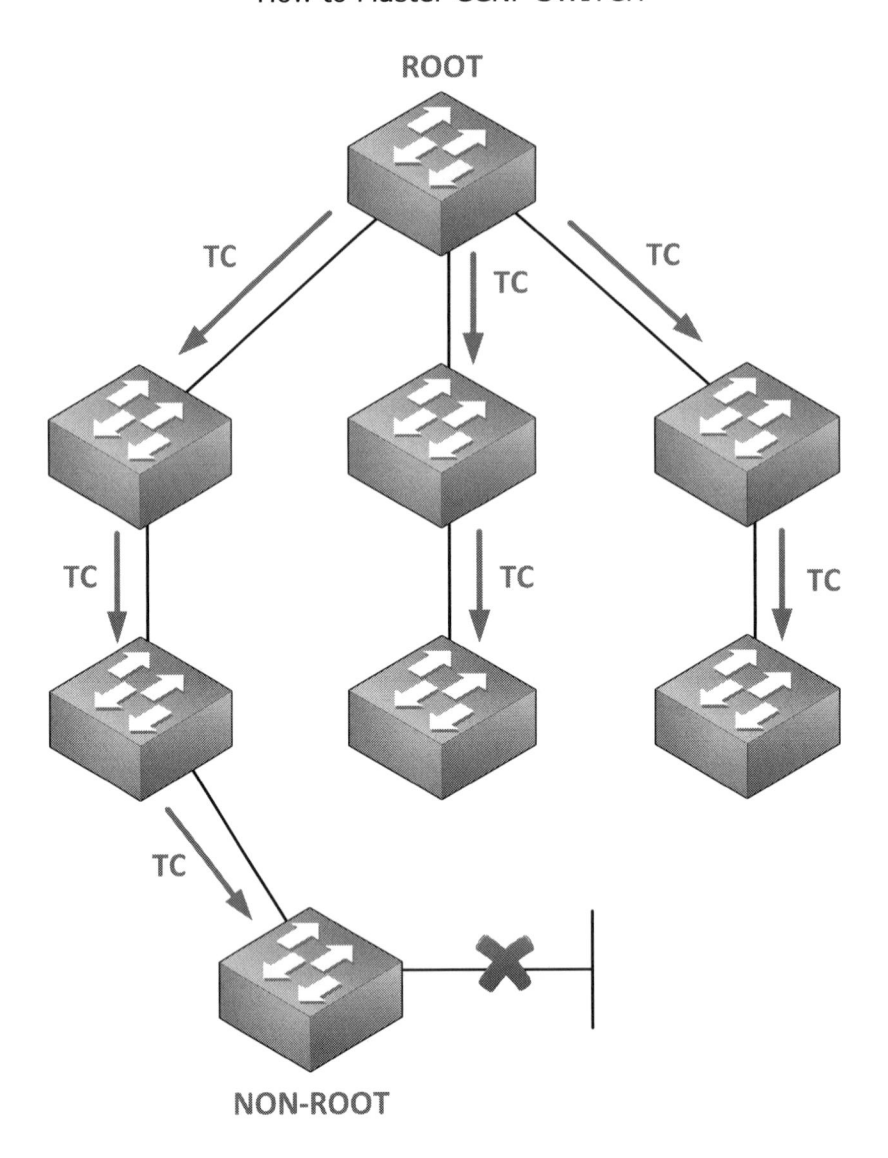

Once the topology change notification reaches the root bridge it will set the **TC (topology change)** bit in the BPDUs it will send. These BPDUs will be forwarded to all the other switches in our network so they can reduce their aging time of the MAC address table. Switches will receives these messages on both forwarding and blocked ports.

Protocol Identifier	Protocol Version Identifier	BPDU Type	Flags	Root Identifier	Root Path Cost	Bridge Identifier	Port Identifier	Message Age	Max Age	Hello Time	Forward Delay

The root bridge will send BPDUs and it will set the flag field to represent the topology change.
That's all there is to it. This is how spanning-tree deals with topology changes in our network. There is one more thing I want to you show you about this mechanism.

6. STP (Spanning Tree Protocol)

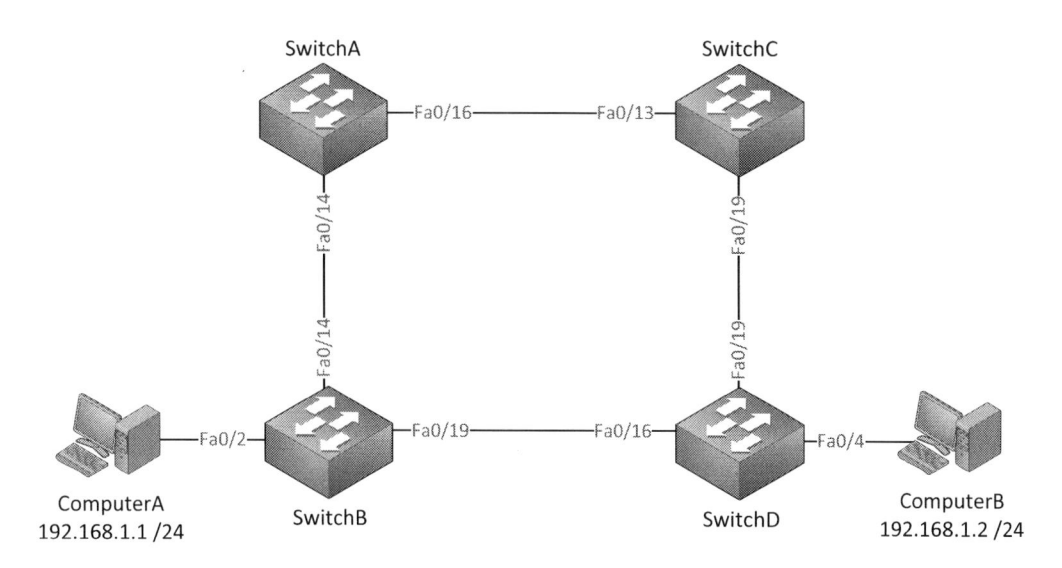

As you can see ComputerA is connected to SwitchB on its fa0/2 interface. Let's see what happens when this interface goes down.

```
SwitchB#show spanning-tree interface fa0/2

Vlan                    Role Sts Cost      Prio.Nbr Type
----------------------- ---- --- --------- -------- --------------------
VLAN0001                Desg FWD 19        128.4    P2p
```

We can see that the fa0/2 interface on SwitchB is designated and forwarding.

```
SwitchB#debug spanning-tree events
Spanning Tree event debugging is on
```

```
SwitchB(config)#interface f0/2
SwitchB(config-if)#shutdown
```

First I enable debug spanning-tree events and then I'll shut the interface.

```
SwitchB STP: VLAN0001 sent Topology Change Notice on Fa0/14
```

Right after shutting down the fa0/2 SwitchB generates a topology change notification and sends it away on its root port.

```
SwitchB(config)#interface f0/2
SwitchB(config-if)#no shutdown
```

Let's bring it back up...

141

```
SwitchB#   STP: VLAN0001 Fa0/2 -> listening
SwitchB# %LINK-3-UPDOWN: Interface FastEthernet0/2, changed
state to up
SwitchB# %LINEPROTO-5-UPDOWN: Line protocol on Interface
FastEthernet0/2, SwitchB# changed state to up
SwitchB#   STP: VLAN0001 Fa0/2 -> learning
SwitchB#   STP: VLAN0001 sent Topology Change Notice on Fa0/14
SwitchB#   STP: VLAN0001 Fa0/2 -> forwarding
```

Once we bring the interface up you can see it goes through the listening and learning state and ends in the forwarding state. The switch generates another topology change notification and sends it on the root port.

What kind of issues could this cause? Imagine we have a network with a LOT of hosts. Each time an interface goes up or down a topology change notification will be generated and ALL switches will set their aging time to 15 seconds. A host will trigger a topology change and if you have a lot of hosts it's possible that you end up with a network that is in a constant state of "topology changes".

Here's a situation that could occur:

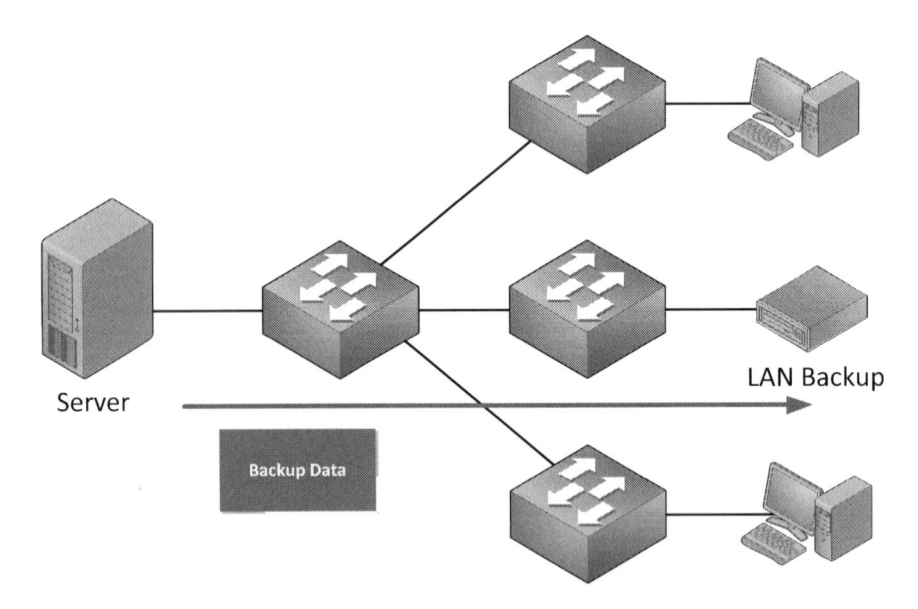

In the picture above I have a server sending a backup to a LAN backup device. This means we'll probably have a lot of unicast traffic from the server to the LAN backup device.

6. STP (Spanning Tree Protocol)

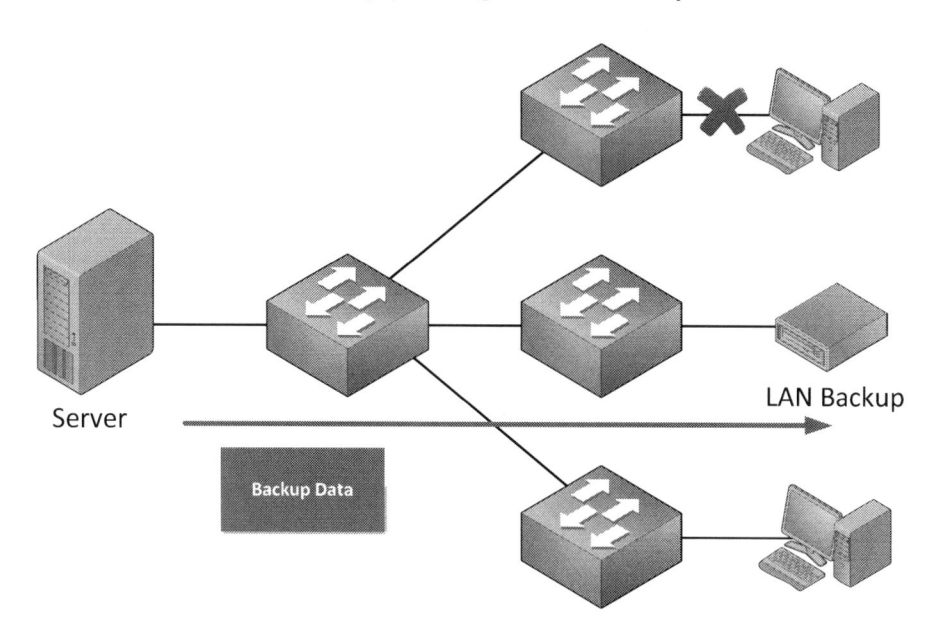

Whenever an interface goes down it will generate a topology change notification and as a result all switches will reduce their aging time of the MAC address table to 15 seconds. All the MAC addresses of the devices will be flushed from the MAC address table.

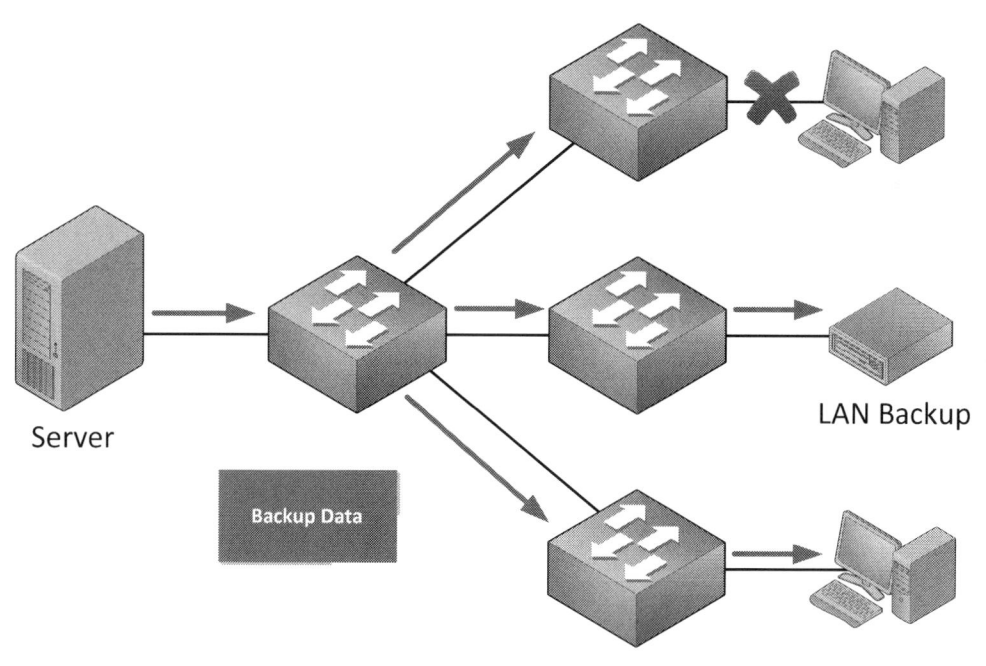

The switches will quickly re-learn the MAC address of the server since its actively sending traffic to the LAN Backup device. If this LAN Backup device is just silently receiving traffic and not sending any traffic itself then there's no way

143

for the switches to re-learn its MAC address.

What happens to unknown MAC unicast traffic? That's right...it's flooded on all interfaces except the one where it originated from. As a result this network will be burdened with traffic until our LAN Backup device sends an Ethernet Frame and the switches re-learn its MAC address.

How can we deal with this drama scenario?

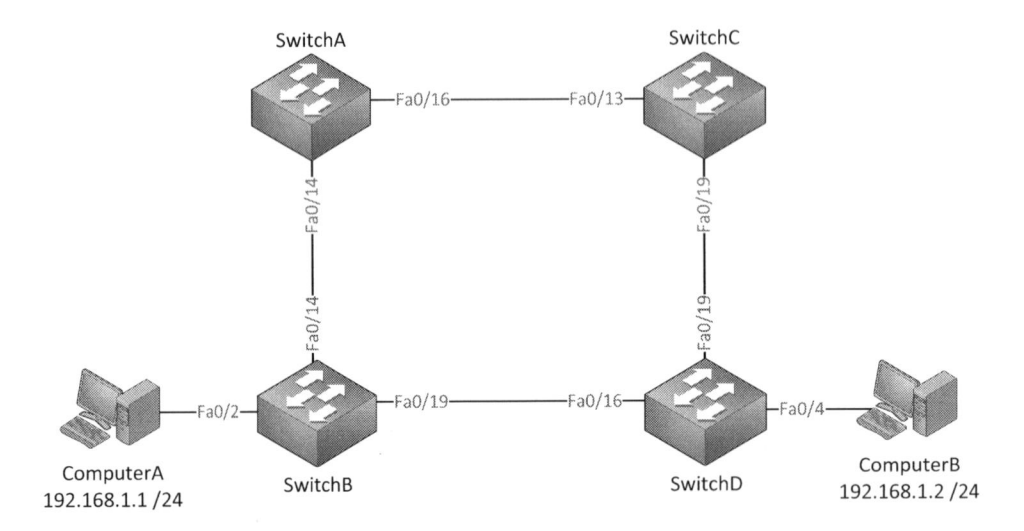

Portfast to the rescue! Portfast is a Cisco proprietary solution to deal with topology changes. It does two things for us:

- Interfaces with portfast enabled that come up will go to **forwarding mode immediately**. It will **skip the listening and learning state**.
- A switch will never generate a topology change notification for an interface that has portfast enabled.

It's a good idea to enable portfast on interfaces that are connected to hosts because these interfaces are likely to go up and down all the time.

6. STP (Spanning Tree Protocol)

Don't enable portfast on an interface to another hub or switch.

```
SwitchB(config)interface fa0/2
SwitchB(config-if)#spanning-tree portfast
%Warning: portfast should only be enabled on ports connected to a single
 host. Connecting hubs, concentrators, switches, bridges, etc...  to this
 interface  when portfast is enabled, can cause temporary bridging loops.
 Use with CAUTION

%Portfast has been configured on FastEthernet0/2 but will only
  have effect when the interface is in a non-trunking mode.
```

```
SwitchD(config)interface fa0/4
SwitchD(config-if)#spanning-tree portfast
%Warning: portfast should only be enabled on ports connected to a single
 host. Connecting hubs, concentrators, switches, bridges, etc... to this
 interface  when portfast is enabled, can cause temporary bridging loops.
 Use with CAUTION

%Portfast has been configured on FastEthernet0/2 but will only
  have effect when the interface is in a non-trunking mode.
```

This is how you enable it on an interface level. Just type in **spanning-tree portfast** on the interface and you are ready to go. You will even get a warning message...(how nice!).

```
SwitchB(config)#spanning-tree portfast default
%Warning: this command enables portfast by default on all interfaces. You
  should now disable portfast explicitly on switched ports leading to hubs,
  switches and bridges as they may create temporary bridging loops.
```

You can also enable it globally with the **spanning-tree portfast default** command. It will enable portfast on all interfaces in **access mode**.

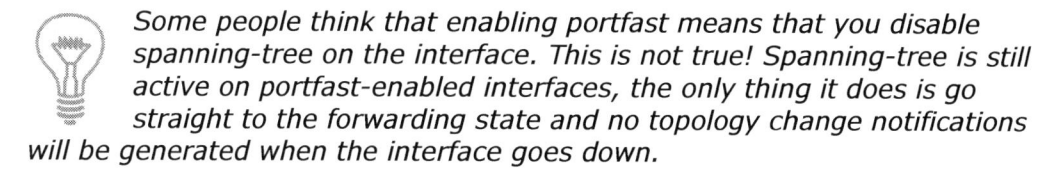

> *Some people think that enabling portfast means that you disable spanning-tree on the interface. This is not true! Spanning-tree is still active on portfast-enabled interfaces, the only thing it does is go straight to the forwarding state and no topology change notifications will be generated when the interface goes down.*

If you ever have to solve a network that has a lot of topology changes there's a useful command you should remember:

```
SwitchB#show spanning-tree detail

 VLAN0001 is executing the ieee compatible Spanning Tree
protocol
   Bridge Identifier has priority 32768, sysid 1, address
0019.569d.5700
   Configured hello time 2, max age 20, forward delay 15
   Current root has priority 4097, address 000f.34ca.1000
   Root port is 16 (FastEthernet0/14), cost of root path is 38
   Topology change flag not set, detected flag not set
   Number of topology changes 10 last change occurred 00:43:29
ago
           from FastEthernet0/2
   Times:  hold 1, topology change 35, notification 2
           hello 2, max age 20, forward delay 15
   Timers: hello 0, topology change 0, notification 0, aging 300
```

Here you can see how many topology changes are detected and which interface was responsible for this. It can help you to track down the source of the topology change notification.

Before we head to the next chapter there are two more features I want to show you:

- **UplinkFast**
- **BackboneFast**

These two features were designed to improve the convergence time of spanning-tree. Let's start with UplinkFast!

6. STP (Spanning Tree Protocol)

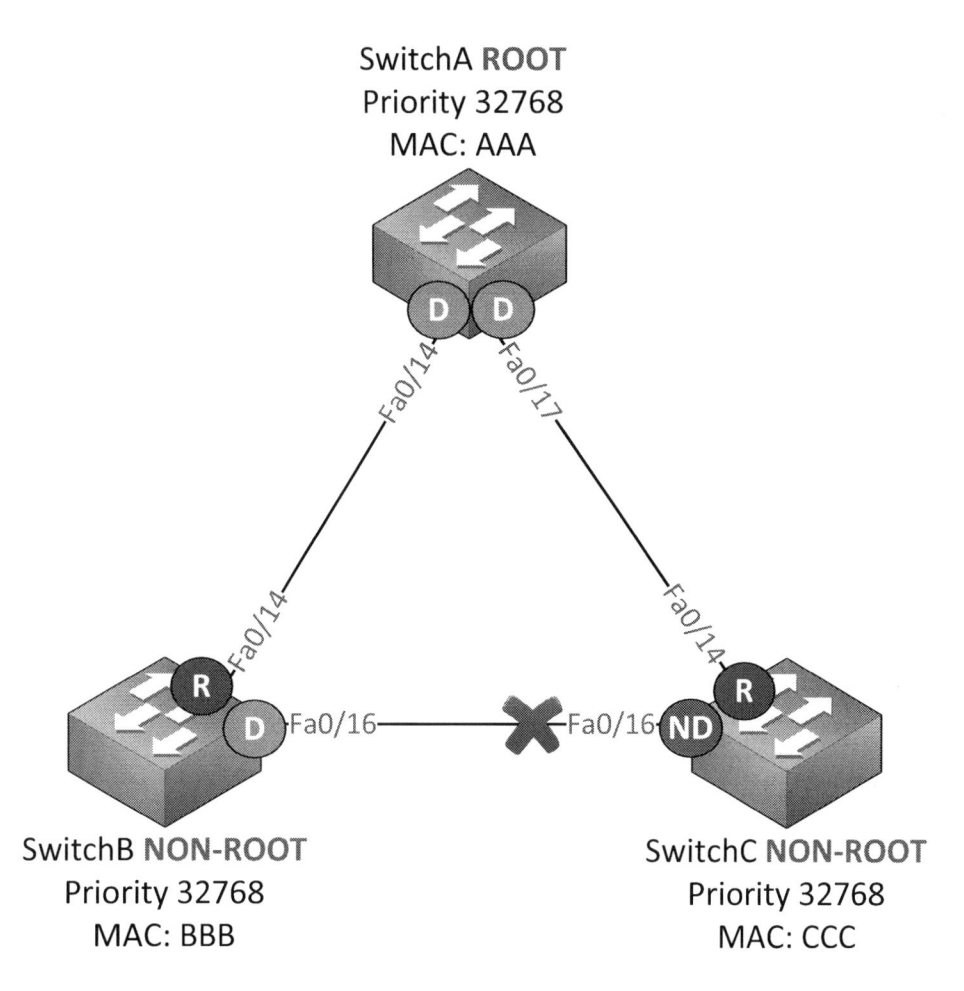

SwitchA **ROOT**
Priority 32768
MAC: AAA

SwitchB **NON-ROOT**
Priority 32768
MAC: BBB

SwitchC **NON-ROOT**
Priority 32768
MAC: CCC

Let's get back to one of our older topologies. Three switches and SwitchA is our root bridge. The fa0/16 interface on SwitchC has been blocked. I'm only using VLAN 1 so nothing fancy here...

If we look at SwitchC we see that the fa0/16 interface has been blocked and fa0/14 is the root port.

147

SwitchA **ROOT**
Priority 32768
MAC: AAA

SwitchB **NON-ROOT**
Priority 32768
MAC: BBB

SwitchC **NON-ROOT**
Priority 32768
MAC: CCC

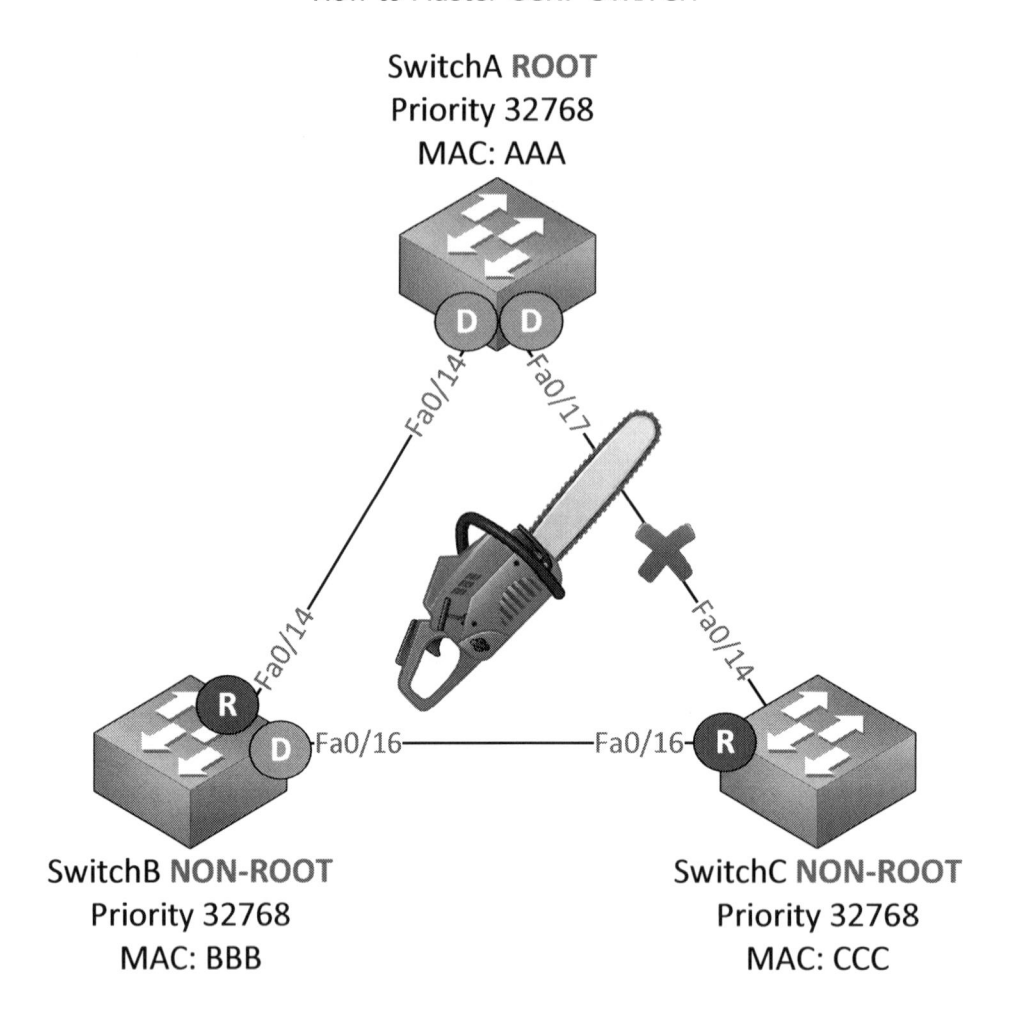

When the fa0/14 interface on SwitchC fails we'll have to use fa0/16 to reach the root bridge. How long does it take for SwitchC to make the transition? Let's find out:

```
SwitchC#debug spanning-tree events
Spanning Tree event debugging is on
```

```
SwitchC(config)#interface fa0/14
SwitchC(config-if)#shutdown
```

Now we'll just wait for the magic to happen...

```
SwitchC#STP: VLAN0001 new root port Fa0/16, cost 38
SwitchC#STP: VLAN0001 Fa0/16 -> listening
SwitchC#STP: VLAN0001 Fa0/16 -> learning
SwitchC#STP: VLAN0001 Fa0/16 -> forwarding
```

BPDUs are originated from the root bridge so if we receive BPDUs on an interface the switch knows it can reach the root bridge on this interface. We

6. STP (Spanning Tree Protocol)

have to go through the blocking (20 seconds), listening (15 seconds) and learning state (15 seconds) so it takes 50 seconds to end up in the forwarding state.

The good thing is that spanning-tree solves the link failure automatically but it also means that we have a downtime of 30 seconds. If you want you can tune the forward delay timer to speed up this process down to roughly 14 seconds.

```
SwitchC(config)#interface fa0/14
SwitchC(config-if)#no shutdown
```

Let's restore connectivity first.

```
SwitchC(config)#spanning-tree uplinkfast
```

Now I'm going to enable **spanning-tree uplinkfast**. This is a global command, you can't configure it on the interface level.

```
SwitchC(config)#interface fa0/14
SwitchC(config-if)#shutdown
```

```
SwitchC# STP: VLAN0001 new root port Fa0/16, cost 3038
SwitchC# %SPANTREE_FAST-7-PORT_FWD_UPLINK: VLAN0001
FastEthernet0/16 moved to Forwarding (UplinkFast).
```

Here's the big difference. When uplinkfast is enabled **a non-designated port will go to forwarding state immediately if the root port fails**. Instead of 50 seconds downtime connectivity is restored immediately.

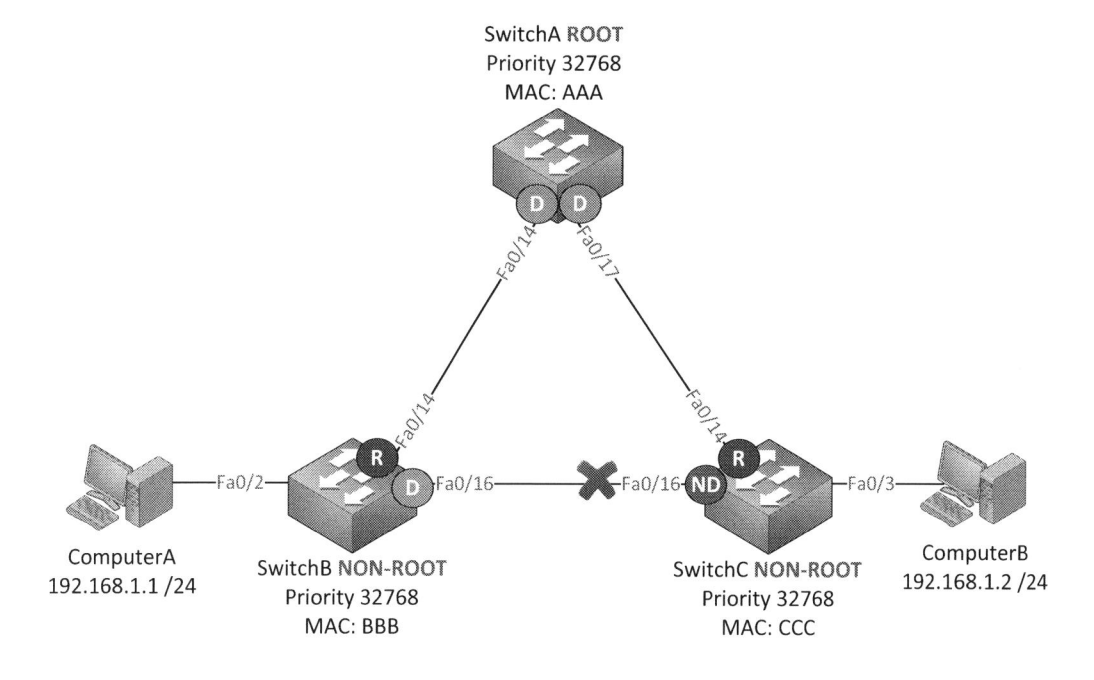

UplinkFast is useful but it will cause a problem with our MAC address tables. In the picture above I added two computers to our topology. Interface fa0/16 on SwitchC is the non-designated port and fa0/14 is the root port.

Let me show you the MAC address tables for all switches:

```
SwitchA#show mac address-table dynamic
          Mac Address Table
-------------------------------------------

Vlan      Mac Address       Type        Ports
----      -----------       --------    -----
  1       000c.2928.5c6c    DYNAMIC     Fa0/14
  1       000c.29e2.03ba    DYNAMIC     Fa0/17
```

```
SwitchB#show mac address-table dynamic
          Mac Address Table
-------------------------------------------

Vlan      Mac Address       Type        Ports
----      -----------       --------    -----
  1       000c.2928.5c6c    DYNAMIC     Fa0/2
  1       000c.29e2.03ba    DYNAMIC     Fa0/14
```

```
SwitchC#show mac address-table dynamic
          Mac Address Table
-------------------------------------------

Vlan      Mac Address       Type        Ports
----      -----------       --------    -----
  1       000c.2928.5c6c    DYNAMIC     Fa0/14
  1       000c.29e2.03ba    DYNAMIC     Fa0/3
```

Here are the MAC addresses of the computers:

- ComputerA: 000c.2928.5c6c
- ComputerB: 000c.29e2.03ba

6. STP (Spanning Tree Protocol)

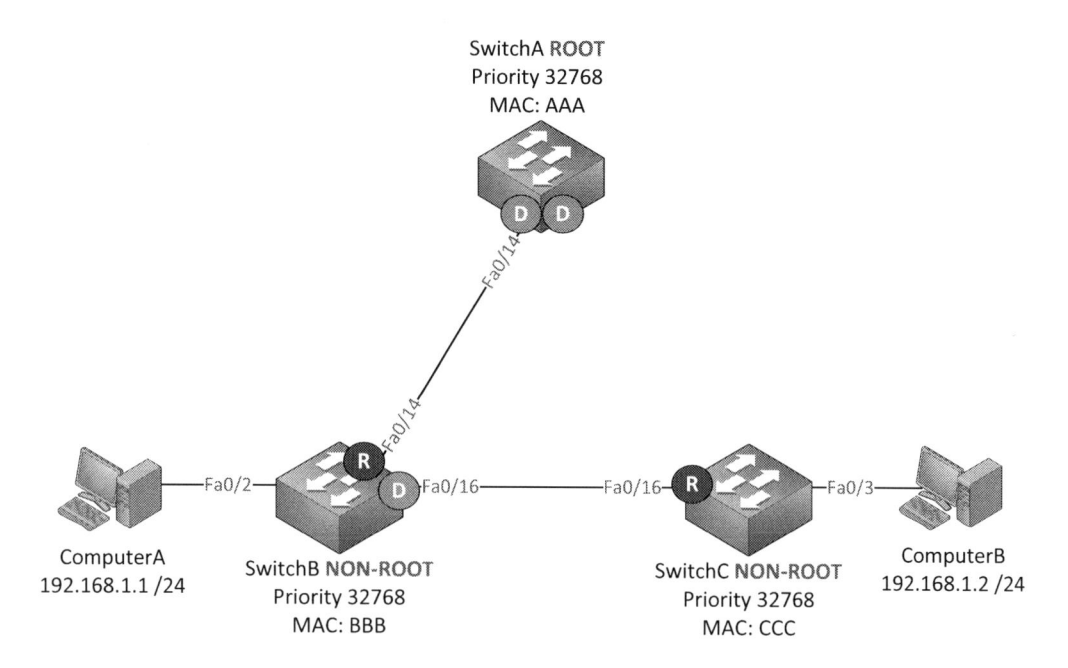

```
SwitchA ROOT
Priority 32768
MAC: AAA
```

```
ComputerA              SwitchB NON-ROOT           SwitchC NON-ROOT            ComputerB
192.168.1.1 /24        Priority 32768             Priority 32768              192.168.1.2 /24
                       MAC: BBB                   MAC: CCC
```

When the link between SwitchA and SwitchC fails, SwitchC will use the fa0/16 interface immediately. However it will take 15 seconds for the topology change mechanism to age out the MAC address table!

```
SwitchB#show mac address-table dynamic
          Mac Address Table
-------------------------------------------

Vlan    Mac Address        Type        Ports
----    -----------        --------    -----
  1     000c.2928.5c6c     DYNAMIC     Fa0/2
  1     000c.29e2.03ba     DYNAMIC     Fa0/14
```

Take a look again at the MAC address table for SwitchB. The MAC address (000c.29e2.03ba) that I highlighted belongs to ComputerB. When SwitchB receives an Ethernet Frame for ComputerB it will be forwarded to SwitchA and it will be dropped! (Well at least for 15 seconds until the topology change mechanism kicks in...).

Of course we have a solution to speed this up, here's what we will do:

How to Master CCNP SWITCH

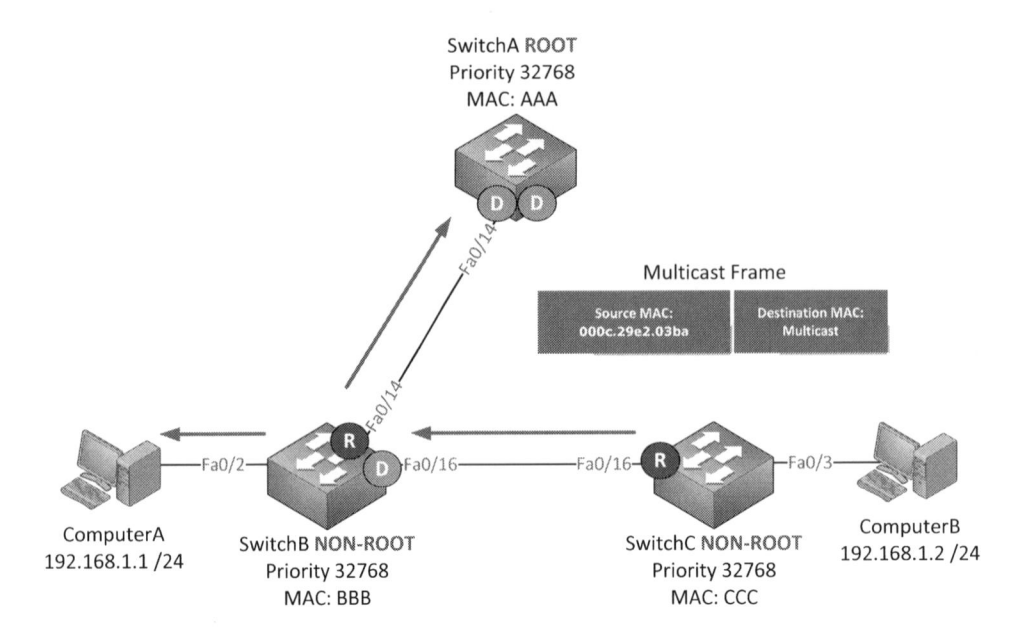

[Network topology diagram showing SwitchA ROOT (Priority 32768, MAC: AAA) at top, connected via Fa0/14 links to SwitchB NON-ROOT (Priority 32768, MAC: BBB) and SwitchC NON-ROOT (Priority 32768, MAC: CCC). SwitchB connects to ComputerA (192.168.1.1 /24) on Fa0/2 and to SwitchC via Fa0/16. SwitchC connects to ComputerB (192.168.1.2 /24) on Fa0/3. A Multicast Frame is shown with Source MAC: 000c.29e2.03ba and Destination MAC: Multicast. Ports marked D (designated) and R (root).]

Once SwitchC switches over to use its non-designated port it will create a **dummy multicast frame.** The source MAC address of this Ethernet Frame will be **all the MAC addresses that it has in its MAC address table**. In my example above this is only the MAC address of ComputerB. The destination multicast address is a proprietary Cisco MAC address.

This multicast frame will be flooded to all other switches so they can update their MAC address tables right away.

Spanning-tree has saved the day again...anything else you need to know? What do you think will happen if I re-enable the fa0/14 interface on SwitchC again (the original root port)?

6. STP (Spanning Tree Protocol)

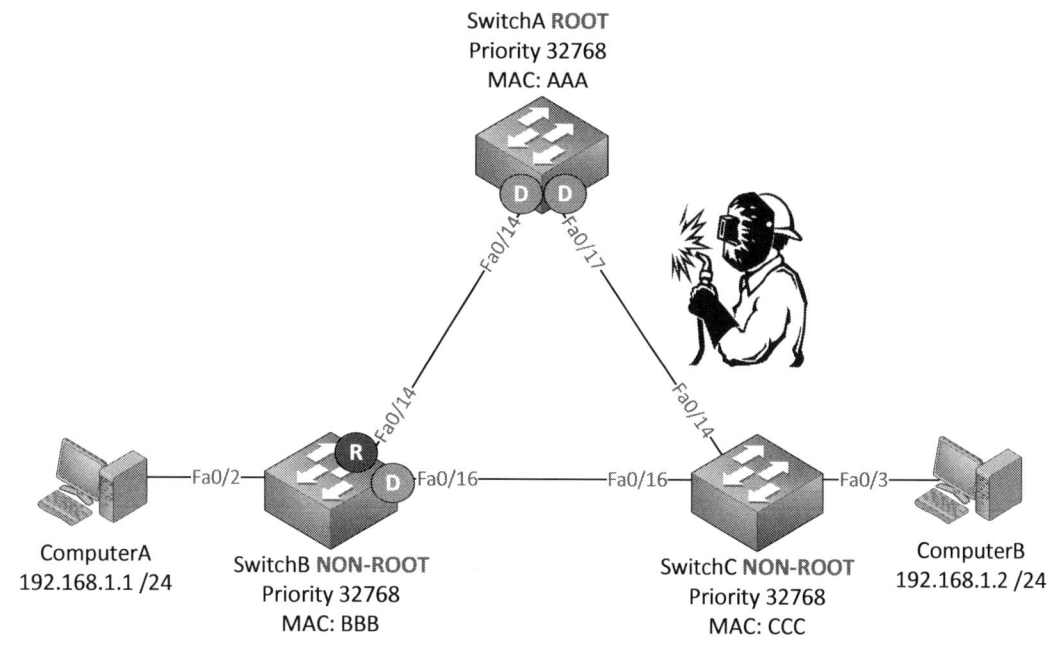

[Network diagram: SwitchA ROOT (Priority 32768, MAC: AAA) at top connected via Fa0/14 and Fa0/17 to SwitchB and SwitchC. SwitchB NON-ROOT (Priority 32768, MAC: BBB) connects Fa0/2 to ComputerA (192.168.1.1 /24) and Fa0/16 to SwitchC. SwitchC NON-ROOT (Priority 32768, MAC: CCC) connects Fa0/3 to ComputerB (192.168.1.2 /24). The link from SwitchA to SwitchC (Fa0/17 - Fa0/14) shows a welder cutting the cable. SwitchB has R (root port) on Fa0/14 and D (designated) on Fa0/16. SwitchA has D on both Fa0/14 and Fa0/17.]

```
SwitchC(config)#interface fa0/14
SwitchC(config-if)#no shutdown
```

Let's bring the interface back up. In my lab it's not as exciting as in the picture…

```
SwitchC# STP: VLAN0001 Fa0/14 -> listening
SwitchC# STP: VLAN0001 Fa0/14: root port delay timer active
SwitchC# STP: VLAN0001 Fa0/14 -> blocking
SwitchC# STP: VLAN0001 new root port Fa0/14, cost 3019
SwitchC# STP: VLAN0001 Fa0/16 -> blocking (uplinkfast)
```

You can see we don't immediately switch back to interface fa0/14. There's no reason to switch back to this interface ASAP because we have a working root port. Even if we would switch back to interface fa0/14 right away we'd still have to wait because the fa0/17 interface on SwitchA will have to go through the listening and learning state (which takes 30 seconds).

That's all I wanted that I wanted to show you about uplinkfast, we'll take a look at backbone fast now.

Backbone Fast is used to recover from an indirect link failure. What does that mean? Let me show you an example of an indirect link failure and how spanning-tree deals with it:

SwitchA ROOT
Priority 32768
MAC: AAA

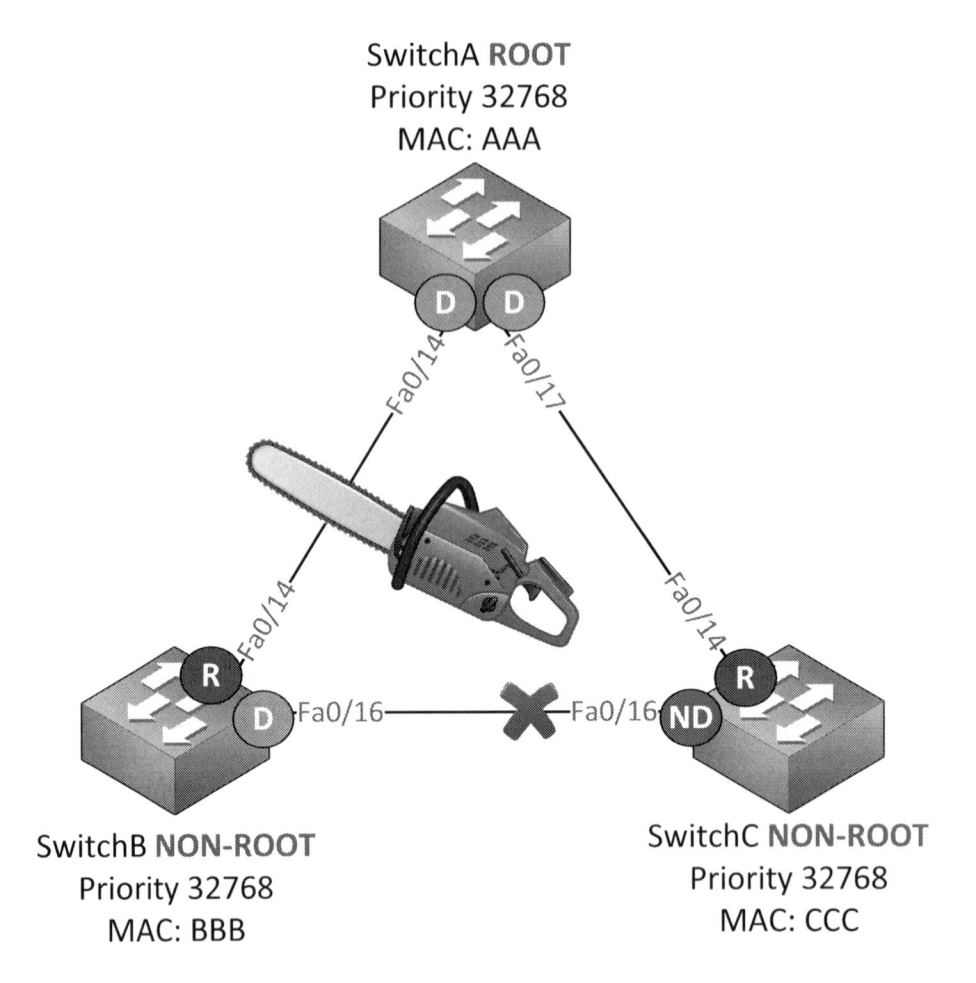

SwitchB NON-ROOT
Priority 32768
MAC: BBB

SwitchC NON-ROOT
Priority 32768
MAC: CCC

Take a look at the picture above. SwitchA is the root bridge and the fa0/16 interface on SwitchC has been blocked. Suddenly the link between SwitchA and SwitchB fails. From SwitchC's perspective this is **an indirect link failure**.

This is what will happen:

1. SwitchB will detect this link failure immediately since it's a directly connected link. Since it doesn't receive any BPDUs from the root anymore it assumes it is now the new root bridge and will send BPDUs towards SwitchC claiming to be the new root.
2. SwitchC will receive these BPDUs from SwitchB but it will realize that this new BPDU is **inferior** compared to the old one it has currently stored on its fa0/16 interface and will **ignore this new BPDU**. When a switch receives an inferior BPDU it means that the neighbor switch has lost its connection to the root bridge.
3. After 20 seconds (default timer) the max age timer will expire for the old BPDU on the fa0/16 interface of SwitchC. The interface will go from blocking to the listening state and will send BPDUs towards SwitchB.

6. STP (Spanning Tree Protocol)

4. SwitchB will receive this BPDU from SwitchC and discovers that he isn't the root bridge. It won't send BPDUs anymore towards SwitchC.
5. The fa0/16 interface on SwitchC will continue from the listening state (15 seconds) to the learning state (15 seconds) and ends up in the forwarding state.

Connectivity is now restored but it took 20 seconds for the max age timer to expire, 15 seconds for the listening state and another 15 seconds for the learning state before we go to the forwarding state. That's a total of 50 seconds downtime. Let's take a look at this situation on our switches:

```
SwitchB#debug spanning-tree events
Spanning Tree event debugging is on
```

```
SwitchC#debug spanning-tree events
Spanning Tree event debugging is on
```

Let's enable our debugging.

```
SwitchA(config)#interface fa0/14
SwitchA(config-if)#shutdown
```

I will shut this interface to simulate an indirect link failure.

```
SwitchB# STP: VLAN0001 we are the spanning tree root
```

SwitchB believes it is the root bridge.

```
SwitchC# STP: VLAN0001 heard root  8193-0019.569d.5700 on Fa0/16
```

SwitchC receives the BPDUs from SwitchB who claims to be the root bridge.

```
SwitchC# STP: VLAN0001 Fa0/16 -> listening
SwitchC# STP: VLAN0001 Fa0/16 -> learning
SwitchC# STP: VLAN0001 Fa0/16 -> forwarding
```

After the max age timer expires (20 seconds) for the old BPDU from SwitchB the fa0/16 interface on SwitchC will go to the listening and learning state and ends up in forwarding state.

```
SwitchB# STP: VLAN0001 heard root  4097-0011.bb0b.3600 on Fa0/16
SwitchB# STP: VLAN0001 new root is 4097, 0011.bb0b.3600 on port
Fa0/16, cost 38
```

The identity crisis of SwitchB comes to an end. It now hears the BPDUs from the root bridge through SwitchC and understands that it's not the root bridge.

Without backbone fast, spanning-tree will discard the inferior BPDUs that

SwitchC receives on its fa0/16 interface and it will have to wait till the max age timer expires (20 seconds).

If we enable backbone fast it will **skip the max age timer** so we can save 20 seconds of time.

```
SwitchA(config)#interface fa0/14
SwitchA(config-if)#no shutdown
```

Let's enable the fa0/14 interface on SwitchA first.

```
SwitchA(config)#spanning-tree backbonefast
```

```
SwitchB(config)#spanning-tree backbonefast
```

```
SwitchC(config)#spanning-tree backbonefast
```

Let's enable backbone fast on all switches. This is a global command (**spanning-tree backbonefast**).

```
SwitchA#debug spanning-tree backbonefast detail
Spanning Tree backbonefast detail debugging is on
```

```
SwitchB#debug spanning-tree events
Spanning Tree event debugging is on
```

```
SwitchC#debug spanning-tree backbonefast detail
Spanning Tree backbonefast detail debugging is on
```

Use the **debug spanning-tree backbonefast detail** command to see real-time information on backbone fast.

```
SwitchA(config)#interface fa0/14
SwitchA(config-if)#shutdown
```

Let's simulate the indirect link failure again...

```
SwitchB# STP: VLAN0001 we are the spanning tree root
```

SwitchB loses its connection to the root bridge and assumes he is now the new root bridge. Nothing new so far...

```
SwitchA# STP FAST: VLAN0001 FastEthernet0/17: sending requested
RLQ response PDU
```

SwitchA receives a new packet called a **(RLQ) Root Link Query** from SwitchC. As soon as SwitchC receives an inferior BPDU it will send a root link

6. STP (Spanning Tree Protocol)

query on its root port and non-designated ports to check if the root bridge is still available.

```
SwitchC# STP FAST: received RLQ response PDU was expected on
VLAN0001 FastEthernet0/14 - resp root id 4097-0011.bb0b.3600
```

SwitchC receives a reply to its root link query on the fa0/14 interface to SwitchA.

```
SwitchC# STP FAST: received_rlq_bpdu on VLAN0001
FastEthernet0/16 - making FastEthernet0/16 a designated port
```

Because SwitchC received a response from the root bridge on its fa0/14 interface it can now skip the max age timer on its f0/16 interface and the interface goes to the listening and learning state right away. We effectively save 20 seconds (max age timer).

Take a good look at the last debug output from SwitchC. It doesn't say that it received something on the fa0/16 interface, it means that it received an answer to the root link query that it did because it received an inferior BPDU on the fa0/16 interface. That's all there is to backbone fast.

Phew! You made it all the way to the end of this chapter. What do you think? If you ask me there's quite some stuff to know about spanning-tree and there is definitely more than meets the eye. If you still feel fuzzy after reading this chapter I would recommend you to re-read it before continuing. Besides reading I also highly recommend to boot up your switches and try some things yourself. It will help you to reinforce your knowledge and it's a good change from reading.

If you want you can try the following lab:

http://gns3vault.com/Switching/pvst-per-vlan-spanning-tree.html

In this lab you'll play with PVST, port priority, different root bridges and changing the cost and different timers.

7. Rapid Spanning Tree

In the previous chapter we took a detailed look at spanning-tree to see how it operates. I spent quite some time at showing you how spanning-tree deals with link failures and how fast it recovers from these events. The original spanning-tree standard works fine but is too slow nowadays for modern networks.

Nowadays we see more and more routing in our networks. Routing protocols like OSPF and EIGRP are much faster than spanning-tree when they have to deal with changes in the network. To keep up with the speed of these routing protocols another flavor of spanning tree was created...**rapid spanning tree**.

Rapid spanning tree is not a revolution of the original spanning tree but an evolution. Behind the scenes some things have been changed to speed up the process, configuration-wise it's the same as what you have seen so far. I will refer to the original spanning tree as 'classic spanning tree'.

Let's dive into rapid spanning tree and we'll see how deep the rabbit hole goes...

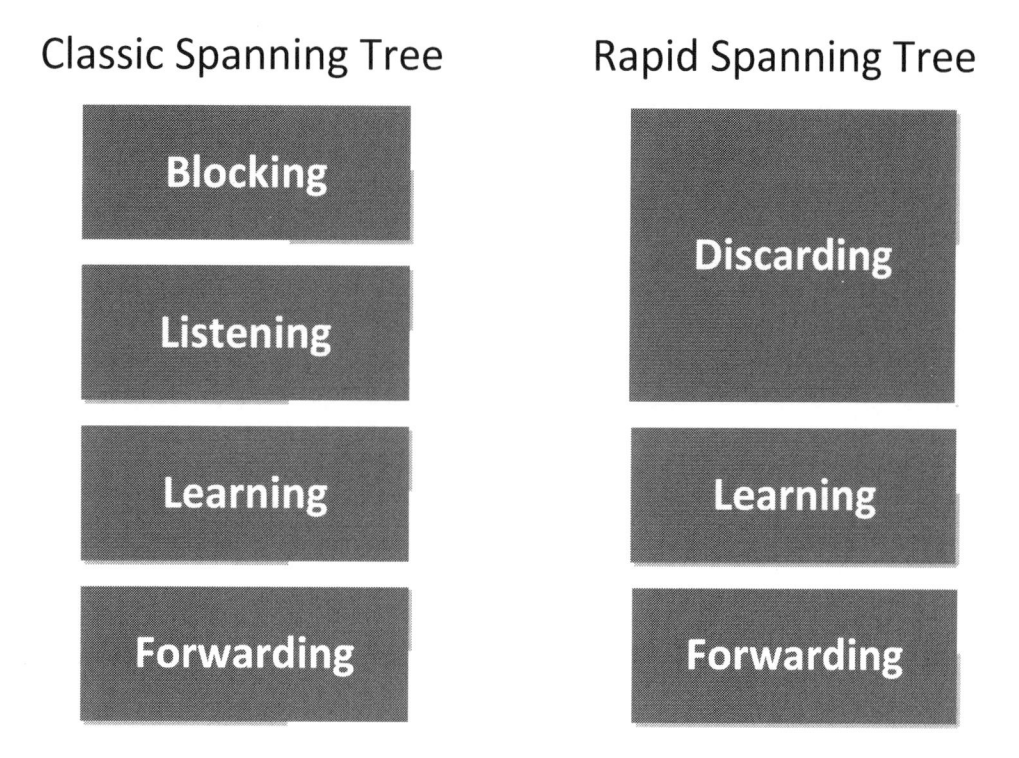

Classic Spanning Tree

- Blocking
- Listening
- Learning
- Forwarding

Rapid Spanning Tree

- Discarding
- Learning
- Forwarding

Remember the port states of spanning tree? We have a blocking, listening, learning and forwarding port state. This is the first difference between spanning tree and rapid spanning tree.

Rapid spanning tree only has three port states:

- **Discarding**
- Learning
- Forwarding

You already know about learning and forwarding but **discarding** is a new port state. Basically it combines the blocking and listening port state.

Classic Spanning Tree	Rapid Spanning Tree	Port active in topology?	Learns MAC Address?
Blocking	Discarding	No	No
Listening	Discarding	Yes	No
Learning	Learning	Yes	Yes
Forwarding	Forwarding	Yes	Yes

Here's a nice overview with the different port states for spanning tree and rapid spanning tree. I've also included whether they are active and if they learn MAC addresses or not.

Do you remember all the other port roles that spanning tree has? Let's do a little review and I'll show you what is different for rapid spanning tree.

7. Rapid Spanning Tree

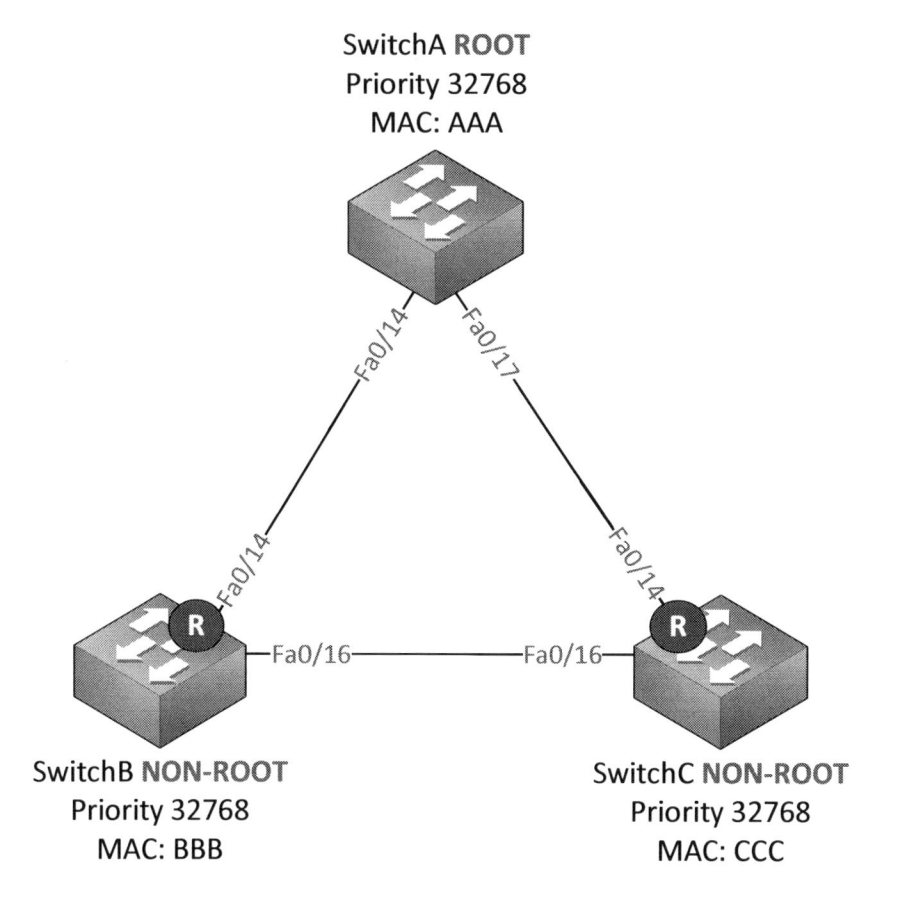

SwitchA ROOT
Priority 32768
MAC: AAA

SwitchB NON-ROOT
Priority 32768
MAC: BBB

SwitchC NON-ROOT
Priority 32768
MAC: CCC

The switch with the best bridge ID (priority + MAC address) becomes the root bridge. The other switches (non-root) have to find the shortest cost path to the root bridge. This is the root port. There's nothing new here, this works exactly the same for rapid spanning tree.

SwitchA **ROOT**
Priority 32768
MAC: AAA

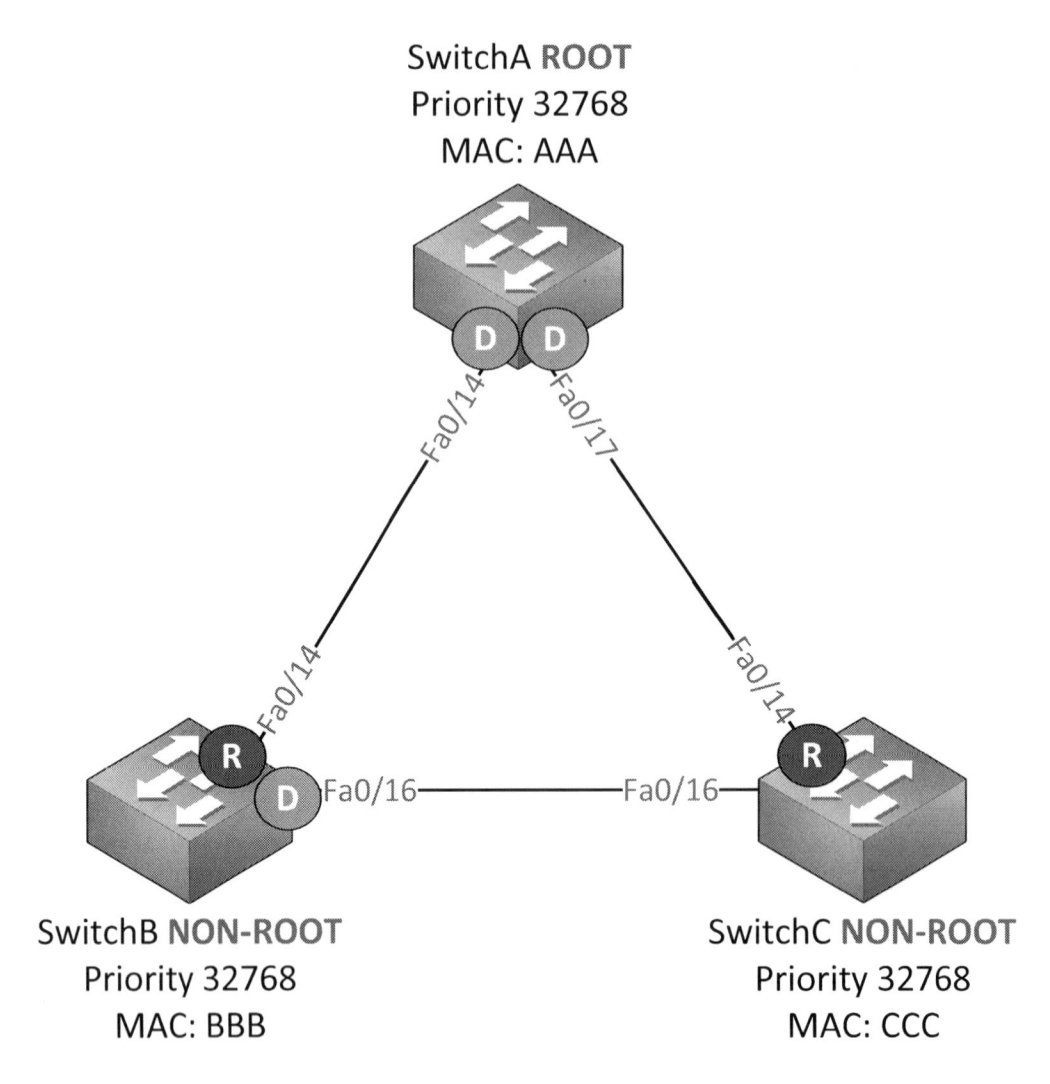

SwitchB **NON-ROOT**
Priority 32768
MAC: BBB

SwitchC **NON-ROOT**
Priority 32768
MAC: CCC

On each segment there can be only one designated port or we'll end up with a loop. The port will become the designated port if it can send the best BPDU. SwitchA as a root bridge will always have the best ports so all of interfaces will be designated. The fa0/16 interface on SwitchB will be the designated port in my example because it has a better bridge ID than SwitchC. There's still nothing new here compared to the classic spanning tree.

7. Rapid Spanning Tree

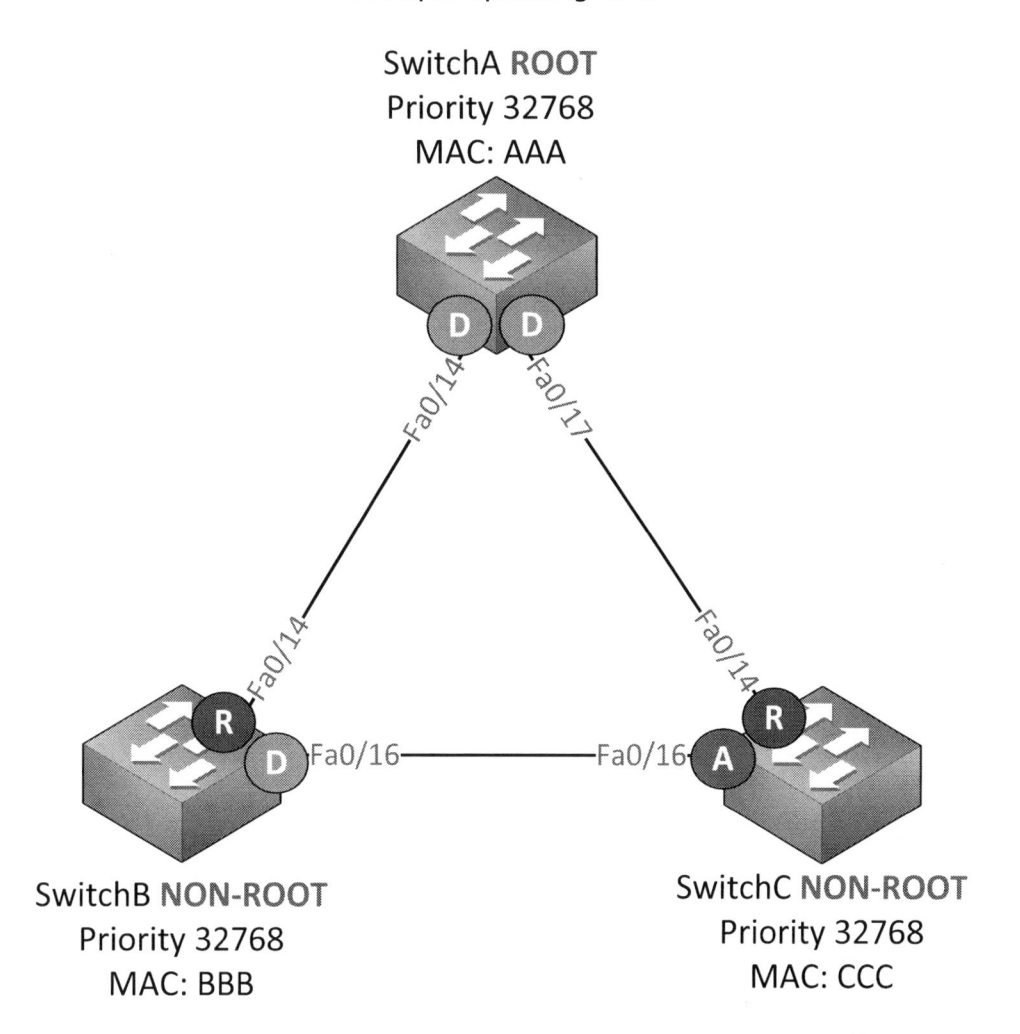

SwitchA ROOT
Priority 32768
MAC: AAA

SwitchB NON-ROOT
Priority 32768
MAC: BBB

SwitchC NON-ROOT
Priority 32768
MAC: CCC

SwitchC receives better BPDUs on its fa0/16 interface from SwitchB and thus it will be blocked. This is the alternate port and it's still the same thing for rapid spanning tree.

SwitchA **ROOT**
Priority 32768
MAC: AAA

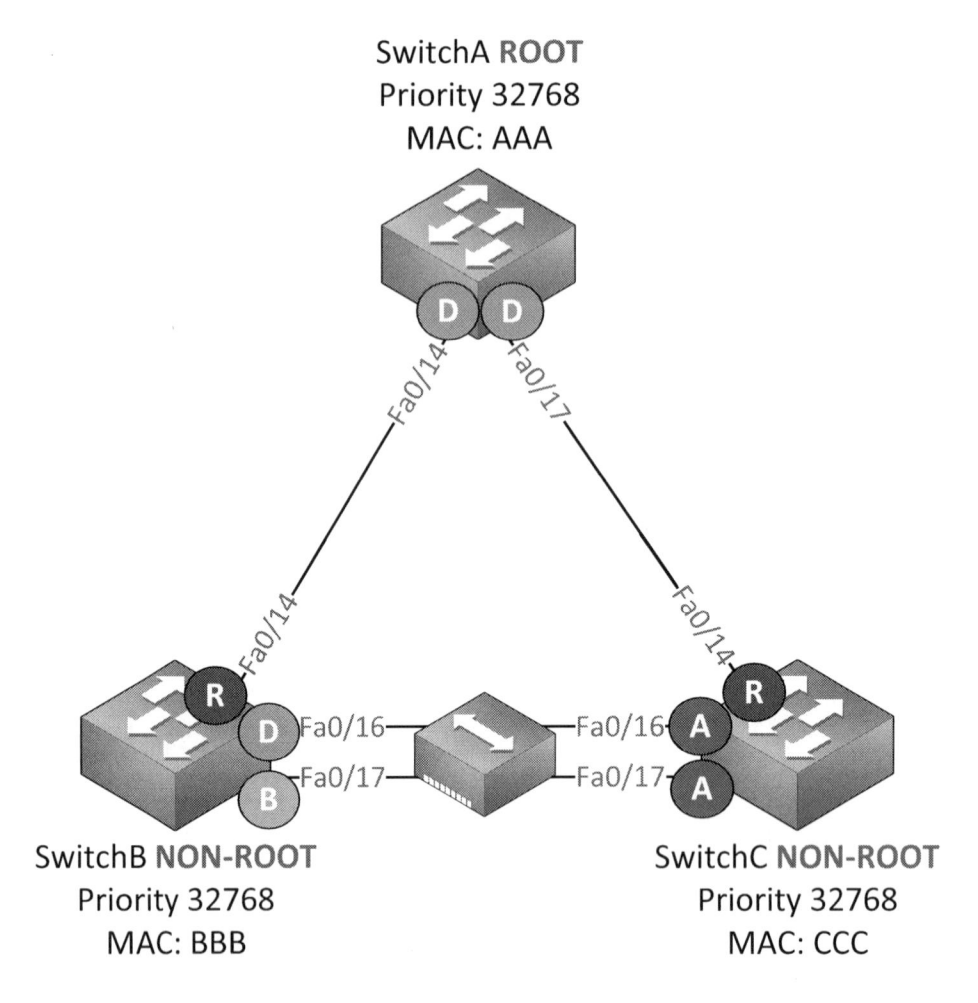

SwitchB **NON-ROOT**
Priority 32768
MAC: BBB

SwitchC **NON-ROOT**
Priority 32768
MAC: CCC

Here is a new port for you, take a look at the fa0/17 interface of SwitchB. It's called a **backup port** and it's new for rapid spanning tree. You are very unlikely to see this port on a production network though. Between SwitchB and SwitchC I've added a hub. Normally (without the hub in between) both fa0/16 and fa0/17 would be designated ports. Because of the hub the fa0/16 and fa0/17 interface on SwitchB are now in the **same collision domain.** Fa0/16 will be elected as the designated port and fa0/17 will become the **backup port** for the fa0/16 interface. The reason that SwitchB sees the fa0/17 interface as a backup port is because it receives its own BPDUs on the fa0/16 and fa0/17 interfaces and understands that it has two connections to the same segment. If you remove the hub the fa0/16 and fa0/17 will both be designated ports just like the classic spanning tree.

7. Rapid Spanning Tree

Rapid Spanning Tree BPDU

| Protocol Identifier | Protocol Version Identifier | BPDU Type | Flags | Root Identifier | Root Path Cost | Bridge Identifier | Port Identifier | Message Age | Max Age | Hello Time | Forward Delay |

| Topology Change | Proposal | Port Role | Learning | Forwarding | Agreement | Topology Change ACK |

The BPDU is different for rapid spanning tree. In the classic spanning tree the **flags** field only had two bits in use:

- Topology change.
- Topology change acknowledgment.

All bits of the flag field are now used. The role of the port that originates the BPDU will be added by using the **port role** field, it has the following options:

- Unknown
- Alternate / Backup port.
- Root port.
- Designated port.

This new BPDU is called a **version 2 BPDU.** Switches running the old version of spanning tree will drop this new BPDU version. In case you are wondering...rapid spanning tree and the old spanning **are compatible!** Rapid spanning tree has a way of dealing with switches running the older spanning tree version.

Let's walk through the other stuff that has been changed:

BPDUs are now sent **every hello time**. Only the root bridge generated BPDUs in the classic spanning tree and those were relayed by the non-root switches if they received it on their root port. Rapid spanning tree works differently...all switches generate BPDUs **every two seconds (hello time).** This is the default hello time but you can change it.

The classic spanning tree uses a max age timer (20 seconds) for BPDUs before they are discarded. Rapid spanning tree works differently! BPDUs are now used as a **keepalive mechanism** similar to what routing protocols like OSPF or EIGRP use. If a switch **misses three BPDUs** from a neighbor switch it will assume connectivity to this switch has been lost and it will remove all MAC addresses immediately.

Rapid spanning tree will **accept inferior BPDUs**. The classic spanning tree ignores them. Does this ring a bell? This is pretty much the backbone fast feature that I showed you in the previous chapter.

165

Transition speed (convergence time) is the most important feature of rapid spanning tree. The classic spanning tree had to walk through the listening and learning state before it would move an interface to the forwarding state, this took 30 seconds with the default timers. The classic spanning tree was based on **timers**.

Rapid spanning **doesn't use timers** to decide whether an interface can move to the forwarding state or not. It will use a **negotiation mechanism** for this. I'll show you how this works in a bit.

Do you remember portfast from the previous chapter? If we enable portfast while running the classic spanning tree it will skip the listening and learning state and put the interface in forwarding state right away. Besides moving the interface to the forwarding state it will also **not generate topology changes** when the interface goes up or down. We still use portfast for rapid spanning tree but it's now referred to as an **edge port**.

Rapid spanning tree can only put interfaces in the forwarding state really fast on **edge ports (portfast)** or **point-to-point interfaces**. It will take a look at the **link type** and there are only two link types:

- Point-to-point (full duplex)
- Shared (half duplex)

Normally we are using switches and all our interfaces are configured as full duplex, rapid spanning tree sees these interfaces as point-to-point. If we introduce a hub to our network we'll have half duplex which is seen as a shared interface to rapid spanning-tree.

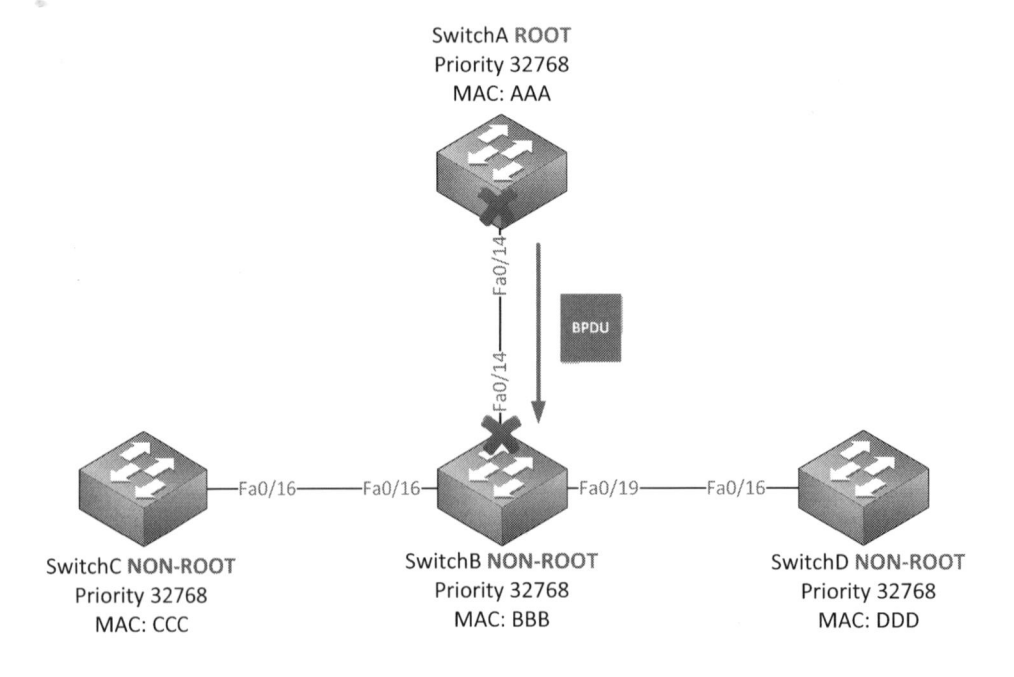

SwitchA **ROOT**
Priority 32768
MAC: AAA

SwitchC **NON-ROOT**
Priority 32768
MAC: CCC

SwitchB **NON-ROOT**
Priority 32768
MAC: BBB

SwitchD **NON-ROOT**
Priority 32768
MAC: DDD

7. Rapid Spanning Tree

Let me describe the rapid spanning tree synchronization mechanism by using the picture above. SwitchA on top is the root bridge. SwitchB, SwitchC and SwitchD are non-root bridges.

As soon as the link between SwitchA and SwitchB comes up their interfaces will be in blocking mode. SwitchB will receive a BPDU from SwitchA and now a **negotiation** will take place called **sync.**

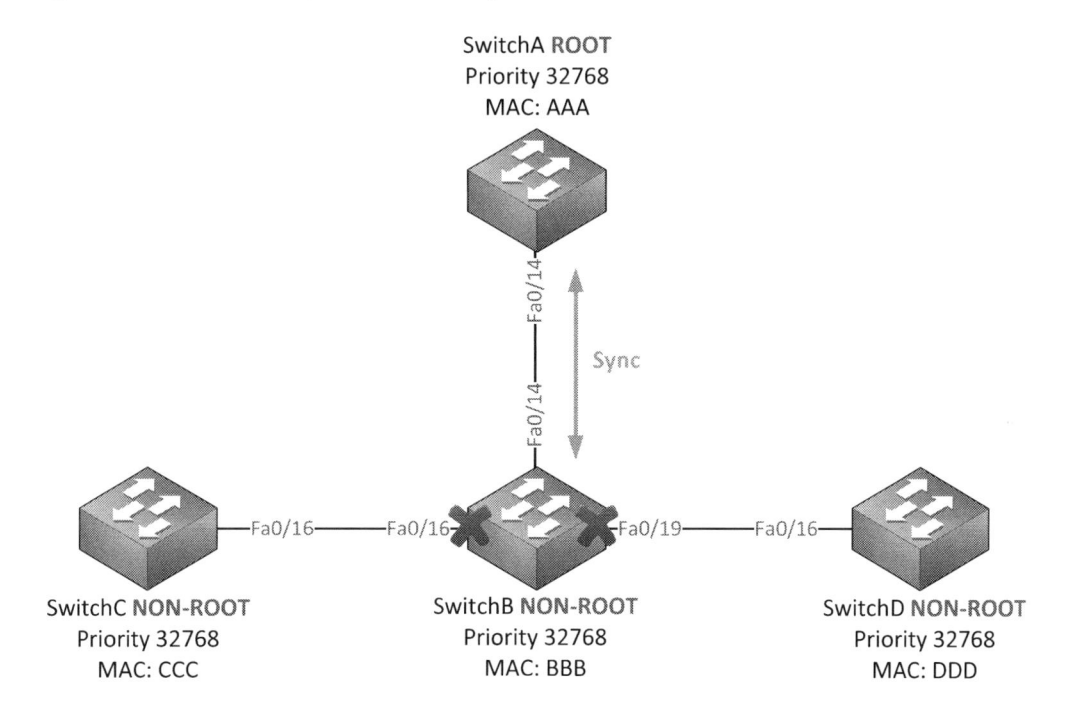

SwitchA ROOT
Priority 32768
MAC: AAA

Fa0/14
Sync
Fa0/14

SwitchC NON-ROOT —Fa0/16——Fa0/16— SwitchB NON-ROOT —Fa0/19——Fa0/16— SwitchD NON-ROOT
Priority 32768   Priority 32768   Priority 32768
MAC: CCC   MAC: BBB   MAC: DDD

After SwitchB received the BPDU from the root bridge it **immediately blocks all its non-edge designated ports**. Non-edge ports are the interfaces that connect to other switches while edge ports are the interfaces that have portfast configured. As soon as SwitchB blocks its non-edge ports the link between SwitchA and SwitchB will go into forwarding state.

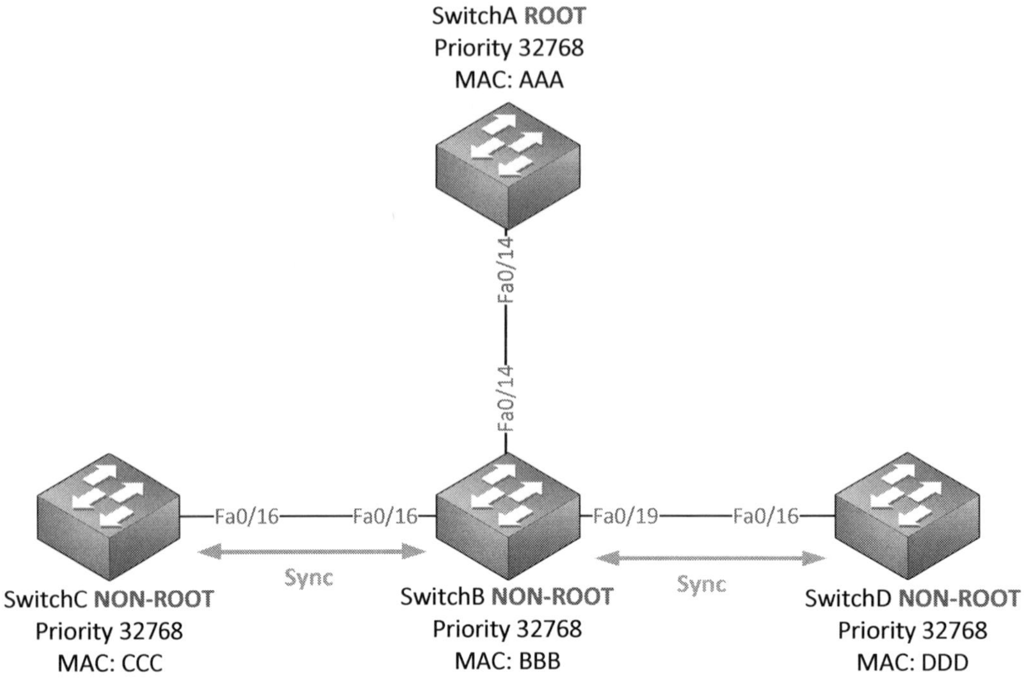
SwitchA ROOT
Priority 32768
MAC: AAA
Fa0/14
Fa0/14
Fa0/16
Fa0/16
Fa0/19
Fa0/16
Sync
Sync
SwitchC NON-ROOT
Priority 32768
MAC: CCC
SwitchB NON-ROOT
Priority 32768
MAC: BBB
SwitchD NON-ROOT
Priority 32768
MAC: DDD

SwitchB will also perform a sync operation with both SwitchC and SwitchD so they can quickly move to the forwarding state.

Are you following me so far? The lesson to learn here is that rapid spanning tree uses this **sync mechanism instead of the "timer-based" mechanism** that the classic spanning tree uses (listening → learning → forwarding). I'm going to show you what this looks like on real switches in a bit.

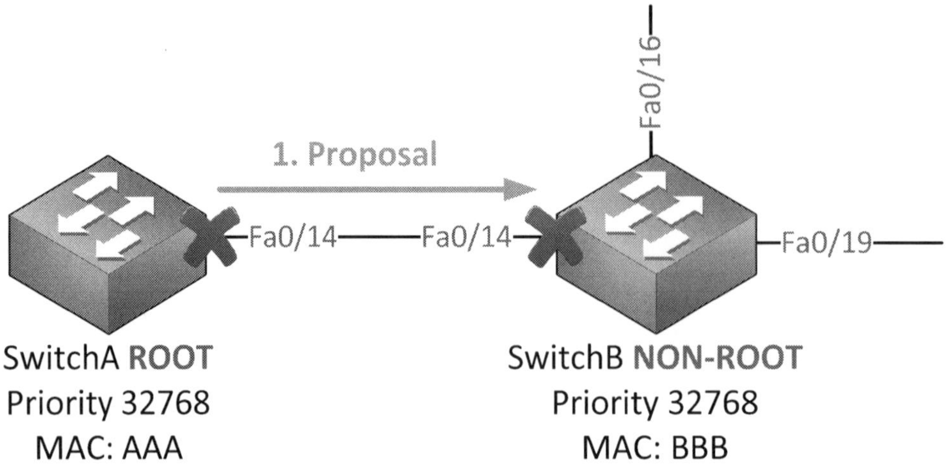
Fa0/16
1. Proposal
Fa0/14
Fa0/14
Fa0/19
SwitchA ROOT
Priority 32768
MAC: AAA
SwitchB NON-ROOT
Priority 32768
MAC: BBB

Let's zoom in on the sync mechanism of rapid spanning tree by taking a detailed look at SwitchA and SwitchB. At first the interfaces will be blocked until they receive a BPDU from each other. At this moment SwitchB will figure

7. Rapid Spanning Tree

out that SwitchA is the root bridge because it has the best BPDU information. The sync mechanism will start because SwitchA will set the **proposal bit** in the flag field of the BPDU.

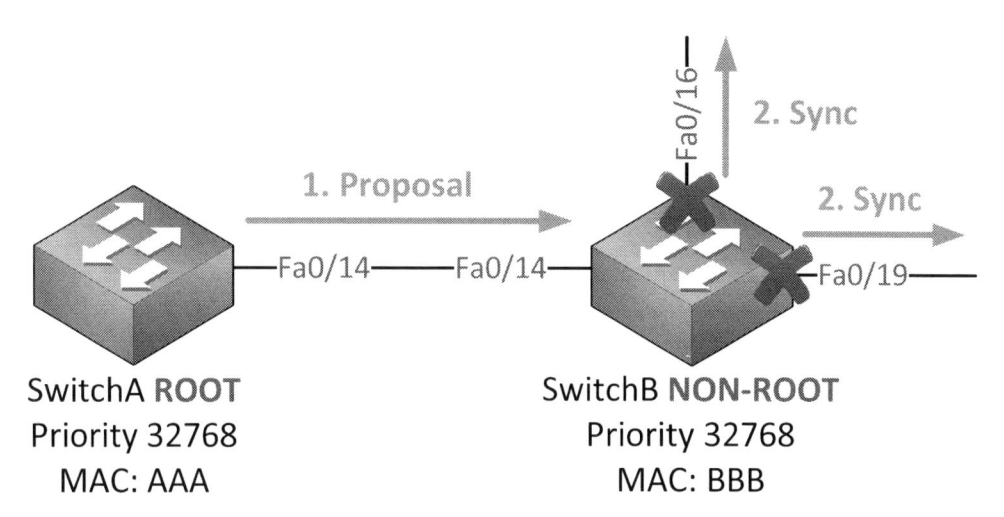

```
                    1. Proposal                    2. Sync
                                                    Fa0/16 ↑
    [SwitchA]──Fa0/14────Fa0/14──[SwitchB]         2. Sync
                                         ──Fa0/19──→

    SwitchA ROOT              SwitchB NON-ROOT
    Priority 32768            Priority 32768
    MAC: AAA                  MAC: BBB
```

SwitchB receives the proposal from SwitchA and realizes it has to do something. It will block all its non-edge interfaces and will start the synchronization towards SwitchC and SwitchD.

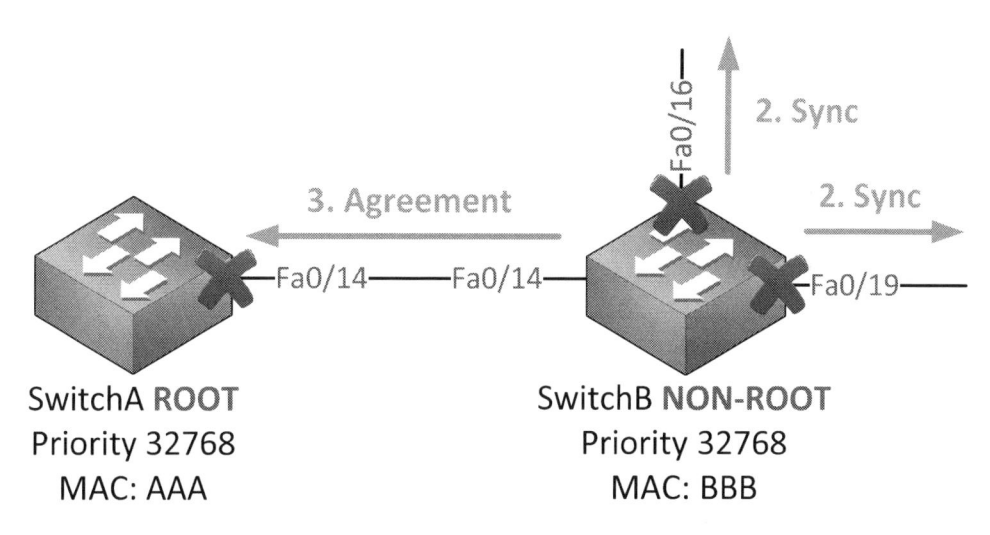

```
                    3. Agreement                    2. Sync
                                                    Fa0/16 ↑
    [SwitchA]←─Fa0/14────Fa0/14──[SwitchB]         2. Sync
                                         ──Fa0/19──→

    SwitchA ROOT              SwitchB NON-ROOT
    Priority 32768            Priority 32768
    MAC: AAA                  MAC: BBB
```

Once SwitchB has its interfaces in sync mode it will let SwitchA know about this by sending an **agreement.**
This agreement is a **copy of the proposal BPDU** where the proposal bit has been switched off and the agreement bit is switched on. The fa0/14 interface on SwitchB will now go into forwarding mode.

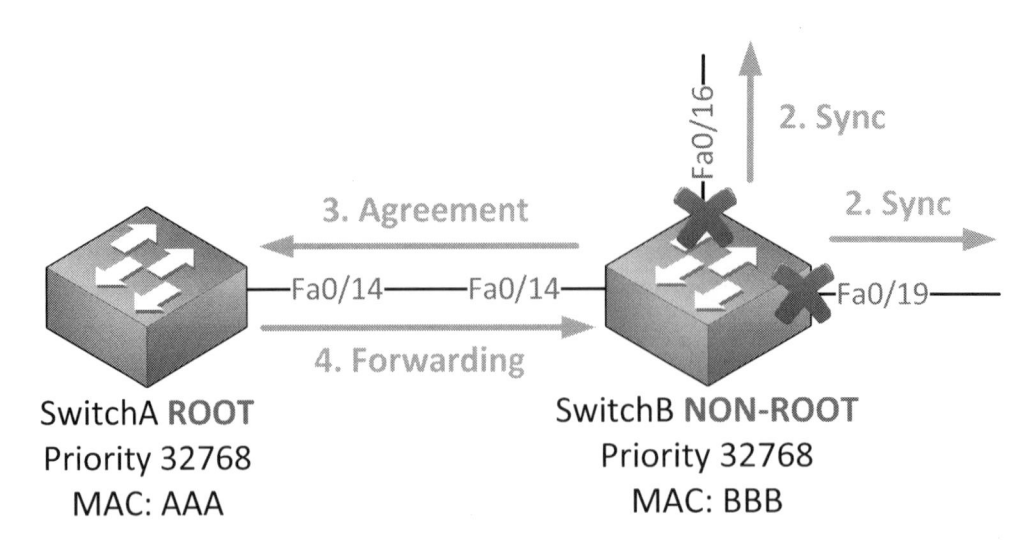

```
                                    Fa0/16↑    2. Sync

                3. Agreement                    2. Sync
         ←──────────────────
         ─Fa0/14──────Fa0/14─            ─Fa0/19─
                4. Forwarding
         ──────────────────→
    SwitchA ROOT                    SwitchB NON-ROOT
    Priority 32768                  Priority 32768
    MAC: AAA                        MAC: BBB
```

Once SwitchA receives the agreement from SwitchB it will put its fa0/14 interface in forwarding mode immediately.

What about the fa0/16 and fa0/19 interface on SwitchB?

7. Rapid Spanning Tree

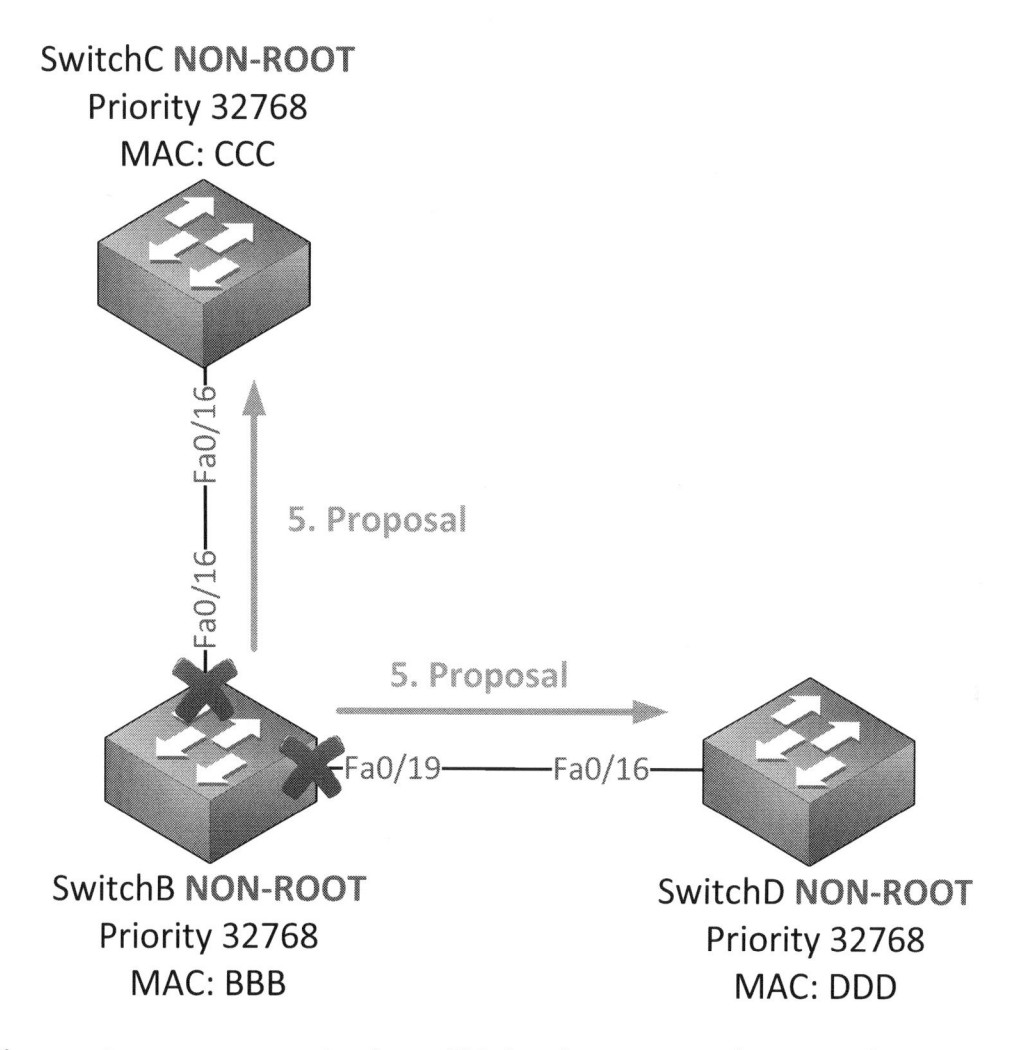

SwitchC NON-ROOT
Priority 32768
MAC: CCC

5. Proposal

5. Proposal

Fa0/19 —— Fa0/16

SwitchB NON-ROOT
Priority 32768
MAC: BBB

SwitchD NON-ROOT
Priority 32768
MAC: DDD

The exact same sync mechanism will take place now on these interfaces. SwitchB will send a proposal on its fa0/16 and fa0/19 interfaces towards SwitchC and SwitchD.

SwitchC NON-ROOT
Priority 32768
MAC: CCC

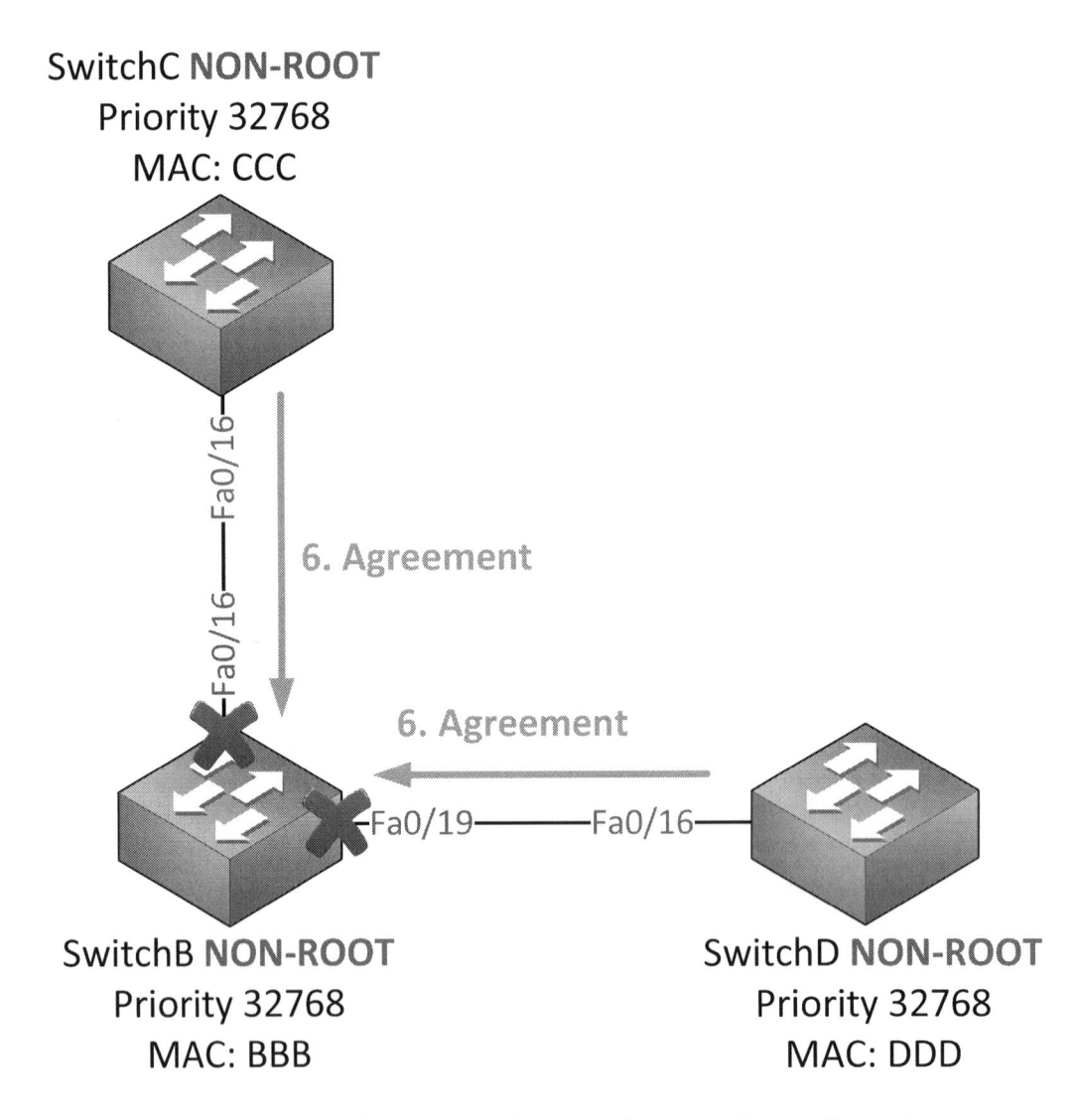

6. Agreement

6. Agreement

SwitchB NON-ROOT
Priority 32768
MAC: BBB

SwitchD NON-ROOT
Priority 32768
MAC: DDD

SwitchC and SwitchD don't have any other interfaces so they will send an agreement back to SwitchB.

7. Rapid Spanning Tree

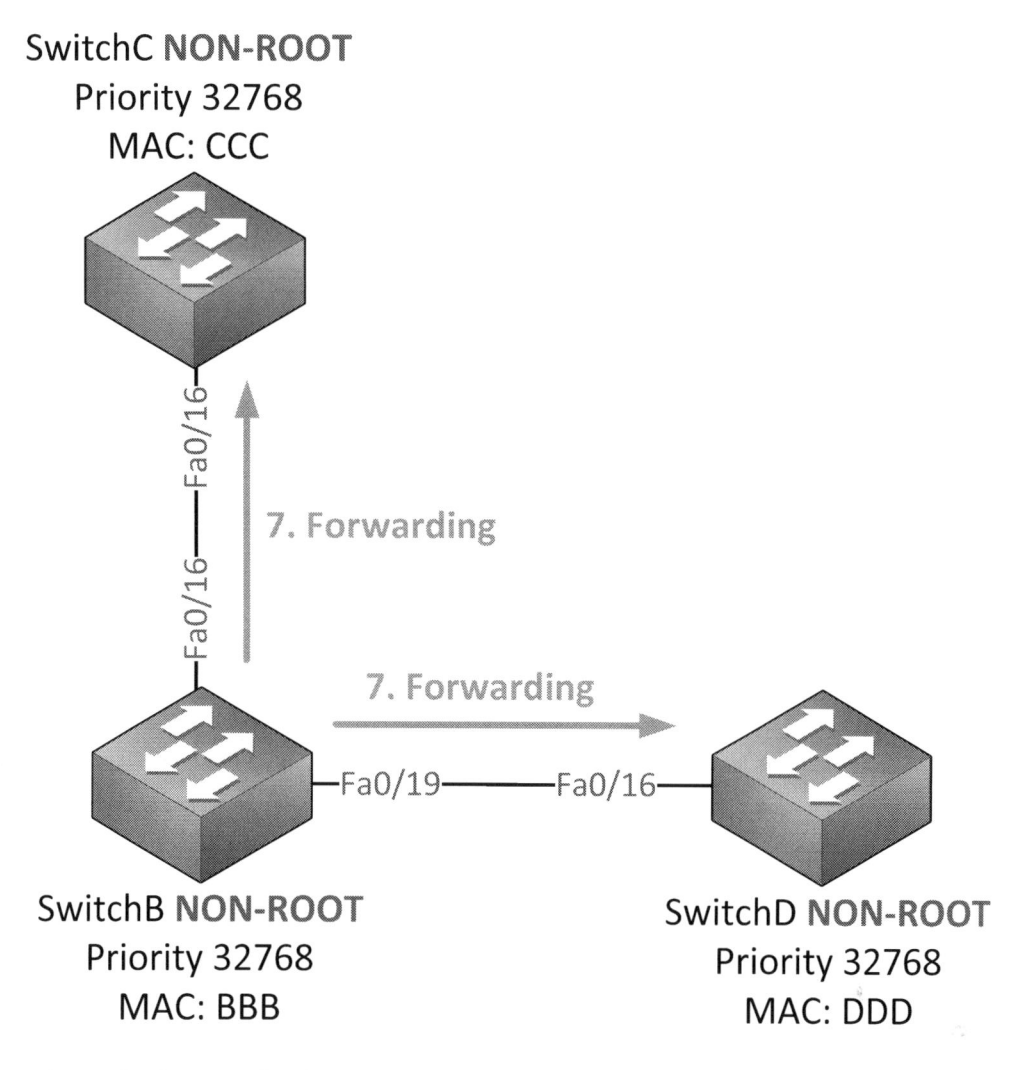

SwitchC NON-ROOT
Priority 32768
MAC: CCC

Fa0/16 — Fa0/16

7. Forwarding

7. Forwarding

Fa0/19————Fa0/16

SwitchB NON-ROOT
Priority 32768
MAC: BBB

SwitchD NON-ROOT
Priority 32768
MAC: DDD

SwitchB will place its fa0/16 and fa0/19 interface in forwarding and we are done. This sync mechanism is just a couple of messages flying back and forth and very fast, it's much faster than the timer-based mechanism of the classic spanning tree!

What else is new with rapid spanning tree? There are three more things I want to show you:

- UplinkFast.
- Topology change mechanism.
- Compatibility with classic spanning tree.

I showed you how **UplinkFast** works in the previous chapter. When you configure the classic spanning tree you have to enable UplinkFast yourself. Rapid spanning tree uses UpLinkFast by default, you don't have to configure it yourself. When a switch loses its root port it will put its alternate port in

forwarding immediately.
The difference is that the classic spanning tree needed multicast frames to update the MAC address tables of all switches.

We don't need this anymore because the topology change mechanism for rapid spanning tree is different.So what's different about the topology change mechanism?

With the classic spanning tree a link failure would trigger a topology change. Using rapid spanning tree a **link failure is not considered as a topology change**. Only non-edge interfaces (leading to other switches) that move to the forwarding state are considered as a topology change. Once a switch detects a topology change this will happen:

- It will start a **topology change while timer** with a value that is twice the hello time. This will be done for all non-edge designated and root ports.
- It will **flush the MAC addresses** that are learned on these ports.
- As long as the topology change while timer is active it will set the topology change bit on BPDUs that are sent out these ports. BPDUs will also be sent out of its root port.

When a neighbor switch receives this BPDU with the topology change bit set this will happen:

- It will clear all its MAC addresses on all interfaces except the one where it received the BPDU with the topology change on.
- It will start a topology change while timer itself and send BPDUs on all designated ports and the root port, setting the topology change bit.

7. Rapid Spanning Tree

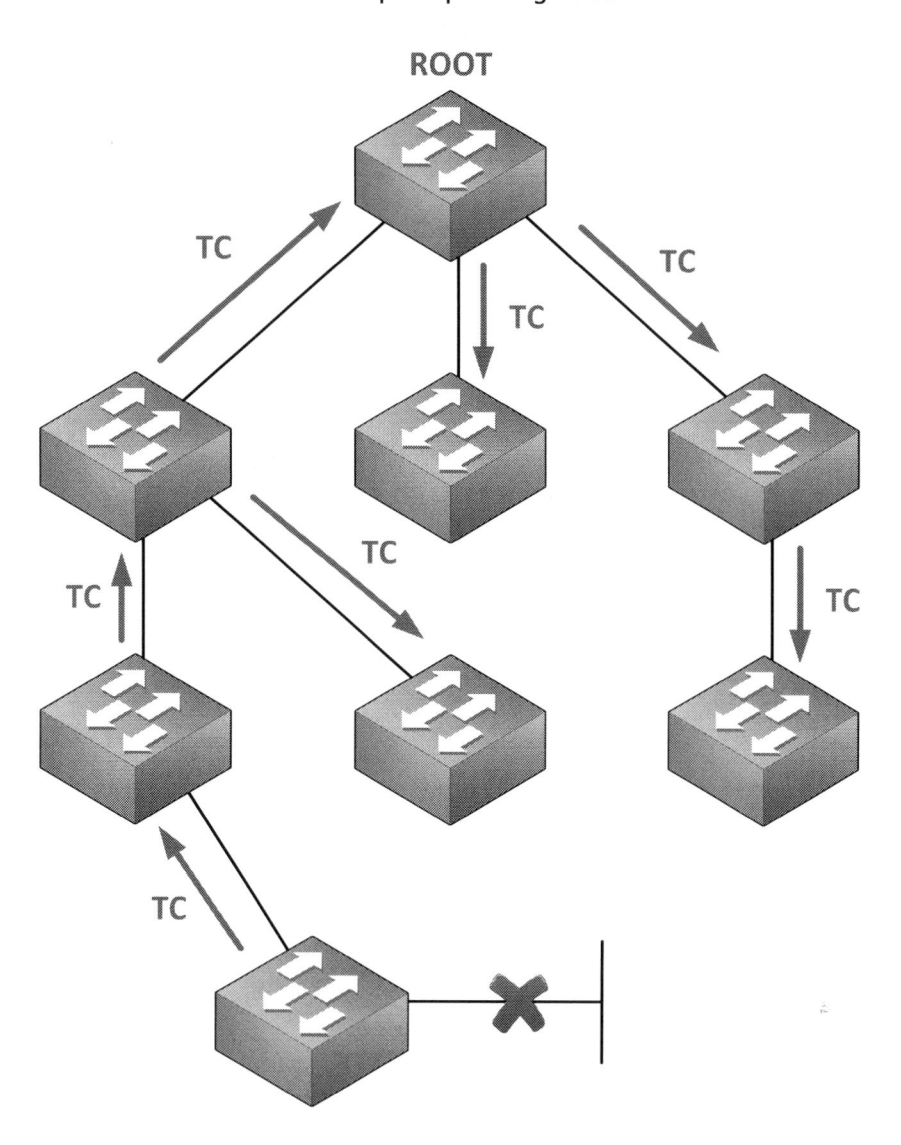

Instead of sending a topology change all the way up to the root bridge like the classic spanning tree does, the topology change is now quickly flooded throughout the network.

SwitchA
Rapid Spanning Tree

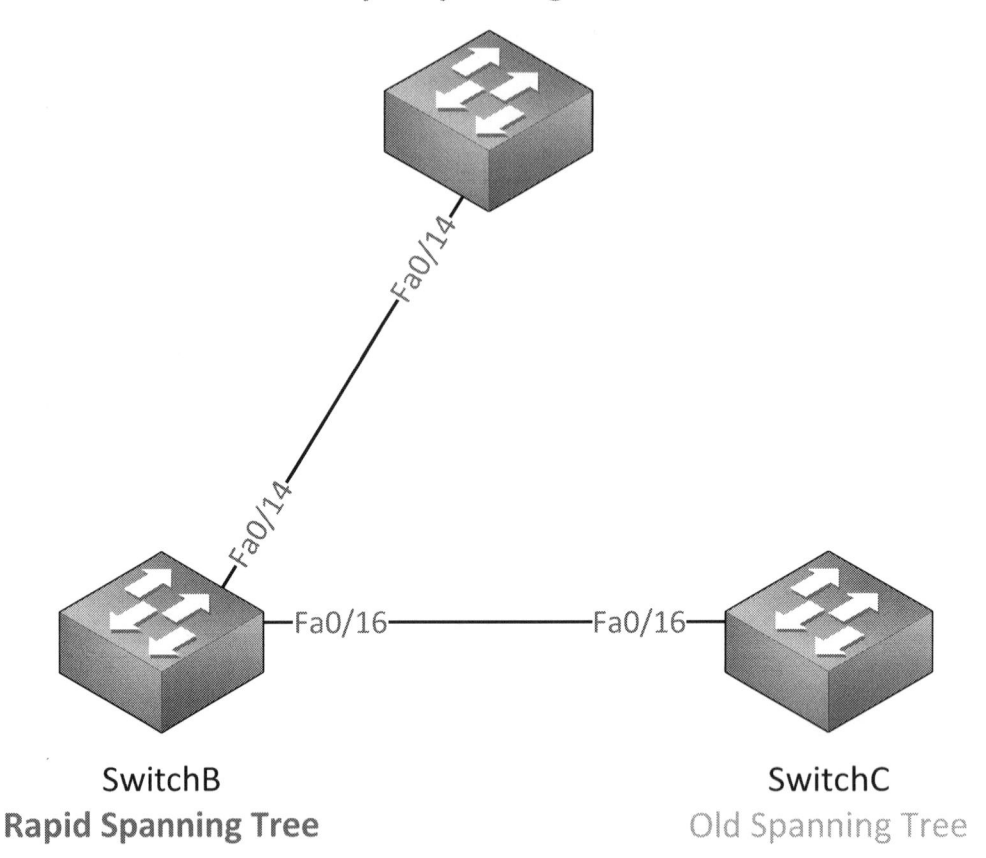

SwitchB
Rapid Spanning Tree

SwitchC
Old Spanning Tree

Last but not least, let's talk about compatibility. The short answer is that rapid spanning tree and classic spanning tree **are compatible.** However when a switch running rapid spanning tree communicates with a switch running classic spanning tree all the Speedy Gonzales features won't work!

In the example above I have my three switches. Between SwitchA and SwitchB we will run rapid spanning tree. Between SwitchB and SwitchC we will fall back to the classic spanning tree.

Seen enough theory? Let's take a look at the configuration of rapid spanning tree!

7. Rapid Spanning Tree

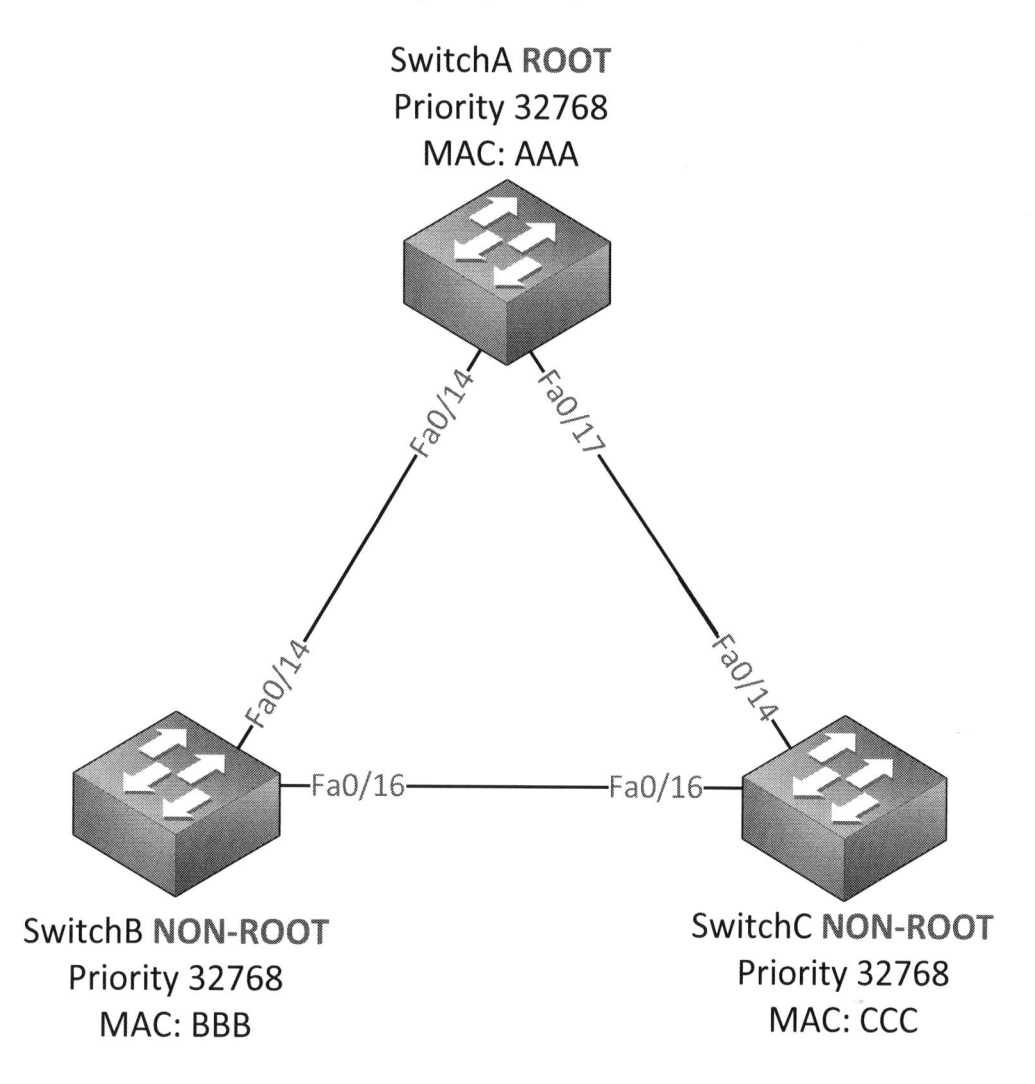

SwitchA ROOT
Priority 32768
MAC: AAA

SwitchB NON-ROOT
Priority 32768
MAC: BBB

SwitchC NON-ROOT
Priority 32768
MAC: CCC

This is the topology I'm going to use. SwitchA will be the root bridge in my example.

```
SwitchA(config)#spanning-tree mode rapid-pvst
```

```
SwitchB(config)#spanning-tree mode rapid-pvst
```

```
SwitchC(config)#spanning-tree mode rapid-pvst
```

That's it...just one command will enable rapid spanning tree on our switches. The implementation of rapid spanning tree is **rapid-pvst**. We are calculating a rapid spanning tree for each VLAN.

First I want to show you the sync mechanism:

```
SwitchA(config)#interface fa0/14
SwitchA(config-if)#shutdown
SwitchA(config)#interface f0/17
SwitchA(config-if)#shutdown
```

I'm going to shut both interfaces on SwitchA to start with.

```
SwitchA#debug spanning-tree events
Spanning Tree event debugging is on
```

```
SwitchB#debug spanning-tree events
Spanning Tree event debugging is on
```

```
SwitchC#debug spanning-tree events
Spanning Tree event debugging is on
```

Second step is to enable debug on all the switches.

```
SwitchA(config)#interface fa0/14
SwitchA(config-if)#no shutdown
```

I'm going to bring the fa0/14 interface back to the land of the living on SwitchA.

```
SwitchA#
setting bridge id (which=3) prio 4097 prio cfg 4096 sysid 1 (on)
id 1001.0011.bb0b.3600
RSTP(1): initializing port Fa0/14
RSTP(1): Fa0/14 is now designated
RSTP(1): transmitting a proposal on Fa0/14
```

The fa0/14 interface on SwitchA will be blocked and it'll send a proposal to SwitchB.

```
SwitchB#
RSTP(1): initializing port Fa0/14
RSTP(1): Fa0/14 is now designated
RSTP(1): transmitting a proposal on Fa0/14
RSTP(1): updt roles, received superior bpdu on Fa0/14
RSTP(1): Fa0/14 is now root port
```

Apparently SwitchB thought it was the root bridge because it says it received a superior BPDU on its fa0/14 interface. It changes its fa0/14 interface to root port.

```
SwitchB# RSTP(1): syncing port Fa0/16
```

7. Rapid Spanning Tree

The fa0/16 interface on SwitchB will go into sync mode. This is the interface that connects to SwitchC.

```
SwitchB#  RSTP(1): synced Fa0/14
RSTP(1): transmitting an agreement on Fa0/14 as a response to a
proposal
```

SwitchB will respond to SwitchA its proposal by sending an agreement.

```
SwitchA# RSTP(1): received an agreement on Fa0/14
%LINK-3-UPDOWN: Interface FastEthernet0/14, changed state to up
%LINEPROTO-5-UPDOWN: Line protocol on Interface
FastEthernet0/14, changed state to up
```

SwitchA receives the agreement from SwitchB and interface fa0/14 will go into forwarding.

```
SwitchB# RSTP(1): transmitting a proposal on Fa0/16
```

SwitchB will send a proposal to SwitchC.

```
SwitchC# RSTP(1): transmitting an agreement on Fa0/16 as a
response to a proposal
```

SwitchC will respond to the proposal of SwitchB and send an agreement.

```
SwitchB# RSTP(1): received an agreement on Fa0/16
%LINK-3-UPDOWN: Interface FastEthernet0/14, changed state to up
%LINEPROTO-5-UPDOWN: Line protocol on Interface
FastEthernet0/14, changed state to up
```

SwitchB receives the agreement from SwitchC and the interface will go into forwarding. That's all there to is it...a quick number of handshakes and the interfaces will move to forwarding without the use of any timers. Let's continue!

```
SwitchA(config)#interface fa0/17
SwitchA(config-if)#no shutdown
```

I'm going to enable this interface so that connectivity is fully restored.

```
SwitchA#show spanning-tree

VLAN0001
  Spanning tree enabled protocol rstp
  Root ID    Priority    4097
             Address     0011.bb0b.3600
             This bridge is the root
             Hello Time  2 sec   Max Age 20 sec   Forward Delay
15 sec

  Bridge ID  Priority    4097    (priority 4096 sys-id-ext 1)
             Address     0011.bb0b.3600
             Hello Time  2 sec   Max Age 20 sec   Forward Delay
15 sec
             Aging Time 300

Interface           Role Sts Cost      Prio.Nbr Type
------------------- ---- --- --------- -------- ----------------
-----------------
Fa0/14              Desg FWD 19        128.16   P2p
Fa0/17              Desg FWD 19        128.19   P2p
```

We can verify that SwitchA is the root bridge. This show command also reveals that we are running rapid spanning tree. Note that the link type is **p2p**. This is because my FastEthernet interfaces are in full duplex by default.

```
SwitchB#show spanning-tree

VLAN0001
  Spanning tree enabled protocol rstp
  Root ID    Priority    4097
             Address     0011.bb0b.3600
             Cost        19
             Port        16 (FastEthernet0/14)
             Hello Time  2 sec   Max Age 20 sec   Forward Delay
15 sec

  Bridge ID  Priority    8193    (priority 8192 sys-id-ext 1)
             Address     0019.569d.5700
             Hello Time  2 sec   Max Age 20 sec   Forward Delay
15 sec
             Aging Time 300

Interface           Role Sts Cost      Prio.Nbr Type
------------------- ---- --- --------- -------- ----------------
-----------------
Fa0/14              Root FWD 19        128.16   P2p
Fa0/16              Desg FWD 19        128.18   P2p
```

```
SwitchC#show spanning-tree
```

7. Rapid Spanning Tree

```
VLAN0001
  Spanning tree enabled protocol rstp
  Root ID    Priority    4097
             Address     0011.bb0b.3600
             Cost        19
             Port        14 (FastEthernet0/14)
             Hello Time   2 sec  Max Age 20 sec  Forward Delay 15 sec

  Bridge ID  Priority    32769  (priority 32768 sys-id-ext 1)
             Address     000f.34ca.1000
             Hello Time   2 sec  Max Age 20 sec  Forward Delay 15 sec
             Aging Time 300

Interface        Role Sts Cost      Prio.Nbr Type
---------------- ---- --- --------- -------- --------------------
Fa0/14           Root FWD 19        128.14   P2p
Fa0/16           Altn BLK 19        128.16   P2p
```

Here are SwitchB and SwitchC. Nothing new here, it's the same information as classic spanning tree.

181

SwitchA ROOT
Priority 32768
MAC: AAA

SwitchB NON-ROOT
Priority 32768
MAC: BBB

SwitchC NON-ROOT
Priority 32768
MAC: CCC

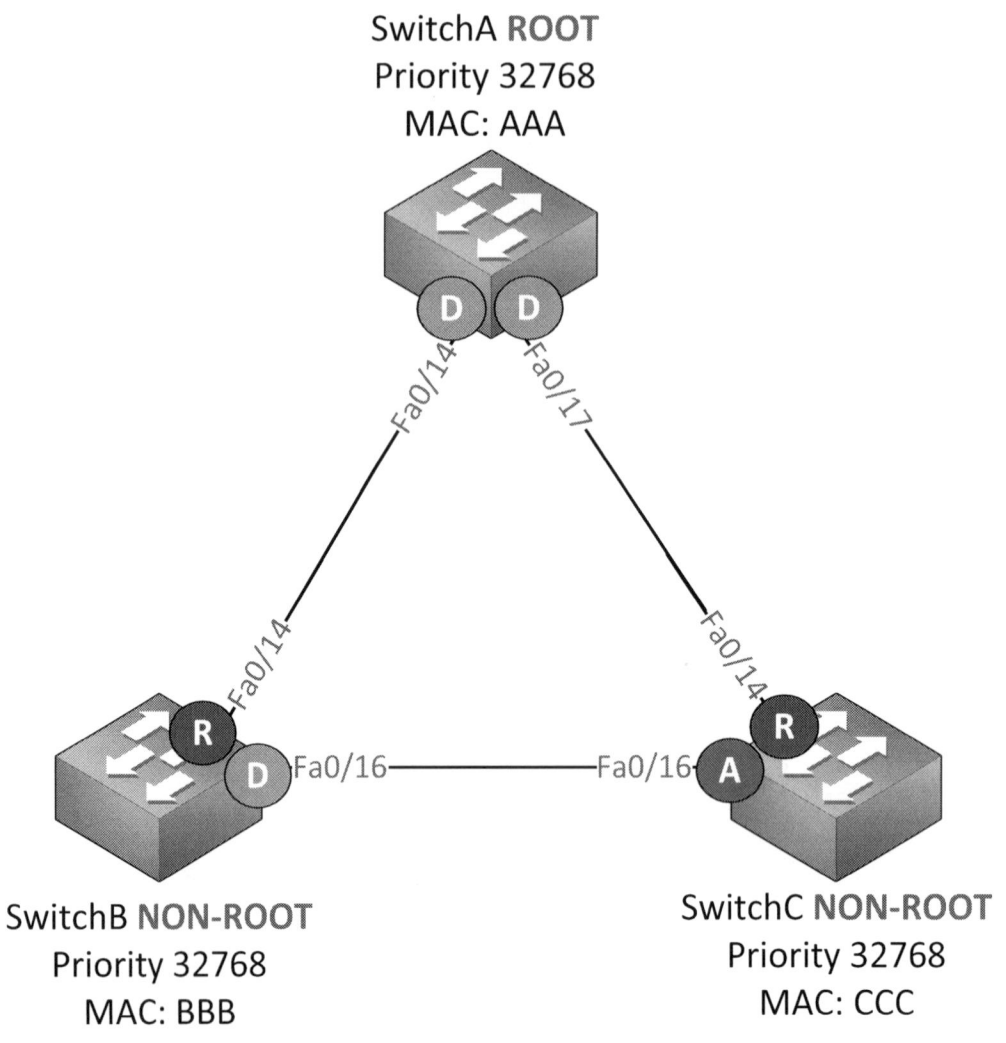

This is what the topology looks at the moment. It's the same as when I showed you the configuration of classic spanning tree.

7. Rapid Spanning Tree

SwitchA ROOT
Priority 32768
MAC: AAA

SwitchB NON-ROOT
Priority 32768
MAC: BBB

SwitchC NON-ROOT
Priority 32768
MAC: CCC

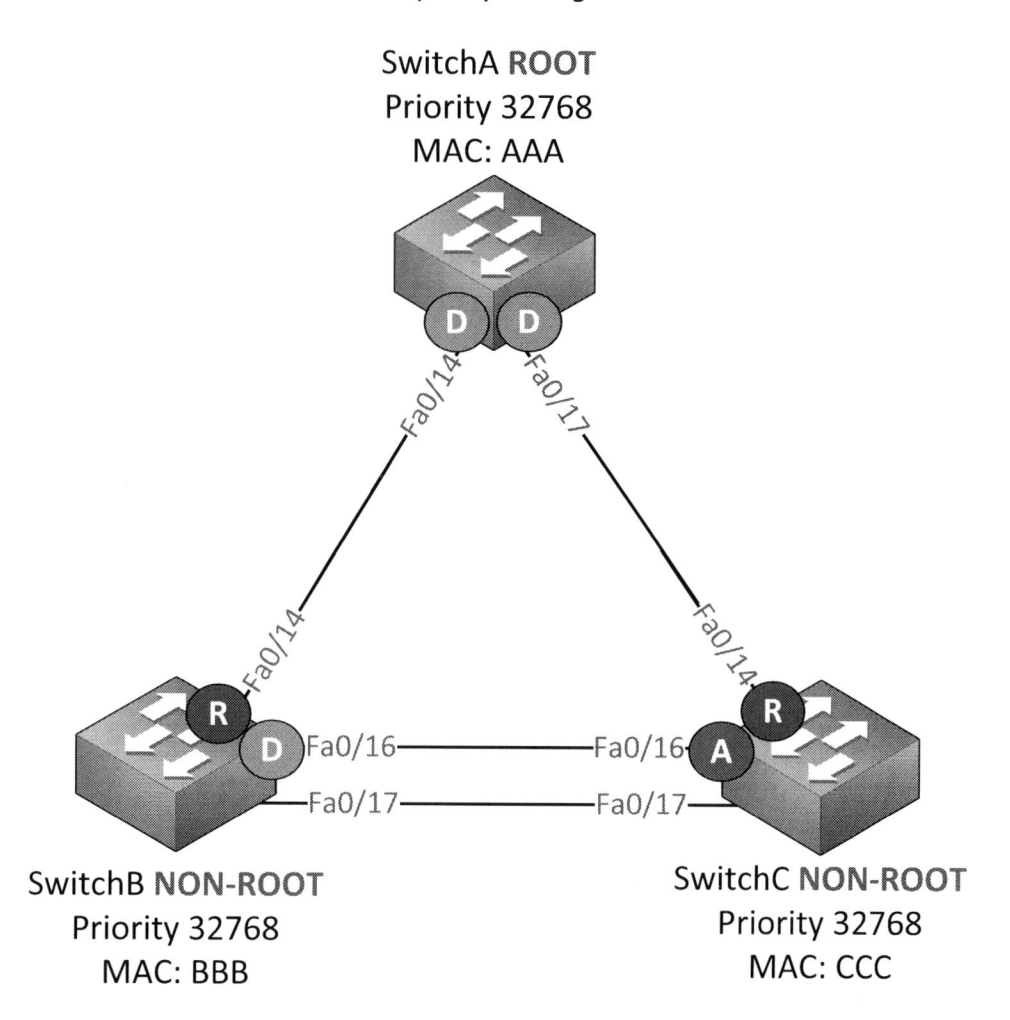

I just added another link between SwitchB and SwitchC. Let's see if this influences our topology.

```
SwitchB#show spanning-tree | begin Interface
Interface            Role Sts Cost      Prio.Nbr Type
-------------------- ---- --- --------- -------- --------------------
Fa0/14               Root FWD 19        128.16   P2p
Fa0/16               Desg FWD 19        128.18   P2p
Fa0/17               Desg FWD 19        128.19   P2p
```

```
SwitchC#show spanning-tree | begin Interface
Interface            Role Sts Cost      Prio.Nbr Type
-------------------- ---- --- --------- -------- --------------------
Fa0/14               Root FWD 19        128.14   P2p
Fa0/16               Altn BLK 19        128.16   P2p
Fa0/17               Altn BLK 19        128.17   P2p
```

Nothing spectacular, we just have another designated port on SwitchB and another alternate port on SwitchC.

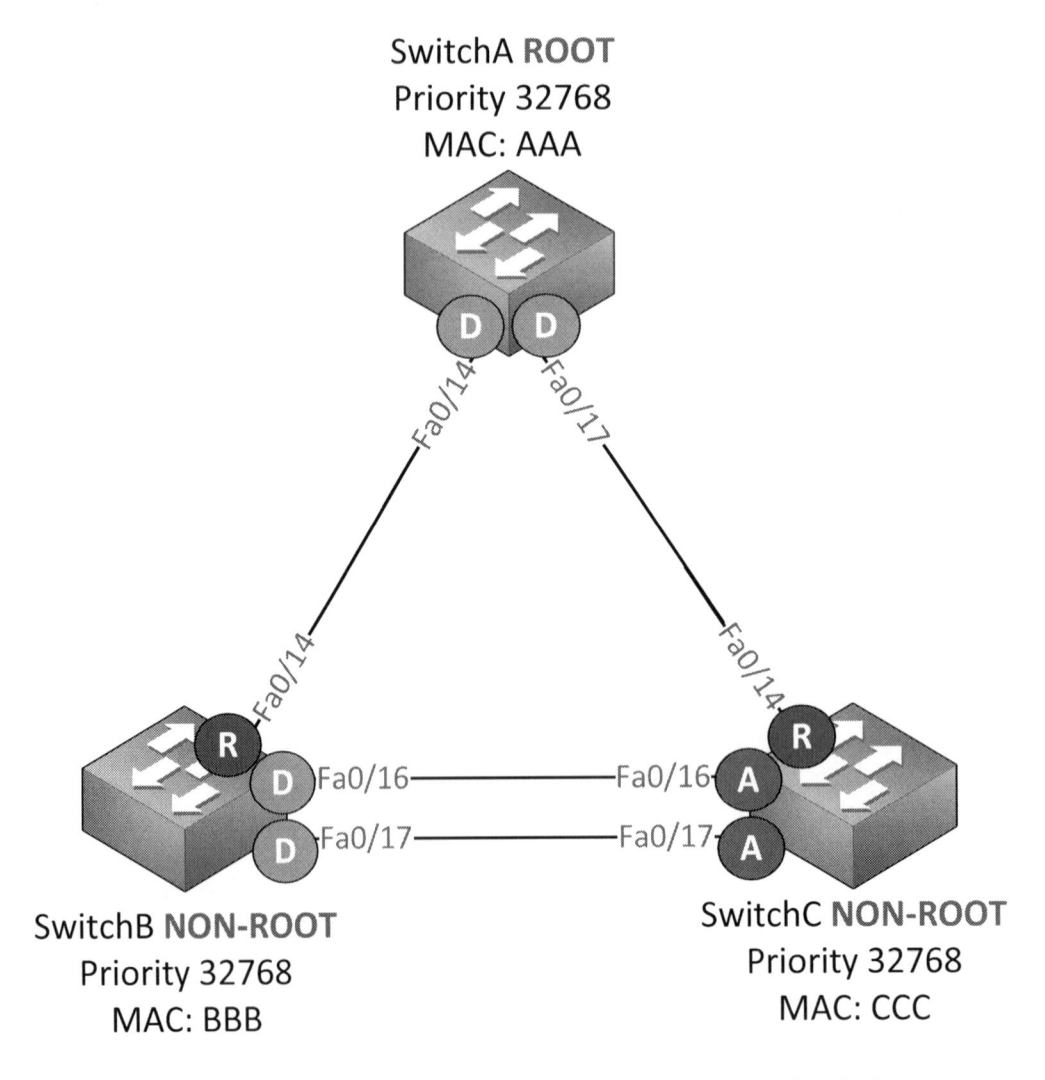

SwitchA **ROOT**
Priority 32768
MAC: AAA

SwitchB **NON-ROOT**
Priority 32768
MAC: BBB

SwitchC **NON-ROOT**
Priority 32768
MAC: CCC

This is the topology at the moment. The reason I just added this link is because I want to show you the difference when I add a hub between SwitchB and SwitchC.

7. Rapid Spanning Tree

SwitchA ROOT
Priority 32768
MAC: AAA

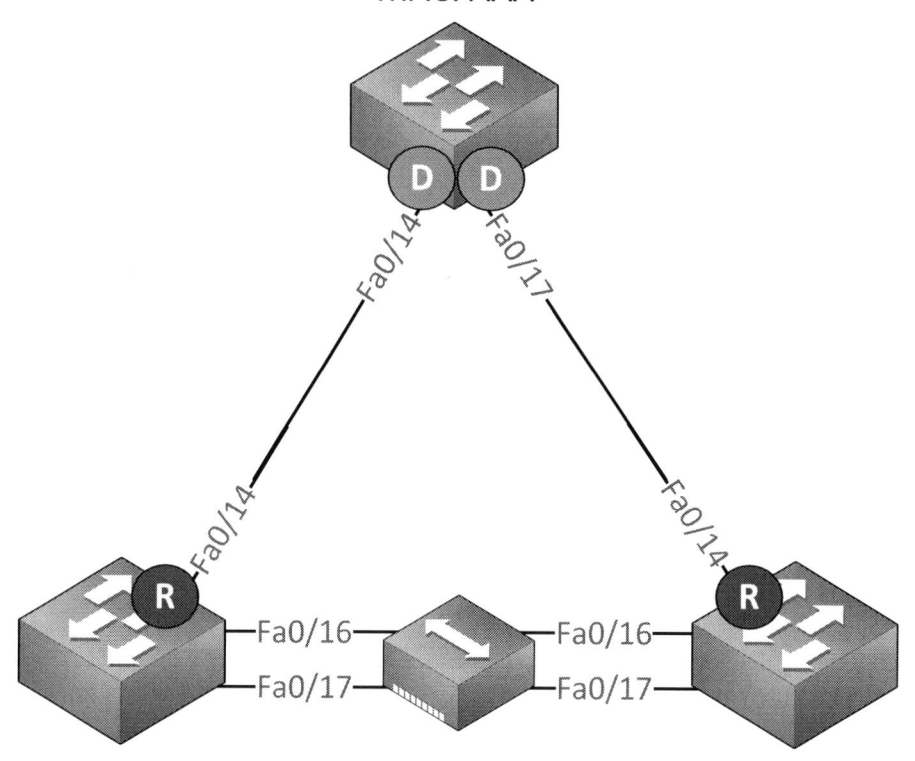

SwitchB NON-ROOT
Priority 32768
MAC: BBB

SwitchC NON-ROOT
Priority 32768
MAC: CCC

```
SwitchB#show spanning-tree | begin Interface

Interface           Role Sts Cost      Prio.Nbr Type
------------------- ---- --- --------- -------- --------------------
Fa0/14              Root FWD 19        128.5    P2p
Fa0/16              Desg FWD 100       128.3    Shr
Fa0/17              Back BLK 100       128.4    Shr
```

```
SwitchC#show spanning-tree | begin Interface

Interface          Role Sts Cost      Prio.Nbr Type
---------          -------- ----      -------- ----
Fa0/14             Root FWD 19        128.5    P2p
Fa0/16             Altn BLK 100       128.3    Shr
Fa0/17             Altn BLK 100       128.4    Shr
```

Here's something new. SwitchB has a backup port. Because of the hub in the middle SwitchB and SwitchC will hear their own BPDUs.
You can also see that the link type is **shr (shared)**. That's because the hub causes these switches to switch their interfaces to half duplex.

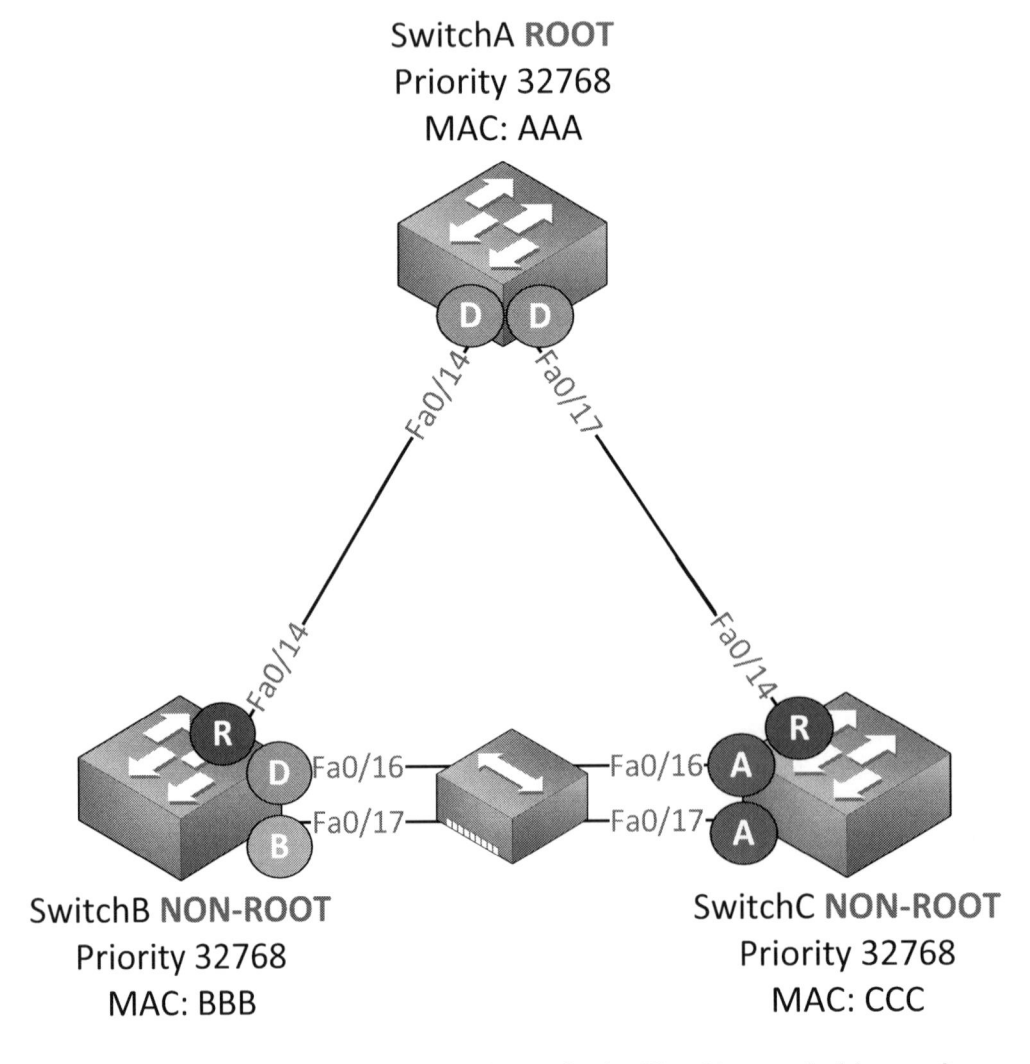

SwitchA **ROOT**
Priority 32768
MAC: AAA

SwitchB **NON-ROOT**
Priority 32768
MAC: BBB

SwitchC **NON-ROOT**
Priority 32768
MAC: CCC

To make the picture complete this is what it looks like. You probably won't ever see the backup port but now you know why it shows up.

7. Rapid Spanning Tree

BPDUs are sent every two seconds (hello time) and if you want to prove this you can take a look at a debug:

```
SwitchB#debug spanning-tree bpdu
```

You can use the **debug spanning-tree bpdu** command to view BPDUs are are sent or received.

```
SwitchB#
STP: VLAN0001 rx BPDU: config protocol = rstp, packet from
FastEthernet0/14  , linktype IEEE_SPANNING , enctype 2, encsize
17
STP: enc 01 80 C2 00 00 00 00 11 BB 0B 36 10 00 27 42 42 03
STP: Data
000002023C10010011BB0B36000000000010010011BB0B360080100000140002
000F00
STP: VLAN0001 Fa0/14:0000 02 02 3C 10010011BB0B3600 00000000
10010011BB0B3600 8010 0000 1400 0200 0F00
RSTP(1): Fa0/14 repeated msg
RSTP(1): Fa0/14 rcvd info remaining 6
RSTP(1): sending BPDU out Fa0/16
RSTP(1): sending BPDU out Fa0/17
STP: VLAN0001 rx BPDU: config protocol = rstp, packet f
```

You will see the contents of the BPDU like above. It's not very useful if you want to see the content of the BPDU but it does show us that SwitchB is receiving BPDUs and sending them on its interfaces.

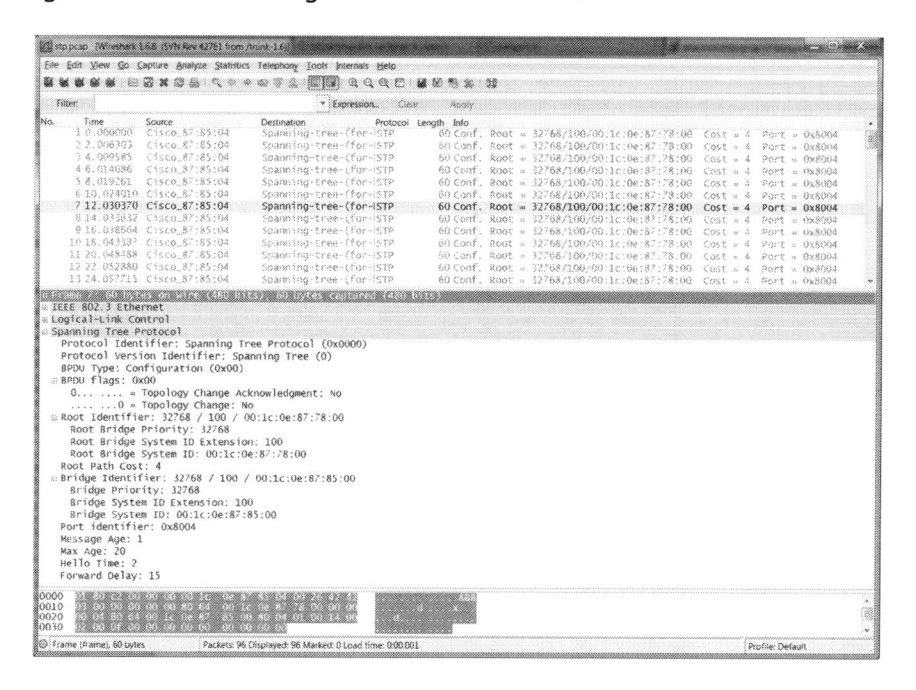

If you do want to look at the contents of a BPDU I recommend you to use wireshark. It shows everything in a nice structured way.

You don't have to capture a BPDU yourself if you don't feel like. The wireshark website has many pre-recorded packet captures.

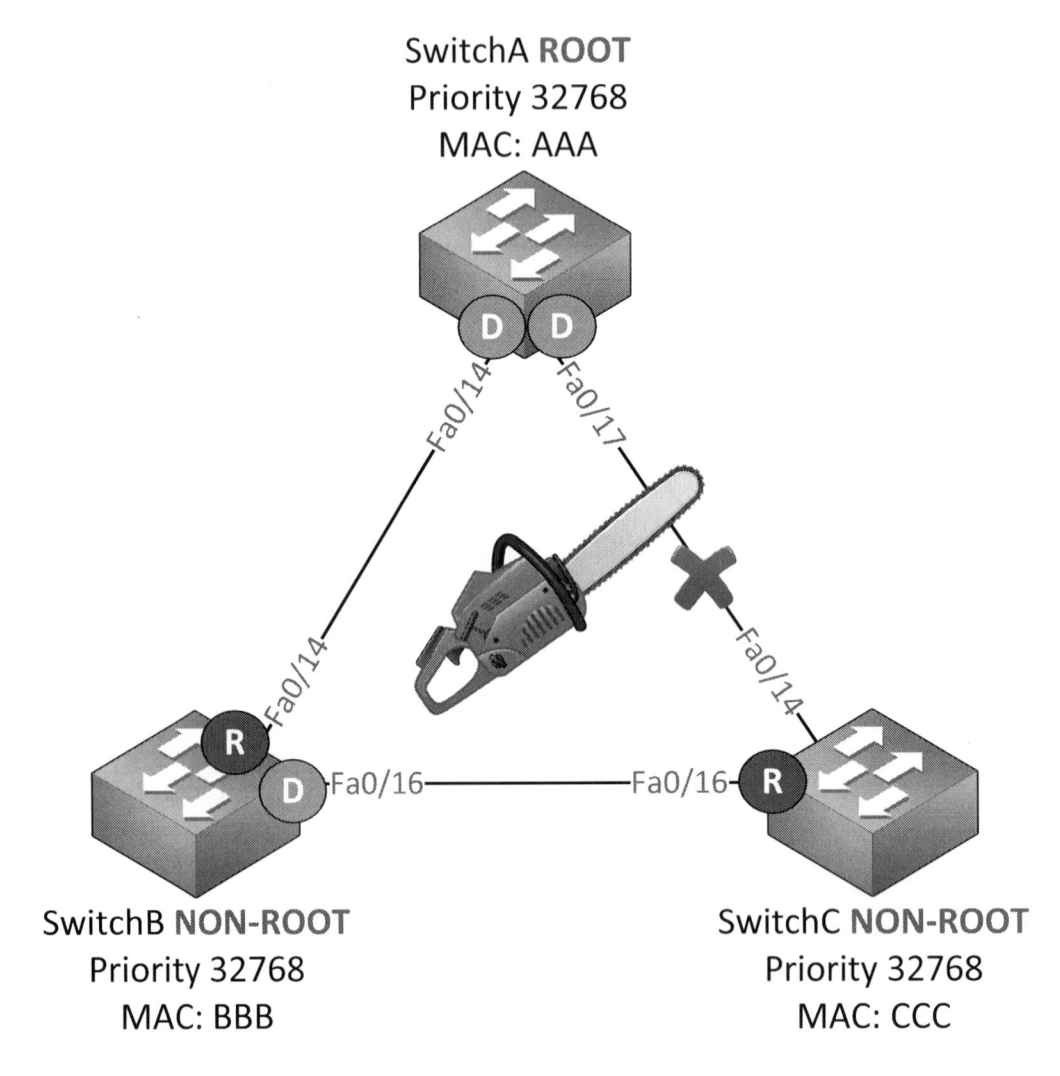

SwitchA **ROOT**
Priority 32768
MAC: AAA

SwitchB **NON-ROOT**
Priority 32768
MAC: BBB

SwitchC **NON-ROOT**
Priority 32768
MAC: CCC

Let's get rid of the hub and do something else…I'm going to simulate a link failure between SwitchA and SwitchC to see how rapid spanning tree deals with this.

```
SwitchA(config)#interface fa0/17
SwitchA(config-if)#shutdown
```

First I'm going to shut the fa0/17 interface on SwitchA.

7. Rapid Spanning Tree

```
SwitchC#
RSTP(1): updt rolesroot port Fa0/14 is going down
RSTP(1): Fa0/16 is now root port
```

SwitchC realized something is wrong with the root port almost immediately and will change the fa0/16 interface from alternate port to root port. This is the equivalent of UplinkFast for classic spanning tree but it's enabled by default for rapid spanning tree.

```
SwitchA(config)#interface fa0/17
SwitchA(config-if)#no shutdown
```

Let's restore connectivity before we continue.

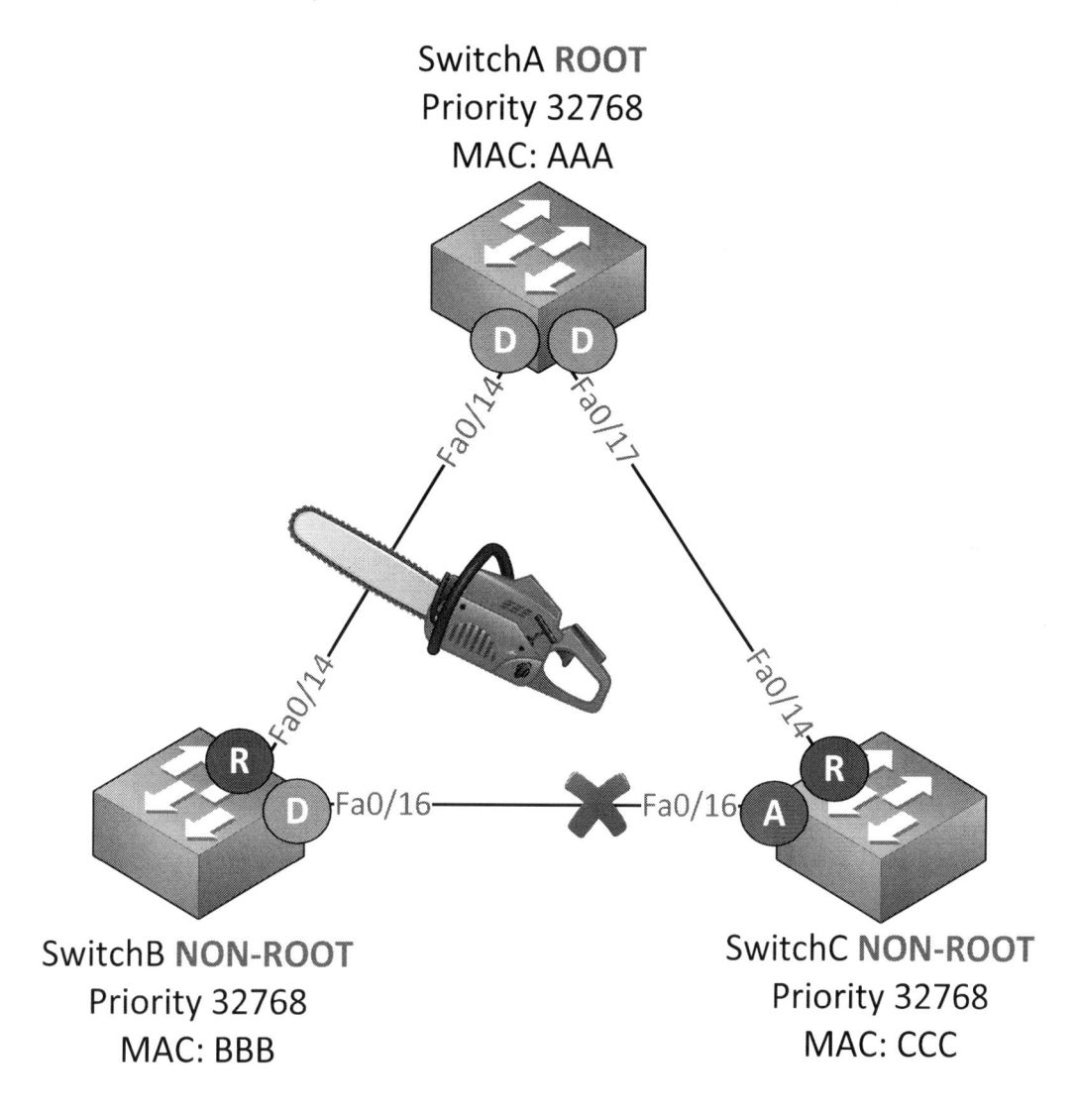

SwitchA ROOT
Priority 32768
MAC: AAA

SwitchB NON-ROOT
Priority 32768
MAC: BBB

SwitchC NON-ROOT
Priority 32768
MAC: CCC

Let's simulate an indirect link failure. In the previous chapter I showed you BackboneFast. A similar mechanism is enabled by default for rapid spanning tree.

```
SwitchA(config)#interface fa0/14
SwitchA(config-if)#shutdown
```

Shutting down this interface will simulate an indirect link failure for SwitchC.

```
SwitchB#
*Mar  1 03:41:20.608: RSTP(1): updt roles, root port Fa0/14 going down
*Mar  1 03:41:20.608: RSTP(1): we become the root bridge
*Mar  1 03:41:20.625: RSTP(1): updt roles, received superior bpdu on Fa0/16
*Mar  1 03:41:20.625: RSTP(1): Fa0/16 is now root port
```

```
SwitchC#
03:41:29: RSTP(1): updt rolessuperior bpdu on Fa0/16 (synced=0)
03:41:29: RSTP(1): Fa0/16 is now designated
```

SwitchB believes it's the root bridge until it receives a superior BPDU from SwitchC. This happens within the blink of an eye.

```
SwitchA(config)#interface fa0/14
SwitchA(config-if)#no shutdown
```

Let's get rid of the shutdown command and continue by looking at edge ports.

7. Rapid Spanning Tree

SwitchA **ROOT**
Priority 32768
MAC: AAA

SwitchB **NON-ROOT**
Priority 32768
MAC: BBB

SwitchC **NON-ROOT**
Priority 32768
MAC: CCC

ComputerA
192.168.1.1 /24

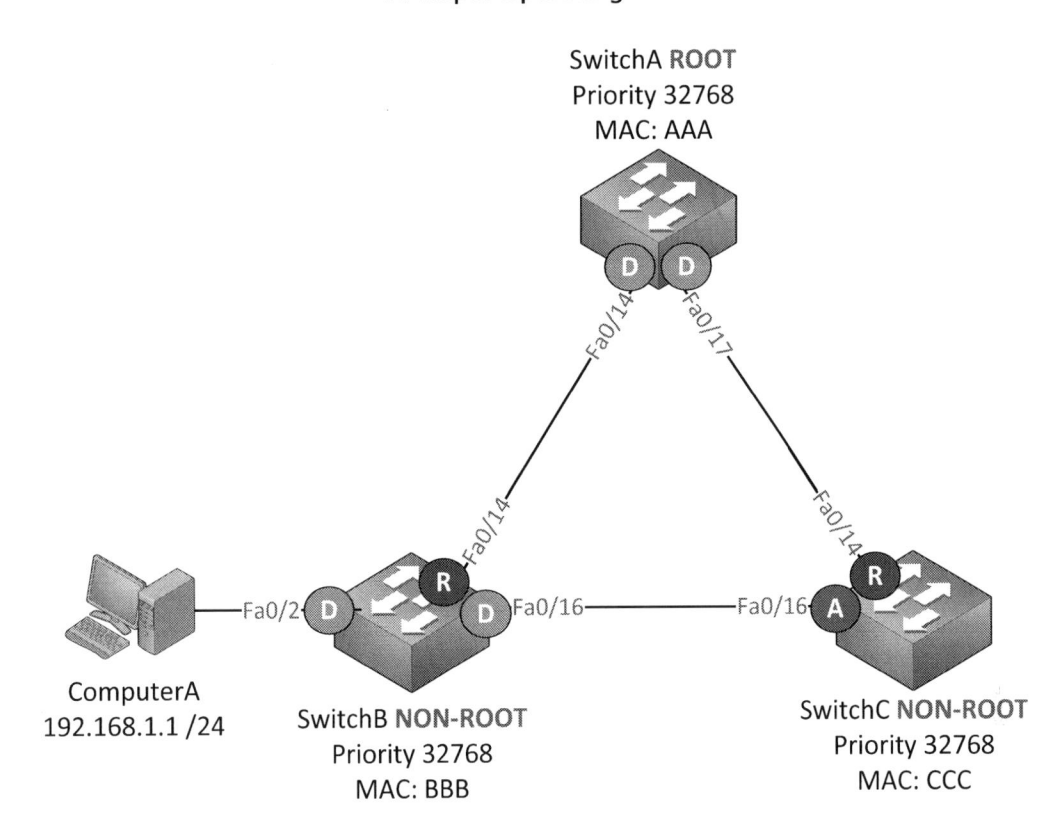

I added ComputerA and it's connected to the fa0/2 interface of SwitchB. Let's see how rapid spanning tree deals with interfaces connected to other devices.

```
SwitchB(config)#interface fa0/2
SwitchB(config-if)#no shutdown
RSTP(1): initializing port Fa0/2
RSTP(1): Fa0/2 is now designated
RSTP(1): transmitting a proposal on Fa0/2
*Mar  1 03:55:35.567: %LINK-3-UPDOWN: Interface FastEthernet0/2,
changed state to up
*Mar  1 03:55:35.710: RSTP(1): transmitting a proposal on Fa0/2
*Mar  1 03:55:36.574: %LINEPROTO-5-UPDOWN: Line protocol on
Interface FastEthernet0/2, changed state to up
*Mar  1 03:55:37.723: RSTP(1): transmitting a proposal on Fa0/2
*Mar  1 03:55:39.736: RSTP(1): transmitting a proposal on Fa0/2
*Mar  1 03:55:41.749: RSTP(1): transmitting a proposal on Fa0/2
*Mar  1 03:55:43.763: RSTP(1): transmitting a proposal on Fa0/2
*Mar  1 03:55:45.776: RSTP(1): transmitting a proposal on Fa0/2
*Mar  1 03:55:47.789: RSTP(1): transmitting a proposal on Fa0/2
*Mar  1 03:55:49.802: RSTP(1): transmitting a proposal on Fa0/2
*Mar  1 03:55:50.398: RSTP(1): Fa0/2 fdwhile Expired
```

You see that it sends a bunch of proposals from the sync mechanism towards the computer. After a while they will expire. The port will end up in forwarding state anyway but it takes a while.

```
SwitchB(config-if)#spanning-tree portfast
%Warning: portfast should only be enabled on ports connected to
a single
 host. Connecting hubs, concentrators, switches, bridges, etc...
to this
 interface  when portfast is enabled, can cause temporary
bridging loops.
 Use with CAUTION

%Portfast has been configured on FastEthernet0/2 but will only
 have effect when the interface is in a non-trunking mode.
```

You have to tell rapid spanning tree that the interface connecting the computer is an edge port. The word "edge" makes sense; it's the border of our spanning tree topology. Enable portfast and you are ready to go.

```
SwitchB(config)#interface fa0/2
SwitchB(config-if)#shutdown
SwitchB(config-if)#no shutdown
```

I'll bring the interface up and down.

```
SwitchB#
RSTP(1): initializing port Fa0/2
RSTP(1): Fa0/2 is now designated
*Mar  1 04:08:32.931: %LINK-3-UPDOWN: Interface FastEthernet0/2,
changed state to up
```

The interface will go to forwarding immediately. Our switch knows that this is the edge of the spanning tree and we don't have to send proposals to it.

```
SwitchB(config)#spanning-tree mode pvst
```

Let's look at compatibility. I'm going to change SwitchB to PVST mode. SwitchA and SwitchC will remain at rapid-PVST.

```
SwitchB(config)#
RSTP(1): updt roles, non-tracked event
setting bridge id (which=3) prio 8193 prio cfg 8192 sysid 1 (on)
id 2001.0019.569d.5700
set portid: VLAN0001 Fa0/2: new port id 8004
STP: VLAN0001 Fa0/2 ->jump to forwarding from blocking
set portid: VLAN0001 Fa0/14: new port id 8010
STP: VLAN0001 Fa0/14 -> listening
set portid: VLAN0001 Fa0/16: new port id 8012
STP: VLAN0001 Fa0/16 -> listening^Z
STP: VLAN0001 heard root  4097-0011.bb0b.3600 on Fa0/16
supersedes   8193-0019.569d.5700
```

7. Rapid Spanning Tree

```
STP: VLAN0001 new root is 4097, 0011.bb0b.3600 on port Fa0/16,
cost 38
STP: VLAN0001 new root port Fa0/14, cost 19
STP: VLAN0001 Fa0/14 -> learning
STP: VLAN0001 Fa0/16 -> learning
STP: VLAN0001 sent Topology Change Notice on Fa0/14
STP: VLAN0001 Fa0/14 -> forwarding
STP: VLAN0001 Fa0/16 -> forwarding
```

SwitchB will throw some information at you. You can see that it receives BPDUs from the root bridge and that the interfaces will have to go through the listening and learning state. When the switches that are talking rapid spanning tree receive a BPDU from the classic spanning tree they will generate classic spanning tree BPDUs themselves so everything keeps working.

```
SwitchA#show spanning-tree | begin Interface
Interface           Role Sts Cost      Prio.Nbr Type
------------------- ---- --- --------- -------- --------------------
Fa0/14              Desg FWD 19        128.16   P2p Peer(STP)
Fa0/17              Desg FWD 19        128.19   P2p
```

```
SwitchB#show spanning-tree | begin Interface
Interface           Role Sts Cost      Prio.Nbr Type
------------------- ---- --- --------- -------- --------------------
Fa0/2               Desg FWD 19        128.4    P2p Edge
Fa0/14              Root FWD 19        128.16   P2p
Fa0/16              Desg FWD 19        128.18   P2p
```

```
SwitchC#show spanning-tree | begin Interface
Interface           Role Sts Cost      Prio.Nbr Type
------------------- ---- --- --------- -------- --------------------
Fa0/14              Root FWD 19        128.14   P2p
Fa0/16              Altn BLK 19        128.16   P2p Peer(STP)
```

We can verify this by looking at the interfaces again. All switches still agree on the port states and everything will function as it should be!

This is the end of the rapid spanning tree chapter. I hope everything makes sense to you. If you haven't done any spanning tree labs up to this moment I highly recommend you to do some labs, take a look at some of the show and debug commands that I showed you in this chapter. If some topics are a little fuzzy to you it might become clearer when you see it in action yourself.

After doing some labs it might be a good idea to reread this chapter or if you feel brave you can continue with the next chapter about MST (Multiple Spanning Tree).

I do have a lab for you left:

http://gns3vault.com/Switching/pvrst-per-vlan-rapid-spanning-tree.html

If you did the previous PVST lab then you'll have no problems with this one because the configuration is similar. If you want to master PVRST I can highly recommend you to try the debugs I showed you in the book yourself so you can see what is going on behind the scenes.

7. Rapid Spanning Tree

8. MST (Multiple Spanning Tree)

In the previous two chapters we talked about (classic) spanning tree and rapid spanning three. **MST (Multiple Spanning Tree)** is the third flavor of spanning tree that you need to know for your CCNP SWITCH exam.

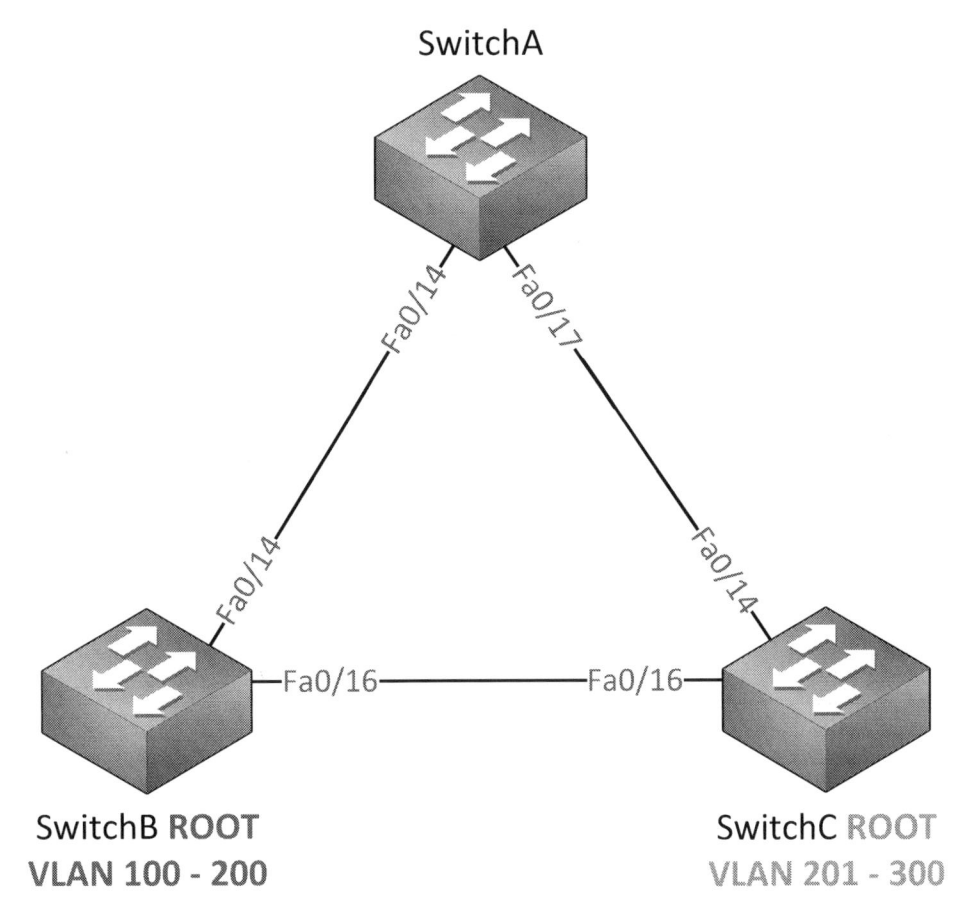

SwitchA

SwitchB **ROOT**
VLAN 100 - 200

SwitchC **ROOT**
VLAN 201 - 300

Take a look at the topology above. We have three switches and a lot of VLANs. There's 199 VLANs in total. If we are running PVST or Rapid PVST this means that we have 199 different calculations for each VLAN. This requires a lot of CPU power and memory.

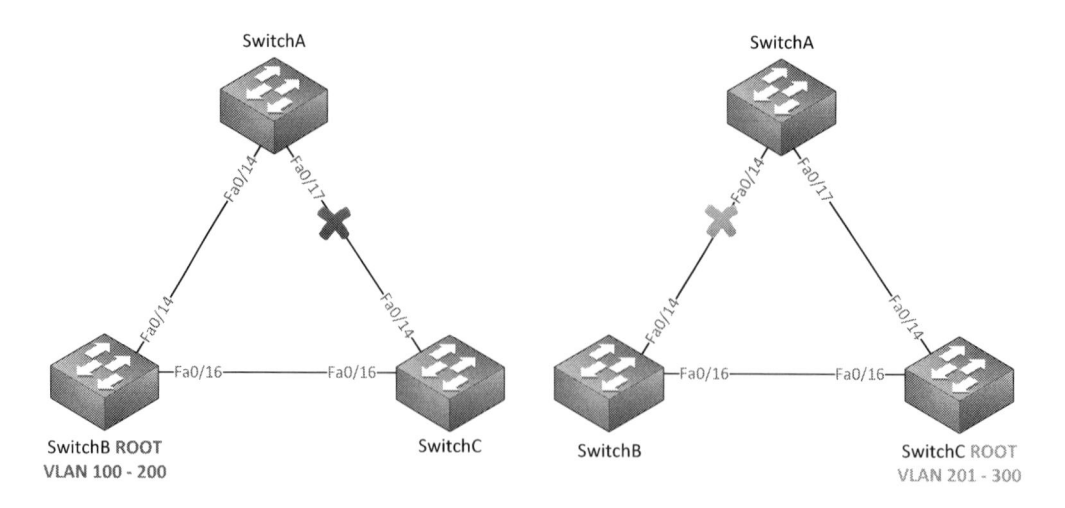

SwitchB is the root bridge for VLAN 100 up to VLAN 200. This probably means that the fa0/17 interface of SwitchA will be blocked. I'll have 100 spanning tree calculations but they all look the same for these VLANs...

The same thing applies for VLAN 201 – 300. SwitchC is the root bridge for VLAN 201 up to 300. The fa0/14 interface on SwitchA will probably be blocked for all these VLANs.

Two different outcomes but I still have 199 different instances of spanning tree running. That's a waste of CPU cycles and memory right?

MST (Multiple Spanning Tree) will do this for us. Instead of calculating a spanning tree for each VLAN we can use **instances** and map VLANS to each instance. For the network above I could do something like this:

- Instance 1: VLAN 100 – 200.
- Instance 2: VLAN 201 – 300.

Sounds logical right? Only two spanning tree calculations (instances) are required for all these VLANs.

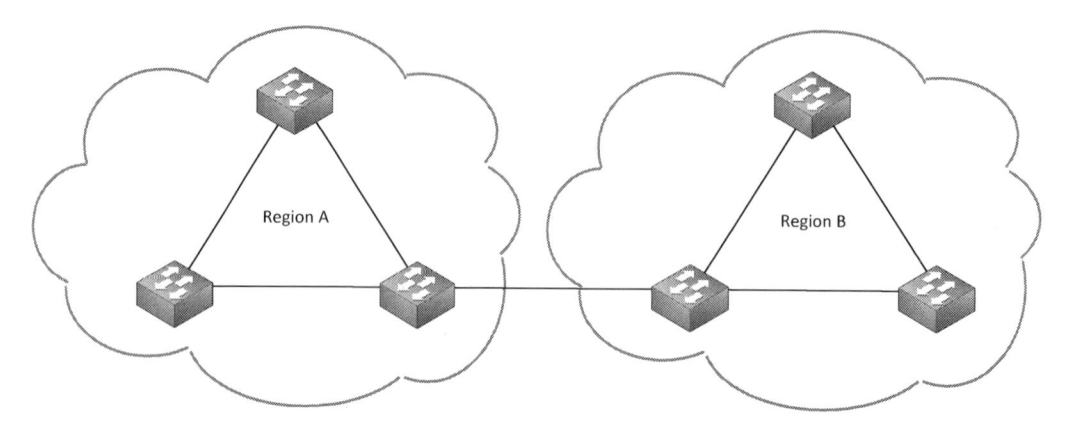

8. MST (Multiple Spanning Tree)

MST works with the concept of **regions.** Switches that are configured to use MST need to find out if their neighbors are running MST. When switches have the **same attributes** they will be in the same region. It's possible to have one or more regions and here are the attributes that need to match:

- MST configuration name.
- MST configuration revision number.
- MST instance to VLAN mapping table.

When switches have the **same attributes** configured they will be in the same region. If the attributes are not the same the switch is seen as being at the boundary of the region. It can be connected to another MST region but also talk to a switch running another version of spanning tree.

The **MST configuration name** is just something you can make up, it's used to identify the MST region. The **MST configuration revision number** is also something you can make up and the idea behind this number is that you can change the number whenever you change your configuration. It doesn't matter what you pick as long as it's the same on all switches within the MST region. VLANs will be mapped to an instance by using the **MST instance to VLAN mapping table**. This is something we have to do ourselves.

MST Region
Instance 0

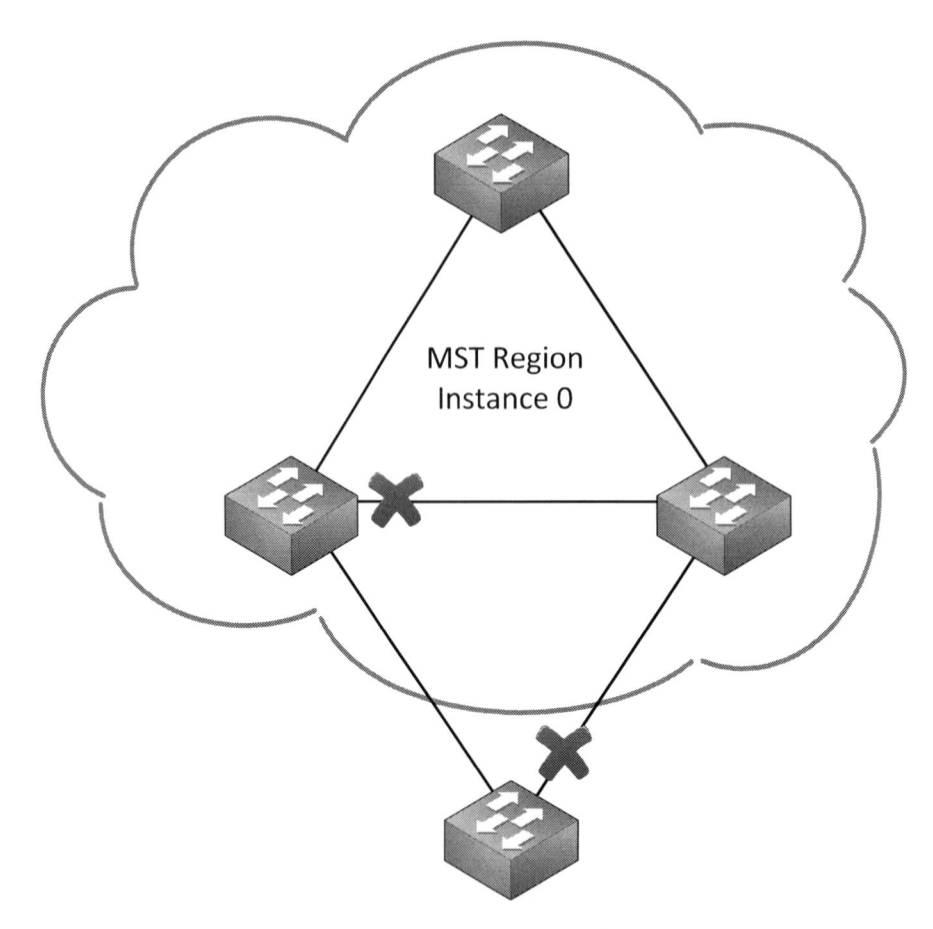

Other version of STP

Within the MST region we will have one instance of spanning tree that will create a loop free topology **within the region.** When you configure MST there is always one default instance used to calculate the topology within the region. We call this the **IST (Internal Spanning Tree).** By default Cisco will use **instance 0** to run the IST. In case you were wondering...its rapid spanning tree that we run within the MST.

8. MST (Multiple Spanning Tree)

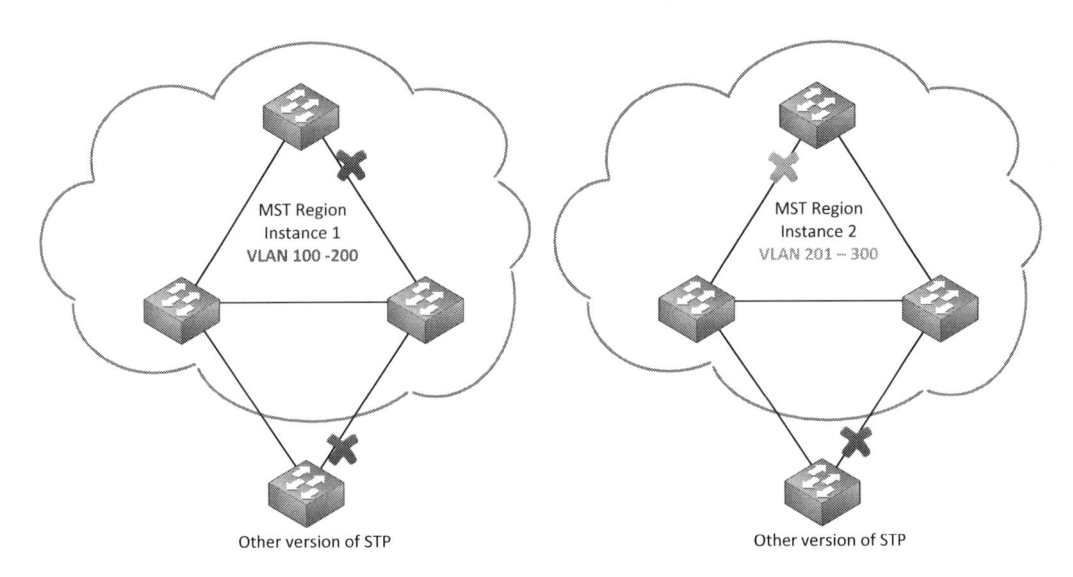

I could create instance 1 for VLAN 100 – 200 and instance 2 for VLAN 201 – 300. Depending on which switch will become root bridge for each instance a different port will be blocked.

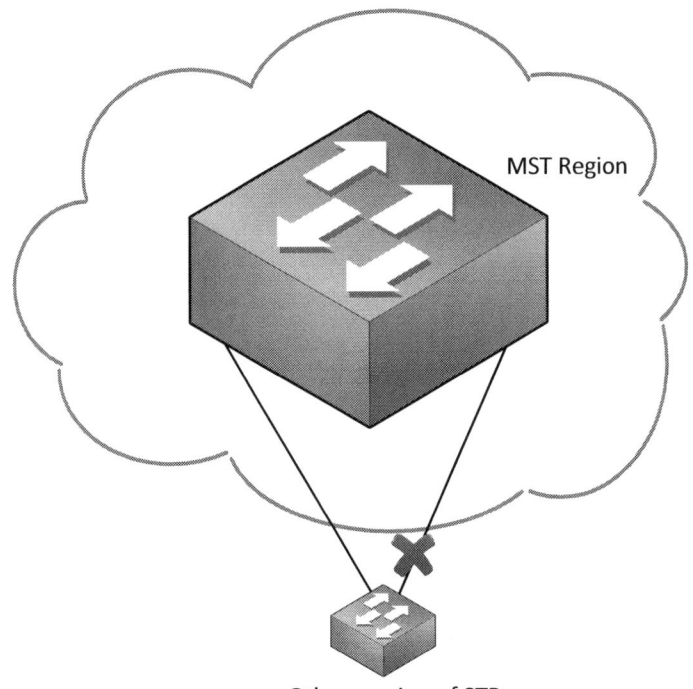

The switch outside the MST region doesn't see what the MST region looks like. For this switch it's like it's talking to one big switch or a 'black box'.

Does this make sense so far? I hope so! Let's have some fun with the configuration.

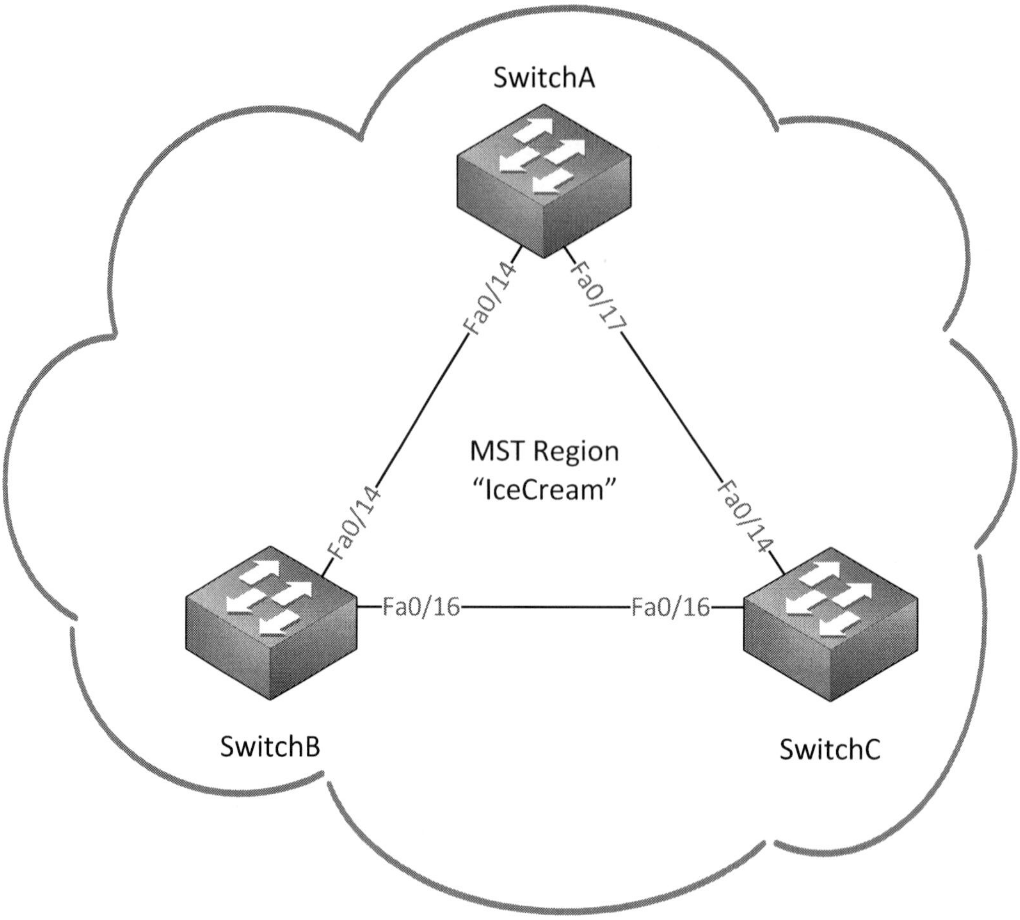
SwitchA
Fa0/14
Fa0/17
MST Region
"IceCream"
Fa0/14
Fa0/14
Fa0/16
Fa0/16
SwitchB
SwitchC

This is the topology that I'm going to use. We'll start with a single MST region with the following attributes:

- MST configuration name: "IceCream"
- MST configuration revision number: 1 (this is just a number that I made up)
- MST instance to VLAN mapping table:
  - Instance 2: VLAN 10, 20 and 30.
  - Instance 3: VLAN 40, 50 and 60.

```
SwitchA(config)#spanning-tree mode mst
```

```
SwitchB(config)#spanning-tree mode mst
```

```
SwitchC(config)#spanning-tree mode mst
```

This is how we enable MST on our switches.

8. MST (Multiple Spanning Tree)

```
%SPANTREE-3-PRESTD_NEIGH: pre-standard MST interaction not
configured (FastEthernet0/16). Please, configure: 'spanning-tree
mst pre-standard' on ports connected to MST pre-standard
switches.
```

Depending on the switches you are using and the IOS version you are running you might see this version. I recommend upgrading your IOS version so you are running the standard version of MST and not the pre-standard that you might find on older IOS versions.

```
SwitchA#show spanning-tree mst configuration
Name       []
Revision   0       Instances configured 1

Instance  Vlans mapped
--------  --------------------------------------------
--------------
0         1-4094
          --------------------------------------------
--------------
```

```
SwitchB#show spanning-tree mst configuration
Name       []
Revision   0       Instances configured 1

Instance  Vlans mapped
--------  --------------------------------------------
--------------
0         1-4094
          --------------------------------------------
--------------
```

```
SwitchC#show spanning-tree mst configuration
Name       []
Revision   0       Instances configured 1

Instance  Vlans mapped
--------  --------------------------------------------
--------------
0         1-4094
          --------------------------------------------
--------------
```

We can use the **show spanning-tree mst configuration** command to see the MST instances. I haven't created any additional instances so only instance 0 is available. You can see that all VLANs are currently mapped to instance 0.

```
SwitchA#show spanning-tree mst

##### MST0    vlans mapped:    1-4094
```

```
Bridge            address 0011.bb0b.3600   priority      32768 (32768
sysid 0)
Root              address 000f.34ca.1000   priority      32768 (32768
sysid 0)
                  port    Fa0/17           path cost     0
Regional Root address 000f.34ca.1000       priority      32768 (32768
sysid 0)
                                           internal cost 200000
rem hops 19
Operational       hello time 2 , forward delay 15, max age 20,
txholdcount 6
Configured        hello time 2 , forward delay 15, max age 20, max
hops     20

Interface         Role Sts Cost      Prio.Nbr Type
---------------   ---- --- --------- -------- --------------------
-------------
Fa0/14            Desg FWD 200000    128.16   P2p
Fa0/17            Root FWD 200000    128.19   P2p
```

You can also use the **show spanning-tree mst** command. We can see the VLAN mapping but also information about the root bridge.

```
SwitchA(config)#interface fa0/14
SwitchA(config-if)#switchport trunk encapsulation dot1q
SwitchA(config-if)#switchport mode trunk
SwitchA(config)#interface fa0/17
SwitchA(config-if)#switchport trunk encapsulation dot1q
SwitchA(config-if)#switchport mode trunk
```

```
SwitchB(config)#interface fa0/14
SwitchB(config-if)#switchport trunk encapsulation dot1q
SwitchB(config-if)#switchport mode trunk
SwitchB(config)#interface fa0/16
SwitchB(config-if)#switchport trunk encapsulation dot1q
SwitchB(config-if)#switchport mode trunk
```

```
SwitchC(config)#interface fa0/14
SwitchC(config-if)#switchport trunk encapsulation dot1q
SwitchC(config-if)#switchport mode trunk
SwitchC(config)#interface fa0/16
SwitchC(config-if)#switchport trunk encapsulation dot1q
SwitchC(config-if)#switchport mode trunk
```

```
SwitchA(config)#vlan 10
SwitchA(config-vlan)#vlan 20
SwitchA(config-vlan)#vlan 30
SwitchA(config-vlan)#vlan 40
SwitchA(config-vlan)#vlan 50
SwitchA(config-vlan)#vlan 60
SwitchA(config-vlan)#exit
```

8. MST (Multiple Spanning Tree)

```
SwitchB(config)#vlan 10
SwitchB(config-vlan)#vlan 20
SwitchB(config-vlan)#vlan 30
SwitchB(config-vlan)#vlan 40
SwitchB(config-vlan)#vlan 50
SwitchB(config-vlan)#vlan 60
SwitchB(config-vlan)#exit
```

```
SwitchC(config)#vlan 10
SwitchC(config-vlan)#vlan 20
SwitchC(config-vlan)#vlan 30
SwitchC(config-vlan)#vlan 40
SwitchC(config-vlan)#vlan 50
SwitchC(config-vlan)#vlan 60
SwitchC(config-vlan)#exit
```

First we have to do our chores. Make sure all interfaces between the switches are in trunk mode and create the VLANs.

```
SwitchA(config)#spanning-tree mst configuration
SwitchA(config-mst)#name IceCream
SwitchA(config-mst)#revision 1
SwitchA(config-mst)#instance 2 vlan 10,20,30
SwitchA(config-mst)#instance 3 vlan 40,50,60
SwitchA(config-mst)#exit
```

```
SwitchB(config)#spanning-tree mst configuration
SwitchB(config-mst)#name IceCream
SwitchB(config-mst)#revision 1
SwitchB(config-mst)#instance 2 vlan 10,20,30
SwitchB(config-mst)#instance 3 vlan 40,50,60
SwitchB(config-mst)#exit
```

```
SwitchC(config)#spanning-tree mst configuration
SwitchC(config-mst)#name IceCream
SwitchC(config-mst)#revision 1
SwitchC(config-mst)#instance 2 vlan 10,20,30
SwitchC(config-mst)#instance 3 vlan 40,50,60
SwitchC(config-mst)#exit
```

This is how we configure MST. First you need the **spanning-tree mst configuration** command to enter the configuration of MST. We set the name by using the **name** command.

Don't forget to set a **revision number** and map the instances with the **instance** command.

```
SwitchA#show spanning-tree mst configuration
Name        [IceCream]
Revision    1       Instances configured 3

Instance    Vlans mapped
--------    ------------------------------------------------------
---------------
0           1-9,11-19,21-29,31-39,41-49,51-59,61-4094
2           10,20,30
3           40,50,60
            ------------------------------------------------------
---------------
```

We can use the show spanning-tree mst configuration command to verify our configuration. You can see that we now have two instances. The VLANS are mapped to instance 2 and 3. All the other VLANs are still mapped to instance 0.

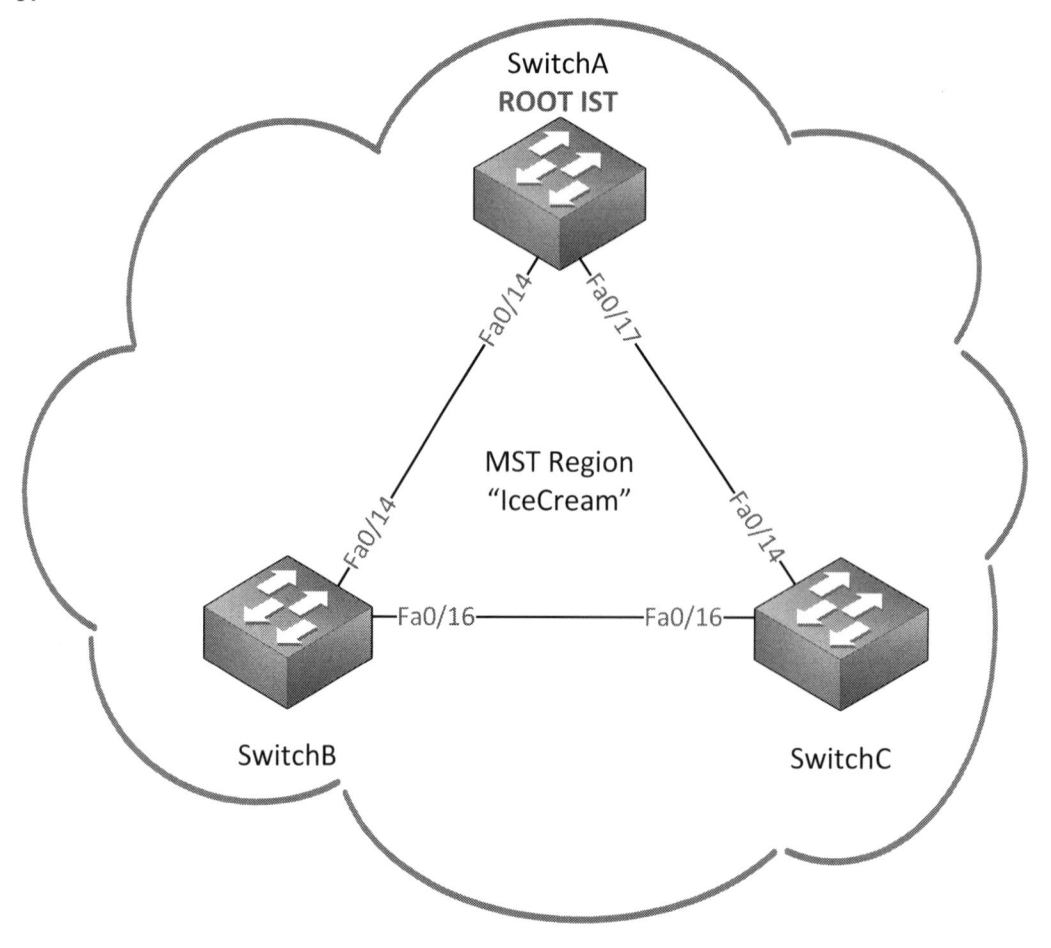

8. MST (Multiple Spanning Tree)

Let's play with the root bridge configuration. Within our region I want to make sure that SwitchA is the root bridge. We'll have to change the priority for the IST (Internal Spanning Tree).

```
SwitchA(config)#spanning-tree mst 0 priority 4096
```

This is how I change the priority for MST instance 0.

```
SwitchA#show spanning-tree mst

##### MST0      vlans mapped:    1-9,11-19,21-29,31-39,41-49,51-
59,61-4094
Bridge          address 0011.bb0b.3600  priority      4096   (4096
sysid 0)
Root            this switch for the CIST
```

Here you can see that SwitchA is the root bridge for the IST. It says CIST which stands for Common and Internal Spanning Tree.

Let's take a look at the interfaces:

```
SwitchA#show spanning-tree mst 0 | begin Interface
Interface           Role Sts Cost      Prio.Nbr Type
----------------    ---- --- --------- -------- --------------------
Fa0/14              Desg FWD 200000    128.16   P2p
Fa0/17              Desg FWD 200000    128.19   P2p
```

```
SwitchB#show spanning-tree mst 0 | begin Interface
Interface           Role Sts Cost      Prio.Nbr Type
----------------    ---- --- --------- -------- --------------------
Fa0/14              Root FWD 200000    128.16   P2p
Fa0/16              Altn BLK 200000    128.18   P2p
```

```
SwitchC#show spanning-tree mst 0 | begin Interface
Interface           Role Sts Cost      Prio.Nbr Type
----------------    ---- --- --------- -------- --------------------
Fa0/14              Root FWD 200000    128.14   P2p
Fa0/16              Desg FWD 200000    128.16   P2p
```

Now we know the state of all interfaces.

SwitchA
ROOT IST

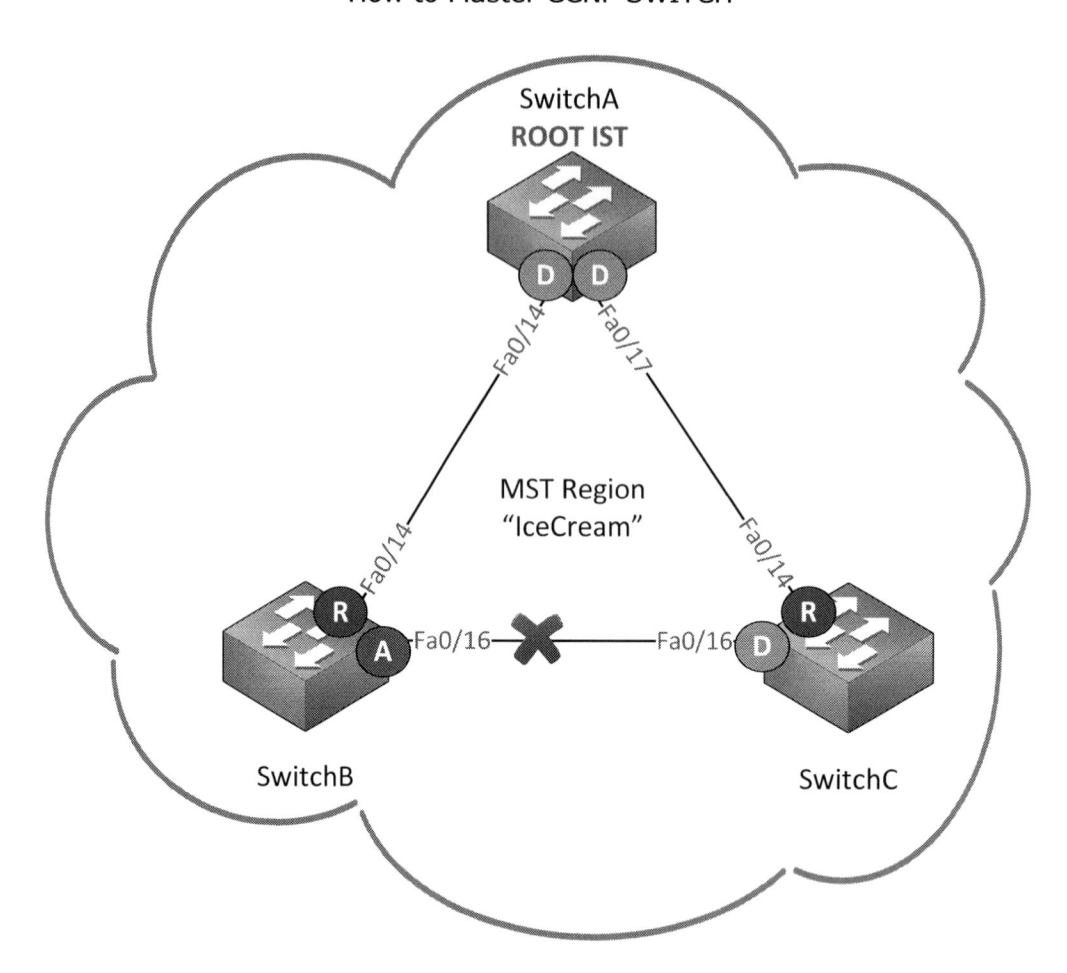

MST Region
"IceCream"

SwitchB   SwitchC

And we can draw a pretty picture so we know what the IST looks like.

Now I want to make some changes to instance 2 so SwitchB will be root bridge:

```
SwitchB(config)#spanning-tree mst 2 priority 4096
```

We'll change the priority on SwitchB for instance 2.

```
SwitchB#show spanning-tree mst 2

##### MST2      vlans mapped:    10,20,30
Bridge          address 0019.569d.5700   priority      4098   (4096
sysid 2)
Root            this switch for MST2
```

This command proves that SwitchB is the root bridge for instance 2.

8. MST (Multiple Spanning Tree)

```
SwitchA#show spanning-tree mst 2 | begin Interface
Interface        Role Sts Cost      Prio.Nbr Type
---------------- ---- --- --------- -------- --------------------
Fa0/14           Root FWD 200000    128.16   P2p
Fa0/17           Altn BLK 200000    128.19   P2p
```

```
SwitchB#show spanning-tree mst 2 | begin Interface
Interface        Role Sts Cost      Prio.Nbr Type
---------------- ---- --- --------- -------- --------------------
Fa0/14           Desg FWD 200000    128.16   P2p
Fa0/16           Desg FWD 200000    128.18   P2p
```

```
SwitchC#show spanning-tree mst 2 | begin Interface
Interface        Role Sts Cost      Prio.Nbr Type
---------------- ---- --- --------- -------- --------------------
Fa0/14           Desg FWD 200000    128.14   P2p
Fa0/16           Root FWD 200000    128.16   P2p
```

This is what instance 2 looks like.

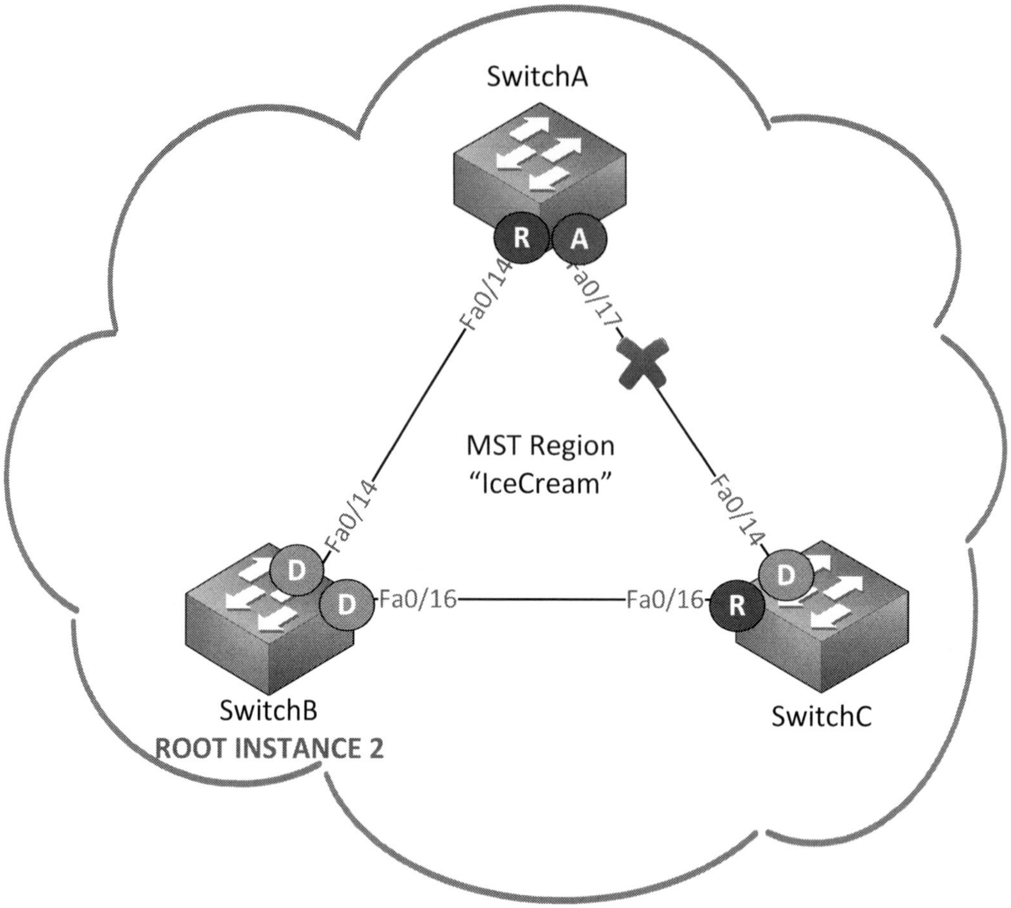
SwitchA
R
A
Fa0/14
Fa0/17
MST Region
"IceCream"
Fa0/14
Fa0/14
D
D
Fa0/16
Fa0/16
R
D
SwitchB
ROOT INSTANCE 2
SwitchC

Here's a fancy picture of instance 2 to show you the port roles. Note that this topology looks different than the one for instance 0.

Last but not least I'm now going to make some changes for instance 3:

```
SwitchC(config)#spanning-tree mst 3 priority 4096
```

SwitchC will become the root bridge for instance 3.

```
SwitchC#show spanning-tree mst 3

##### MST3    vlans mapped:   40,50,60
Bridge        address 000f.34ca.1000  priority      4099  (4096
sysid 3)
Root          this switch for MST3
```

SwitchC is now the root bridge for instance 3.

8. MST (Multiple Spanning Tree)

```
SwitchA#show spanning-tree mst 3 | begin Interface
Interface           Role Sts Cost      Prio.Nbr Type
------------------- ---- --- --------- -------- --------------------
Fa0/14              Desg FWD 200000    128.16   P2p
Fa0/17              Root FWD 200000    128.19   P2p
```

```
SwitchB#show spanning-tree mst 3 | begin Interface
Interface           Role Sts Cost      Prio.Nbr Type
------------------- ---- --- --------- -------- --------------------
Fa0/14              Altn BLK 200000    128.16   P2p
Fa0/16              Root FWD 200000    128.18   P2p
```

```
SwitchC#show spanning-tree mst 3 | begin Interface
Interface           Role Sts Cost      Prio.Nbr Type
------------------- ---- --- --------- -------- --------------------
Fa0/14              Desg FWD 200000    128.14   P2p
Fa0/16              Desg FWD 200000    128.16   P2p
```

Check the port states just to be sure...

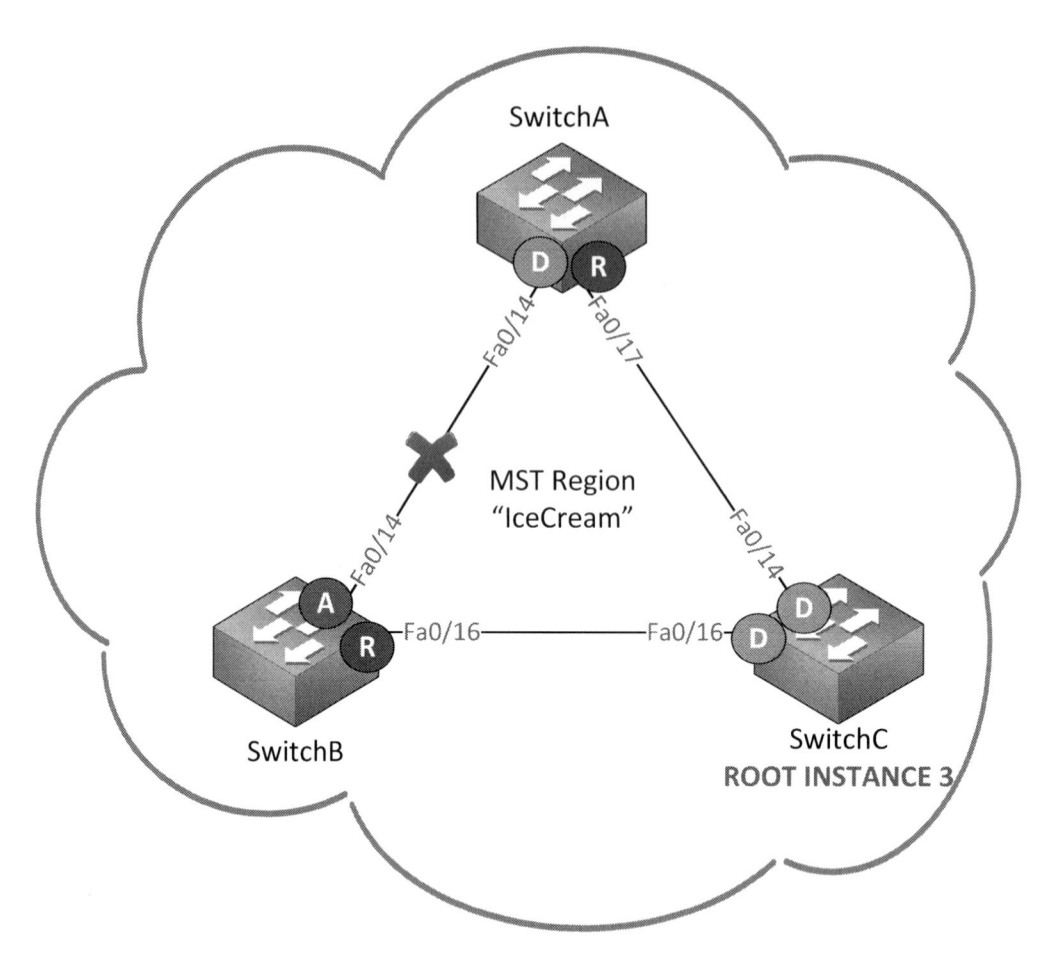

And here's the topology picture for instance 3.

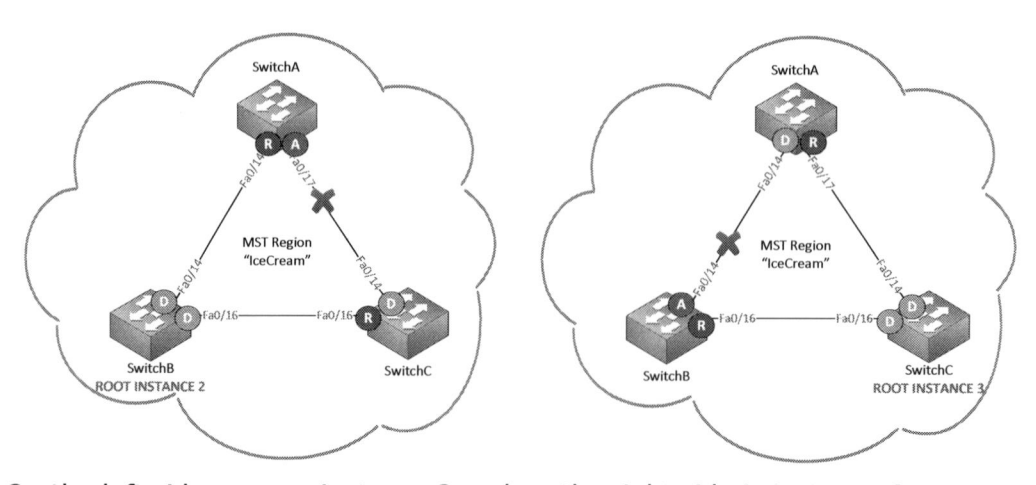

On the left side you see instance 2 and on the right side is instance 3.

8. MST (Multiple Spanning Tree)

By changing the root bridge per instance we end up with different topologies:

- Instance 2: fa0/17 on SwitchA is blocked for VLAN 10, 20 and 30.
- Instance 3: fa0/14 on SwitchB is blocked for VLAN 40, 50 and 60.

Is this making sense so far? I sure hope so!

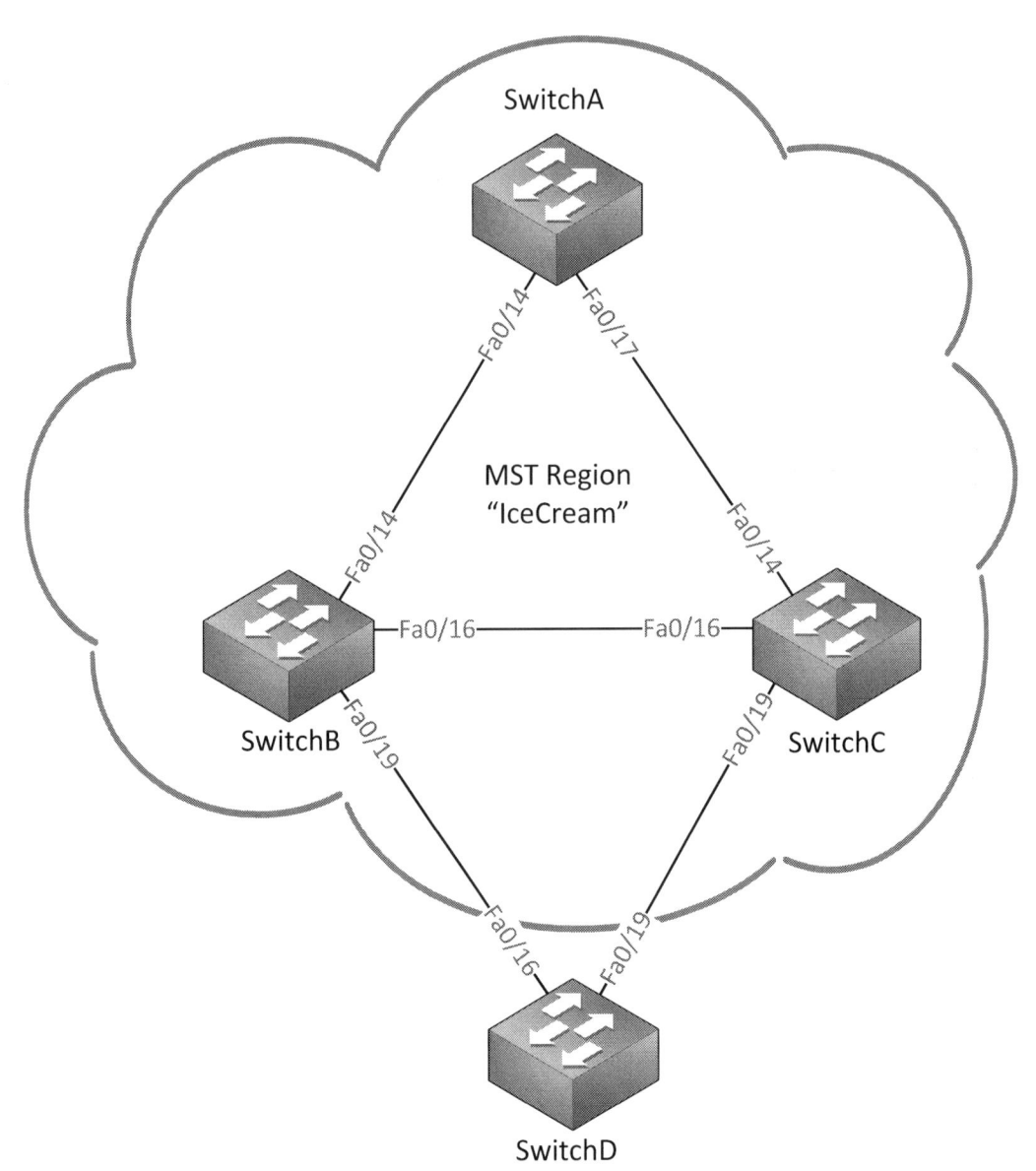

What if I add SwitchD to our topology? I'm not going to configure MST on it but I'll let it run PVST. Will it see the details of our MST region? Let's find out!

```
SwitchD(config)#spanning-tree mode pvst
```

PVST is the default on most Cisco switches but I'm showing it here so you really know I'm running PVST.

```
SwitchD(config)#interface fa0/16
SwitchD(config-if)#switchport trunk encapsulation dot1q
SwitchD(config-if)#switchport mode trunk
SwitchD(config)#interface fa0/19
SwitchD(config-if)#switchport trunk encapsulation dot1q
SwitchD(config-if)#switchport mode trunk
```

```
SwitchD(config)#vlan 10
SwitchD(config-vlan)#vlan 20
SwitchD(config-vlan)#vlan 30
SwitchD(config-vlan)#vlan 40
SwitchD(config-vlan)#vlan 50
SwitchD(config-vlan)#vlan 60
SwitchD(config-vlan)#exit
```

I want to make sure that we have trunk to SwitchB and SwitchC and that SwitchD knows about all the VLANs.

```
SwitchD#show spanning-tree vlan 1

VLAN0001
  Spanning tree enabled protocol ieee
  Root ID    Priority    4096
             Address     0011.bb0b.3600
             Cost        19
             Port        19 (FastEthernet0/19)
             Hello Time   2 sec  Max Age 20 sec  Forward Delay 15 sec

  Bridge ID  Priority    32769  (priority 32768 sys-id-ext 1)
             Address     0009.7c36.2880
             Hello Time   2 sec  Max Age 20 sec  Forward Delay 15 sec
             Aging Time 300

Interface           Role Sts Cost      Prio.Nbr Type
------------------- ---- --- --------- -------- --------------------
Fa0/16              Altn BLK 19        128.16   P2p
Fa0/19              Root FWD 19        128.19   P2p
```

This is what SwitchD sees about VLAN 1. Keep in mind this VLAN was mapped to instance 0. It sees SwitchA as the root bridge and you can see which port is in forwarding and blocking mode.

```
SwitchD#show spanning-tree vlan 10
```

8. MST (Multiple Spanning Tree)

```
VLAN0010
  Spanning tree enabled protocol ieee
  Root ID    Priority    4096
             Address     0011.bb0b.3600
             Cost        19
             Port        19 (FastEthernet0/19)
             Hello Time   2 sec  Max Age 20 sec  Forward Delay
15 sec

  Bridge ID  Priority    32778  (priority 32768 sys-id-ext 10)
             Address     0009.7c36.2880
             Hello Time   2 sec  Max Age 20 sec  Forward Delay
15 sec
             Aging Time 300

Interface           Role Sts Cost      Prio.Nbr Type
------------------- ---- --- --------- -------- -----------------
----------------
Fa0/16              Altn BLK 19        128.16   P2p
Fa0/19              Root FWD 19        128.19   P2p
```

Here's VLAN 10 which is mapped to instance 2. SwitchD sees SwitchA as the root bridge for this VLAN even though we configured SwitchB as the root bridge for instance 2. This is perfectly normal because **MST will only advertise BPDUs from the IST to the outside world**. We won't see any information from instance 2 or instance 3 on SwitchD.

```
SwitchD#show spanning-tree vlan 40

VLAN0040
  Spanning tree enabled protocol ieee
  Root ID    Priority    4096
             Address     0011.bb0b.3600
             Cost        19
             Port        19 (FastEthernet0/19)
             Hello Time   2 sec  Max Age 20 sec  Forward Delay
15 sec

  Bridge ID  Priority    32808  (priority 32768 sys-id-ext 40)
             Address     0009.7c36.2880
             Hello Time   2 sec  Max Age 20 sec  Forward Delay
15 sec
             Aging Time 300

Interface           Role Sts Cost      Prio.Nbr Type
------------------- ---- --- --------- -------- -----------------
----------------
Fa0/16              Altn BLK 19        128.16   P2p
Fa0/19              Root FWD 19        128.19   P2p
```

VLAN 40 is mapped to instance 3 but you can see that SwitchD sees SwitchA as the root bridge. SwitchD receives the same BPDU for all VLANS.

This is everything that I wanted to explain to you about MST. You have now seen (classic) spanning tree, rapid spanning tree and multiple spanning tree. Is your head spinning now? Spanning-tree isn't as heavily tested on the CCNP SWITCH exam as I think they should but it's a really important topic if you work with real life networks. Most LAN networks have plenty of switches so you'll have to deal with spanning-tree and it's important to feel familiar with this protocol.

You've come a long way from the first spanning tree chapter, climbing your way through rapid spanning tree and multiple spanning tree. There's one spanning tree chapter left which is about the spanning tree toolkit. Don't worry it's all downhill from now on!

If you want to configure MST yourself take a look at this lab:

http://gns3vault.com/Switching/mst-multiple-spanning-tree.html

8. MST (Multiple Spanning Tree)

9. Spanning Tree Toolkit

By now you should have a good understanding of spanning tree. Spanning tree is an important topic. There are many things that could go wrong with it and in this chapter we'll walk through a number of tools we can use to protect our spanning tree topology.

Let's start with an overview:

- PortFast: we have seen this one in the spanning tree and rapid spanning tree chapter. It will configure an access port as an edge port so it goes to forwarding mode immediately.
- **BPDUGuard:** This will disable (err-disable) an interface that has PortFast configured if it receives a BPDU.
- **BPDUFilter:** This will suppress BPDUs on interfaces.
- **RootGuard:** This will prevent a neighbor switch from becoming a root bridge, even if it has the best bridge ID.
- UplinkFast: we have seen this one in the spanning tree chapter. It improves convergence time.
- BackboneFast: we have seen this one as well in the spanning tree chapter. It improves convergence time if you have an indirect link failure.

UplinkFast and BackboneFast are not required for rapid spanning tree because it's already implemented by default. We'll start with **BPDUguard**:

How to Master CCNP SWITCH

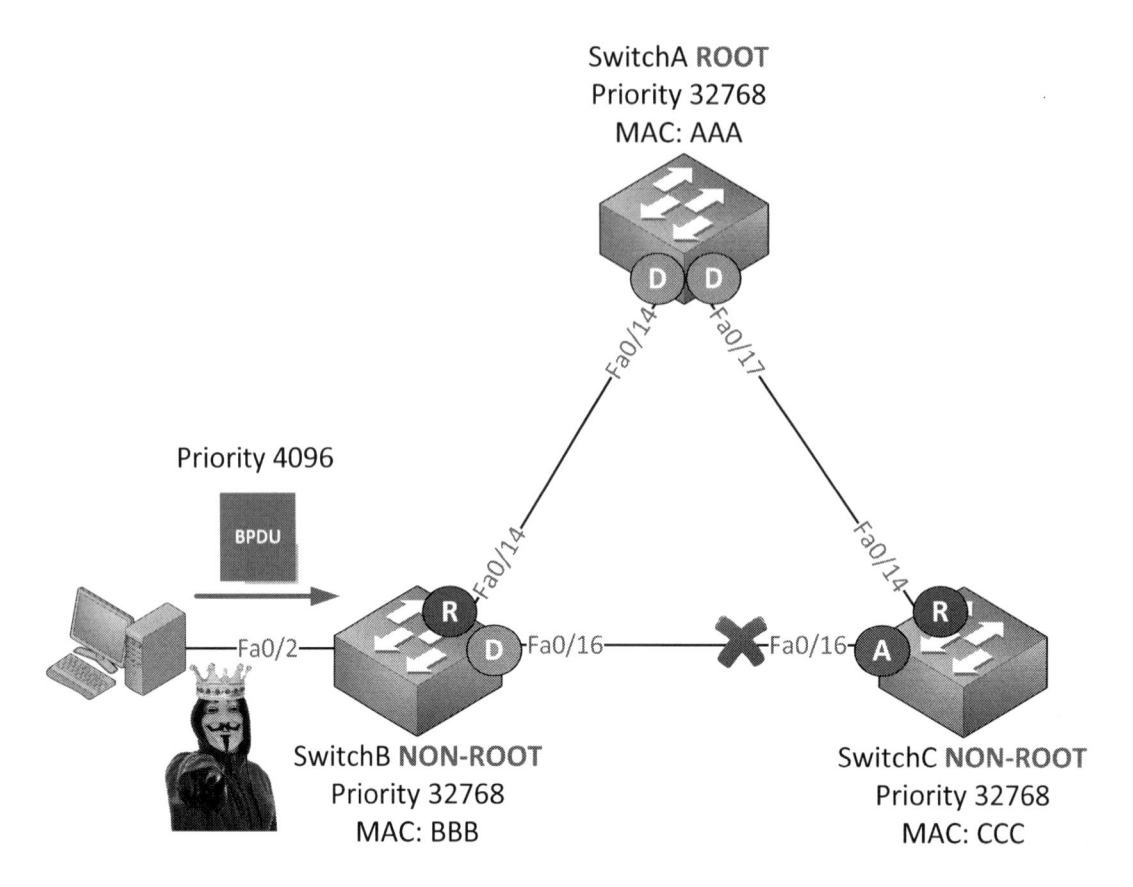

SwitchA ROOT
Priority 32768
MAC: AAA

Priority 4096

SwitchB NON-ROOT
Priority 32768
MAC: BBB

SwitchC NON-ROOT
Priority 32768
MAC: CCC

In my topology above we have a perfectly working spanning tree topology. By default spanning tree will send and receive BPDUs on all interfaces. In our example we have a computer on the fa0/2 interface of SwitchB. Someone with ~~curious~~ hostile intentions could start a tool that generates BPDUs with a superior bridge ID. What'll happen is that our switches will believe that the root bridge can now be reached through SwitchB and we'll have a spanning tree re-calculation. Doesn't sound like a good idea right?

9. Spanning Tree Toolkit

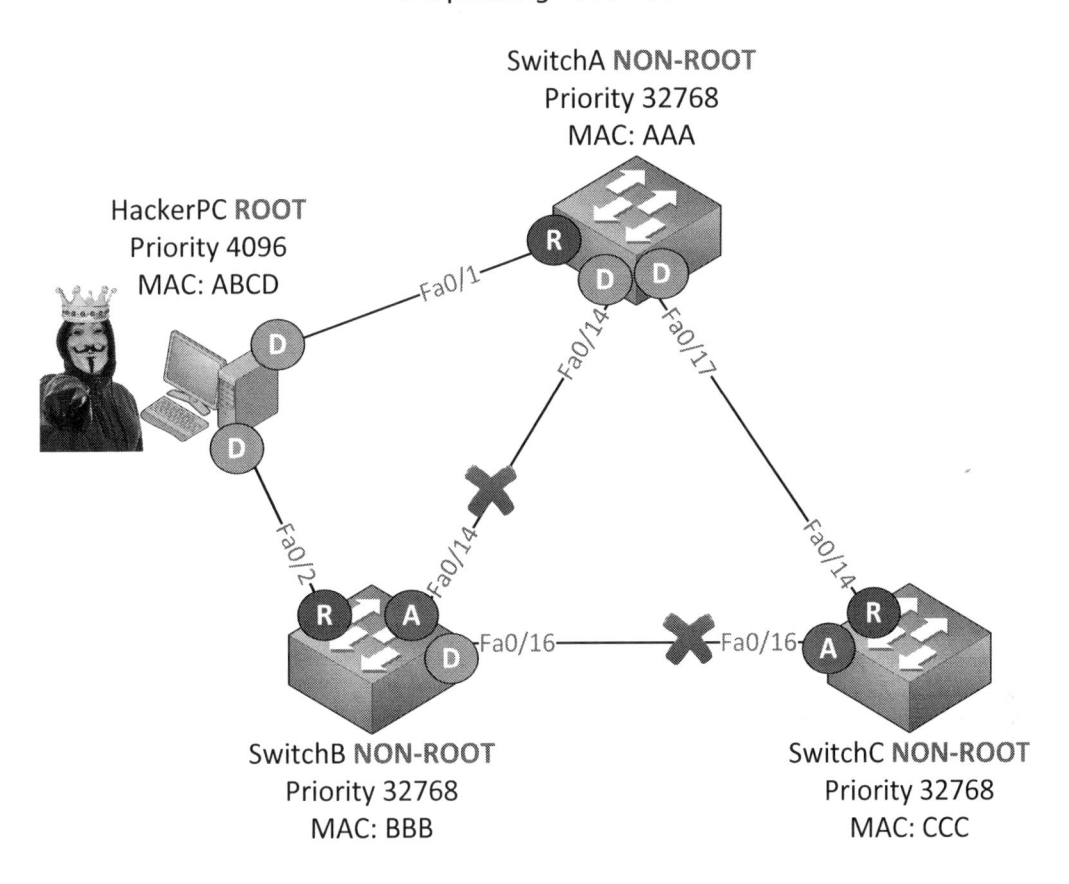

SwitchA NON-ROOT
Priority 32768
MAC: AAA

HackerPC ROOT
Priority 4096
MAC: ABCD

SwitchB NON-ROOT
Priority 32768
MAC: BBB

SwitchC NON-ROOT
Priority 32768
MAC: CCC

You could even do a man in the middle attack without anyone knowing. Imagine I connect my computer to two switches. If I become the root bridge all traffic from SwitchA or SwitchC towards SwitchB will flow through me. I'll run Wireshark and wait till the magic happens.

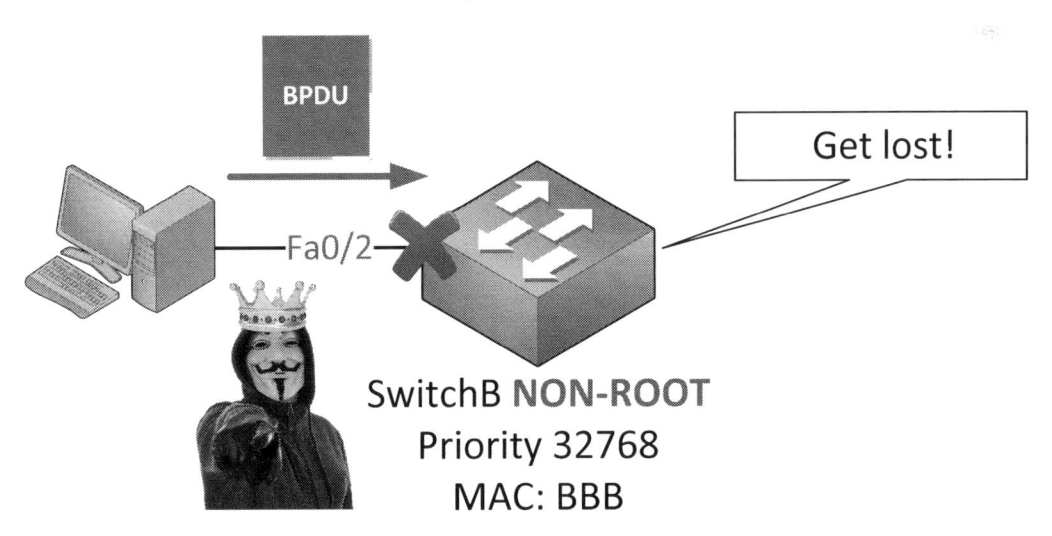

Get lost!

SwitchB NON-ROOT
Priority 32768
MAC: BBB

BPDUguard will ensure that when we receive a BPDU on an interface that the interface will go into **err-disable mode**.

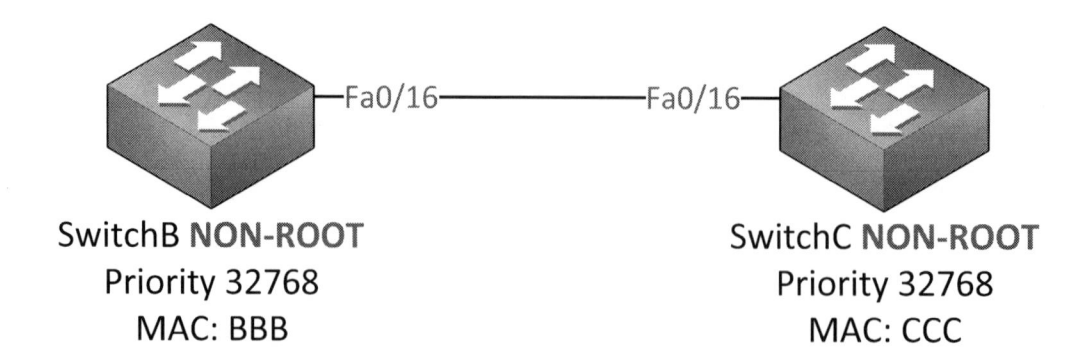

SwitchB **NON-ROOT** Fa0/16————Fa0/16 SwitchC **NON-ROOT**
Priority 32768   Priority 32768
MAC: BBB   MAC: CCC

To demonstrate BPDUguard I'm going to use two switches. I'll configure the fa0/16 interface of SwitchB so it will go into err-disable mode if it receives a BPDU from SwitchC.

```
SwitchB(config)#interface fa0/16
SwitchB(config-if)#spanning-tree bpduguard enable
```

This is how you enable it on the interface. Keep in mind normally you will never do this between switches; you should configure this on the interfaces in access mode that connect to computers.

```
SwitchB#
%SPANTREE-2-BLOCK_BPDUGUARD: Received BPDU on port Fa0/16 with
BPDU Guard enabled. Disabling port.
%PM-4-ERR_DISABLE: bpduguard error detected on Fa0/16, putting
Fa0/16 in err-disable state
: %LINEPROTO-5-UPDOWN: Line protocol on Interface
FastEthernet0/16, changed state to down
%LINEPROTO-5-UPDOWN: Line protocol on Interface Vlan1, changed
state to down
*Mar  1 00:19:32.089: %LINK-3-UPDOWN: Interface
FastEthernet0/16, changed state to down
```

Uh oh...there goes our interface.

```
SwitchB(config-if)#no spanning-tree bpduguard
SwitchB(config-if)#shutdown
SwitchB(config-if)#no shutdown
```

Get rid of BPDUguard and do a shut/no shut to get the interface back up and running.

```
SwitchB(config)#spanning-tree portfast bpduguard
```

You can also use the **spanning-tree portfast bpduguard** command. This will globally activate BPDUguard on all interfaces that have portfast enabled.

9. Spanning Tree Toolkit

```
SwitchB(config)#spanning-tree portfast default
```

Portfast can also be enabled globally for all interfaces running in access mode.

```
SwitchB#show spanning-tree summary
Switch is in pvst mode
Root bridge for: none
Extended system ID           is enabled
Portfast Default             is enabled
PortFast BPDU Guard Default  is enabled
Portfast BPDU Filter Default is disabled
Loopguard Default            is disabled
EtherChannel misconfig guard is enabled
UplinkFast                   is disabled
BackboneFast                 is disabled
Configured Pathcost method used is short
```

Here's a useful command so you can verify your configuration. You can see that portfast and BPDUGuard have been enabled globally.

BPDUGuard will put the interface in err-disable mode. It's also possible to filter BPDU messages by using **BPDUfilter**. BPDUfilter can be configured **globally** or on the **interface level** and there's a difference:

- Global: if you enable BPDUfilter globally any interface with portfast enabled will **become a standard port**.
- Interface: if you enable BPDUfilter on the interface it will **ignore** incoming BPDUs and it will **not send** any BPDUs.

You have to be careful when you enable BPDUfilter on interfaces. You can use it on interfaces in access mode that connect to computers but make sure you never configure it on interfaces connected to other switches; if you do you might end up with a loop.

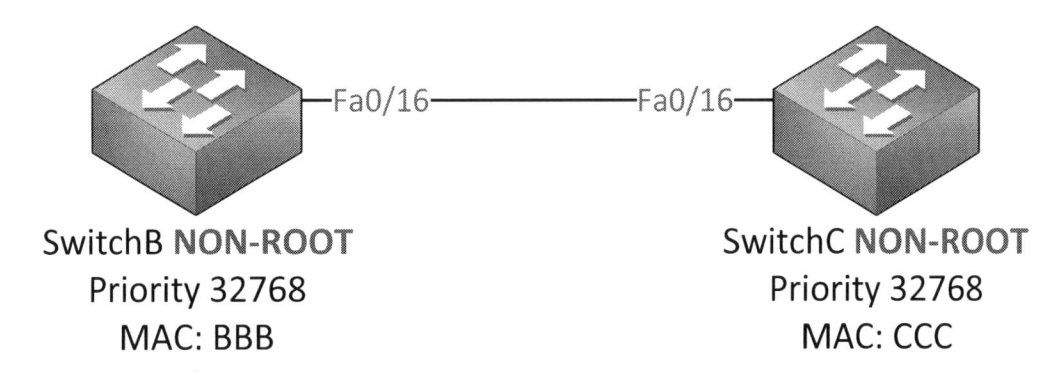

SwitchB **NON-ROOT**
Priority 32768
MAC: BBB

SwitchC **NON-ROOT**
Priority 32768
MAC: CCC

I'm going to use SwitchB and SwitchC again to demonstrate BPDUfilter.

223

Let's enable it:

```
SwitchB(config)#interface fa0/16
SwitchB(config-if)#spanning-tree portfast trunk
SwitchB(config-if)#spanning-tree bpdufilter enable
```

It will stop sending BPDUs and it will ignore whatever is received.

```
SwitchB#debug spanning-tree bpdu
```

You won't see any exciting messages but if you enable BPDU debugging you'll notice that it **doesn't send** any BPDUs anymore. If you want you can also enable BPDU debugging on SwitchC and you'll see that you **won't receive** any from SwitchB.

```
SwitchB(config)#interface fa0/16
SwitchB(config-if)#no spanning-tree bpdufilter enable
```

Let's get rid of the BPDUfilter command on the interface level.

```
SwitchB(config)#spanning-tree portfast bpdufilter default
```

You can also use the global command for BPDUfilter. This will enable BPDUfilter on all interfaces that have portfast.

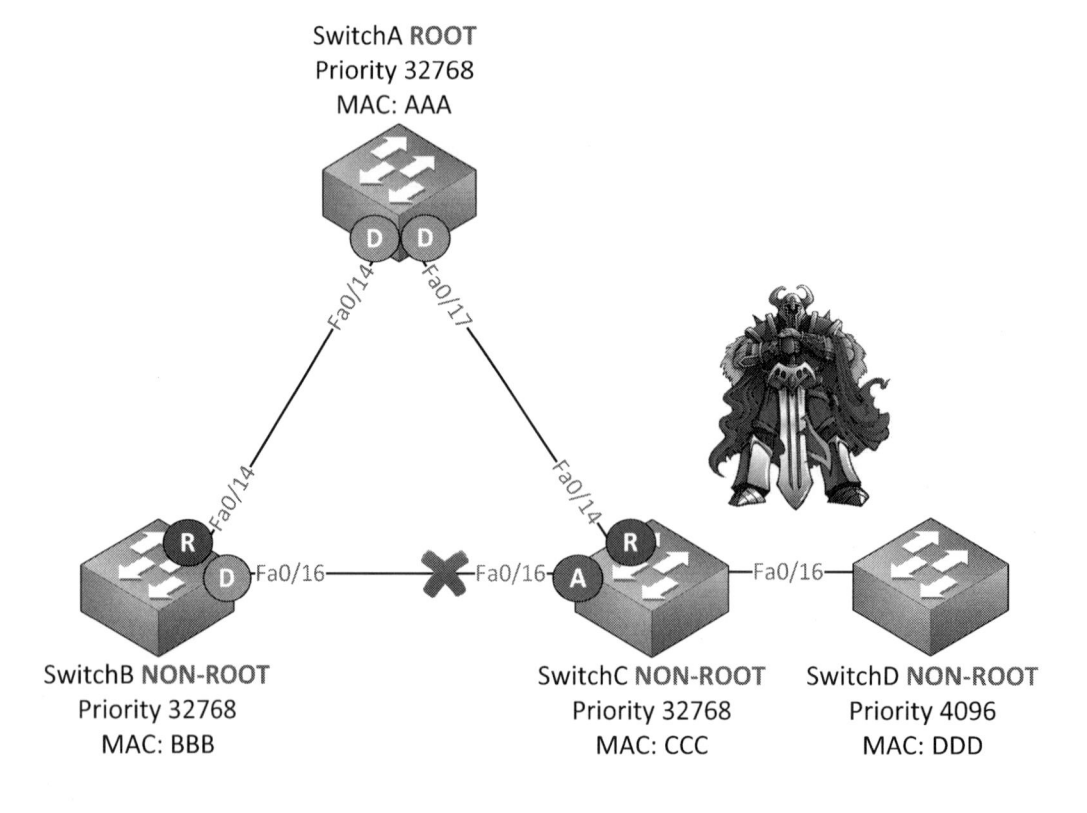

SwitchA **ROOT**
Priority 32768
MAC: AAA

SwitchB **NON-ROOT**
Priority 32768
MAC: BBB

SwitchC **NON-ROOT**
Priority 32768
MAC: CCC

SwitchD **NON-ROOT**
Priority 4096
MAC: DDD

9. Spanning Tree Toolkit

Another option we have to protect our spanning tree is to use **RootGuard**. Simply said RootGuard will make sure you don't accept a certain switch as a root bridge. BPDUs are sent and processed normally but if a switch suddenly sends a BPDU with a superior bridge ID you won't accept it as the root bridge. Normally SwitchD would become the root bridge because it has the best bridge ID, fortunately we have RootGuard on SwitchC so it's not going to happen!

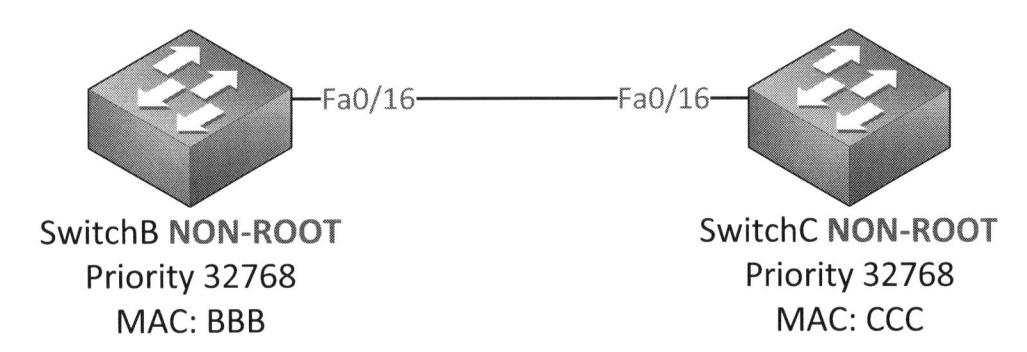

SwitchB **NON-ROOT**
Priority 32768
MAC: BBB

SwitchC **NON-ROOT**
Priority 32768
MAC: CCC

Let me show you the configuration by using SwitchB and SwitchC.

```
SwitchB(config)#spanning-tree vlan 1 priority 4096
```

Let's make sure that SwitchC is NOT the root bridge.

```
SwitchB(config)#interface fa0/16
SwitchB(config-if)#spanning-tree guard root
%SPANTREE-2-ROOTGUARD_CONFIG_CHANGE: Root guard enabled on port FastEthernet0/16.
```

This is how we enable RootGuard on the interface.

```
SwitchB#debug spanning-tree events
Spanning Tree event debugging is on
```

Don't forget to enable debugging if you want to see the action.

```
SwitchC(config)#spanning-tree vlan 1 priority 0
```

Let's upset SwitchB by changing the priority to the lowest value possible (0) on SwitchC. Normally it should now become the root bridge.

```
SwitchB#
STP: VLAN0001 heard root    1-000f.34ca.1000 on Fa0/16
supersedes   4097-0019.569d.5700
%SPANTREE-2-ROOTGUARD_BLOCK: Root guard blocking port FastEthernet0/16 on VLAN0001.
```

Here goes...SwitchB will not accept SwitchC as a root bridge. It will block the interface for this VLAN.

```
SwitchB#show spanning-tree inconsistentports

Name                     Interface                 Inconsistency
------------------------ ------------------------- -------------------
VLAN0001                 FastEthernet0/16          Root Inconsistent

Number of inconsistent ports (segments) in the system : 1
```

Here's another useful command to check if root guard is doing its work.

Spanning-tree is become more secure by the minute! There is one more thing we have to think about however...

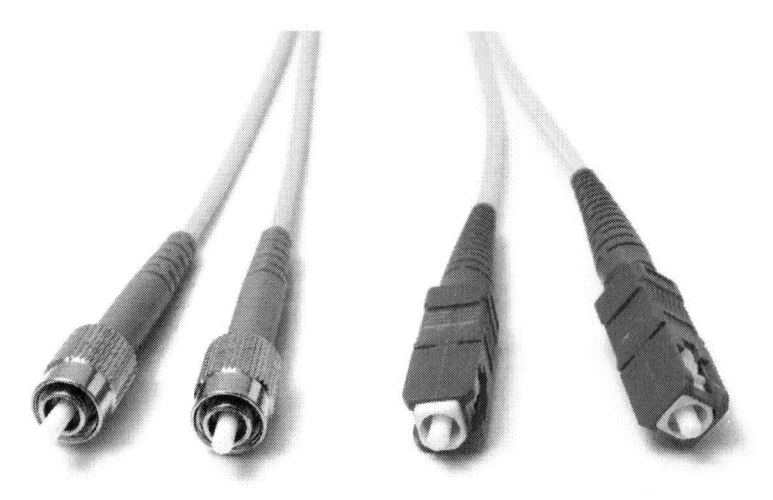

If you ever used fiber cables you might have noticed that there is a different connector to transmit and receive traffic. If one of the cables (transmit or receive) fails we'll have a **unidirectional link failure** and this can cause spanning tree loops. There are two protocols that can take care of this problem:

- LoopGuard
- UDLD

Let's start by taking a close look at what will happen if we have a unidirectional link failure.

9. Spanning Tree Toolkit

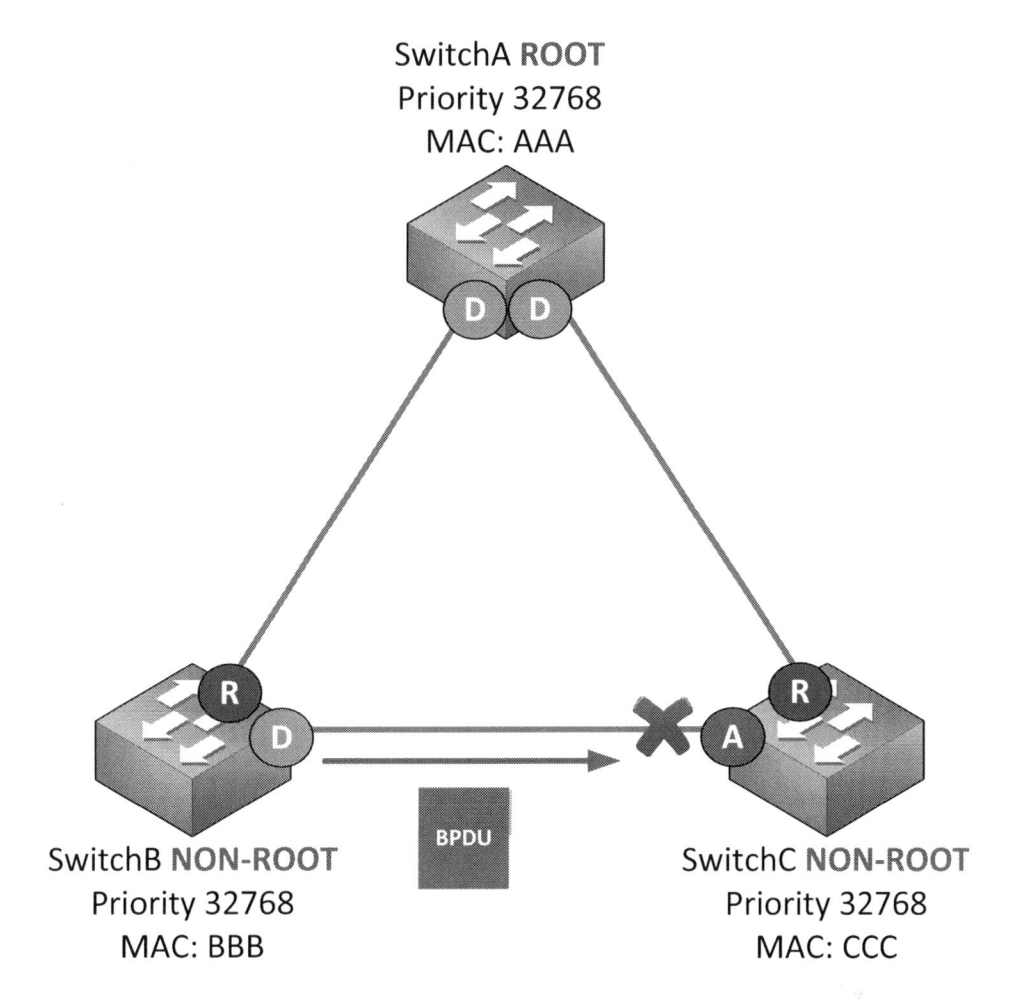

SwitchA ROOT
Priority 32768
MAC: AAA

SwitchB NON-ROOT
Priority 32768
MAC: BBB

SwitchC NON-ROOT
Priority 32768
MAC: CCC

Imagine the links between the switches are fiber links. In reality there's a different connector for transmit and receive. SwitchC is receiving BPDUs from SwitchB and as a result the interface has become an alternate port and is in blocking mode.

SwitchA **ROOT**
Priority 32768
MAC: AAA

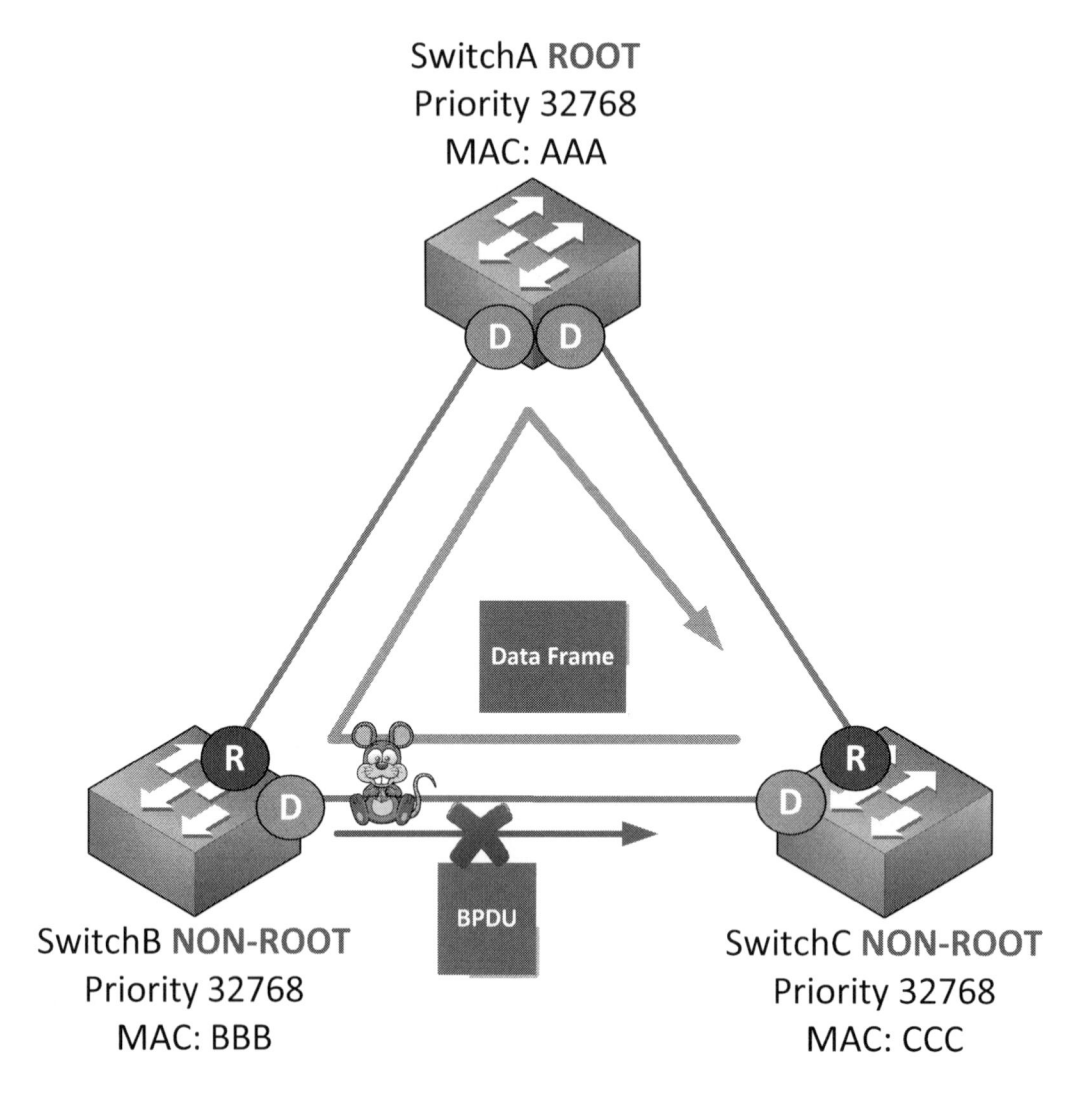

SwitchB **NON-ROOT**
Priority 32768
MAC: BBB

SwitchC **NON-ROOT**
Priority 32768
MAC: CCC

Now something goes wrong...the transmit connector on SwitchB towards SwitchC ~~was eaten by mice~~ failed due to unknown reasons. As a result SwitchC is not receiving any BPDUs from SwitchB but it can still send traffic to SwitchB.

Because SwitchC is not receiving anymore BPDUs on its alternate port it will go into forwarding mode. We now have a **one way loop** as indicated by the green arrow.

9. Spanning Tree Toolkit

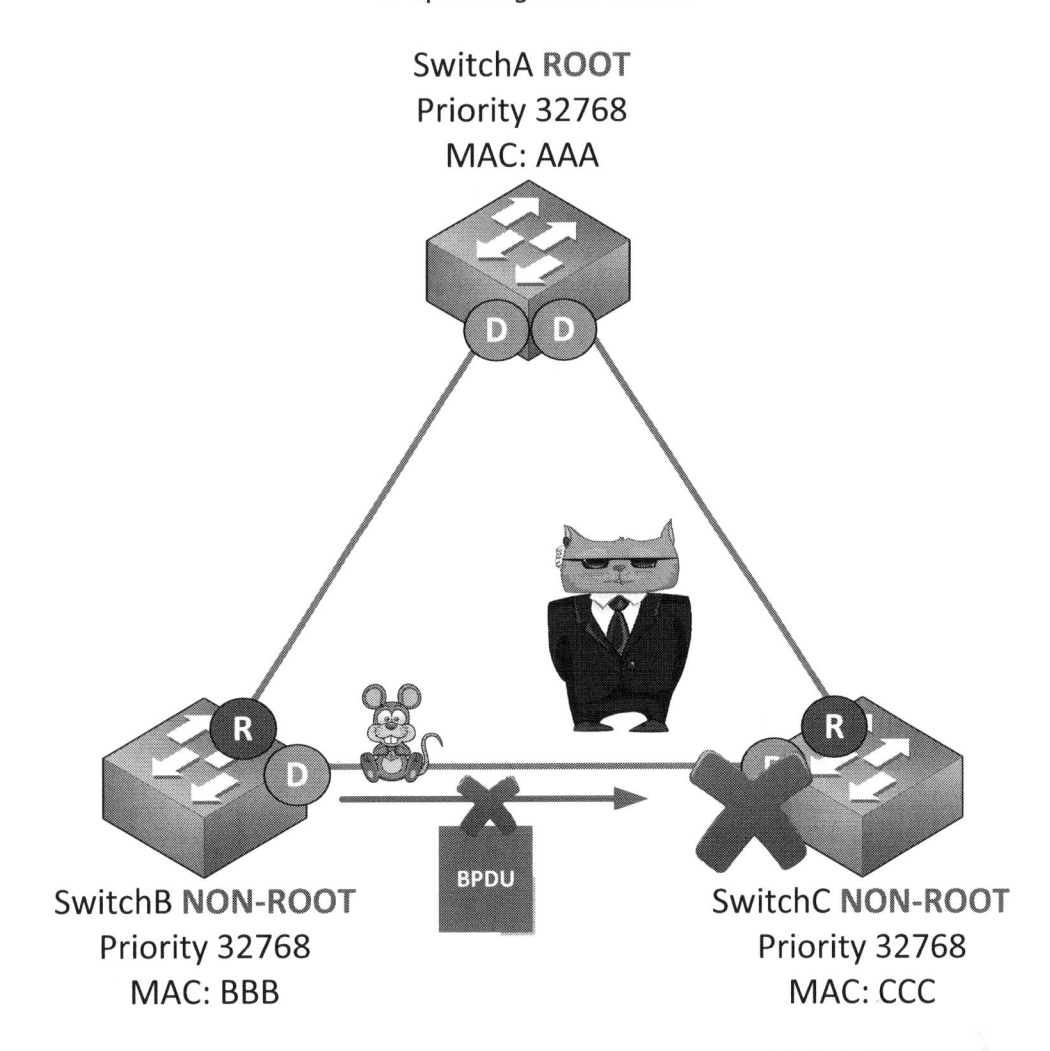

SwitchA ROOT
Priority 32768
MAC: AAA

SwitchB NON-ROOT
Priority 32768
MAC: BBB

SwitchC NON-ROOT
Priority 32768
MAC: CCC

One of the methods we can use to solve our unidirectional link failure is to configure **LoopGuard.** When a switch is sending but not receiving BPDUs on the interface, LoopGuard will place the interface in the **loop-inconsistent state** and block all traffic!

SwitchA ROOT
Priority 32768
MAC: AAA

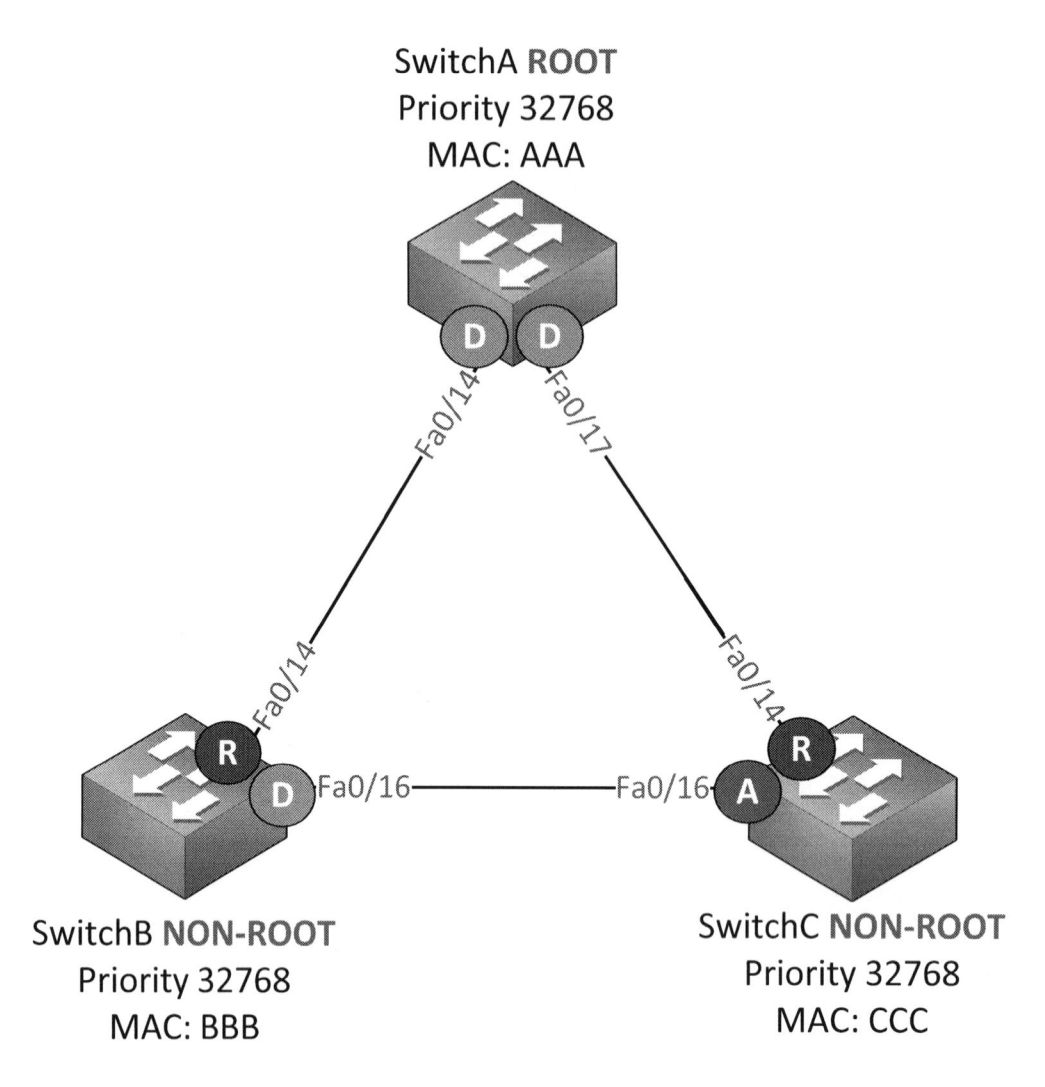

SwitchB NON-ROOT
Priority 32768
MAC: BBB

SwitchC NON-ROOT
Priority 32768
MAC: CCC

I'm going to use this topology again to demonstrate LoopGuard.

```
SwitchA(config)#spanning-tree loopguard default
```

```
SwitchB(config)#spanning-tree loopguard default
```

```
SwitchC(config)#spanning-tree loopguard default
```

Use the **spanning-tree loopguard default** command to enable LoopGuard globally.

```
SwitchB(config)#interface fa0/16
SwitchB(config-if)#spanning-tree portfast trunk
SwitchB(config-if)#spanning-tree bpdufilter enable
```

I don't have any fiber connectors so I'm unable to create a unidirectional link

9. Spanning Tree Toolkit

failure. I can simulate it however by using BPDUfilter on SwitchB's fa0/16 interface. SwitchC won't receive any BPDUs anymore on its alternate port which will cause it to go into forwarding mode.

```
SwitchC#
*Mar  1 00:17:14.431: %SPANTREE-2-LOOPGUARD_BLOCK: Loop guard
blocking port FastEthernet0/16 on VLAN0001.
```

Normally this would cause a loop but luckily we have LoopGuard configured. You can see this error message appearing in your console, problem solved!

```
SwitchC(config-if)#spanning-tree guard loop
```

If you want you don't have to configure LoopGuard globally, you can also do it on the interface level like this.

Another protocol we can use to deal with unidirectional link failures is called **UDLD (UniDirectional Link Detection).** This protocol is not part of the spanning tree toolkit but it does help us to prevent loops.

Simply said UDLD is a layer 2 protocol that works like a keepalive mechanism. You send hello messages, you receive them and life is good. As soon as you still send hello messages but don't receive them anymore you know something is wrong and we'll block the interface.

SwitchA **ROOT**
Priority 32768
MAC: AAA

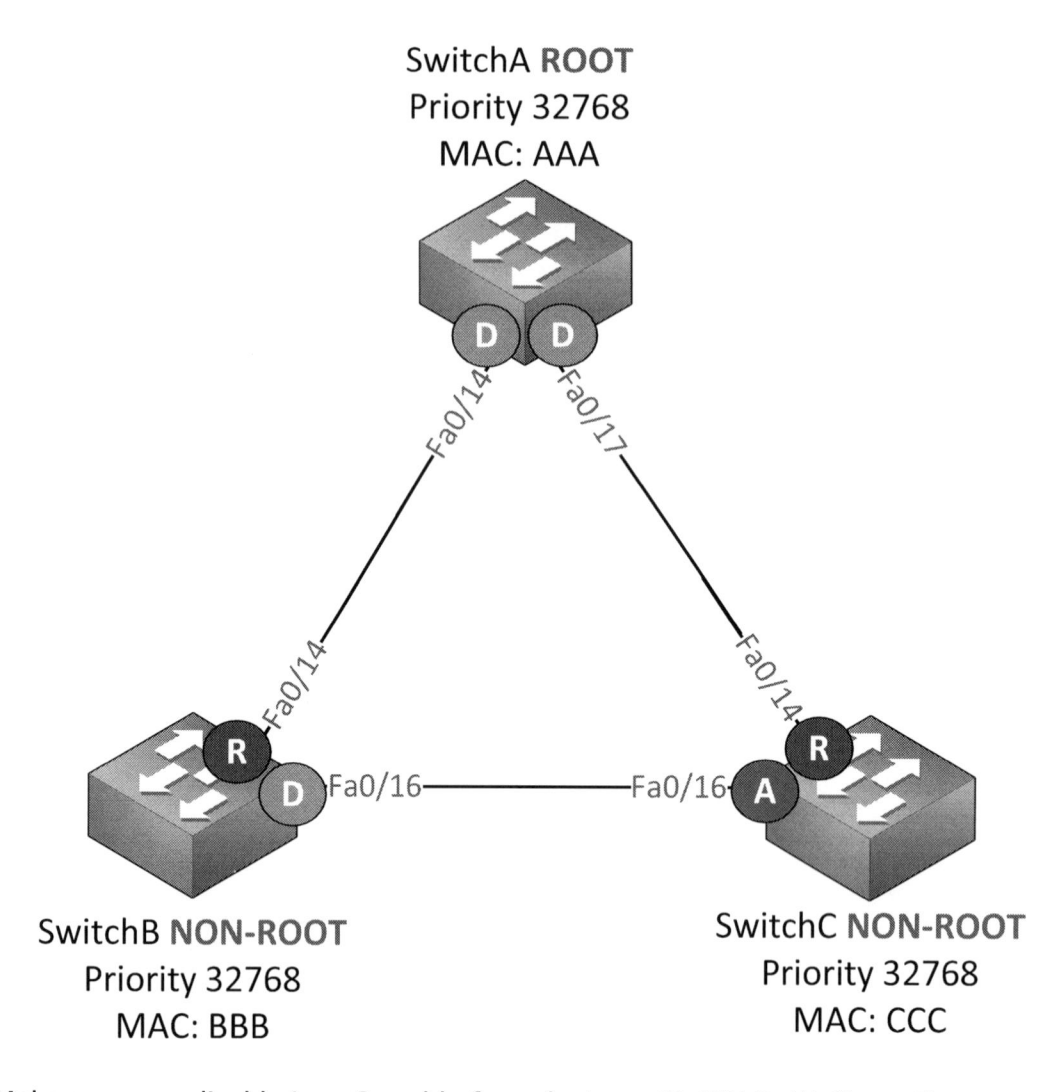

SwitchB **NON-ROOT**
Priority 32768
MAC: BBB

SwitchC **NON-ROOT**
Priority 32768
MAC: CCC

Make sure you disable LoopGuard before playing with UDLD. We'll use the same topology to demonstrate UDLD.

```
SwitchA(config)#udld ?
  aggressive  Enable UDLD protocol in aggressive mode on fiber
ports except
              where locally configured
  enable      Enable UDLD protocol on fiber ports except where
locally
              configured
  message     Set UDLD message parameters
```

There are a number of methods how you can configure UDLD. You can do it globally with the udld command but this will only activate UDLD **for fiber links**!

9. Spanning Tree Toolkit

There are two options for UDLD:

- **Normal** (default)
- **Aggressive**

When you set UDLD to **normal** it will mark the port as **undetermined** but it won't shut the interface when something is wrong. This is only used to "inform" you but it won't stop loops.

Aggressive is a better solution, when it loses connectivity to a neighbor it will send a UDLD frame 8 times in a second. If the neighbor does not respond the interface will be put in **err-disable** mode.

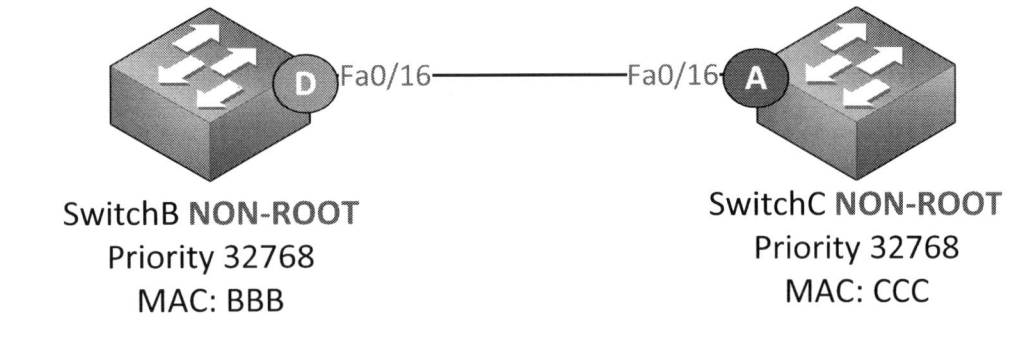

```
D Fa0/16————————Fa0/16 A
```

SwitchB **NON-ROOT**
Priority 32768
MAC: BBB

SwitchC **NON-ROOT**
Priority 32768
MAC: CCC

```
SwitchB(config)#interface fa0/16
SwitchB(config-if)#udld port aggressive
```

```
SwitchC(config)#interface fa0/16
SwitchC(config-if)#udld port aggressive
```

We'll use SwitchB and SwitchC to demonstrate UDLD. I'll use aggressive mode so we can see that the interface goes down when something is wrong.

```
SwitchB#debug udld events
UDLD events debugging is on
SwitchC#
New_entry = 34422DC (Fa0/16)
Found an entry from same device (Fa0/16)
Cached entries = 2 (Fa0/16)
Entry (0x242BB9C) deleted: 1 entries cached
Cached entries = 1 (Fa0/16)
Checking if multiple neighbors (Fa0/16)
Single neighbor detected (Fa0/16)
Checking if link is bidirectional (Fa0/16)
Found my own ID pair in 2way conn list (Fa0/16)
```

If you want to see that UDLD is working you can try a debug.

Now the tricky part will be to simulate a unidirectional link failure. LoopGuard was easier because it was based on BPDUs. UDLD runs its own layer 2 protocol by using the proprietary MAC address 0100.0ccc.cccc.

```
SwitchC(config)#mac access-list extended UDLD-FILTER
SwitchC(config-ext-macl)#deny any host 0100.0ccc.cccc
SwitchC(config-ext-macl)#permit any any
SwitchC(config-ext-macl)#exit
SwitchC(config)#interface fa0/16
SwitchC(config-if)#mac access-group UDLD-FILTER in
```

This is a creative way to cause trouble. By filtering the MAC address of UDLD it will think that there is an unidirectional link failure!

```
SwitchB#
UDLD FSM updated port, bi-flag udld_empty_echo, phase
udld_detection (Fa0/16)
timeout timer = 0 (Fa0/16)
Phase set to EXT.  (Fa0/16)
New_entry = 370CED0 (Fa0/16)
Found an entry from same device (Fa0/16)
Cached entries = 2 (Fa0/16)
Entry (0x3792BE0) deleted: 1 entries cached
Cached entries = 1 (Fa0/16)
Zero IDs in 2way conn list (Fa0/16)
Zero IDs in 2way conn list (Fa0/16)
UDLD disabled port, packet received in extended detection
(Fa0/16)
%UDLD-4-UDLD_PORT_DISABLED: UDLD disabled interface Fa0/16,
unidirectional link detected
%PM-4-ERR_DISABLE: udld error detected on Fa0/16, putting Fa0/16
in err-disable state
```

You'll see a lot of debug information flying by but the end result will be that the port is now in err-disable state.

```
SwitchB#show udld fastEthernet 0/16

Interface Fa0/16
---
Port enable administrative configuration setting: Enabled / in
aggressive mode
Port enable operational state: Enabled / in aggressive mode
Current bidirectional state: Unidirectional
Current operational state: Disabled port
```

You can verify it by using the **show udld** command.

LoopGuard and UDLD both solve the same problem: Unidirectional Link failures.

9. Spanning Tree Toolkit

They have some overlap but there are a number of differences, here's an overview:

	LoopGuard	UDLD
Configuration	Global / per port	Global (for fiber) / per port
Per VLAN?	Yes	No, per port
Autorecovery	Yes	Yes but you need to configure err-disable timeout.
Protection against STP failures because of unidirectional links	Yes – need to enable it on all root and alternate ports	Yes – need to enable it on all interfaces.
Protection against STP failures because of software failures (not sending BPDUs)	Yes	No
Protection against miswiring (switching fiber transmit/receive connector)	No	Yes

There is one last topic I want to explain to you, it's not a spanning tree protocol but it's about redundant links so I'll park it here. It's called **FlexLinks.**

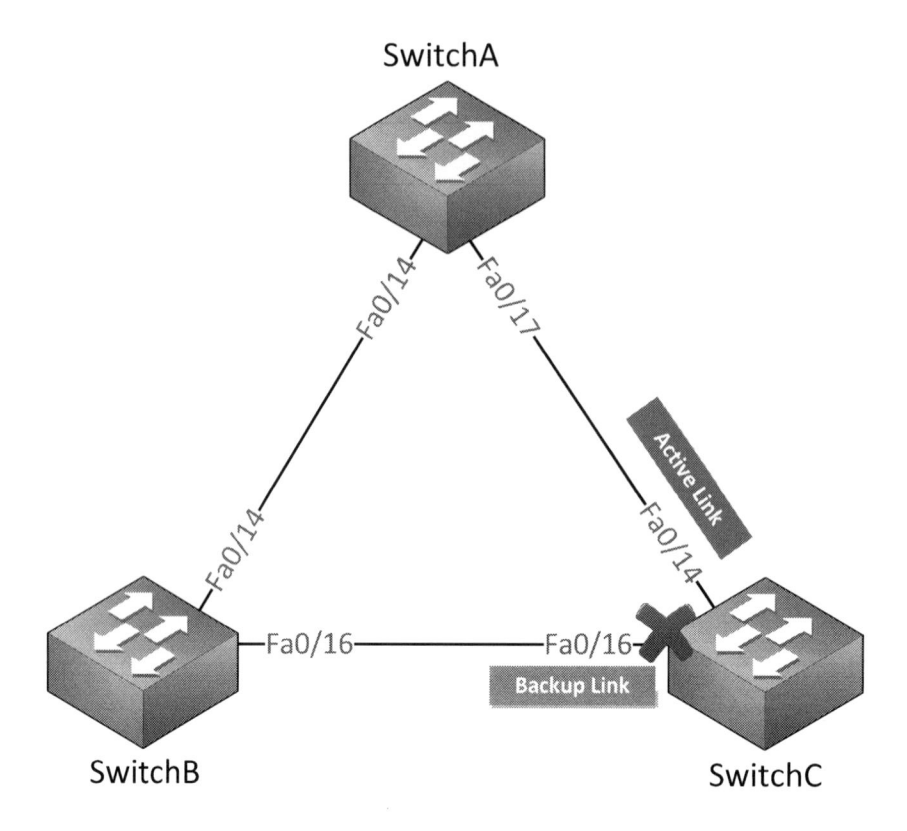

Here's the deal: When you configure **FlexLinks** you'll have an **active** and **standby** interface. I can configure this on SwitchC:

- Fa0/14 will be the active interface.
- Fa0/16 will be the backup interface (this one is blocked!).

When you configure interfaces as FlexLinks they will **not send BPDUs**. There is no way to detect loops because **we don't run spanning-tree** on them. Whenever our active interface fails the backup interface will take over.

```
SwitchC(config)#interface fa0/14
SwitchC(config-if)#switchport backup interface fa0/16
```

This is how we make interface fa0/16 a backup of interface fa0/14.

```
SwitchC#
%SPANTREE-6-PORTDEL_ALL_VLANS: FastEthernet0/14 deleted from all
Vlans
%SPANTREE-6-PORTDEL_ALL_VLANS: FastEthernet0/16 deleted from all
Vlans
```

You can see spanning-tree is being disabled for these interfaces.

9. Spanning Tree Toolkit

```
SwitchC#show interfaces switchport backup

Switch Backup Interface Pairs:

Active Interface      Backup Interface      State
-------------------------------------------------------------
FastEthernet0/14      FastEthernet0/16      Active Up/Backup
Standby
```

Verify our configuration with the **show interfaces switchport backup** command. That's all there is to it. It's an interesting solution because we don't need spanning-tree anymore. After all only one interface is active at any moment.

```
SwitchC(config)#interface f0/14
SwitchC(config-if)#shutdown
```

Let's shut the active interface…

```
SwitchC#show interfaces switchport backup

Switch Backup Interface Pairs:

Active Interface      Backup Interface      State
-------------------------------------------------------------
FastEthernet0/14      FastEthernet0/16      Active
Down/Backup Up
```

You can see that fa0/16 has gone active. That's all there is to it.

This is it! The end of spanning-tree in this book. You've seen (classic) spanning tree, rapid spanning tree, multiple spanning tree and a couple of cool features to protect it. How do you feel by now? Maybe you think routing is more fun? :) This is all you need to know for your CCNP SWITCH exam.

If you want some practice I highly recommend you to try the following labs:

http://gns3vault.com/Switching/spanning-tree-bpdu-guard.html

http://gns3vault.com/Switching/spanning-tree-bpdu-filter.html

http://gns3vault.com/Switching/spanning-tree-root-guard.html

http://gns3vault.com/Switching/spanning-tree-loop-guard.html

http://gns3vault.com/Switching/udld-unidirectional-link-detection.html

http://gns3vault.com/Switching/flex-links-backup-interface.html

9. Spanning Tree Toolkit

10. Etherchannel (Link Aggregation)

In this chapter we'll take a look at **etherchannel** which is also known as link **aggregation**. Etherchannels is a technology that lets you bundle multiple physical links into a single logical link. We'll take a look at how it works and what the advantages of etherchannel are.

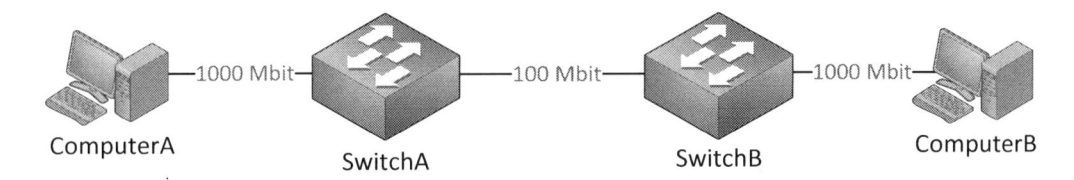

Take a look at the picture above. I have two switches and two computers connected to the switches. The computers are connected with 1000 Mbit interfaces while the link between the switches is only 100 Mbit. If one of the computers would send traffic that exceeds 100 Mbit of bandwidth we'll have congestion and traffic will be dropped. There are two solutions to this problem:

- Replace the link in between the switches with something faster, 1000Mbit or maybe even 10 gigabit if you feel like.
- Add multiple links and bundle them into an etherchannel.

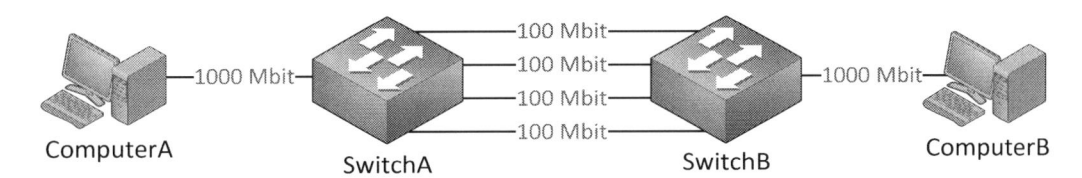

In the picture above I have added a couple of extra links. The problem with this setup is that we have a loop so spanning tree would block 3 out of 4 links.

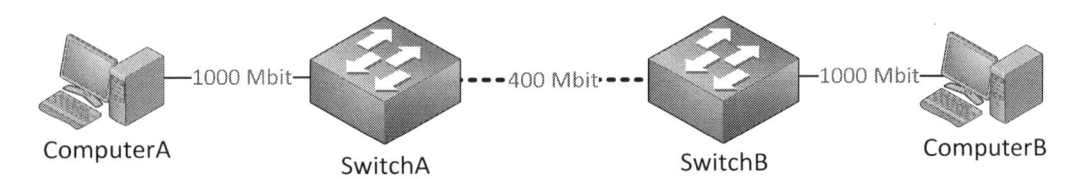

The cool thing about etherchannel is that it will bundle all physical links into a logical link with the combined bandwidth. By combining 4x 100 Mbit I now have a 400 Mbit link. Spanning tree sees this link as **one logical link so there are no loops!**

Etherchannel will do load balancing among the different links that we have and it takes care of redundancy. Once one of the links fails it will keep working and use the links that we have left. There's a maximum to the number of links you can use: **8 physical interfaces**.
If you want to configure an Etherchannel there are two protocols you can

241

choose from:

- **PAgP (Cisco proprietary)**
- **LACP (IEEE standard)**

These protocols can dynamically configure an etherchannel. It's also possible to configure a static etherchannel without these protocols doing the negotiation of the link for you. If you are going to create an etherchannel you need to make sure that all ports have the same configuration:

- Duplex has to be the same.
- Speed has to be there same.
- Same native AND allowed VLANs.
- Same switchport mode (access or trunk).

PAgp and LACP will check if the configuration of the interfaces that you use are the same.

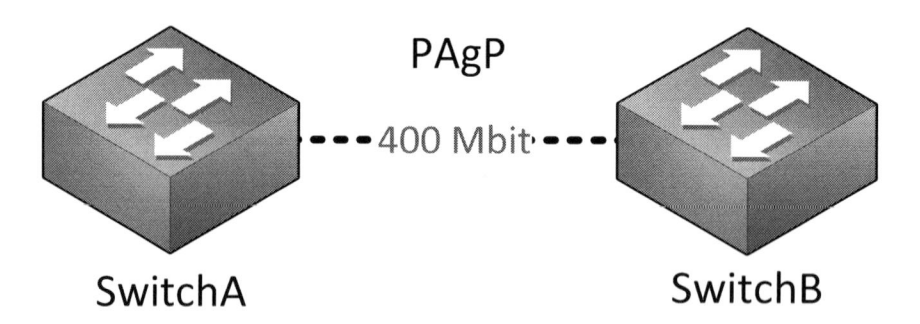

PAgP

---400 Mbit---

SwitchA   SwitchB

If you want to configure PAgP you have a number of options you can choose from, an interface can be configured as:

- **On** (interface becomes member of the etherchannel but does not negotiate).
- **Desirable** (interface will actively ask the other side to become an etherchannel).
- **Auto** (interface will wait passively for the other side to ask to become an etherchannel).
- **Off** (no etherchannel configured on the interface).

Let me show you the configuration of PAgP and how the different options work!

10. Etherchannel (Link Aggregation)

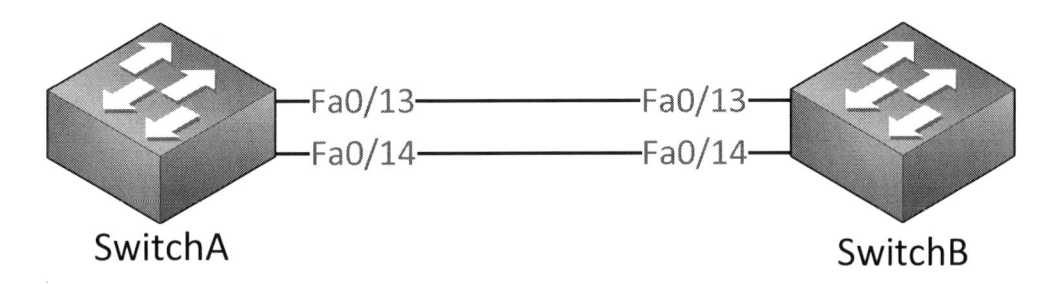

I'll use SwitchA and SwitchB to demonstrate PAgP. We'll use two interfaces to bundle into a single logical link.

```
SwitchA(config)#interface fa0/13
SwitchA(config-if)#channel-group 1 mode ?
  active     Enable LACP unconditionally
  auto       Enable PAgP only if a PAgP device is detected
  desirable  Enable PAgP unconditionally
  on         Enable Etherchannel only
  passive    Enable LACP only if a LACP device is detected
```

First we go to the interface level where we can create a **channel-group**. I'm going to use channel-group number 1. Above you can see the different options that we have for PAgP and LACP.

```
SwitchA(config)#interface fa0/13
SwitchA(config-if)#channel-group 1 mode desirable
Creating a port-channel interface Port-channel 1
SwitchA(config)#interface fa0/14
SwitchA(config-if)#channel-group 1 mode desirable
```

I configure SwitchA for PAgP desirable mode. It will actively ask SwitchB to become an Etherchannel this way.

```
SwitchB(config)#interface fa0/13
SwitchB(config-if)#channel-group 1 mode auto
SwitchB(config)#interface fa0/14
SwitchB(config-if)#channel-group 1 mode auto
```

Here's the configuration of SwitchB. I used the PAgP auto mode so it will respond to requests to become an etherchannel.

```
SwitchA %LINK-3-UPDOWN: Interface Port-channel1, changed state to up
```

```
SwitchB %LINK-3-UPDOWN: Interface Port-channel1, changed state to up
```

You'll see a message on your switches like mine above. The switch will create a port-channel interface.

```
SwitchA(config)#interface port-channel 1
SwitchA(config-if)#switchport trunk encapsulation dot1q
SwitchA(config-if)#switchport mode trunk
```

```
SwitchB(config)#interface port-channel 1
SwitchB(config-if)#switchport trunk encapsulation dot1q
SwitchB(config-if)#switchport mode trunk
```

The port-channel interface can be configured. I've set mine to use 802.1Q encapsulation and to become a trunk.

```
SwitchA#show etherchannel 1 port-channel
        Port-channels in the group:
        ---------------------------

Port-channel: Po1
------------

Age of the Port-channel   = 0d:00h:10m:16s
Logical slot/port   = 2/1         Number of ports = 2
GC                  = 0x00010001      HotStandBy port = null
Port state          = Port-channel Ag-Inuse
Protocol            =    PAgP
Port security       = Disabled

Ports in the Port-channel:

Index   Load   Port     EC state          No of bits
------+------+------+------------------+-----------
  0     00     Fa0/13   Desirable-Sl       0
  0     00     Fa0/14   Desirable-Sl       0

Time since last port bundled:    0d:00h:00m:07s    Fa0/14
Time since last port Un-bundled: 0d:00h:04m:08s    Fa0/13
```

Here's one way to verify your configuration. Use the show etherchannel port-channel command to check if the port-channel is active or not.

10. Etherchannel (Link Aggregation)

You can also see that we are using PAgP. Interface fa0/13 and fa0/14 are both in use for this etherchannel.

```
SwitchA#show etherchannel summary
Flags:  D - down         P - bundled in port-channel
        I - stand-alone  s - suspended
        H - Hot-standby (LACP only)
        R - Layer3       S - Layer2
        U - in use       f - failed to allocate aggregator

        M - not in use, minimum links not met
        u - unsuitable for bundling
        w - waiting to be aggregated
        d - default port


Number of channel-groups in use: 1
Number of aggregators:           1

Group  Port-channel  Protocol    Ports
------+-------------+-----------+-----------------------------------
1      Po1(SU)          PAgP     Fa0/13(P)   Fa0/14(P)
```

If you have many etherchannels you can also use the **show etherchannel summary** command. It will give you a quick overview of all the etherchannels and the interfaces that are in use.

```
SwitchA#show interfaces fa0/14 etherchannel
Port state      = Up Mstr In-Bndl
Channel group = 1              Mode = Desirable-Sl   Gcchange = 0
Port-channel  = Po1            GC   = 0x00010001     Pseudo port-
channel = Po1
Port index    = 0              Load = 0x00           Protocol = 
PAgP

Flags:  S - Device is sending Slow hello.  C - Device is in
Consistent state.
        A - Device is in Auto mode.         P - Device learns on
physical port.
        d - PAgP is down.
Timers: H - Hello timer is running.         Q - Quit timer is
running.
        S - Switching timer is running.     I - Interface timer
is running.

Local information:
                                    Hello    Partner   PAgP
Learning   Group
Port        Flags State  Timers   Interval  Count     Priority
Method   Ifindex
```

245

```
Fa0/14      SC U6/S7    H    30s  1           128         Any         5001

Partner's information:

                Partner                 Partner             Partner
Partner   Group
Port            Name                    Device ID           Port        Age
Flags     Cap.
Fa0/14          SwitchB                 0019.569d.5700 Fa0/14           19s
SAC       10001

Age of the port in the current state: 0d:00h:02m:37s
```

The third method to verify your etherchannel is to use the **show interfaces etherchannel** command. In my example I am looking at the information of my fa0/14 interface. Besides information of our local switch you can also see the interface of our neighbor switch (SwitchB in my example).

The last thing I want to share with you about PAgP are the different modes you can choose from:

- On
- Desirable
- Auto
- Off

I have configured SwitchA to use desirable and SwitchB to use auto mode. Not all the different combinations work:

	On	Desirable	Auto	Off
On	Yes	No	No	No
Desirable	No	Yes	Yes	No
Auto	No	Yes	No	No
Off	No	No	No	No

Here's an overview with all the different options. Keep in mind that configuring your etherchannel as "on" doesn't use any negotiation so it will fail if the other side is configured for auto or desirable.

LACP is similar to PAgP. You also have different options to choose from when you configure the interface:

- **On** (interfaces becomes member of the etherchannel but does not negotiate).
- **Active** (interface will actively ask the other side to become an etherchannel).
- **Passive** (interface will wait passively for the other side to ask to become an etherchannel).
- **Off** (no etherchannel configured on the interface).

10. Etherchannel (Link Aggregation)

It's basically the same thing as PAgP but the terminology is different. Let's configure LACP to see what it does.

```
SwitchA(config)#default interface fa0/13
Interface FastEthernet0/13 set to default configuration
SwitchA(config)#default interface fa0/14
Interface FastEthernet0/14 set to default configuration
```

```
SwitchB(config)#default interface fa0/13
Interface FastEthernet0/13 set to default configuration
SwitchB(config)#default interface fa0/14
Interface FastEthernet0/14 set to default configuration
```

```
SwitchA(config)#no interface port-channel1
```

```
SwitchB(config)#no interface port-channel1
```

Don't forget to clean up PAgP before you start playing with LACP.

```
SwitchA(config-if)#interface fa0/13
SwitchA(config-if)#channel-group 1 mode active
Creating a port-channel interface Port-channel 1
SwitchA(config-if)#interface f0/14
SwitchA(config-if)#channel-group 1 mode active
```

I'll configure SwitchA to use LACP active mode.

```
SwitchB(config)#interface fa0/13
SwitchB(config-if)#channel-group 1 mode passive
Creating a port-channel interface Port-channel 1
SwitchB(config-if)#interface fa0/14
SwitchB(config-if)#channel-group 1 mode passive
```

SwitchB will use LACP passive mode.

```
SwitchA#show etherchannel 1 port-channel
        Port-channels in the group:
        ---------------------------

Port-channel: Po1    (Primary Aggregator)

------------

Age of the Port-channel   = 0d:00h:03m:04s
Logical slot/port   = 2/1          Number of ports = 2
HotStandBy port = null
Port state          = Port-channel Ag-Inuse
Protocol            =    LACP
```

247

```
Port security           = Disabled

Ports in the Port-channel:

Index   Load   Port       EC state            No of bits
------+------+------+------------------+-----------
  0     00    Fa0/13     Active                  0
  0     00    Fa0/14     Active                  0

Time since last port bundled:    0d:00h:00m:54s      Fa0/14
```

We can use the show etherchannel port-channel command again to verify our configuration again. As you can see the protocol is now LACP and interfaces fa0/13 and fa0/14 are active.

The configuration of PAgP and LACP is similar. Keep in mind that PAgP can only be used between Cisco devices while LACP is a IEEE standard, you can use it to form etherchannels with devices from other vendors.

	On	Active	Passive	Off
On	Yes	No	No	No
Active	No	Yes	Yes	No
Passive	No	Yes	No	No
Off	No	No	No	No

Here's an overview with the different modes and combinations for LACP. It's similar to PAgP but now we have the active and passive mode.

Last thing I want to show you about etherchannel is load-balancing:

```
SwitchA#show etherchannel load-balance
EtherChannel Load-Balancing Configuration:
        src-mac

EtherChannel Load-Balancing Addresses Used Per-Protocol:
Non-IP:  Source MAC address
  IPv4:  Source MAC address
  IPv6:  Source MAC address
```

Use the **show etherchannel load-balance** command to see what the default configuration is. As you can see our etherchannel load-balances based on the source MAC address.

```
SwitchA(config)#port-channel load-balance ?
  dst-ip          Dst IP Addr
  dst-mac         Dst Mac Addr
  src-dst-ip      Src XOR Dst IP Addr
  src-dst-mac     Src XOR Dst Mac Addr
  src-ip          Src IP Addr
```

10. Etherchannel (Link Aggregation)

```
src-mac         Src Mac Addr
```

You can use the global **port-channel load-balance** command to change this behavior. You can see you can choose between source/destination MAC/IP address or a combination of source/destination.

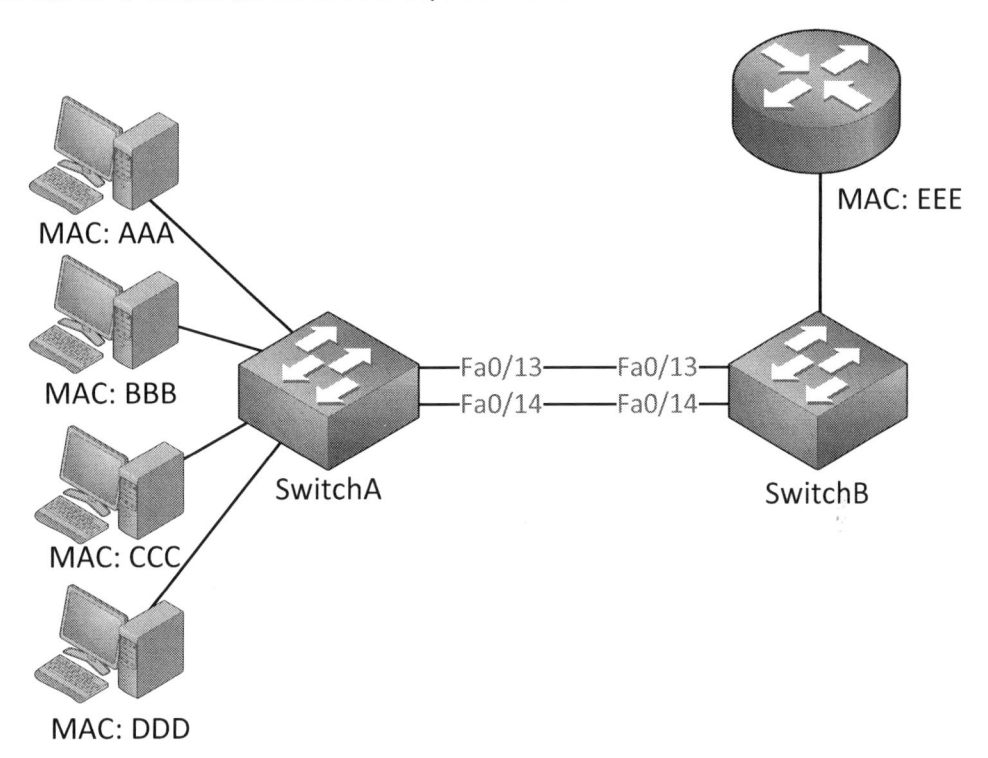

Why should you care about load balancing? Take a look at the picture above. We have 4 computers and one router on the right side. The default load-balancing mechanism is source MAC address. This means that **ALL** traffic from **one** MAC address will be sent down one and the same physical interface, for example:

- MAC address AAA will be sent using SwitchA's fa0/13 interface.
- MAC address BBB will be sent using SwitchA's fa0/14 interface.
- MAC address AAA will be sent using SwitchA's fa0/13 interface.
- MAC address BBB will be sent using SwitchA's fa0/14 interface.

Since we have multiple computers this is fine, both physical links on SwitchA will be used for our etherchannel so depending on how much traffic the computers send it will be close to a 1:1 ratio.

It's a different story for SwitchB since we only have one router with MAC address EEE. It will pick one of the physical interfaces so **ALL** traffic from the router will be sent down interface fa0/13 **OR** fa0/14. One of the physical links won't be used at all...

249

```
SwitchB(config)#port-channel load-balance dst-mac
```

If this is the case it's better to change the load balancing mechanism. If we switch it to destination MAC address on SwitchB traffic from our router to the computer will be load-balanced amongst the different physical interfaces because we have multiple computers with different destination MAC addresses.

This is all I have for you on etherchannels. Before you continue to the next chapter why not try to configure some PAgP and LACP etherchannels yourself? Here's a lab for you:

http://gns3vault.com/Switching/pagp-lacp-etherchannel.html

10. Etherchannel (Link Aggregation)

11. InterVLAN routing

In this chapter we are going to take a look at routing between VLANs. When we want communication between different VLANs we'll need a device that can do routing. We could use an external router but it's also possible to use a **multilayer switch** (aka layer 3 switches).

Let's look at the different options!

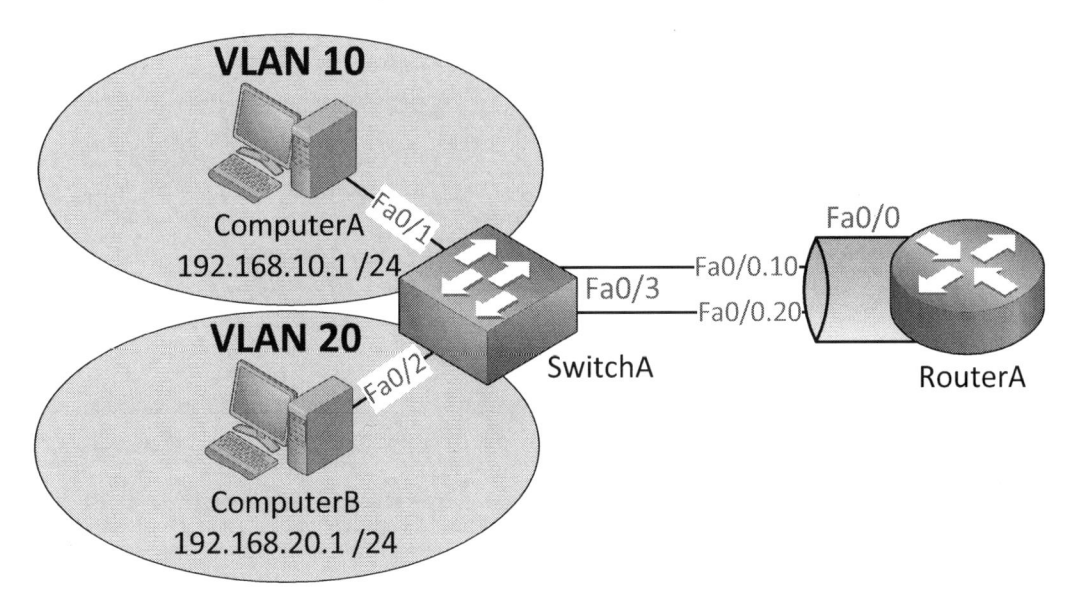

If you studied CCNA this picture should ring a bell. This is the **router on a stick** setup. SwitchA has two VLANs so we have two different subnets. If we want communication between these VLANs we'll have to use a device that can do routing. In this example we'll use a router for the job. RouterA will need access to both VLANs so we'll create a 802.1Q trunk between SwitchA and RouterA.

```
SwitchA(config)#interface fa0/3
SwitchA(config-if)#switchport trunk encapsulation dot1q
SwitchA(config-if)#switchport mode trunk
SwitchA(config-if)#switchport trunk allowed vlan 10,20
```

This is how we configure SwitchA. Make interface fa0/3 a trunk port and for security measures I made sure that only VLAN 10 and 20 are allowed.

```
RouterA(config)#interface fa0/0.10
RouterA(config-subif)#encapsulation dot1Q 10
RouterA(config-subif)#ip address 192.168.10.254 255.255.255.0
RouterA(config)#interface fa0/0.20
RouterA(config-subif)#encapsulation dot1Q 20
RouterA(config-subif)#ip address 192.168.20.254 255.255.255.0
```

Create two sub-interfaces on the router and tell it to which VLAN they belong. Don't forget to add an IP address for each VLAN.

```
RouterA#show ip route
*Mar  1 00:02:14.811: %SYS-5-CONFIG_I: Configured from console by console
Codes: C - connected, S - static, R - RIP, M - mobile, B - BGP
       D - EIGRP, EX - EIGRP external, O - OSPF, IA - OSPF inter area
       N1 - OSPF NSSA external type 1, N2 - OSPF NSSA external type 2
       E1 - OSPF external type 1, E2 - OSPF external type 2
       i - IS-IS, su - IS-IS summary, L1 - IS-IS level-1, L2 - IS-IS level-2
       ia - IS-IS inter area, * - candidate default, U - per-user static route
       o - ODR, P - periodic downloaded static route

Gateway of last resort is not set

C    192.168.10.0/24 is directly connected, FastEthernet0/0.10
C    192.168.20.0/24 is directly connected, FastEthernet0/0.20
```

The router will be able to route because these two networks are directly connected.

```
C:\Documents and Settings\ComputerA>ipconfig

Windows IP Configuration

Ethernet adapter Local Area Connection:

        Connection-specific DNS Suffix  . :
        IP Address. . . . . . . . . . . . : 192.168.10.1
        Subnet Mask . . . . . . . . . . . : 255.255.255.0
        Default Gateway . . . . . . . . . : 192.168.10.254
```

```
C:\Documents and Settings\ComputerB>ipconfig

Windows IP Configuration

Ethernet adapter Local Area Connection:

        Connection-specific DNS Suffix  . :
        IP Address. . . . . . . . . . . . : 192.168.20.1
        Subnet Mask . . . . . . . . . . . : 255.255.255.0
        Default Gateway . . . . . . . . . : 192.168.20.254
```

Don't forget to set your IP address and gateway on the computers.

11. InterVLAN routing

```
C:\Documents and Settings\ComputerA>ping 192.168.20.1

Pinging 192.168.20.1 with 32 bytes of data:

Reply from 192.168.20.1: bytes=32 time<1ms TTL=128
Reply from 192.168.20.1: bytes=32 time<1ms TTL=128
Reply from 192.168.20.1: bytes=32 time<1ms TTL=128
Reply from 192.168.20.1: bytes=32 time<1ms TTL=128

Ping statistics for 192.168.1.2:
    Packets: Sent = 4, Received = 4, Lost = 0 (0% loss),
Approximate round trip times in milli-seconds:
    Minimum = 0ms, Maximum = 0ms, Average = 0ms
```

That's how you do it. So why would you want to use a solution like this? It's cheap! You don't need a multilayer switch for your routing. Any layer 2 switch will do.
The Cisco Catalyst 2960 is a layer 2 switch; the cheapest multilayer switch is the Cisco Catalyst 3560. Compare the price on those two and you'll see what I'm talking about.

Some of the disadvantages of this solution is that your router is a single point of failure and that traffic flows up and down on the same link which might cause congestion.

So what other solutions do we have?

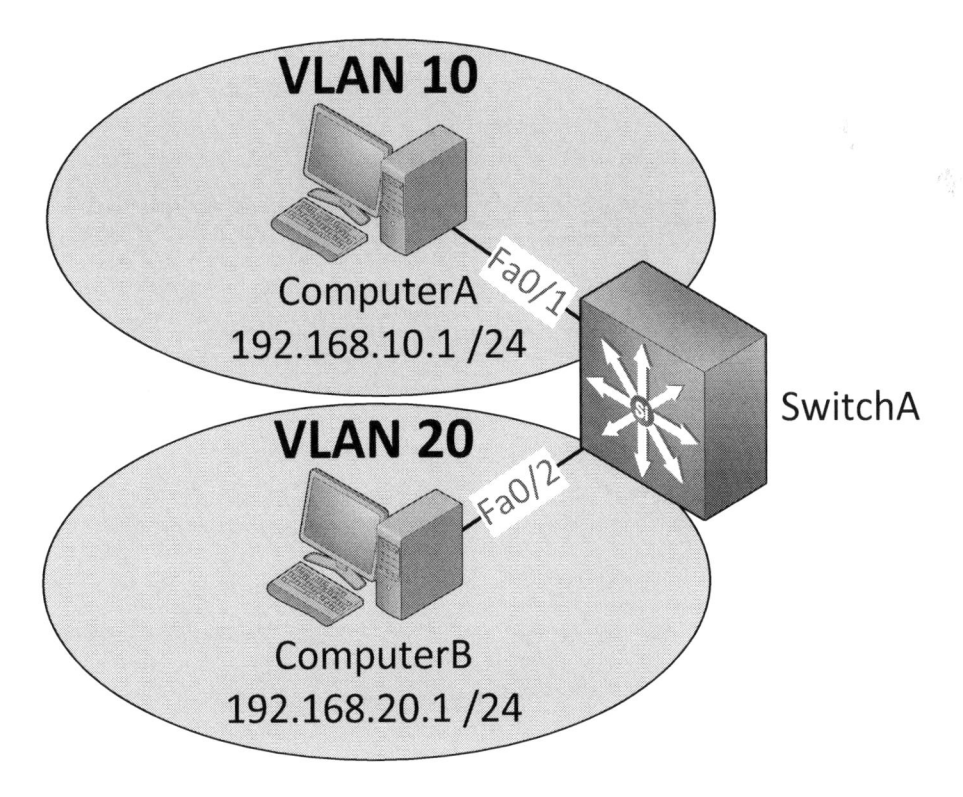

VLAN 10
ComputerA
192.168.10.1 /24
Fa0/1

VLAN 20
ComputerB
192.168.20.1 /24
Fa0/2

SwitchA

255

Finally a new icon to use! This is the picture of a multilayer switch. This switch has routing capabilities! I can configure something called a **SVI (Switch Virtual Interface)** for each VLAN and put an IP address on it. This IP address can be used for computers as their default gateway.

```
SwitchA(config)#ip routing
SwitchA(config)#interface vlan 10
SwitchA(config-if)#no shutdown
SwitchA(config-if)#ip address 192.168.10.254 255.255.255.0
SwitchA(config)#interface vlan 20
SwitchA(config-if)#no shutdown
SwitchA(config-if)#ip address 192.168.20.254 255.255.255.0
```

Start by enabling routing using the **ip routing** command. If you forget this your switch won't build a routing table! Next step is to create a SVI for VLAN 10 and 20 and configure IP addresses on them. This configuration might look familiar if you worked with layer 2 switches before. On a layer 2 switch like the Cisco Catalyst 2950/2960 we also have a SVI but you can only use it for remote management.

Once you create a SVI and type no shutdown it will normally be "up" since it's only a virtual interface, there are however a number of requirements or it will show up as "down":

- The VLAN has to **exist** in the VLAN database and it should be **active**.
- At least one access or trunk port should use this VLAN actively and it should be in spanning-tree forwarding mode.

Simply said: the VLAN has to be active somehow or your SVI will go down.

11. InterVLAN routing

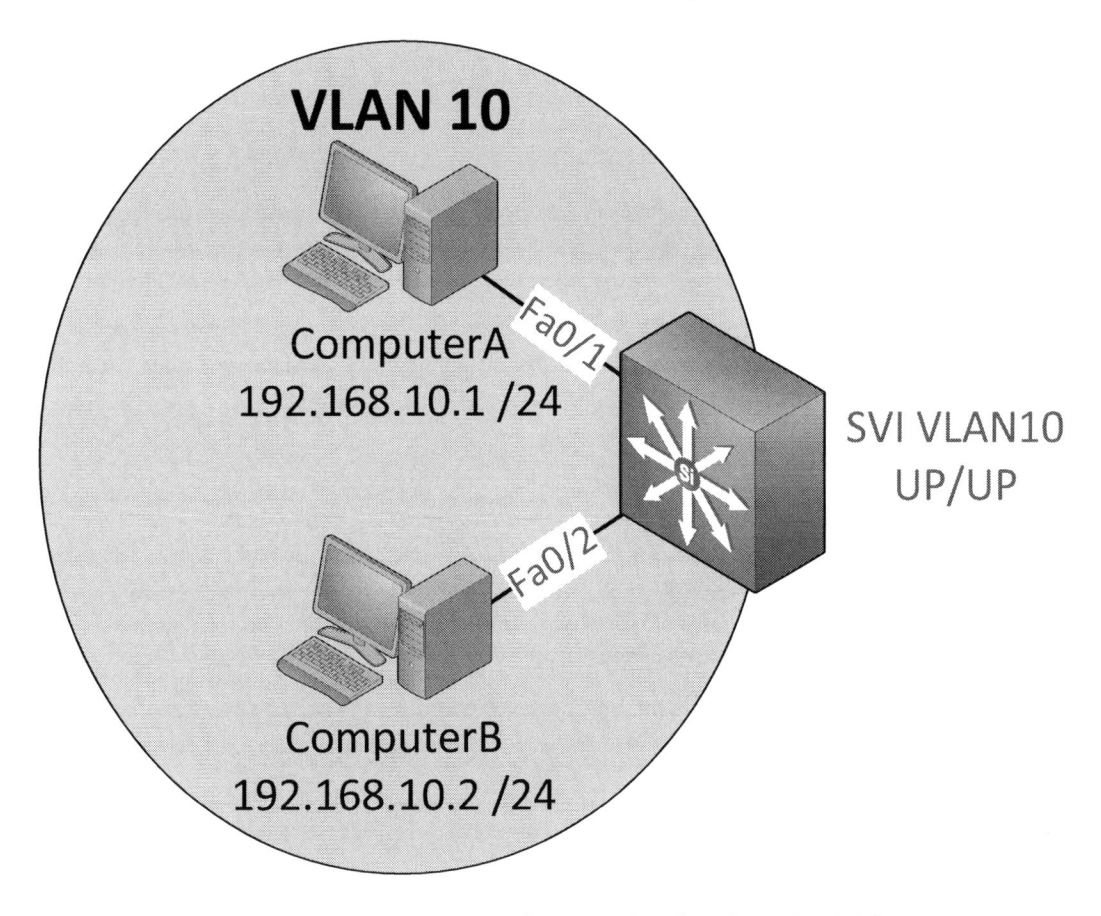

I have two computers in VLAN 10 and created a SVI for VLAN 10.

```
SwitchA#show ip interface brief vlan 10
Interface            IP-Address      OK? Method Status
Protocol
Vlan10               192.168.10.254  YES manual up            up
```

You'll see that the status says up/up so that's good.

257

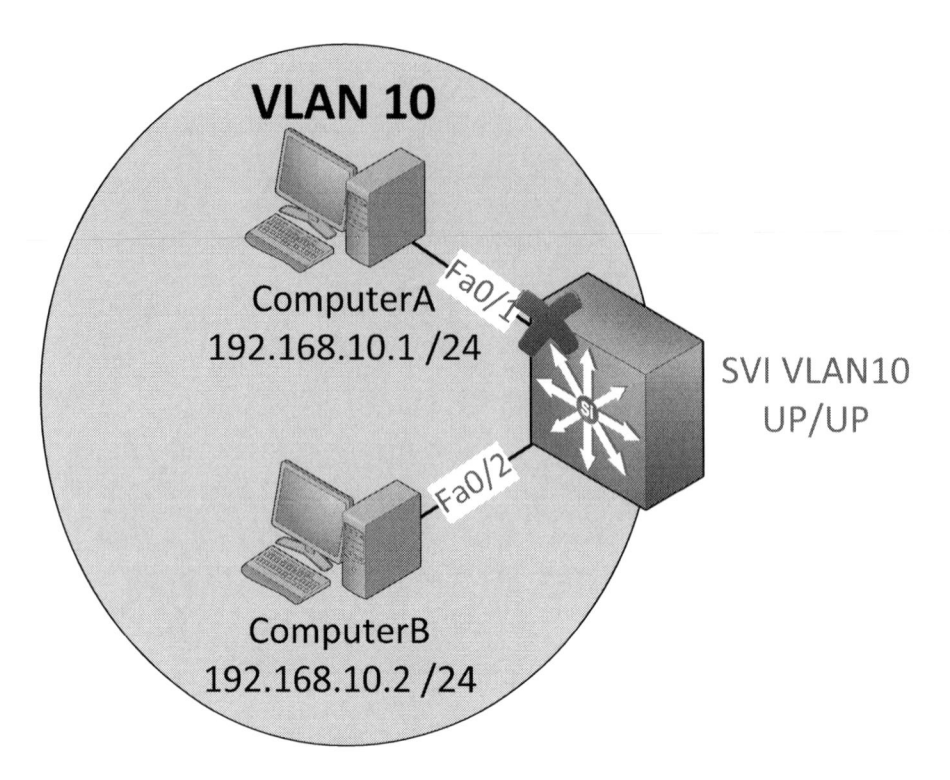

If I shutdown one interface nothing will change, my SVI will still show up/up because interface fa0/2 is still active.

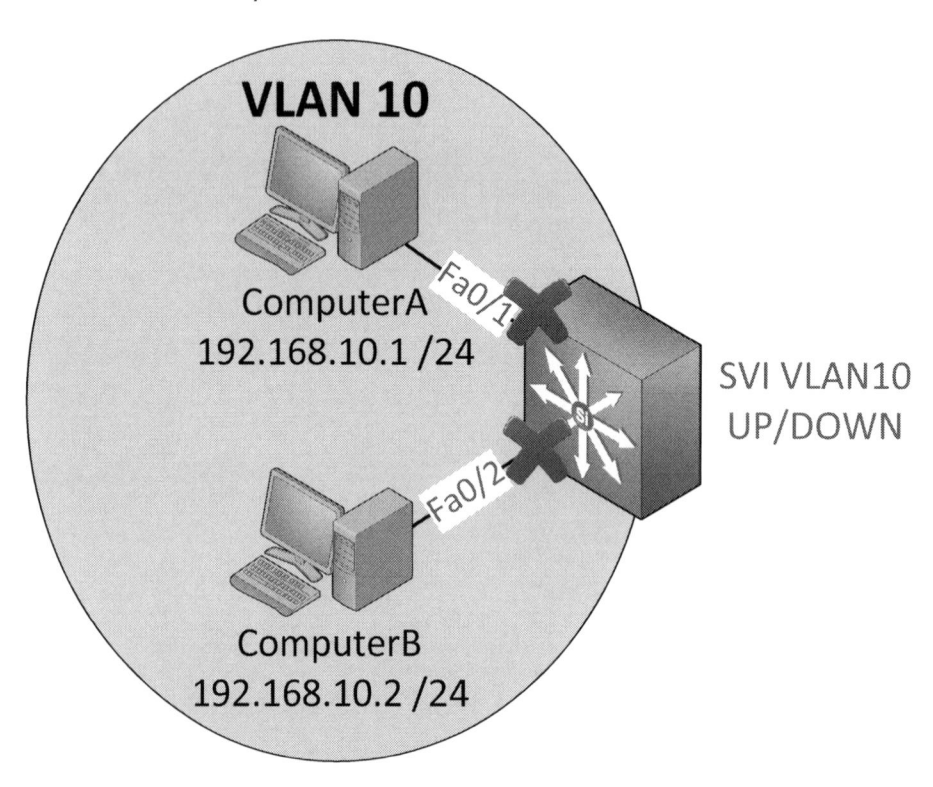

11. InterVLAN routing

```
SwitchA#show ip interface brief vlan 10
Interface              IP-Address      OK? Method Status
Protocol
Vlan10                 192.168.10.254  YES manual up
down
```

Once I shut both interfaces we don't have anything active anymore in VLAN 10. As a result the SVI will go to up/down.

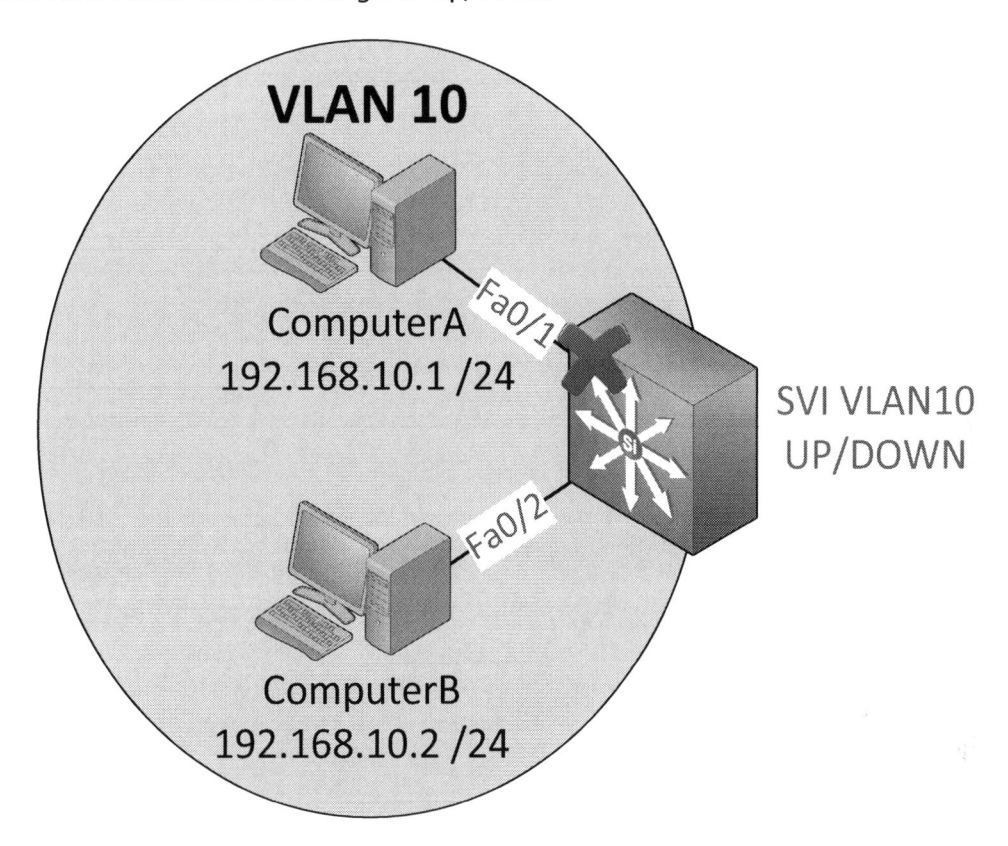

Now if I want I can exclude an interface from the SVI state. Imagine I want to make sure that whatever happens to interface fa0/2 doesn't influence the SVI state.

```
SwitchA(config)#interface fa0/2
SwitchA(config-if)#switchport autostate exclude
```

I can use the **switchport autostate exclude** command. This means it won't influence the state of the SVI interface anymore. Fa0/1 is the only interface that can now influence the SVI state, as soon as it goes down you'll see that SVI state go down as well, even though fa0/2 is still up and running.

Enough about the SVI, there's another method we can use our multilayer switch for routing. By default all interfaces on a switch are **switchports** (layer 2) but we can change them to **routed ports** (layer 3). A routed port is the exact same interface as what we use on a router.

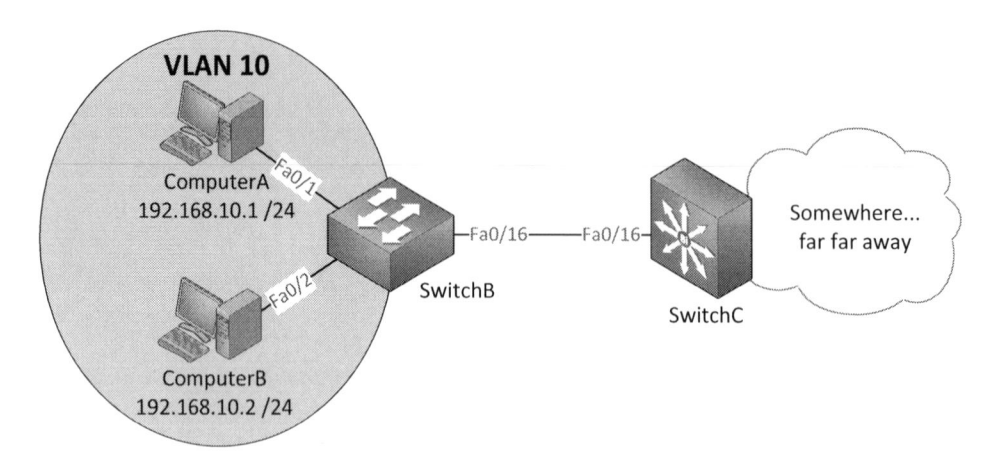

Here's an example of the routed port. SwitchB is a layer 2 switch and SwitchC is a multilayer switch. The fa0/16 interface on SwitchC has been configured as a router port so it can be used as the default gateway for the clients in VLAN 10.

```
SwitchB(config)#interface fa0/16
SwitchB(config-if)#switchport mode access
SwitchB(config-if)#switchport access vlan 10
```

I'm going to configure the fa0/16 interface to SwitchC as a normal access port and put it in VLAN 10.

```
SwitchC(config)#interface fa0/16
SwitchC(config-if)#no switchport
SwitchC(config-if)#ip address 192.168.10.254 255.255.255.0
```

Make it a routed port by typing **no switchport** and put an IP address on it, it can now be used by the computers as a gateway!

There are two things you should remember about this routed port:

- It's no longer a switchport so it's not associated with any VLAN.
- It's a routed port but it doesn't support sub-interfaces like a router does.

What should you use? The SVI or the routed port? If you only have one interface in a VLAN it's fine to use the routed port, configure an IP address on it and you are ready to go. If you have multiple interfaces in a VLAN you should use the SVI.

11. InterVLAN routing

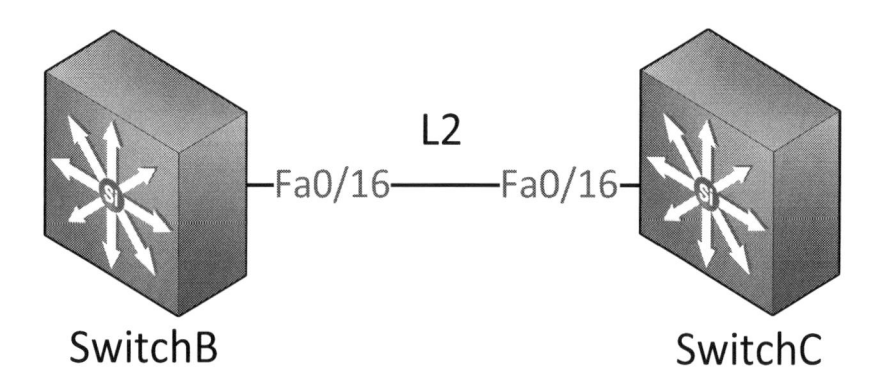

SwitchB ——Fa0/16———L2———Fa0/16—— SwitchC

Multilayer switches can **use routing protocols.** Let me show you an example. I have two multilayer switches and the link in between is layer 2.

```
SwitchB(config-if)#switchport trunk encapsulation dot1q
SwitchB(config-if)#switchport mode trunk
```

```
SwitchC(config-if)#switchport trunk encapsulation dot1q
SwitchC(config-if)#switchport mode trunk
```

I'm creating a 802.1q trunk in between the switches but it doesn't matter what you pick. I also could have used access interfaces and use a single VLAN.

```
SwitchB(config)#vlan 10
SwitchB(config)#interface vlan 10
SwitchB(config-if)#ip address 192.168.10.1 255.255.255.0
```

```
SwitchC(config)#vlan 10
SwitchC(config)#interface vlan 10
SwitchC(config-if)#ip address 192.168.10.2 255.255.255.0
```

Create a SVI interface on each Switch and configure an IP address.

```
SwitchC#ping 192.168.10.1

Type escape sequence to abort.
Sending 5, 100-byte ICMP Echos to 192.168.10.1, timeout is 2
seconds:
!!!!!
Success rate is 100 percent (5/5), round-trip min/avg/max =
1/3/4 ms
```

The switches can reach each other so the SVI interfaces and trunk are working.

```
SwitchB(config)#ip routing
SwitchB(config)#router eigrp 10
SwitchB(config-router)#network 192.168.10.0
```

```
SwitchB(config)#ip routing
SwitchC(config)#router eigrp 10
SwitchC(config-router)#network 192.168.10.0
```

Let's configure EIGRP to see if we can form a neighbor adjacency.

```
SwitchB %DUAL-5-NBRCHANGE: EIGRP-IPv4:(10) 10: Neighbor
192.168.10.2 (Vlan10) is up: new adjacency
```

There goes...the switches have found each other.

```
SwitchC#show ip eigrp neighbors
EIGRP-IPv4:(10) neighbors for process 10
H   Address                 Interface       Hold Uptime    SRTT
RTO Q   Seq
                                            (sec)          (ms)
Cnt Num
0   192.168.10.1            Vl10            13 00:01:25    1
200 0   1
```

We have successfully configured EIGRP between these two switches using the SVI interfaces.

We can also do this with the routed ports!

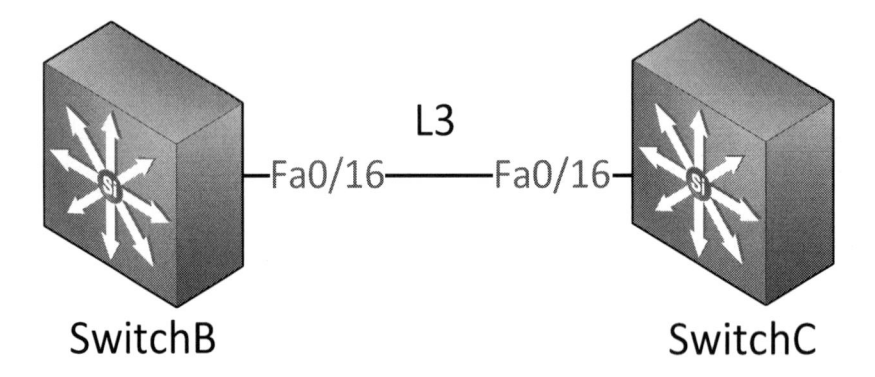

L3
SwitchB —Fa0/16———Fa0/16— SwitchC

Same switches but now I'm going to make the link in between layer 3 by using the routed ports.

```
SwitchB(config)#no interface vlan 10
SwitchB(config)#interface fa0/16
SwitchB(config-if)#no switchport
SwitchB(config-if)#ip address 192.168.10.1 255.255.255.0
```

```
SwitchC(config)#no interface vlan 10
SwitchC(config)#interface fa0/16
SwitchC(config-if)#no switchport
SwitchC(config-if)#ip address 192.168.10.2 255.255.255.0
```

11. InterVLAN routing

Get rid of the SVI interfaces and change the interfaces to routed ports. Don't forget to add an IP address.

```
SwitchB(config)#router ospf 10
SwitchB(config-router)#network 192.168.10.0 0.0.0.255 area 0
```

```
SwitchC(config-if)#router ospf 10
SwitchC(config-router)#network 192.168.10.0 0.0.0.255 area 0
```

Let's configure OSPF this time just for fun!

```
SwitchB#show ip ospf neighbor

Neighbor ID      Pri    State         Dead Time    Address
Interface
192.168.10.2      1     FULL/DR       00:00:37     192.168.10.2
FastEthernet0/16
```

We have established an OSPF neighbor adjacency by using the routed ports!

If you use your multilayer switch as a gateway for clients you might want to use it as a DHCP server as well. This is no problem at all.

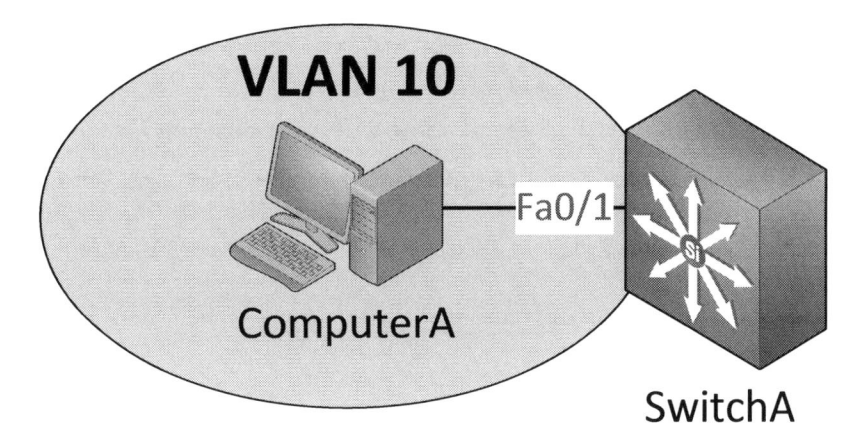

Here's an example for SwitchA. There's one computer in VLAN 10.

```
SwitchA(config)#interface vlan 10
SwitchA(config-if)#ip address 192.168.10.254 255.255.255.0
SwitchA(config)#interface fa0/1
SwitchA(config-if)#switchport access vlan 10
```

First I'll create the SVI, put an IP address on it and make sure ComputerA is in VLAN 10. You can also use a routed port if you like.

```
SwitchA(config)#ip dhcp pool VLAN10POOL
SwitchA(dhcp-config)#network 192.168.10.0 255.255.255.0
```

```
SwitchA(dhcp-config)#default-route 192.168.10.254
SwitchA(config)#ip dhcp excluded-address 192.168.10.254
```

Here's a fairly simple example of a DHCP pool. You can pick any name you like for the pool. Type in the network and that's it. I've also added a gateway with the default-route command. Optionally you can exclude a number of IP addresses.

```
SwitchA#debug ip dhcp server packet
DHCPD: incoming interface name is Vlan10
DHCPD: DHCPDISCOVER received from client 0100.0c29.285c.6c on
interface Vlan10.
DHCPD: Sending DHCPOFFER to client 0100.0c29.285c.6c
(192.168.10.1).
DHCPD: Check for IPe on Vlan10
DHCPD: creating ARP entry (192.168.10.1, 000c.2928.5c6c).
DHCPD: unicasting BOOTREPLY to client 000c.2928.5c6c
(192.168.10.1).
DHCPD: incoming interface name is Vlan10
DHCPD: DHCPREQUEST received from client 0100.0c29.285c.6c.
DHCPD: Sending DHCPACK to client 0100.0c29.285c.6c
(192.168.10.1).
DHCPD: Check for IPe on Vlan10
DHCPD: creating ARP entry (192.168.10.1, 000c.2928.5c6c).
DHCPD: unicasting BOOTREPLY to client 000c.2928.5c6c
(192.168.10.1).
```

With the **debug ip dhcp server packet** command you can actually see what is going on when a computer requests an IP address. There are four messages that DHCP uses:

- DHCP Discover
- DHCH Offer
- DHCP Request
- DHCP Acknowledgement

The computer sends an **DHCP Discover** because it's looking for an IP address. This message is **broadcasted** within the VLAN. The DHCP server will reply with the **DHCP Offer** message, this contains all the information the computer needs. The computer will reply with a **DHCP request** because it likes what it sees. The final step is a **DHCP Acknowledgement** from the DHCP server.

```
SwitchA#show ip dhcp binding
IP address         Client-ID/         Lease expiration           Type
         Hardware address
192.168.10.1       0100.0c29.285c.6c          Mar 01 1993 04:33 AM
Automatic
```

Use the **show ip dhcp binding** command to check the current leases.

11. InterVLAN routing

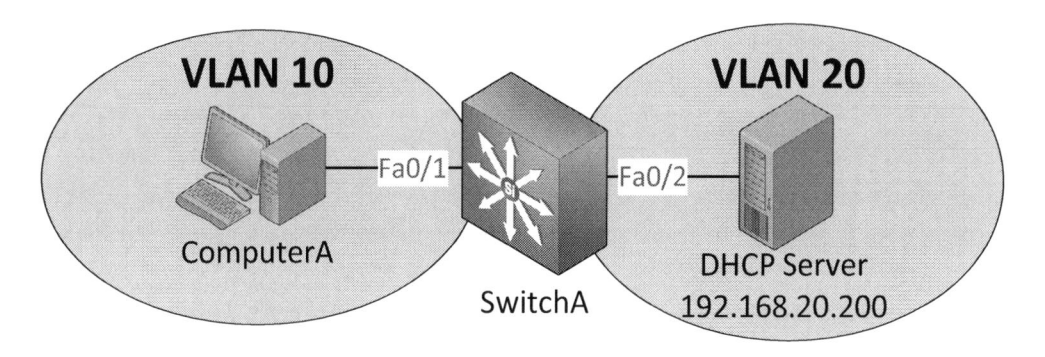

When a device is looking for a DHCP server it will send a DHCP Discover message. This is broadcasted within the VLAN. What do we have to do if the DHCP server is not on the same VLAN? We can use the **ip helper** command to fix this. In the example above I have a computer in VLAN 10 and the DHCP server is in VLAN 20.

```
SwitchA(config)#interface vlan 10
SwitchA(config-if)#ip address 192.168.10.254 255.255.255.0
SwitchA(config-if)#ip helper 192.168.20.200
SwitchA(config)#interface vlan 20
SwitchA(config-if)#ip address 192.168.20.254 255.255.255.0
SwitchA(config)#interface fa0/1
SwitchA(config-if)#switchport access vlan 10
SwitchA(config)#interface fa0/2
SwitchA(config-if)#switchport access vlan 20
```

The key to this configuration is the **ip helper** command. When SwitchA hears a DHCP discover message in VLAN 10 it will pass it along to the DHCP server in VLAN 20 as a unicast IP packet. The DHCP server will forward the lease to SwitchA so it can be delivered to ComputerA.

That's all that I have for you about routing! You have now learned the difference between layer 2 and multilayer switches, the next chapter will be about **CEF (Cisco Express Forwarding)** where we take a look at all the steps a multilayer switch has to take before it can forward an IP packet.

If you want to practice the configuration of routing, the SVI and the routed ports I have a couple of labs for you:

http://gns3vault.com/Network-Services/router-on-a-stick.html

http://gns3vault.com/Switching/switch-svi-interface-and-routing.html

You can also play around with DHCP if you want:

http://gns3vault.com/Network-Services/dhcp-server.html

12. CEF (Cisco Express Forwarding)

Perhaps you have heard about the term "wirespeed" before. It's something the marketing department likes to use when it comes to selling networking equipment. It means that packets can be forwarded without any noticeable delay. Oh btw, for the remaining of this chapter the words "multilayer switch" and "router" are the same thing. Everything that I explain about the multilayer switches from now on also applies to routers. Let's take a look at the difference between layer 2 and multilayer switches from the switch's perspective:

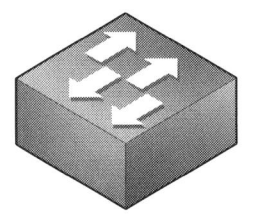

- Switch within VLANs.
- Filter traffic based on layer 2

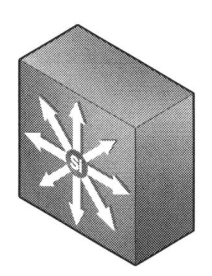

Layer 2 Switch

- Switch within VLANs.
- Route between VLANs.
- Filter traffic based on layer 2 or 3.

Multilayer switch

You know that layer 2 switches only will switch Ethernet frames within a VLAN, and if we want we can filter traffic based on layer 2 (for example with port-security). The multilayer switch can do the same but is also able to route between VLANS and filter on layer 3 or 4 using access-lists.

Forwarding on layer 2 is based on the destination MAC address. Our switch learns the source MAC addresses on incoming frames and it builds the MAC address table. Whenever an Ethernet frame enters one of our interfaces, we'll check the MAC address table to find the destination MAC address and we'll send it out the correct interface.

Forwarding on layer 3 is based on the destination IP address. Forwarding happens when the switch receives an IP packet where the source IP address is in a **different subnet** than the destination IP address.

When our multilayer switch receives an IP packet with its **own MAC address as the destination** in the Ethernet header there are two possibilities:

- If the destination IP address is an address that is configured on the multilayer switch then the IP packet was destined for this switch.
- If the destination IP address is an address that is not configured on the multilayer switch then we have to act as a gateway and "route" the packet. This means we'll have to do a lookup in the routing table to check for the **longest match**. Also we have to check if the IP packet is allowed if you configured an ACL.

Back in the days...switching was done at **hardware speed** while routing was done in **software**. Nowadays both switching and routing is done at hardware speed. In the remaining of this chapter you'll learn why.

Let's take a look at the difference between handling Ethernet Frames and IP Packets:

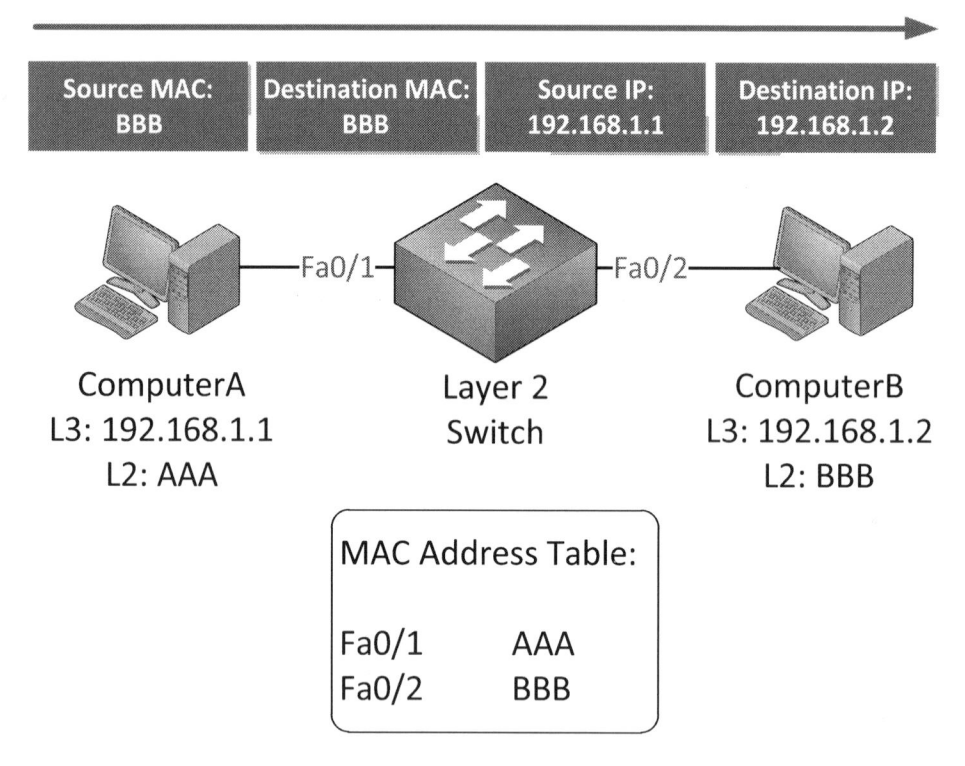

| Source MAC: BBB | Destination MAC: BBB | Source IP: 192.168.1.1 | Destination IP: 192.168.1.2 |

ComputerA
L3: 192.168.1.1
L2: AAA

Layer 2 Switch

ComputerB
L3: 192.168.1.2
L2: BBB

MAC Address Table:

Fa0/1   AAA
Fa0/2   BBB

The life of a layer 2 switch is simple:

1. The switch will verify the checksum of the Ethernet frame to make it sure it's not corrupted or altered.
2. The switch receives an Ethernet frame and adds the source MAC address to the MAC address table.
3. The switch forwards the Ethernet frame to the correct interface if it knows the destination MAC address. If not, it will be flooded.

There is **no alteration** of the Ethernet frame!

Now let's see what we have to do when we receive an IP packet on a

12. CEF (Cisco Express Forwarding)

multilayer switch:

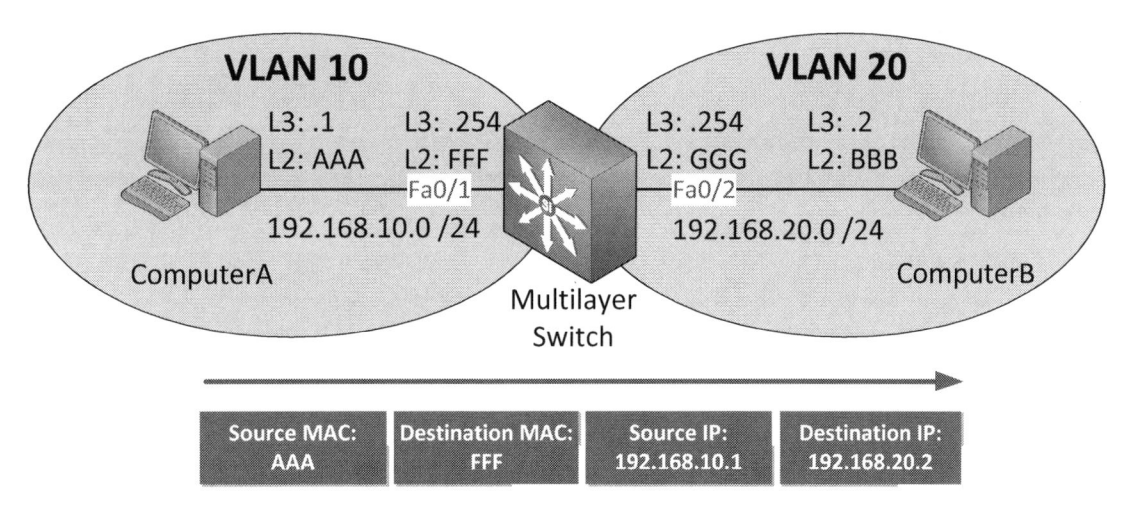

In the example above ComputerA is sending an IP packet towards computerB. Note that they are in different subnets so we will have to route it. When our multilayer switch receives the IP packet this is what will happen:

1. The switch will verify the checksum of the Ethernet frame to make it sure it's not corrupted or altered.
2. The switch will verify the checksum of the IP packet to make it sure it's not corrupted or altered.

The multilayer switch will check the routing table, notices that 192.168.20 /24 is directly connected and the following will happen:

1. Check the ARP table to see if there's a layer 2 to 3 mapping for ComputerB. If there is no mapping the multilayer switch will send an ARP request.
2. The destination MAC address changes from FFF (Multilayer switch Fa0/1) to BBB (ComputerB).
3. The source MAC address changes from AAA (ComputerA) to GGG (Multilayer switch Fa0/2).
4. The TTL (time to live) field in the IP packet is decreased by 1 and because of this the IP header checksum will be recalculated.
5. The Ethernet frame checksum must be recalculated.
6. The Ethernet frame carrying the IP packet will be sent out of the interface towards ComputerB.

As you can see there are quite some steps involved if we want to route IP packets.

When we look at multilayer switches there is a "separation of duties". We have to build a table for the MAC addresses, fill a routing table, ARP requests, check if an IP packet matches an access-list etc and we need to forward our IP packets. These tasks are divided between the "**control plane**" and the "**data**

plane". Let me give you an illustration:

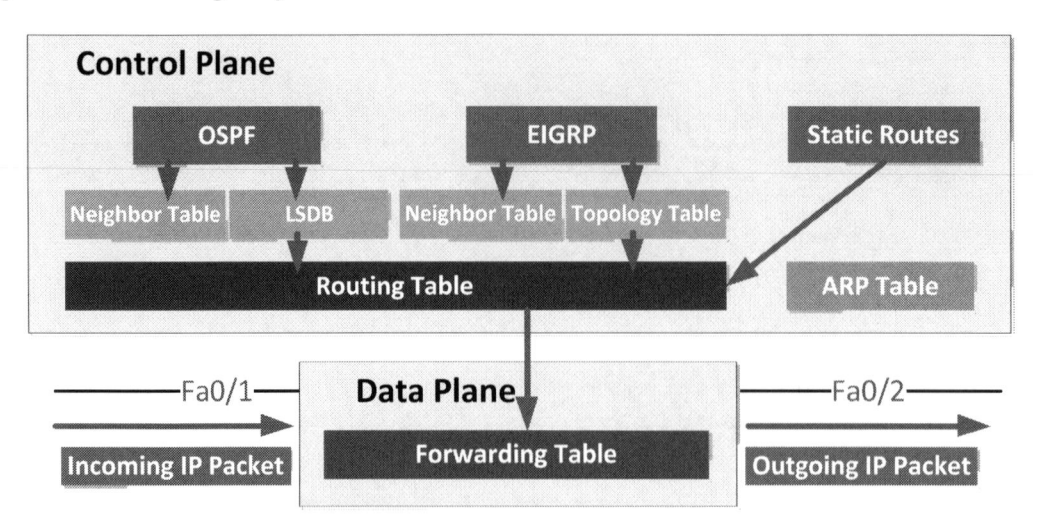

The control plane is responsible for exchanging routing information using routing protocols, building a routing table and ARP table. The data plane is responsible for the actual forwarding of IP packets. The routing table isn't very suitable for fast forwarding because we have to deal with **recursive routing**. What is recursive routing? Let me give you an example:

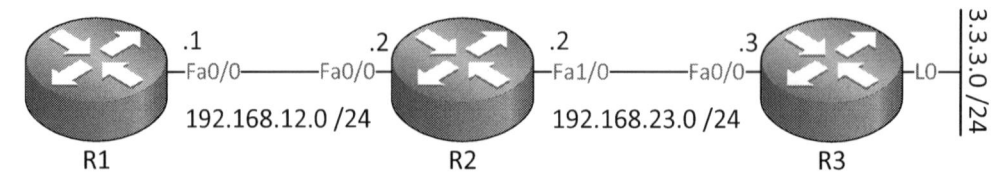

In the example above I have three routers. R3 has a loopback interface that we want to reach from R1. I will use static routes for reachability:

```
R1(config)#ip route 3.3.3.0 255.255.255.0 192.168.23.3
R1(config)#ip route 192.168.23.0 255.255.255.0 192.168.12.2
```

The first static route is to reach the loopback0 interface of R3 and points to the FastEthernet0/0 interface of R3.

12. CEF (Cisco Express Forwarding)

The second static route is required to reach network 192.168.23.0/24.

```
R1#show ip route
Codes: C - connected, S - static, R - RIP, M - mobile, B - BGP
       D - EIGRP, EX - EIGRP external, O - OSPF, IA - OSPF inter area
       N1 - OSPF NSSA external type 1, N2 - OSPF NSSA external type 2
       E1 - OSPF external type 1, E2 - OSPF external type 2
       i - IS-IS, su - IS-IS summary, L1 - IS-IS level-1, L2 - IS-IS level-2
       ia - IS-IS inter area, * - candidate default, per-user static route
       o - ODR, P - periodic downloaded static route

Gateway of last resort is not set

C    192.168.12.0/24 is directly connected, FastEthernet0/0
     3.0.0.0/24 is subnetted, 1 subnets
S       3.3.3.0 [1/0] via 192.168.23.3
S    192.168.23.0/24 [1/0] via 192.168.12.2
```

Whenever R1 wants to reach 3.3.3.0/24 we have to do 3 lookups:

- The first lookup is to check the entry for 3.3.3.0 /24. It's there and the next hop IP address is 192.168.23.3
- The second lookup is for 192.168.23.3. There's an entry and the next hop IP address is 192.168.12.2.
- The third and last lookup is for 192.168.12.2. There's an entry and it is directly connected.

R1 has to check the routing table 3 times before it knows where to send its traffic. Doesn't sound very efficient right? Doing multiple lookups to reach a certain network is called **recursive routing**.

Most of the time all incoming and outgoing IP packets will be processed and forwarded by the data plane but there are some exceptions, first let me show you this picture:

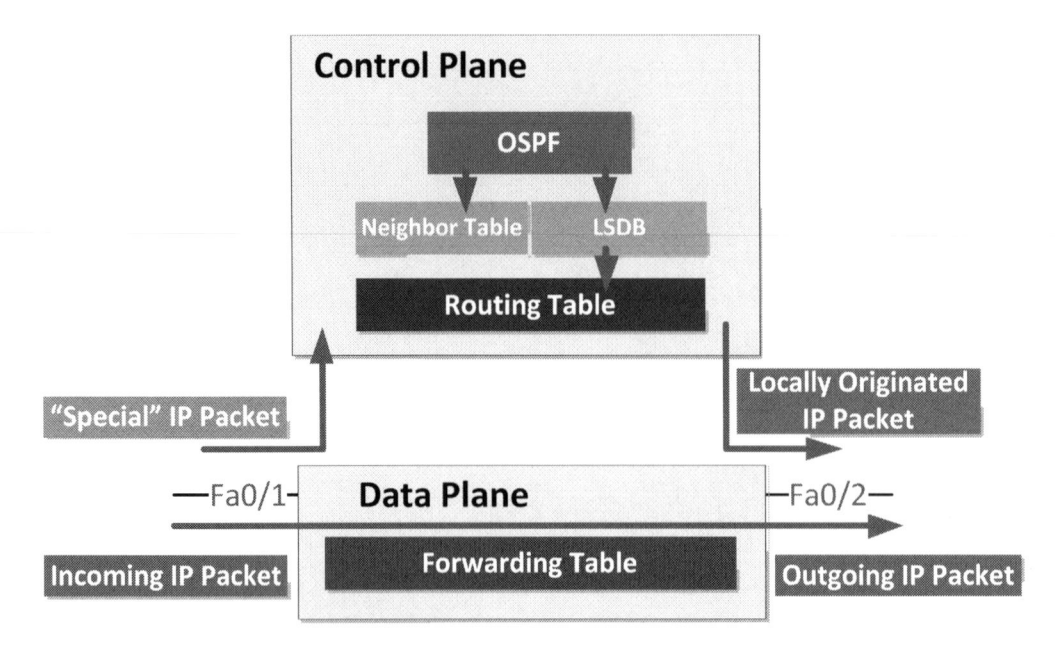

```
                    Control Plane
                    ┌─────────────────────────┐
                    │        OSPF             │
                    │  Neighbor Table  LSDB   │
                    │     Routing Table       │
                    └─────────────────────────┘
"Special" IP Packet                    Locally Originated IP Packet
       ─Fa0/1─   Data Plane   ─Fa0/2─
Incoming IP Packet   Forwarding Table   Outgoing IP Packet
```

Most of the IP packets can be forwarded by the data plane. However there are some "special" IP packets that can't be forwarded by the data plane immediately and they are sent to the control plane, here are some examples:

- IP packets that are destined for one of the IP addresses of the multilayer switch.
- Routing protocol traffic like OSPF, EIGRP or BGP.
- IP packets that have some of the options set in the IP header.
- IP packets with an expired TTL.

The control plane can forward outgoing IP packets to the data plane or use its own forwarding mechanism to determine the outgoing interface and the next hop IP address. An example of this is local policy based routing. If you have never heard about policy based routing, don't worry...it's covered in CCNP ROUTE.

Our multilayer switch has many more steps to take than the layer 2 switches so theoretically it should be slower right?

One reason that multilayer switches are able to forward frames and packets at wirespeed is because of special hardware called ASICs in the dataplane.

Information like MAC addresses, the routing table or access-lists are stored into these ASICs. The tables are stored in **content-addressable memory (CAM)** and **ternary content addressable memory (TCAM)**.

- The CAM table is used to store layer 2 information like:
    - The source MAC address.
    - The interface where we learned the MAC address on.
    - To which VLAN the MAC address belongs.

12. CEF (Cisco Express Forwarding)

Table lookups are fast! Whenever the switch receives an Ethernet frame it will use a hashing algorithm to create a "key" for the destination MAC address + VLAN and it will compare this hash to the already hashed information in the CAM table. This way it is able to quickly lookup information in the CAM table.

- The TCAM table is used to store "higher layer" information like:
    - Access-lists.
    - Quality of service information.
    - Routing table.
- The TCAM table can match on 3 different values:
    - 0 = Don't look.
    - 1 = Compare.
    - X = Any value acceptable.
- Longest match will return a hit.
- Useful for a lookup where we don't need an exact match. (routing table or ACLs for example).

Because there are 3 values we call it *ternary*.

So why are there 2 types of tables?

When we look for a MAC address we always require an **exact match**. We require the exact MAC address if we want to forward an Ethernet frame. The MAC address table is stored in a CAM table.

Whenever we need to match an IP packet against the routing table or an access-list we **don't always need an exact match**. For example an IP packet with destination address 192.168.20.44 will match:

- 192.168.20.44 /32
- 192.168.20.0 /24
- 192.168.0.0 /16

Information like the routing table are stored in a TCAM table for this reason. We can decide whether all or some bits have to match.

Here's an example of a TCAM table:

TCAM L3 Prefix Lookup

192.168.10.22

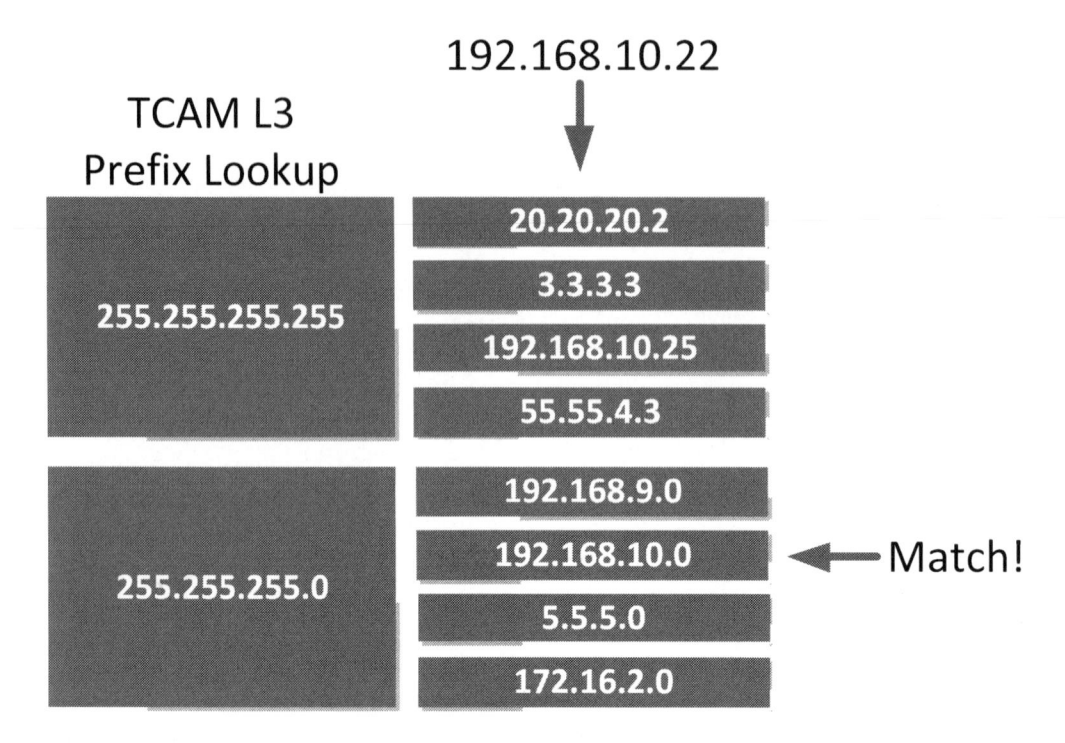

255.255.255.255:
- 20.20.20.2
- 3.3.3.3
- 192.168.10.25
- 55.55.4.3

255.255.255.0:
- 192.168.9.0
- 192.168.10.0 ← Match!
- 5.5.5.0
- 172.16.2.0

If we want to match IP address 192.168.10.22 the multilayer switch will first see if there's a "most specific match". There is nothing that matches 192.168.10.22 /32 so we'll continue if there is anything else that matches. In this case there is an entry that matches 192.168.10.0 /24. The example above applies to routing table lookups, access-lists but also quality of service, VLAN access-lists and more.

Now you know all the steps a multilayer switch has to take when it has to forward ip packets, the control/data plane and that we use different tables stored in special hardware called ASICs. Let's take a closer look at the actual 'forwarding' of IP packets.

There are different **switching methods** to forward IP packets.

12. CEF (Cisco Express Forwarding)

Here are the different switching options:

- **Process switching**:
    - All packets are examined by the CPU and all forwarding decisions are made in software...very slow!
- **Fast switching** (also known as **route caching**):
    - The first packet in a flow is examined by the CPU; the forwarding decision is cached in hardware for the next packets in the same flow. This is a faster method.
- **(CEF) Cisco Express Forwarding** (also known as **topology based switching**):
    - Forwarding table created in hardware beforehand. All packets will be switched using hardware. This is the fastest method but there are some limitations. Multilayer switches and routers use CEF.

When using **process switching** the router will remove the header for each Ethernet frame, look for the destination IP address in the routing table for each IP packet and then forward the Ethernet frame with the rewritten MAC addresses and CRC to the outgoing interface. Everything is done in software so this is very CPU-intensive.

Fast switching is more efficient because it will lookup the first IP packet but it will store the forwarding decision in the fast switching cache. When the routers receive Ethernet frames carrying IP packets in the same flow it can use the information in the cache to forward them to the correct outgoing interface.

The default for routers is **CEF (Cisco Express Forwarding)**. Let's take a closer look at CEF:

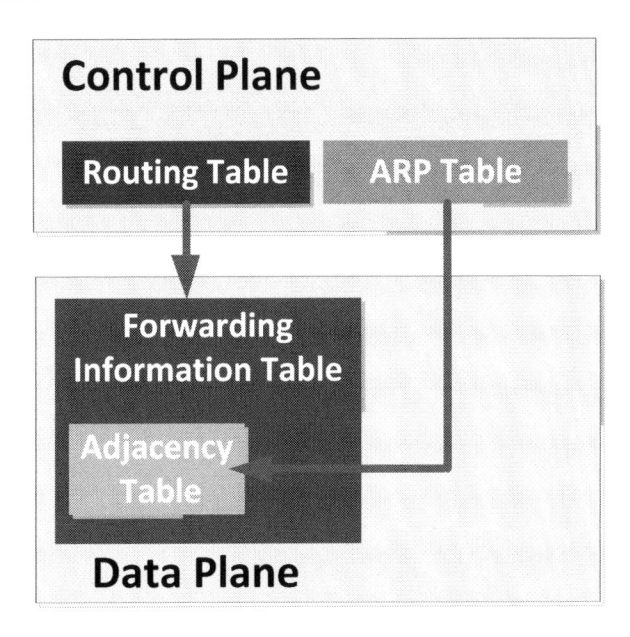

How to Master CCNP SWITCH

The multilayer switch will use the information from tables that are built by the (control plane) **to build hardware tables**. It will use the routing table to build **the FIB (Forwarding Information Base)** and the ARP table to build the **adjacency table**. This is the fastest switching method because we now have all the layer 2 and 3 information required to forward IP packets in hardware.

Are you following me so far? Let's take a look at the forwarding information table and the adjacency table on some routers. If you want to follow me along you can take a look at your multilayer switch OR use routers in GNS3:

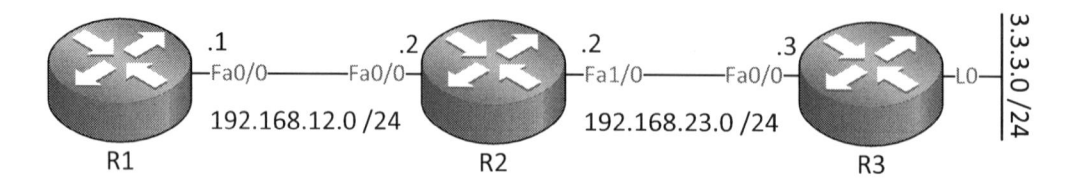

I'll use the same topology that I showed you earlier. 3 routers and R3 has a loopback0 interface. I'll use static routes to have full connectivity:

```
R1(config)#ip route 3.3.3.0 255.255.255.0 192.168.23.3
R1(config)#ip route 192.168.23.0 255.255.255.0 192.168.12.2
```

```
R2(config)#ip route 3.3.3.0 255.255.255.0 192.168.23.3
```

```
R3(config)#ip route 192.168.12.0 255.255.255.0 192.168.23.2
```

These are the static routes that I'll use.
Now let me show you the routing and FIB table:

```
R1#show ip route
Codes: C - connected, S - static, R - RIP, M - mobile, B - BGP
       D - EIGRP, EX - EIGRP external, O - OSPF, IA - OSPF inter area
       N1 - OSPF NSSA external type 1, N2 - OSPF NSSA external type 2
       E1 - OSPF external type 1, E2 - OSPF external type 2
       i - IS-IS, su - IS-IS summary, L1 - IS-IS level-1, L2 - IS-IS level-2
       ia - IS-IS inter area, * - candidate default, U - per-user static route
       o - ODR, P - periodic downloaded static route

Gateway of last resort is not set

C    192.168.12.0/24 is directly connected, FastEthernet0/0
     3.0.0.0/24 is subnetted, 1 subnets
S       3.3.3.0 [1/0] via 192.168.23.3
S    192.168.23.0/24 [1/0] via 192.168.12.2
```

276

12. CEF (Cisco Express Forwarding)

```
R1#show ip cef
Prefix                  Next Hop              Interface
0.0.0.0/0               drop                  Null0 (default route
handler entry)
0.0.0.0/32              receive
3.3.3.0/24              192.168.12.2          FastEthernet0/0
192.168.12.0/24         attached              FastEthernet0/0
192.168.12.0/32         receive
192.168.12.1/32         receive
192.168.12.2/32         192.168.12.2          FastEthernet0/0
192.168.12.255/32       receive
192.168.23.0/24         192.168.12.2          FastEthernet0/0
224.0.0.0/4             drop
224.0.0.0/24            receive
255.255.255.255/32      receive
```

Show ip cef reveals the FIB table to us. You can see there's quite some stuff in the FIB table, let me explain some of the entries:

- 0.0.0.0/0 is for the null0 interface. When we receive IP packets that match this rule then it will be dropped.
- 0.0.0.0/32 is for all-zero broadcasts. Forget about this one since we don't use it anymore.
- 3.3.3.0/24 is the entry for the loopback0 interface of R3. Note that the next hop is 192.168.12.2 and NOT 192.168.23.3 as in the routing table!
- 192.168.12.0/24 is our directly connected network.
- 192.168.12.0/32 is reserved for the exact network address.
- 192.168.12.1/32 is the IP address on interface FastEthernet 0/0.
- 192.168.12.2/32 is the IP address on R2's FastEthernet 0/0 interface.
- 192.168.12.255/32 is the broadcast address for network 192.168.12.0/24.
- 224.0.0.0/4 matches all multicast traffic. It will be dropped if multicast support is disabled globally.
- 224.0.0.0/24 matches all multicast traffic that is reserved for local network control traffic (for example OSPF, EIGRP).
- 255.255.255.255/32 is the broadcast address for a subnet.

Let's take a detailed look at the entry for network 3.3.3.0 /24:

```
R1#show ip cef 3.3.3.0
3.3.3.0/24, version 8, epoch 0, cached adjacency 192.168.12.2
0 packets, 0 bytes
  via 192.168.23.3, 0 dependencies, recursive
    next hop 192.168.12.2, FastEthernet0/0 via 192.168.23.0/24
    valid cached adjacency
```

The version number tells us how often this CEF entry was updated since the table was generated. We can see that in order to reach 3.3.3.0/24 we need to go to 192.168.23.3 and that a recursive lookup is required. The next hop is 192.168.12.2. It also says that it's a **valid cached adjacency**. There are a number of different adjacencies:

- **Null adjacency**: used to send packets to the null0 interface.
- **Drop adjacency**: you'll see this for packets that can't be forwarded because of encapsulation errors, routes that cannot be resolved or protocols that are not supported.
- **Discard adjacency**: This is for packets that have to be discarded because of an access-list or other policy.
- **Punt adjacency**: Used for packets that are sent to the control plane for processing.

Packets that are not forwarded by CEF are handled by the CPU. If you have many of those packets then you might see performance issues. You can see how many packets have been handled by the CPU:

```
R1#show cef not-cef-switched
CEF Packets passed on to next switching layer
Slot  No_adj No_encap Unsupp'ted Redirect  Receive  Options
Access       Frag
RP          0       0          0         0        17        0
0           0
```

You can use the **show cef not-cef-switched** command to verify this; the number of packets are listed per reason:

- **No_adj**: adjacency is incomplete.
- **No_encap**: ARP information is incomplete.
- **Unsupp'ted**: packet has features that are not supported.
- **Redirect**: ICMP redirect.
- **Receive**: These are the packets that were destined for an IP address configured on a layer 3 interface, packets that are meant for our router.
- **Options:** There are IP options in the header of the packet.
- **Access:** access-list evaluation failure.
- **Frag:** packet fragmention error.

We can also take a look at the adjacency table that stores the layer 2 information for each entry:

```
R1#show adjacency summary
Adjacency Table has 1 adjacency
  Table epoch: 0 (1 entry at this epoch)

  Interface                    Adjacency Count
  FastEthernet0/0              1
```

You can use the **show adjacency summary** command to take a quick look how many adjacencies we have. An adjacency is a mapping from layer 2 to 3 and comes from the ARP table.

12. CEF (Cisco Express Forwarding)

```
R1#show adjacency
Protocol Interface                 Address
IP       FastEthernet0/0           192.168.12.2(9)
```

R1 only has a single interface that is connected to R2. You can see the entry for 192.168.12.2 which is the FastEthernet 0/0 interface of R2. Let's zoom in on this entry:

```
R1#show adjacency detail
Protocol Interface                 Address
IP       FastEthernet0/0           192.168.12.2(9)
                                   0 packets, 0 bytes
                                   CC011D800000CC001D8000000800
                                   ARP         03:55:00
                                   Epoch: 0
```

We can see there's an entry for 192.168.12.2 and it says:

CC011D800000CC001D8000000800

What does this number mean? It's the MAC addresses that we require and the Ethertype...let me break it down for you:

- CC011D800000 is the MAC address of R2's FastEthernet0/0 interface.

```
R2#show interfaces fastEthernet 0/0
FastEthernet0/0 is up, line protocol is up
  Hardware is AmdFE, address is cc01.1d80.0000 (bia
cc01.1d80.0000)
```

- CC001D800000 is the MAC address of R1's FastEthernet0/0 interface.

```
R1#show interfaces fastEthernet 0/0
FastEthernet0/0 is up, line protocol is up
  Hardware is AmdFE, address is cc00.1d80.0000 (bia
cc00.1d80.0000)
```

- 0800 is the Ethertype. 0x800 stands for IPv4.

Thanks to the FIB and adjacency table we have all the layer 2 and 3 information that we require to rewrite and forward packets. Keep in mind before actually forwarding the packet we first have to rewrite the header information:

- Source MAC address.
- Destination MAC address.
- Ethernet frame checksum.
- IP Packet TTL.
- IP Packet Checksum.

Once this is done we can forward the packet. Now you have an idea what CEF is about and how packets are dealt with.

Every now and then students ask me what the difference is between routers and switches since a multilayer switch can route, and a router can do switching if you want.

Courtesy of Cisco Systems, Inc. Unauthorized use not permitted.

The difference is getting smaller but switches normally only use Ethernet. If you buy a Cisco Catalyst 3560 or 3750 you'll only have Ethernet interfaces. They have ASICs so switching of frames can be done at wire speed. Routers on the other hand have other interfaces like serial links, wireless and they can be upgraded with modules for VPN, VoIP etc. You can't configure stuff like NAT/PAT on a (small) switch. The line is getting thinner however...

Routers are used for routing, layer 2 switches for switching but multilayer switches can do a combination of both. Maybe your switch is doing 80% switching and 20% routing or vice versa. The TCAM can be "programmed" to make use of optimal resources by using SDM templates.

SDM (Switching Database Manager) is used on Cisco Catalyst switches to manage the memory usage of the TCAM. For example, a switch that is only used for switching won't require any memory to store IPv4 routing information. On the other hand, a switch that is only used as a router won't need much memory to store MAC addresses.

SDM offers a number of templates that we can use on our switch.

12. CEF (Cisco Express Forwarding)

Here's an example of a Cisco Catalyst 3560 switch:

```
SW1#show sdm prefer
 The current template is "desktop default" template.
 The selected template optimizes the resources in
 the switch to support this level of features for
 8 routed interfaces and 1024 VLANs.

  number of unicast mac addresses:                 6K
  number of IPv4 IGMP groups + multicast routes:   1K
  number of IPv4 unicast routes:                   8K
    number of directly-connected IPv4 hosts:       6K
    number of indirect IPv4 routes:                2K
  number of IPv4 policy based routing aces:        0
  number of IPv4/MAC qos aces:                     0.5K
  number of IPv4/MAC security aces:                1K
```

Above you can see that the current template is "desktop default" and you can see how much memory it reserves for the different items. Here's an example of the other templates:

```
SW1#show sdm prefer ?
  access              Access bias
  default             Default bias
  dual-ipv4-and-ipv6  Support both IPv4 and IPv6
  ipe                 IPe bias
  routing             Unicast bias
  vlan                VLAN bias
  |                   Output modifiers
  <cr>
```

Here are the SDM templates for the switch. We can change the template with the **sdm prefer** command:

```
SW1(config)#sdm prefer vlan
Changes to the running SDM preferences have been stored, but cannot take effect
until the next reload.
Use 'show sdm prefer' to see what SDM preference is currently active.
```

You have to reload before it takes effect:

```
SW1#reload
```

281

Now let's check the template again:

```
SW1#show sdm prefer
 The current template is "desktop vlan" template.
 The selected template optimizes the resources in
 the switch to support this level of features for
 8 routed interfaces and 1024 VLANs.

   number of unicast mac addresses:                  12K
   number of IPv4 IGMP groups + multicast routes:    1K
   number of IPv4 unicast routes:                    0
   number of IPv4 policy based routing aces:         0
   number of IPv4/MAC qos aces:                      0.5K
   number of IPv4/MAC security aces:                 1K
```

Compared to the "desktop default" template we now have double the storage for unicast MAC addresses. There is nothing reserved for IPv4 routes though.

It's a good idea to set the SDM template to match something for the intended use of your switch. If you are doing both switching and routing and unsure about what template to pick then you might want to look at the current usage of the TCAM, here's how to do it:

```
SW1#show platform tcam utilization

CAM Utilization for ASIC# 0                        Max
Used
                                                   Masks/Values
Masks/values

 Unicast mac addresses:                            784/6272
13/26
 IPv4 IGMP groups + multicast routes:              144/1152
6/26
 IPv4 unicast directly-connected routes:           784/6272
13/26
 IPv4 unicast indirectly-connected routes:         272/2176
8/44
 IPv4 policy based routing aces:                   0/0
0/0
 IPv4 qos aces:                                    768/768
260/260
 IPv4 security aces:                               1024/1024
27/27
```

My (lab) switch isn't doing much but you can see how the TCAM is filled at the moment. Now you have something to compare with the SDM templates.

12. CEF (Cisco Express Forwarding)

If you want to see CEF in action I would recommend you to play with the commands I just showed you when you are doing labs. Just take a look at the FIB and adjacency tables when you are doing some routing labs. To practice the SDM template, try switching the template once and also compare the different SDM templates to see their differences.

13. SPAN and RSPAN

Cisco Catalyst Switches have a feature called SPAN (Switch Port Analyzer) that lets you **copy all traffic from a source port or source VLAN** to a destination interface. This is very useful for a number of reasons:

- If you want to use wireshark to capture traffic from an interface that is connected to a workstation, server, phone or anything else you want to sniff.
- Redirect all traffic from a VLAN to an IDS / IPS.
- Redirect all VoIP calls from a VLAN so you can record the calls.

The source can be an interface or a VLAN, the destination is an interface. You can choose if you want to forward **transmitted, received or both directions** to the destination interface.

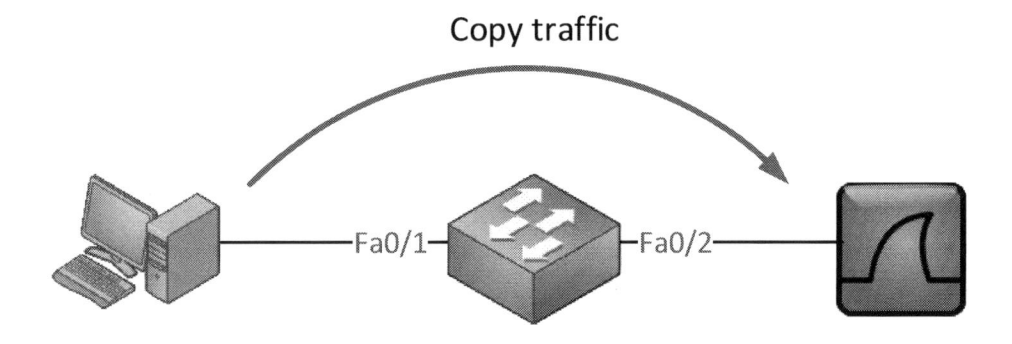

When you use a destination interface on the same switch as your switch we call it SPAN, when the destination is a remote interface on another switch we call it **RSPAN** (Remote SPAN). When using RSPAN you need to use a VLAN for your RSPAN traffic so that traffic can travel from the source switch to the destination switch.

Copy traffic

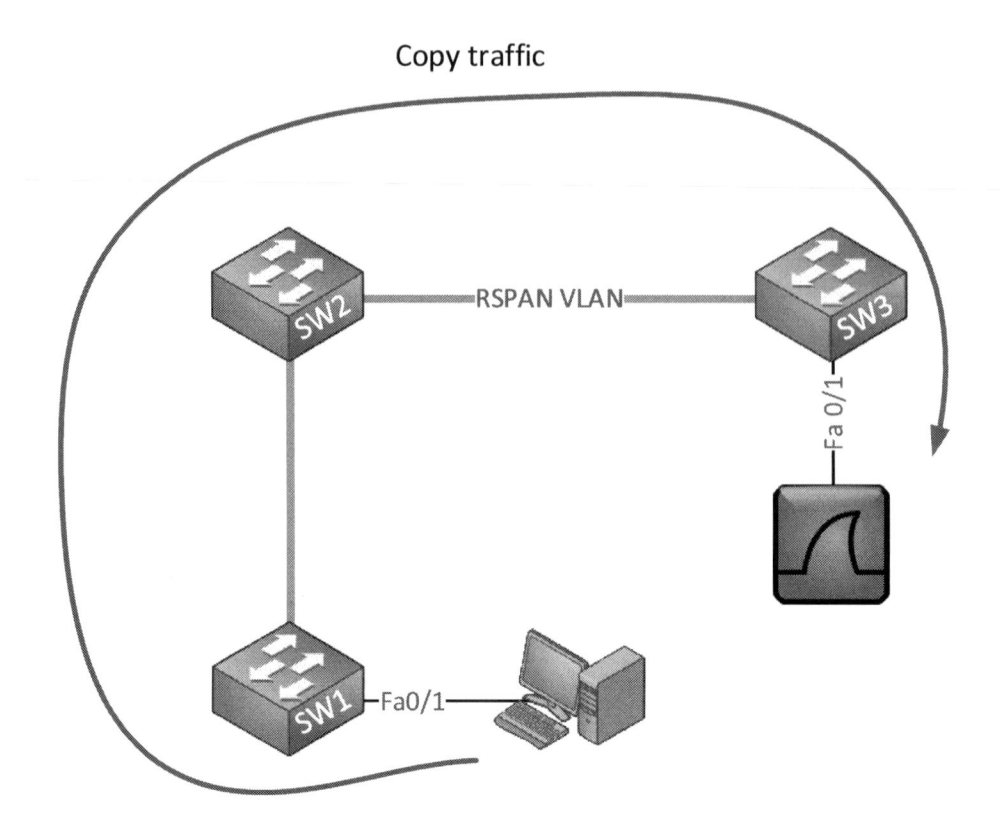

When you use RSPAN you need to use a VLAN that carries the traffic that you are copying. In the picture above you see SW1 which will copy the traffic from the computer onto a "RSPAN VLAN". SW2 doesn't do anything with it while SW3 receives the traffic and forwards it to a computer that has wireshark running. Make sure the trunks between the switches **allow the RSPAN VLAN**.

SPAN and RSPAN are great tools but there are some restrictions:

- The source interface can be anything…switchport, routed port, access port, trunk port, etherchannel, etc.
- When you configure a trunk as the source interface it will copy traffic from all VLANs, however there is an option to filter this.
- You can use multiple source interfaces or a single VLAN, but you can't mix interfaces and VLANs.
- It's very simple to overload an interface. When you select an entire VLAN as the source and use a 100Mbit destination interface…it might be too much.
- When you configure a destination port you will lose its configuration. When you remove SPAN, the configuration is restored. In short…you can't use the destination interface for anything else besides receiving traffic.

13. SPAN and RSPAN

- Layer 2 frames like CDP, VTP, DTP and spanning-tree BPDUs are not copied by default but you can tell SPAN/RSPAN to copy them anyway.

This should give you an idea of what SPAN / RSPAN are capable of. The configuration is pretty straight-forward so let me give you some examples…let's start with SPAN:

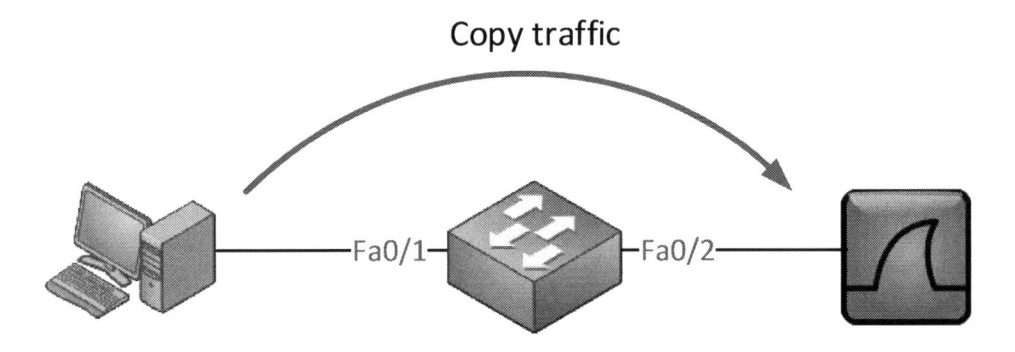

Copy traffic

—Fa0/1— —Fa0/2—

```
Switch(config)#monitor session 1 source interface fa0/1
Switch(config)#monitor session 1 destination interface fa0/2
```

These commands are pretty straight-forward. We use a session number (1) and select a source and destination interface. You can verify the configuration like this:

```
Switch#show monitor session 1
Session 1
---------
Type                   : Local Session
Source Ports           :
    Both               : Fa0/1
Destination Ports      : Fa0/2
    Encapsulation      : Native
          Ingress      : Disabled
```

As you can see, by default it will copy traffic that is transmitted and received (both) to the destination port. If you only want the capture the traffic going in one direction you have to specify it like this:

```
Switch(config)#monitor session 1 source interface fa0/1 ?
  ,     Specify another range of interfaces
  -     Specify a range of interfaces
  both  Monitor received and transmitted traffic
  rx    Monitor received traffic only
  tx    Monitor transmitted traffic only
```

Just add rx or tx and you are ready to go. If interface FastEthernet 0/1 were a

287

trunk you could add a filter to select the VLANs you want to forward:

```
Switch(config)#monitor session 1 filter vlan 1 - 100
```

This will filter VLAN 1 – 100 from being forwarded. If you don't want to use an interface as the source but a VLAN, you can do it like this:

```
Switch(config)#monitor session 2 source vlan 1
Switch(config)#monitor session 2 destination interface fa0/3
```

I am unable to use session 1 for this because I am already using source interfaces for that session. It's also impossible to use the same destination interface for another session. This is why I created another session number and picked FastEthernet 0/3 as a destination. So far so good? Let's look at RSPAN!

This is the topology we will use:

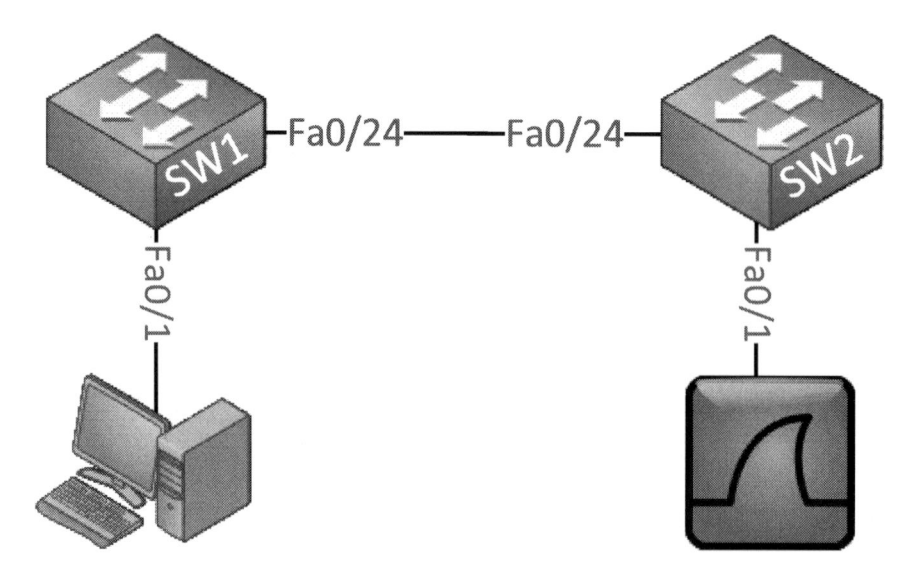

The idea is to forward traffic from FastEthernet 0/1 on SW1 to FastEthernet 0/1 on SW2. There are a couple of things we have to configure here:

```
SW1(config)#vlan 100
SW1(config-vlan)#remote-span
```

```
SW2(config)#vlan 100
SW2(config-vlan)#remote-span
```

First we need to create the VLAN and tell the switches that it's a RSPAN vlan.

13. SPAN and RSPAN

This is something that is easily forgotten. Secondly we will configure the link between the two switches as a trunk:

```
SW1(config)#interface fastEthernet 0/24
SW1(config-if)#switchport trunk encapsulation dot1q
SW1(config-if)#switchport mode trunk
```

```
SW2(config)#interface fastEthernet 0/24
SW2(config-if)#switchport trunk encapsulation dot1q
SW2(config-if)#switchport mode trunk
```

Now we can configure RSPAN:

```
SW1(config)#monitor session 1 source interface fastEthernet 0/1
SW1(config)#monitor session 1 destination remote vlan 100
```

This selects FastEthernet 0/1 as the source and VLAN 100 as the destination...

```
SW2(config)#monitor session 1 source remote vlan 100
SW2(config)#monitor session 1 destination interface fastEthernet 0/1
```

And on SW2 we select VLAN 100 as the source and FastEthernet 0/1 as its destination. Here's the output of the show monitor session command:

```
SW1#show monitor session 1
Session 1
---------
Type                   : Remote Source Session
Source Ports           :
    Both               : Fa0/1
Dest RSPAN VLAN        : 100
```

```
SW2#show monitor session 1
Session 1
---------
Type                   : Remote Destination Session
Source RSPAN VLAN      : 100
Destination Ports      : Fa0/1
    Encapsulation      : Native
          Ingress      : Disabled
```

All traffic from FastEthernet 0/1 on SW1 will now be copied to interface FastEthernet 0/1 on SW2. That's all there is to it!

14. High Availability / Switch Virtualization

In the first chapter of this book you learned about campus network designs and how we use different layers and "switch blocks" to create a hierarchical design that has redundant links.

You also learned in the spanning-tree chapters how spanning-tree creates a loop-free topology by blocking some of the redundant links. The thing with spanning-tree is that we have a loop-free topology, we have redundancy but **we can't use all the redundant links** for forwarding. Here's an illustration to visualize this:

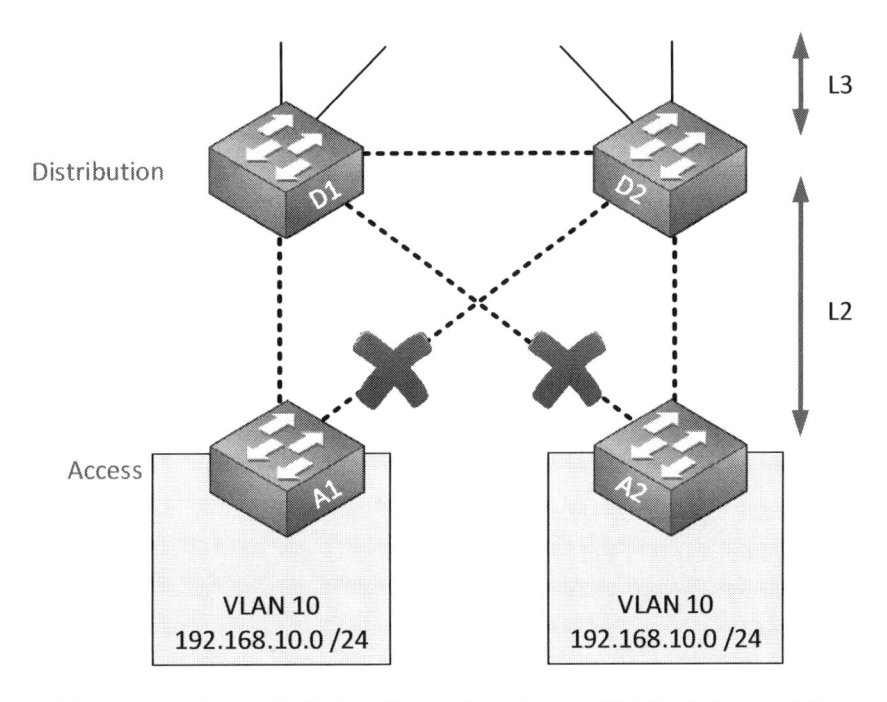

The dashed lines are layer 2 links. Spanning-tree will block two of these links to create a loop-free topology. Another issue with this topology is that we do have redundancy in the distribution (and core) layer but we don't have redundancy in the access layer.

When one of the distribution layer switches fails, the other one can take over. We don't have this luxury in the access layer…when either of the switches fails then the other one can't take over.

One way of solving this problem is to create a **logical switch**. Cisco switches offer some technologies to convert two or more physical switches into a single logical switch, it will look like this:

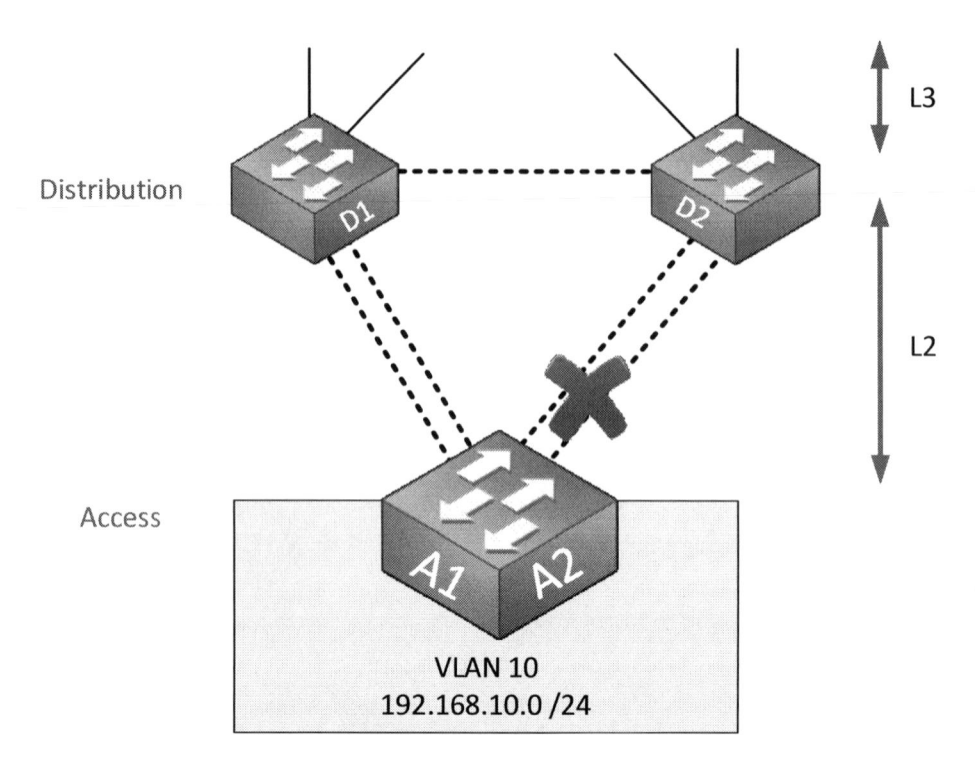

A1 and A2 are two physical switches but they are combined into a single logical switch. The distribution layer switches think that they are connected to one access layer switch. The uplink pairs to each distribution layer switch can be combined into an Etherchannel.

When the link between D1 and D2 is a layer 2 link, spanning-tree will still have to block one of the etherchannels.

We can improve this topology by doing the same thing in the distribution layer, combining the two physical distribution layer switches into a single logical switch:

14. High Availability / Switch Virtualization

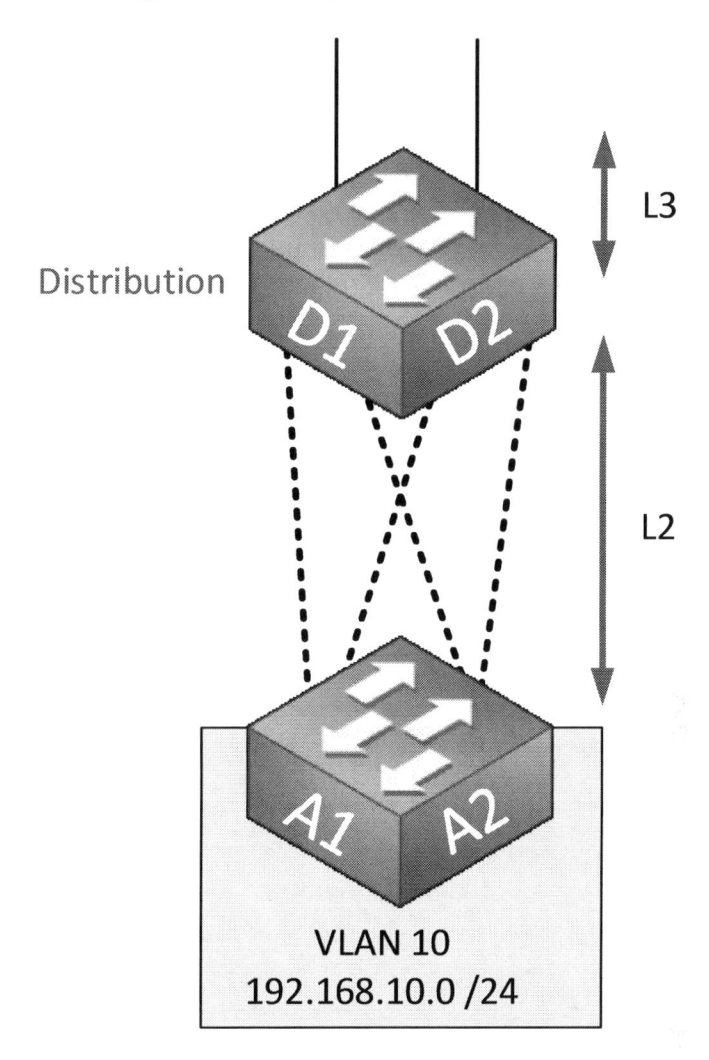

Distribution

VLAN 10
192.168.10.0 /24

The two distribution layer switches are now combined into a single logical switch. The four links between the switch pairs can be combined into a **single etherchannel**. Since we now have a single link between the two logical switches, spanning-tree doesn't have to block anything. Normally we can't create an etherchannel that spans multiple physical switches. By creating logical switches, this is no problem. An etherchannel like this between multiple physical switches is also called **Multi-Chassis Etherchannel**.

Combining multiple physical switches into logical switches makes our network topology a LOT simpler, here's a "before and after" example:

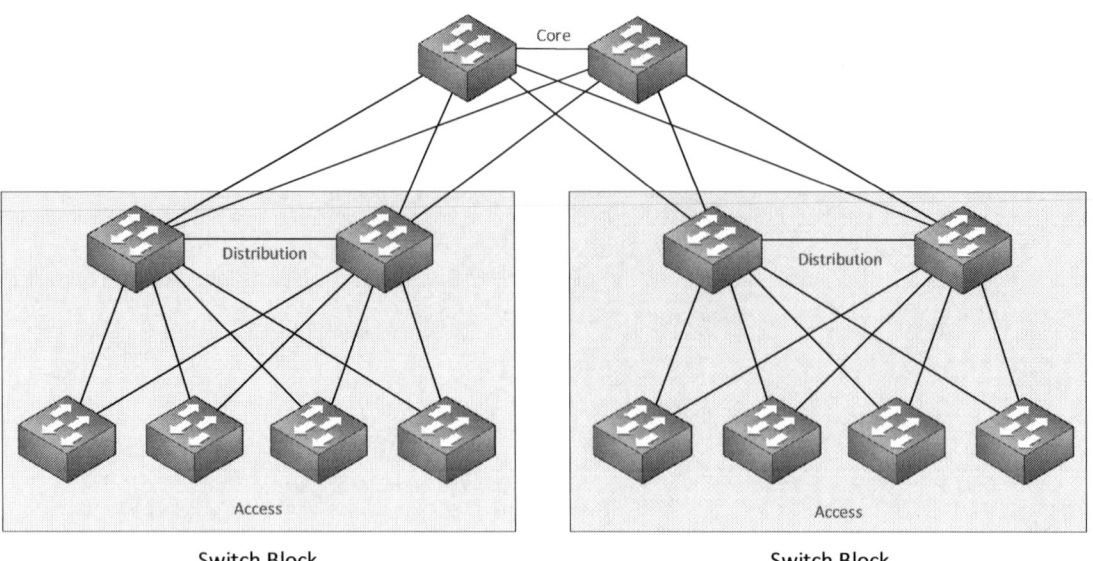

How to Master CCNP SWITCH

Above you see the "regular" network design with only physical switches. Here's what it looks like with "logical" switches:

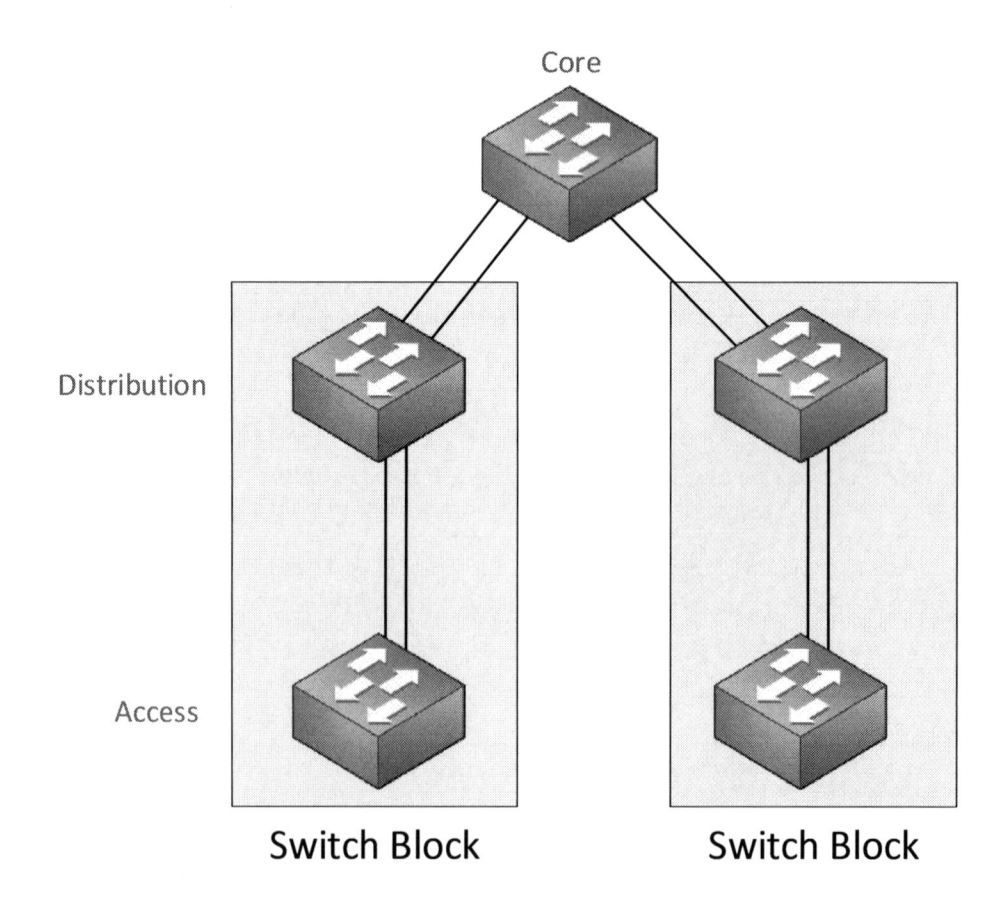

Switch Block   **Switch Block**

14. High Availability / Switch Virtualization

The picture above looks really clean and simple. Each switch picture represents multiple physical switches that have been combined into a single logical switch. The redundant links between each switch pair can be configured as an Etherchannel.

You should now have an idea of the advantages of combining physical switches into logical switches. Let's take a look at the technologies that can achieve this.

The first technology is called Stackwise. Stackwise is typically used for access layer switches and available on models like the 3750, 3750-X and 3850.

Switches that support Stackwise use a special stacking cable to connect the switches to each other. Each switch has two stacking connectors that are used to "daisy-chain" (loop) the switches together. Each switch is connected to the one below it and the bottom switch will be connected to the one on top.

The Stackwise cable is like an extension of the switching fabric of the switches. When an Ethernet frame has to be moved from one physical switch to another, the Stackwise "loop" is used. The advantage of using a cabled loop is that you can remove one switch from the stack, the loop will be broken but the stack will keep working.

One switch in the stack becomes the **master** that does all "management tasks" for the stack. All other switches are **members**. If the master fails, another member will become the new member.

To select a master, Stackwise uses an election process that checks for the following criteria (in order of importance):

1. **User priority**: we can configure a priority to decide which switch becomes the master.
2. **Hardware / software priority**: The switch with the most extensive feature set has a higher priority than another switch (for example: IP Services vs IP base).
3. **Default Configuration**: A switch that already has a configuration will take precedence over switches with no configuration.
4. **Uptime**: The switch with the longest uptime.
5. **MAC address**: The switch with the lowest MAC address.

It makes sense to choose the master ourselves so normally we use user priority to configure the master.
Once the stack has been created, the configuration of the switches is the same as if it were one single switch...they share the same management IP address, hostname, etc.

Here's a picture of the stacking connectors, this is the rear of a Cisco Catalyst 3750 switch:

Courtesy of Cisco Systems, Inc. Unauthorized use not permitted.

You can see the two connectors on the left side...Stack1 and Stack 2. Here's what the Stackwise cable looks like:

Let's take a look at the configuration of Stackwise. I'll use two 3750 switches

14. High Availability / Switch Virtualization

for this. Make sure they are all powered off and then cable them like this:

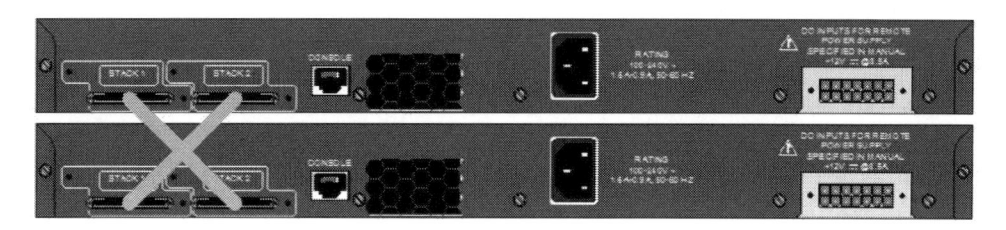

First I will start the switch that I want to become the Master, i'll use the one on top for this. Once you start it with the cables connected, you'll see some Stackwise information during boot:

```
SM: Detected stack cables at PORT1 PORT2

Waiting for Stack Master Election...
SM: Waiting for other switches in stack to boot...
######################################################
SM: All possible switches in stack are booted up

Election Complete
Switch 1 booting as Master
Waiting for Port download...Complete

%STACKMGR-4-SWITCH_ADDED: Switch 1 has been ADDED to the stack
%STACKMGR-5-SWITCH_READY: Switch 1 is READY
%STACKMGR-4-STACK_LINK_CHANGE: Stack Port 1 Switch 1 has changed
to state DOWN
%STACKMGR-4-STACK_LINK_CHANGE: Stack Port 2 Switch 1 has changed
to state DOWN
%STACKMGR-5-MASTER_READY: Master Switch 1 is READY
```

Our switch detected the stacking cables and does an election to see who will become the master. By default each switch will think that it's switch number 1 and the master. I'll change the user priority to make sure that this switch will always be selected as the master:

```
SW1(config)#switch 1 priority 15
Changing the Switch Priority of Switch Number 1 to 15
Do you want to continue?[confirm]
New Priority has been set successfully
```

To make sure the new user priority will be used, we'll save our configuration and reboot the switch:

```
SW1#copy running-config startup-config
SW1#reload
```

Once SW1 is back up and running, we'll power on the second switch. This is

297

what you will see on the console:

```
SW2#
SM: Detected stack cables at PORT1 PORT2

Waiting for Stack Master Election...

Election Complete
Switch 2 booting as Member, Switch 1 elected Master
HCOMP: Compatibility check PASSED
Waiting for feature sync....
Waiting for Port download...Complete
Stack Master is ready
```

You can see that the election was succesful, the second switch has become the member. This is looking good so let's verify our work

```
SW1#show switch
Switch/Stack Mac Address : 0011.214e.d180
                                       H/W     Current
Switch#   Role    Mac Address      Priority Version  State
-----------------------------------------------------------
*1        Master  0011.214e.d180      15      0       Ready
 2        Member  0016.c762.6c80       1      0       Ready
```

The **show switch** command tells us that we have a master and member, you can also see the user priority and the switch numbers. We can also verify if both stack connectors are used or not:

```
SW1#show switch stack-ports
   Switch #    Port 1       Port 2
   --------    ------       ------
      1          Ok           Ok
      2          Ok           Ok
```

Both switches have two stack ports that are up and running. We can also check the bandwidth that Stackwise offers:

```
SW1#show switch stack-ring speed

Stack Ring Speed         : 32G
Stack Ring Configuration: Full
Stack Ring Protocol      : StackWise
```

This tells us the ring speed is 32 Gbit and the configuration is "Full". This means that we have a daisy-chained loop, if you only use a single Stackwise cable then this command will show only 16 Gbit for the ring speed and the ring configuration will be "Half".

Our two switches have been combined into a single logical switch, here's what

14. High Availability / Switch Virtualization

the interface numbers now look like:

```
SW1#show ip interface brief | include Fast
FastEthernet1/0/1      unassigned      YES unset   down
down
FastEthernet1/0/2      unassigned      YES unset   down
down
FastEthernet1/0/3      unassigned      YES unset   down
down
FastEthernet1/0/4      unassigned      YES unset   down
down
[output omitted]
FastEthernet2/0/1      unassigned      YES unset   down
down
FastEthernet2/0/2      unassigned      YES unset   down
down
FastEthernet2/0/3      unassigned      YES unset   down
down
FastEthernet2/0/4      unassigned      YES unset   down
down
[output omitted]
```

The interfaces on the first switch use the FastEthernet1/0/X format and the interfaces on the second switch use the FastEthernet2/0/X format.

That's all there is to configuring Stackwise. The next technology we will look at is supervisor redundancy.

Cisco has a number of switches that are based on a chassis (for example the 4500R, 6500 and 8500) that has slots that we can use for switching modules. The chassis requires a "supervisor module" which does all the management tasks. You can insert a second supervisor in the chassis for redundancy. When the first one fails, the second one will take over. The same thing applies to power, these chassis' offer redundant power supplies.

The first supervisor that boots will become the active supervisor for the chassis. The second one will be in standby, it will take over when the active supervisor fails.

There are a number of different "redundancy" modes that the supervisors can use:

- **RPR (Route Processor Redundancy)**: The redundant supervisor is partially booted and initialized. When the active supervisor fails, the standby supervisor has to reload every module in the switch and initialize all supervisor functions. This is the slowest redundancy method. Failover takes at least 2 minutes.
- **RPR+ (Route Processor Redundancy Plus)**: The redundant supervisor boots and is initialized. Layer 2 and 3 functions are not started, when the active supervisor fails then the standby supervisor

will finish its initialization without reloading switch modules. Failover takes at least 30 seconds.
- **Stateful Switchover (SSO)**: The redundant supervisor is fully booted and initialized. The startup and running configuration is synced between the active and standby supervisor. Layer 2 information is synced between the supervisors, hardware forwarding can continue even during a failover. Interface states are also maintained so that you won't see any flapping interfaces during failover. This is the fastest method and can be done in about 0-3 seconds.

Here's a graphical overview with the differences between RPR, RPR+ and SSO:

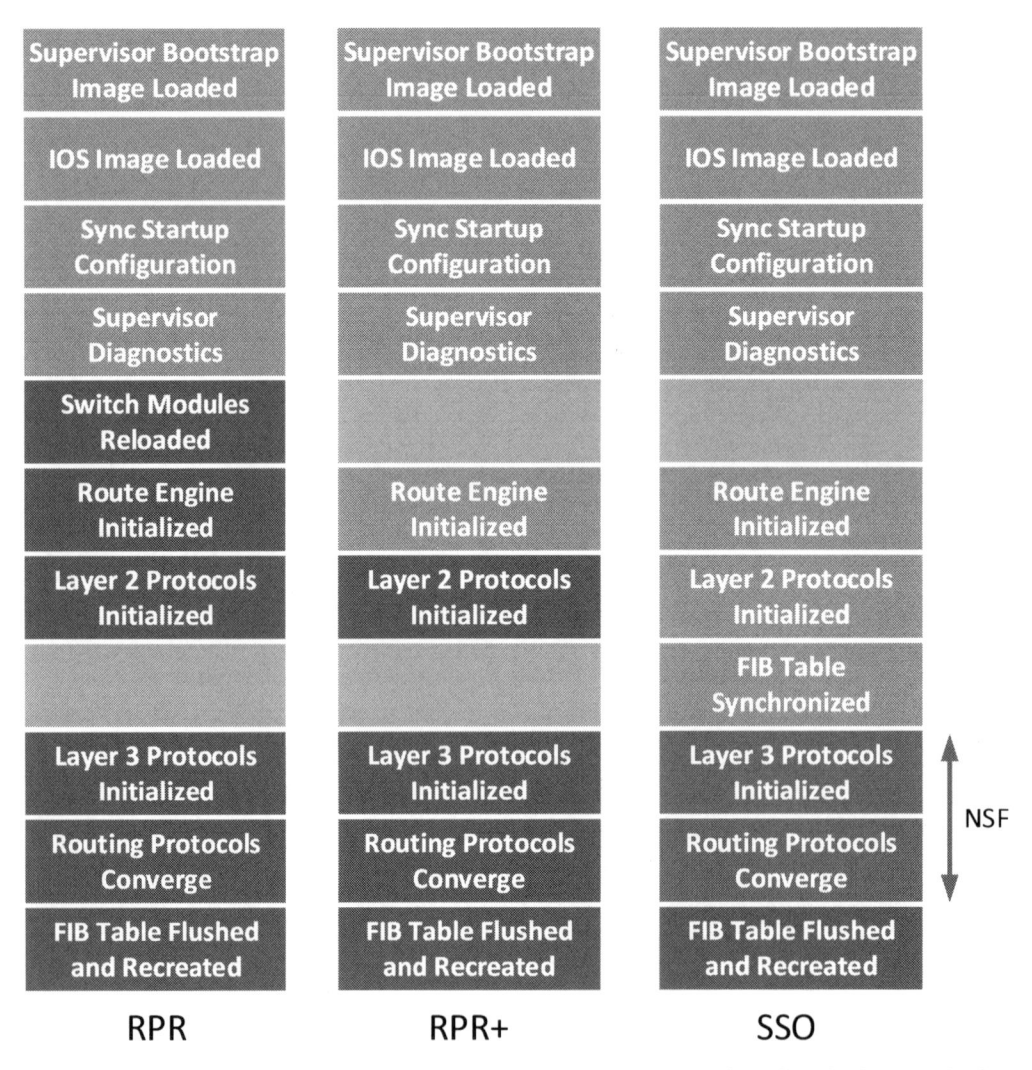

RPR	RPR+	SSO
Supervisor Bootstrap Image Loaded	Supervisor Bootstrap Image Loaded	Supervisor Bootstrap Image Loaded
IOS Image Loaded	IOS Image Loaded	IOS Image Loaded
Sync Startup Configuration	Sync Startup Configuration	Sync Startup Configuration
Supervisor Diagnostics	Supervisor Diagnostics	Supervisor Diagnostics
Switch Modules Reloaded		
Route Engine Initialized	Route Engine Initialized	Route Engine Initialized
Layer 2 Protocols Initialized	Layer 2 Protocols Initialized	Layer 2 Protocols Initialized
		FIB Table Synchronized
Layer 3 Protocols Initialized	Layer 3 Protocols Initialized	Layer 3 Protocols Initialized
Routing Protocols Converge	Routing Protocols Converge	Routing Protocols Converge
FIB Table Flushed and Recreated	FIB Table Flushed and Recreated	FIB Table Flushed and Recreated

NSF

The light items on top are what the standby supervisor has loaded, the dark items are the things it still has to do when it has to take over from the active supervisor.

By default the active supervisor will sync the startup configuration and configuration register values with the standby supervisor. We can however configure some other things that should be synchronized. Here's how to configure the supervisor:

```
Switch(config)#redundancy
Switch(config-red)#main-cpu
```

First you need to enter the main CPU configuration mode. Now we can specify what should be synchronized:

```
Switch(config-r-mc)#auto-sync bootvar
```

With the auto-sync command we can tell the supervisors that it should also sync the bootvar.

If you use SSO then you can also use the **NSF (NonStop Forwarding)** feature. NSF is used to rebuild the RIB (Routing Information Base) after the supervisor failover has occurred. The RIB is then used to generate the FIB (Fowarding Information Base) for CEF (Cisco Express Forwarding) which is then downloaded to any switch modules or hardware that support CEF.

NSF can also get help from other NSF-aware neighbors. If another router supports NSF then they can send routing information to the standby supervisor so that it can rebuild its tables quickly. The routing protocols have to support NSF though...BGP, EIGRP, OSPF and IS-IS support this. You have to enable this for each routing protocol, here's an example:

```
Switch(config)# router bgp 1
Switch(config-router)# bgp graceful-restart
```

```
Switch(config)# router eigrp 1
Switch(config-router)# nsf
```

```
Switch(config)# router ospf 1
Switch(config-router)# nsf
```

Besides redundancy within a single chassis, the chassis platforms also support a feature similar to Stackwise.

Some of these switches support VSS, this allows us to configure two identical chassis' to function as one **logical switch.** To create this logical switch we need to link the two chassis' together with multiple interfaces. This link is called a **VSL (Virtual Switch Link).**

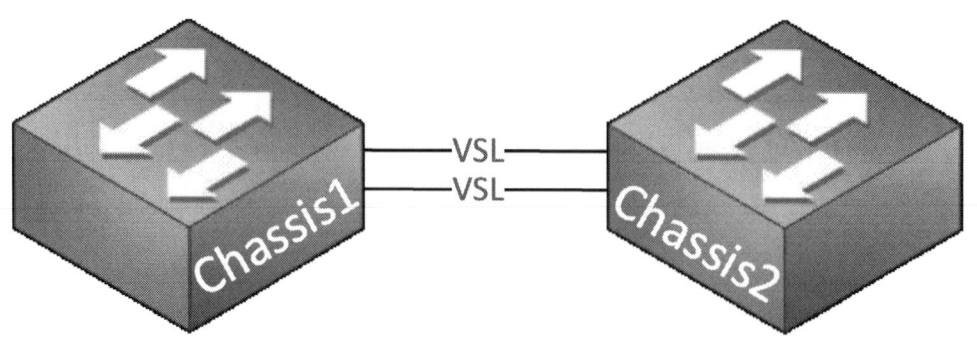

Just like Stackwise, the two chassis' will operate as a single logical switch. When a supervisor in one chassis fails, the supervisor in the other chassis can take over.

That's all we have on high availability and switch virtualization. Some of these topics might be hard to practice since you need access to specific switches. Make sure you are familiar with the general concepts and you should be fine for the exam.

14. High Availability / Switch Virtualization

15. Gateway Redundancy (VRRP, GLBP, HSRP)

In this chapter we'll take a look at different protocols for **gateway redundancy.** So what is gateway redundancy and why do we need it? Let's start with an example!

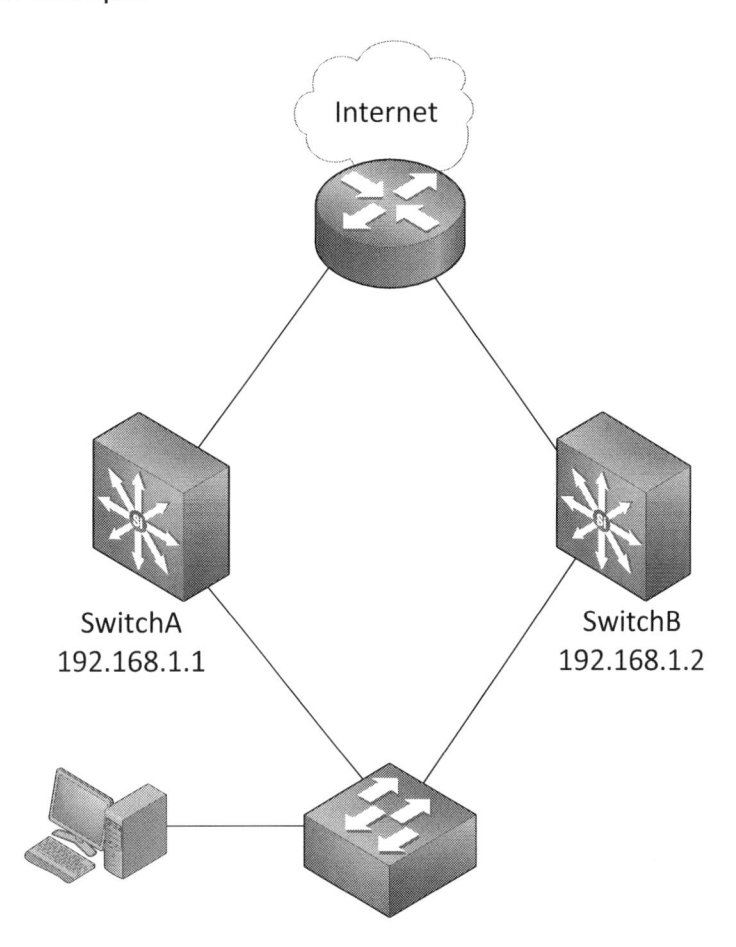

The network in the picture above is fairly simple. I have one computer connected to a switch. In the middle you'll find two multilayer switches (SwitchA and SwitchB) that both have an IP address that could be used as the default gateway for the computer. Behind SwitchA and SwitchB there's a router that is connected to the Internet.

Which gateway should we configure on the computer? SwitchA or SwitchB? You can only configure a one gateway after all...

How to Master CCNP SWITCH

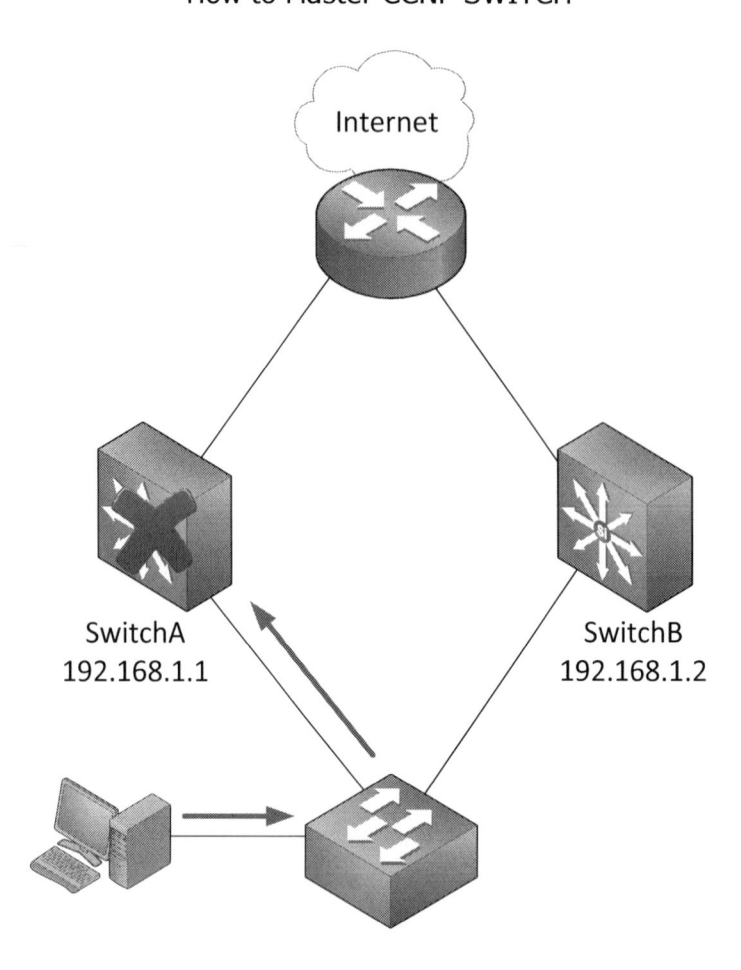

SwitchA
192.168.1.1

SwitchB
192.168.1.2

If we pick SwitchA and it crashes, the computer won't be able to get out of its own subnet because it only knows about **one** default gateway.

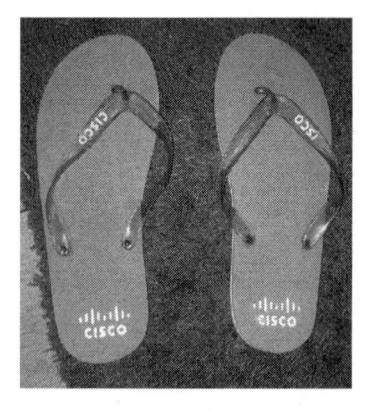

For all you Microsoft, Linux, MacOS, FreeBSD, [insert random operating system here] people. There are methods so you can configure multiple gateways and gateway failover on your operating system but since we are wearing our network engineer flip flops today we'll use a network solution to deal with gateway redundancy.

P.S. – Yes those are my Cisco flip flops from a Cisco Summer Barbecue.
P.P.S. – No I don't dare to wear them in public, they stay in the closet where they belong ;)

15. Gateway Redundancy (VRRP, GLBP, HSRP)

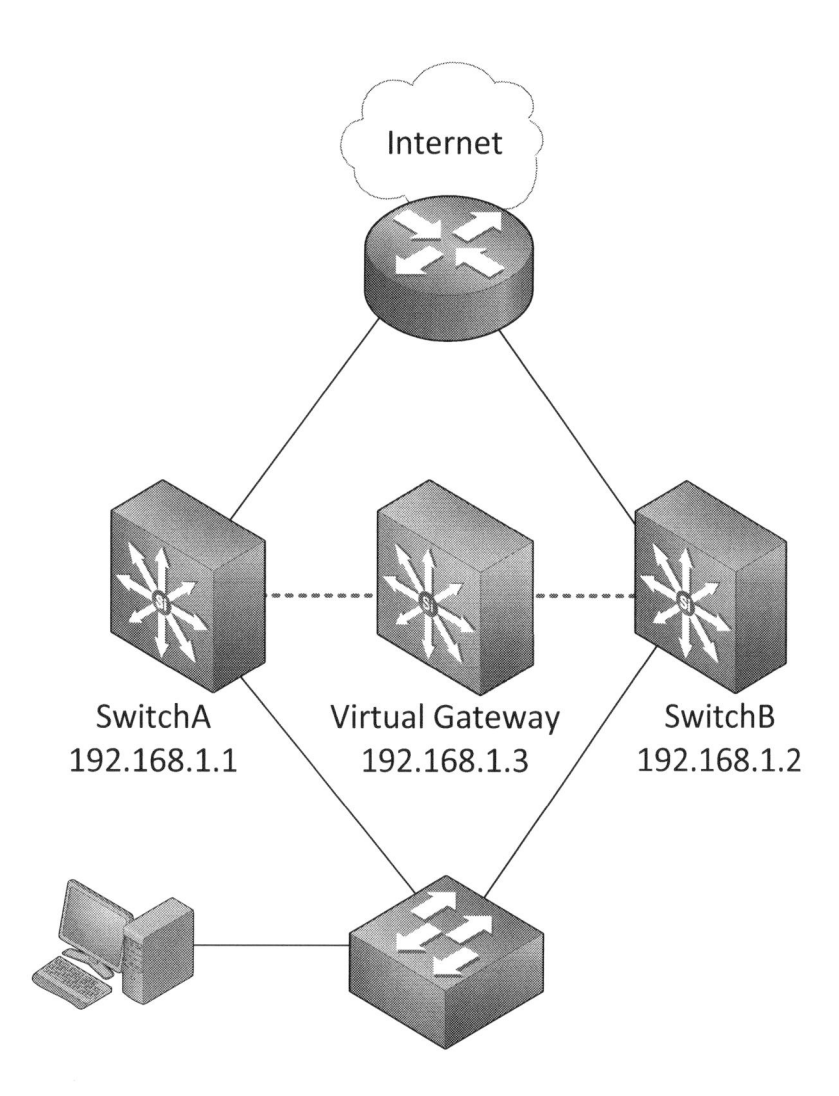

[Network diagram: Internet connected to a router, which connects to SwitchA (192.168.1.1), Virtual Gateway (192.168.1.3), and SwitchB (192.168.1.2). These connect down to a switch and a computer.]

We are going to create a **virtual gateway** to solve the gateway problem. Between SwitchA and SwitchB we'll create a virtual gateway with its own IP address, in my example this is 192.168.1.3.

The computer will use 192.168.1.3 as its default gateway. One of the switches will be the active gateway and in case it fails the other one will take over.

There are three different protocols than can create a virtual gateway:

- **HSRP (Hot Standby Routing Protocol)**
- **VRRP (Virtual Router Redundancy Protocol)**
- **GLBP (Gateway Load Balancing Protocol)**

These protocols all work similar but there are a number of differences. We'll start with the configuration of HSRP which is a **Cisco proprietary** protocol. Oh by the way…HSRP, VRRP and GLBP are protocols that work perfectly in GNS3 so if you want to follow me along...boot up some emulated routers!

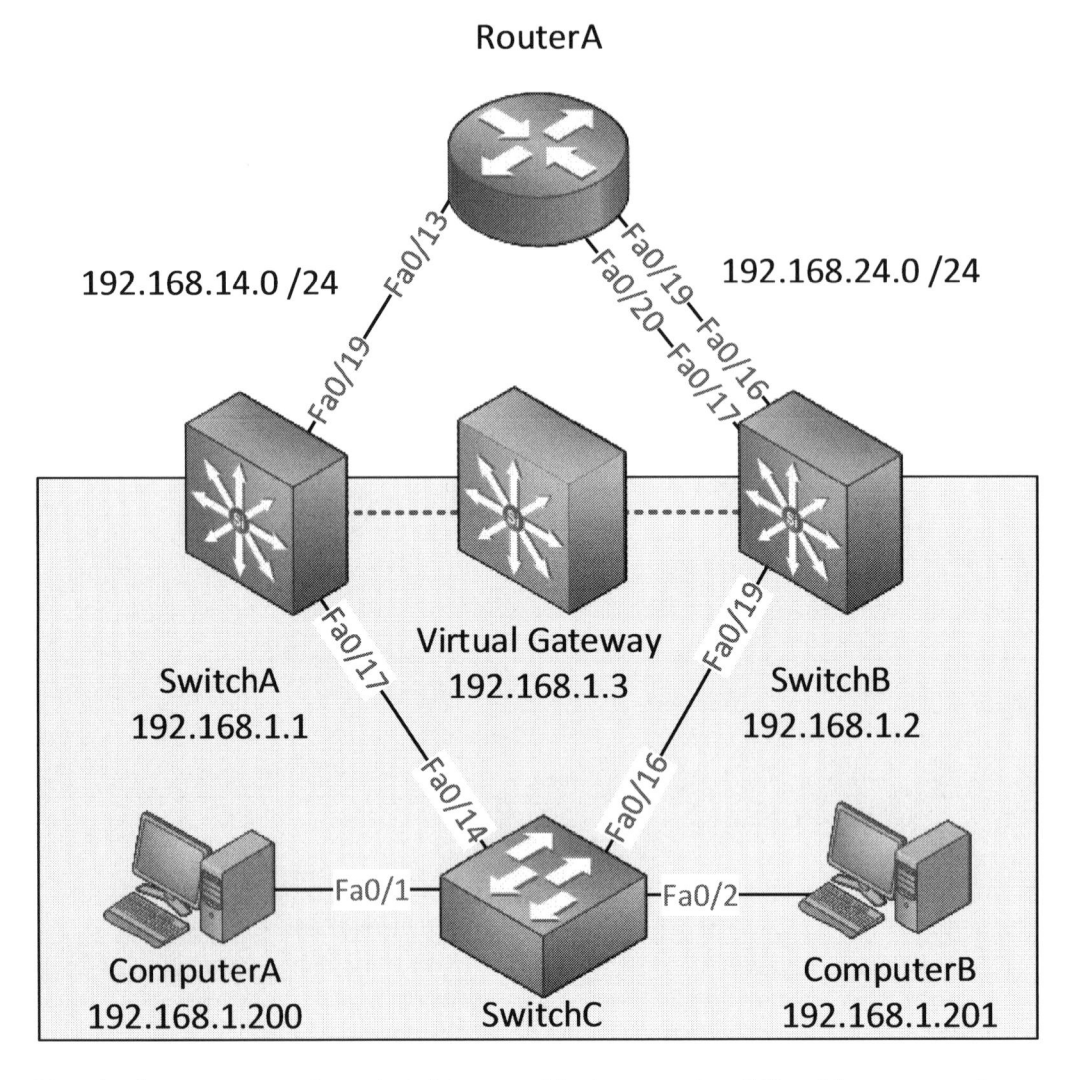

RouterA

192.168.14.0 /24   192.168.24.0 /24

SwitchA
192.168.1.1

Virtual Gateway
192.168.1.3

SwitchB
192.168.1.2

ComputerA
192.168.1.200

SwitchC

ComputerB
192.168.1.201

Here's the same topology but I have added a couple of IP addresses and interface numbers, this is what we have:

- SwitchA, SwitchB, SwitchC and ComputerA are in VLAN1 and we'll use the 192.168.1.0 /24 subnet.
- The link between SwitchA and RouterA is a layer 3 link and uses 192.168.14.0 /24 as the subnet.
- The link between SwitchB and RouterA is also a layer 3 link and uses 192.168.24.0 /24 as the subnet.
- 192.168.1.3 will be the default gateway for ComputerA.

15. Gateway Redundancy (VRRP, GLBP, HSRP)

Let me show you the configuration!

```
SwitchA(config)#interface fa0/17
SwitchA(config-if)#no switchport
SwitchA(config-if)#ip address 192.168.1.1 255.255.255.0
```

```
SwitchB(config)#interface fa0/19
SwitchB(config-if)#no switchport
SwitchB(config-if)#ip address 192.168.1.2 255.255.255.0
```

I'm using layer 3 ports on SwitchA and SwitchB. You can also use the SVI interfaces if you like it really doesn't make a difference.

```
SwitchA(config)#interface fa0/19
SwitchA(config-if)#no switchport
SwitchA(config-if)#ip address 192.168.14.1 255.255.255.0
```

```
SwitchB(config)#interface fa0/16
SwitchB(config-if)#no switchport
SwitchB(config-if)#ip address 192.168.24.2 255.255.255.0
```

We will make the interfaces on SwitchA and SwitchB towards RouterA layer 3 as well. Don't forget to configure an IP address.

```
RouterA(config)#interface fa0/13
RouterA(config-if)#no shutdown
RouterA(config-if)#ip address 192.168.14.4 255.255.255.0
```

```
RouterA(config)#interface fa0/19
RouterA(config-if)#no shutdown
RouterA(config-if)#ip address 192.168.24.4 255.255.255.0
```

```
RouterA(config)#interface loopback 0
RouterA(config-if)#ip address 1.1.1.1 255.255.255.0
```

Interfaces on routers are in shutdown by default so don't forget to type no shutdown. I'm creating a loopback0 interface so we have something to ping.

```
SwitchA(config)#ip routing
SwitchA(config)#ip route 1.1.1.0 255.255.255.0 192.168.14.4
```

```
SwitchB(config)#ip routing
SwitchB(config)#ip route 1.1.1.0 255.255.255.0 192.168.24.4
```

SwitchA and SwitchB have no idea how to reach the loopback0 interface on RouterA so I'm going to help them with a static route. Don't forget to enable IP routing because it's disabled by default.

```
SwitchA(config)#interface fa0/17
SwitchA(config-if)#standby 1 ip 192.168.1.3
```

```
SwitchB(config)#interface fa0/19
SwitchB(config-if)#standby 1 ip 192.168.1.3
```

Use the **standby** command to configure HSRP. 192.168.1.3 will be the virtual gateway IP address. The "1" is the group number for HSRP. It doesn't matter what you pick just make sure it's the same on both devices.

```
SwitchA#
%HSRP-5-STATECHANGE: FastEthernet0/17 Grp 1 state Speak ->
Standby
%HSRP-5-STATECHANGE: FastEthernet0/17 Grp 1 state Standby ->
Active
```

```
SwitchB#
%HSRP-5-STATECHANGE: FastEthernet0/19 Grp 1 state Speak ->
Standby
```

Depending on which switch you configured first you'll see these messages. One of the switches will be the active gateway.

```
C:\Documents and Settings\ComputerA>ipconfig

Windows IP Configuration


Ethernet adapter Local Area Connection:

        IP Address. . . . . . . . . . . . : 192.168.1.100
        Subnet Mask . . . . . . . . . . . : 255.255.255.0
        Default Gateway . . . . . . . . . : 192.168.1.3
```

We can test HSRP by changing the default gateway on ComputerA. I'll set it to the virtual IP address 192.168.1.3.

```
C:\Documents and Settings\ComputerA>ping 192.168.1.3

Pinging 192.168.1.3 with 32 bytes of data:

Reply from 192.168.1.3: bytes=32 time<1ms TTL=128
Reply from 192.168.1.3: bytes=32 time<1ms TTL=128
Reply from 192.168.1.3: bytes=32 time<1ms TTL=128
Reply from 192.168.1.3: bytes=32 time<1ms TTL=128

Ping statistics for 192.168.1.3:
    Packets: Sent = 4, Received = 4, Lost = 0 (0% loss),
Approximate round trip times in milli-seconds:
    Minimum = 0ms, Maximum = 0ms, Average = 0ms
```

15. Gateway Redundancy (VRRP, GLBP, HSRP)

As you can see we can successfully reach the virtual gateway IP address.

That wasn't too bad right? Only one command and HSRP works! There are a couple of other things we can do however.

```
SwitchA#show ip arp
Protocol   Address          Age (min)   Hardware Addr    Type   Interface
Internet   192.168.14.4         49      0009.7c36.2880   ARPA   FastEthernet0/19
Internet   192.168.14.1          -      0011.bb0b.3642   ARPA   FastEthernet0/19
Internet   192.168.1.1           -      0011.bb0b.3641   ARPA   FastEthernet0/17
Internet   192.168.1.3           -      0000.0c07.ac01   ARPA   FastEthernet0/17
Internet   192.168.1.2          33      0019.569d.5741   ARPA   FastEthernet0/17
```

192.168.1.3 is our virtual IP address. What about the MAC address? It's also virtual as you can see:

0000.0c07.ac01 is the MAC address that we have. HSRP uses the **0000.0c07.acXX** MAC address where XX is the **HSRP group number**. In my example I configured HSRP group number 1.

```
SwitchA#show standby
FastEthernet0/17 - Group 1
  State is Active
    2 state changes, last state change 01:02:09
  Virtual IP address is 192.168.1.3
  Active virtual MAC address is 0000.0c07.ac01
    Local virtual MAC address is 0000.0c07.ac01 (v1 default)
  Hello time 3 sec, hold time 10 sec
    Next hello sent in 0.769 secs
  Preemption disabled
  Active router is local
  Standby router is 192.168.1.2, priority 100 (expires in 9.111 sec)
  Priority 100 (default 100)
  IP redundancy name is "hsrp-Fa0/17-1" (default)
```

```
SwitchB#show standby
FastEthernet0/19 - Group 1
  State is Standby
    1 state change, last state change 01:01:51
  Virtual IP address is 192.168.1.3
  Active virtual MAC address is 0000.0c07.ac01
    Local virtual MAC address is 0000.0c07.ac01 (v1 default)
  Hello time 3 sec, hold time 10 sec
    Next hello sent in 2.959 secs
  Preemption disabled
  Active router is 192.168.1.1, priority 100 (expires in 8.608 sec)
  Standby router is local
  Priority 100 (default 100)
  IP redundancy name is "hsrp-Fa0/19-1" (default)
```

Use the **show standby** command to verify your configuration. There's a couple of interesting things here:

- We can see the virtual IP address here (192.168.1.3).
- It also shows the virtual MAC address (0000.0c07.ac01).
- You can see which router is active or in standby mode.
- The hello time is 3 seconds and the hold time is 10 seconds.
- Preemption is disabled.

The active router will **respond to ARP requests** from computers and it will be actively forwarding packets from them. It will send hello messages to the routers that are in standby mode. Routers in standby mode will listen to the hello messages, if they don't receive anything from the active router they will wait for the **hold time to expire** before taking over. The hold time is 10 seconds by default which is pretty slow; we'll see how to speed this up in a bit.

Each HSRP router will go through a number of states before it ends up as an active or standby router, this is what will happen:

State	Explanation
Initial	This is the first state when HSRP starts. You'll see this just after you configured HSRP or when the interface just got enabled.
Listen	The router knows the virtual IP address and will listen for hello messages from other HSRP routers.
Speak	The router will send hello messages and will join the election to see which router will become active or standby.
Standby	The router didn't become the active router but will keep sending hello messages. If the active router fails it will take over.
Active	The router will actively forward packets from clients and sends hello messages.

15. Gateway Redundancy (VRRP, GLBP, HSRP)

We can see all these steps with a debug command.

```
SwitchA(config)#interface fa0/17
SwitchA(config-if)#shutdown
```

```
SwitchB(config)#interface fa0/19
SwitchB(config-if)#shutdown
```

I'm going to shut the interfaces so we can see all the states for HSRP from the beginning.

```
SwitchA#debug standby events
HSRP Events debugging is on
```

Use the **debug standby events** command so we can take a look.

```
SwitchA#
HSRP: Fa0/17 Grp 1 Init: a/HSRP enabled
HSRP: Fa0/17 Grp 1 Init -> Listen
HSRP: Fa0/17 Grp 1 Redundancy "hsrp-Fa0/17-1" state Init ->
Backup
HSRP: Fa0/17 Grp 1 Listen: c/Active timer expired (unknown)
HSRP: Fa0/17 Grp 1 Listen -> Speak
HSRP: Fa0/17 Grp 1 Standby router is local
HSRP: Fa0/17 Grp 1 Speak -> Standby
HSRP: Fa0/17 Grp 1 Standby: c/Active timer expired (unknown)
HSRP: Fa0/17 Grp 1 Active router is local
HSRP: Fa0/17 Grp 1 Standby router is unknown, was local
HSRP: Fa0/17 Grp 1 Standby -> Active
%HSRP-5-STATECHANGE: FastEthernet0/17 Grp 1 state Standby ->
Active
HSRP: Fa0/17 Grp 1 Redundancy "hsrp-Fa0/17-1" state Standby ->
Active
```

I filtered out some debug information but you can clearly see the different states we go through before we end up in the active state.

```
SwitchB#debug standby events
HSRP Events debugging is on
```

Let's enable the debug on SwitchB as well.

```
SwitchB(config-if)#interface fa0/16
SwitchB(config-if)#no shutdown
```

313

Get the interface up and running.

```
SwitchB#
HSRP: Fa0/19 Grp 1 Init: a/HSRP enabled
HSRP: Fa0/19 Grp 1 Init -> Listen
HSRP: Fa0/19 Grp 1 Listen -> Speak
HSRP: Fa0/19 Grp 1 Speak -> Standby
HSRP: Fa0/19 Grp 1 Active router is local
HSRP: Fa0/19 Grp 1 Standby router is unknown, was local
HSRP: Fa0/19 Grp 1 Standby -> Active
%HSRP-5-STATECHANGE: FastEthernet0/19 Grp 1 state Standby -> Active
HSRP: Fa0/19 Grp 1 Redundancy "hsrp-Fa0/19-1" state Standby -> Active
HSRP: Fa0/19 Grp 1 Hello  in  192.168.1.1 Active  pri 100 vIP 192.168.1.3
HSRP: Fa0/19 Grp 1 Active: h/Hello rcvd from lower pri Active router (100/192.168.1.1)
HSRP: Fa0/19 Grp 1 Redundancy group hsrp-Fa0/19-1 state Active -> Active
HSRP: Fa0/19 Grp 1 Redundancy group hsrp-Fa0/19-1 state Active -> Active
HSRP: Fa0/19 Grp 1 Standby router is 192.168.1.1
```

SwitchB will go through the same states. In the debug you can see it receives a hello message from SwitchA and decides that SwitchA has a lower priority and SwitchB takes over the role as the active router.

```
SwitchA#
%HSRP-5-STATECHANGE: FastEthernet0/17 Grp 1 state Active -> Speak
%HSRP-5-STATECHANGE: FastEthernet0/17 Grp 1 state Speak -> Standby
```

We can confirm this by looking at SwitchA. You can see that it is now in the standby state because SwitchB is active.

By default the switch with the **highest priority** will become the active HSRP device. If the priority is the same then the **highest IP address** will be the tie-breaker.

```
SwitchA#show standby | include Priority
   Priority 100 (default 100)
```

```
SwitchB#show standby | include Priority
   Priority 100 (default 100)
```

Both switches have a **priority of 100 by default** so the IP address is the tie-breaker. SwitchB has a higher IP address so it became active.

15. Gateway Redundancy (VRRP, GLBP, HSRP)

```
SwitchA(config)#interface fa0/17
SwitchA(config-if)#standby 1 priority 150
```

Let's say I want to make sure SwitchA becomes the active router. We can do this by using the **standby priority** command.

```
SwitchA#show standby
FastEthernet0/17 - Group 1
  State is Standby
    16 state changes, last state change 00:27:52
  Virtual IP address is 192.168.1.3
  Active virtual MAC address is 0000.0c07.ac01
    Local virtual MAC address is 0000.0c07.ac01 (v1 default)
  Hello time 3 sec, hold time 10 sec
    Next hello sent in 0.039 secs
  Preemption disabled
  Active router is 192.168.1.2, priority 100 (expires in 8.960 sec)
  Standby router is local
  Priority 150 (configured 150)
  IP redundancy name is "hsrp-Fa0/17-1" (default)
```

We can confirm SwitchA has a higher priority but SwitchB is still active. Once HSRP has decided which device should be active it will **stay active until it goes down**. We can overrule this if we want though...

```
SwitchA#show standby brief
                   P indicates configured to preempt.
                   |
Interface  Grp Prio P State   Active        Standby         Virtual IP
Fa0/17     1   150    Active  local         192.168.1.2     192.168.1.3
```

```
SwitchB#show standby brief
                   P indicates configured to preempt.
                   |
Interface  Grp Prio P State   Active        Standby         Virtual IP
Fa0/19     1   100    Standby 192.168.1.1   local           192.168.1.3
```

The **show standby brief** command is another nice method to check your HSRP configuration.

```
SwitchA(config)#interface fa0/17
SwitchA(config-if)#standby 1 preempt
```

We can use **preempt** to ensure the device with the highest priority becomes active immediately.

315

```
SwitchA#
%HSRP-5-STATECHANGE: FastEthernet0/17 Grp 1 state Standby ->
Active
```

```
SwitchB#
HSRP: Fa0/19 Grp 1 Redundancy "hsrp-Fa0/19-1" state Active ->
Speak
HSRP: Fa0/19 Grp 1 Speak -> Standby
HSRP: Fa0/19 Grp 1 Redundancy "hsrp-Fa0/19-1" state Speak ->
Standby
```

There goes…SwitchA is now active and SwitchB goes to standby!

```
SwitchA(config)#interface fa0/17
SwitchA(config-if)#standby 1 authentication text secret
```

```
SwitchB(config)#interface fa0/19
SwitchB(config-if)#standby 1 authentication text secret
```

If you want you can enable authentication for HSRP. You can choose between **plaintext** and **MD5.** Here's an example of plaintext.

```
SwitchA(config)#interface fa0/17
SwitchA(config-if)#standby 1 authentication md5 key-string
md5pass
```

```
SwitchB(config)#interface fa0/19
SwitchB(config-if)#standby 1 authentication md5 key-string
md5pass
```

Here's an example for MD5 authentication.

```
SwitchA#show standby | include time
  Hello time 3 sec, hold time 10 sec
```

By default HSRP is pretty slow. SwitchB is my standby router and it will wait for 10 seconds (hold time) before it will become active once SwitchA fails. That means we'll have 10 seconds of downtime…

```
SwitchA(config)#interface fa0/17
SwitchA(config-if)#standby 1 timers msec 100 msec 300
```

```
SwitchB(config)#interface fa0/19
SwitchB(config-if)#standby 1 timers msec 100 msec 300
```

We can speed things up by changing the timers with the **standby timers** command. We can even use millisecond values. I've set the hello time to 100 milliseconds and the hold timer to 300 milliseconds. Make sure your hold time

15. Gateway Redundancy (VRRP, GLBP, HSRP)

is at **least three times** the hello timer.

```
SwitchA(config)#interface fa0/17
SwitchA(config-if)#standby 1 preempt
SwitchA(config-if)#standby 1 preempt delay minimum 60
```

```
SwitchB(config)#interface fa0/19
SwitchB(config-if)#standby 1 preempt
SwitchB(config-if)#standby 1 preempt delay minimum 60
```

Remember preemption that I just showed you? By default preemption will take effect immediately but it might be a good idea to use a delay. If a router or reboots it might need some time to "converge". Maybe OSPF or EIGRP need to form neighbor adjacencies or spanning-tree isn't ready yet unblocking ports. I've changed the delay for preemption to 60 seconds, this way we make sure this device won't become active until its uplinks are up and running.

```
SwitchA(config)#interface fa0/17
SwitchA(config-if)#standby 1 version 2
```

```
SwitchB(config)#interface fa0/19
SwitchB(config-if)#standby 1 version 2
```

Depending on the router or switch model you might have the option to use HSRP version 2. You can change the version by using the **standby version** command.

	HSRPv1	**HSRPv2**
Group numbers	0 – 255	0 – 4095
Virtual MAC Address	0000.0c07.acXX (XX = group number)	0000.0c9f.fxxx (XXX = group number)
Multicast address	224.0.0.2	224.0.0.102

HSRP version 1 and version 2 are **not compatible** so make sure you use the same version on both devices.

How to Master CCNP SWITCH

RouterA

192.168.14.0 /24   192.168.24.0 /24

SwitchA
192.168.1.1
Priority 150
Active

Virtual Gateway
192.168.1.3

SwitchB
192.168.1.2
Priority 100
Standby

ComputerA
192.168.1.200

SwitchC

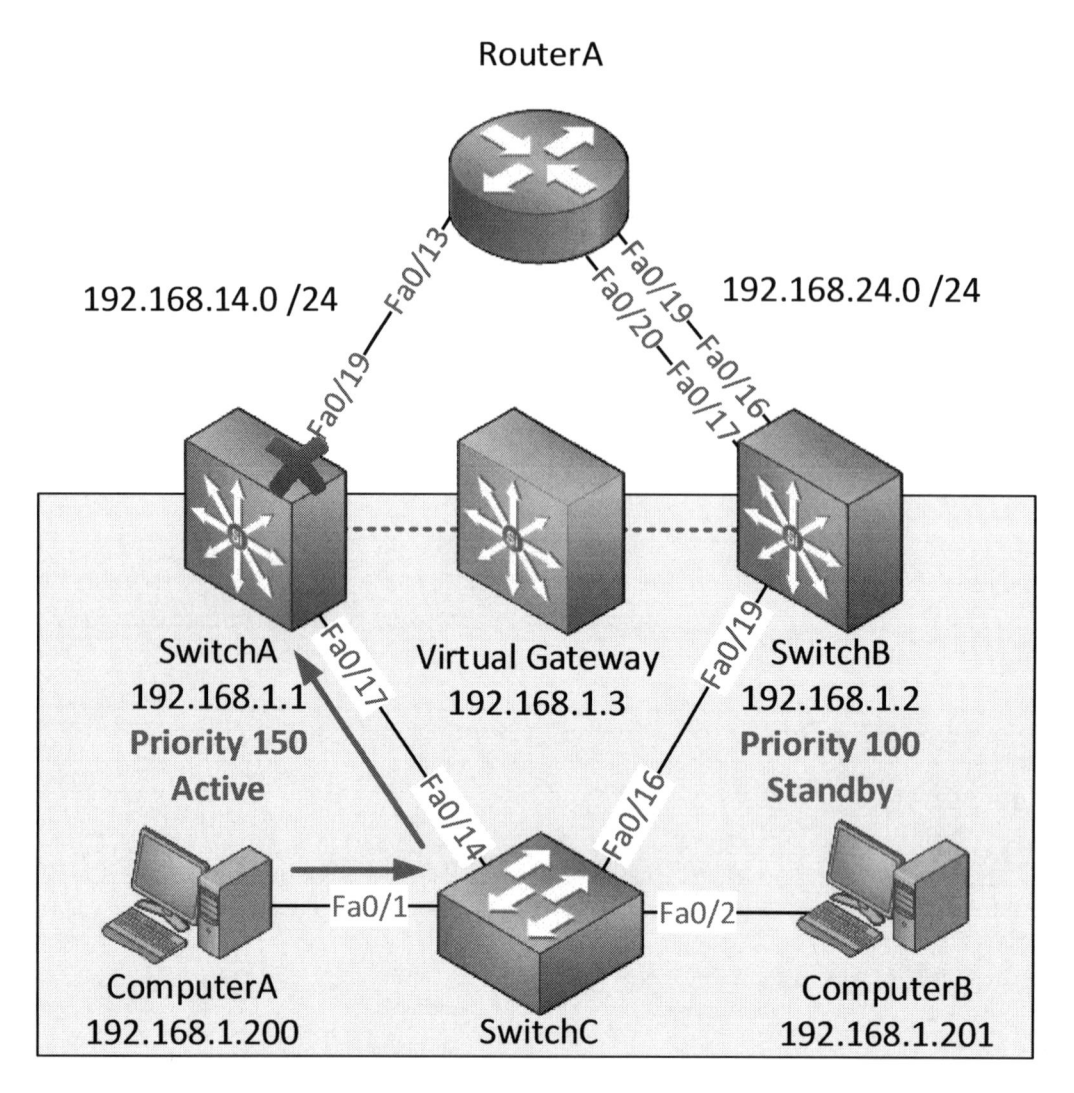

ComputerB
192.168.1.201

There is one more thing I'd like to show you about HSRP. In the picture above SwitchA is the active router because we changed the priority to 150. That's great but what if the fa0/19 interface on SwitchA fails? It will be the active router but it doesn't have a direct path to RouterA anymore. When this happens it will send an ICMP redirect to the computer. It would be better if SwitchB becomes the active router in case this happens.

HSRP offers a feature called **interface tracking**. We can select an interface to track and if it fails we will give it a **penalty**.

15. Gateway Redundancy (VRRP, GLBP, HSRP)

This way your priority will decrease and another device can become the active router.

```
SwitchA(config)#interface fa0/17
SwitchA(config-if)#standby 1 preempt
```

```
SwitchB(config)#interface fa0/19
SwitchB(config-if)#standby 1 preempt
```

We already configured preemption on SwitchA before but I need to make sure I configure this on SwitchB as well. We want to make sure the device with the highest priority will always be the active router.

```
SwitchA(config-if)#standby 1 track fastEthernet 0/19
```

This is how you configure interface tracking. Use the **standby track** command.

```
SwitchA(config)#interface fa0/19
SwitchA(config-if)#shutdown
```

We will shut the interface to simulate a link failure.

```
SwitchA#show standby | include Priority
  Priority 140 (configured 150)
```

You can see the priority is now 140 instead of the 150 that we configured. Interface tracking will **decrement your priority with 10 by default.** This will not be enough to make SwitchA surrender its active state so we'll have to change it.

```
SwitchA(config)#interface fa0/17
SwitchA(config-if)#standby 1 track fastEthernet 0/19 60
```

We can change the decrement value to something between 1 and 255. I've set mine to 60.

```
SwitchA#show standby | include Priority
  Priority 90 (configured 150)
```

```
SwitchA#
%HSRP-5-STATECHANGE: FastEthernet0/17 Grp 1 state Active -> Speak
%HSRP-5-STATECHANGE: FastEthernet0/17 Grp 1 state Speak -> Standby
```

You can see the priority is now 90 which is lower than SwitchB (100). As a result SwitchA will go to the standby state and SwitchB will move to the active

319

state.

```
SwitchA(config)#track 1 ?
  interface  Select an interface to track
  ip         IP protocol
  list       Group objects in a list
  rtr        Response Time Reporter (RTR) entry
```

Interface tracking is useful but it will only check the state of the interface. We can also check some other things. For example you can check if a certain prefix is in the routing table or not. We can also use **IP SLA** which is pretty cool.

```
SwitchA(config)#interface fa0/17
SwitchA(config-if)#no standby 1 track fastEthernet 0/19 60
```

Let's get rid of the interface tracking so we can do something with a higher coolness factor.

```
SwitchA(config)#ip sla 1
SwitchA(config-ip-sla)#icmp-echo 192.168.14.4
SwitchA(config)#ip sla schedule 1 start-time now life forever
SwitchA(config)#track 1 rtr 1 reachability
SwitchA(config)#interface fa0/19
SwitchA(config-if)#standby 1 track 1 decrement 60
```

IP SLA can be used for many things. One of them is to generate a ping to a destination every X seconds and we can combine this with object tracking. In the example above I have created IP SLA instance 1 which will send a ping to IP address 192.168.14.4. IP SLA can be run on a schedule, I've set it to start right away and run forever. Using the **track rtr** command I combined IP SLA with object tracking. Last step is to enable HSRP interface tracking and combine it with object tracking using the standby track command.

```
RouterA(config)#interface fa0/13
RouterA(config-if)#shutdown
```

Once I shut the fa0/13 interface on RouterA we will be unable to ping IP address 192.168.14.4.

```
SwitchA#
%HSRP-5-STATECHANGE: FastEthernet0/17 Grp 1 state Active ->
Speak
%HSRP-5-STATECHANGE: FastEthernet0/17 Grp 1 state Speak ->
Standby
```

And as a result SwitchA will go from active to the standby state. Tracking the reachability of an IP address might be a better idea than tracking the "state" of an interface. It's possible that an interface shows up/up but that it's impossible

15. Gateway Redundancy (VRRP, GLBP, HSRP)

to get any IP packets to the other side. You could also use IP SLA to see if a certain server or other device is reachable.

This is everything I want to show you about HSRP. We'll continue by taking a look at VRRP!

VRRP is very similar to HSRP; if you understood HSRP you'll have no trouble with VRRP which is a **standard protocol** defined by the IETF in RFC 3768. Configuration-wise it's pretty much the same but there are a couple of differences.

Let's start with an overview:

	HSRP	**VRRP**
Protocol	Cisco proprietary	IETF – RFC 3768
Number of groups	16 groups maximum	255 groups maximum
Active/Standby	1 active, 1 standby and multiple candidates.	1 active and several backups.
Virtual IP Address	Different from real IP addresses on interfaces	Can be the same as the real IP address on an interface.
Multicast address	224.0.0.2	224.0.0.18
Tracking	Interfaces or Objects	Objects
Timers	Hello timer 3 seconds, hold time 10 seconds.	Hello timer 1 second, hold time 3 seconds.
Authentication	Supported	Not supported in RFC 3768

As you can see there are a number of differences between HSRP and VRRP. Nothing too fancy however. HSRP is a cisco proprietary protocol so you can only use it between Cisco devices.

RouterA

192.168.14.0 /24   192.168.24.0 /24

SwitchA
192.168.1.1

Virtual Gateway
192.168.1.3

SwitchB
192.168.1.2

ComputerA
192.168.1.200

SwitchC

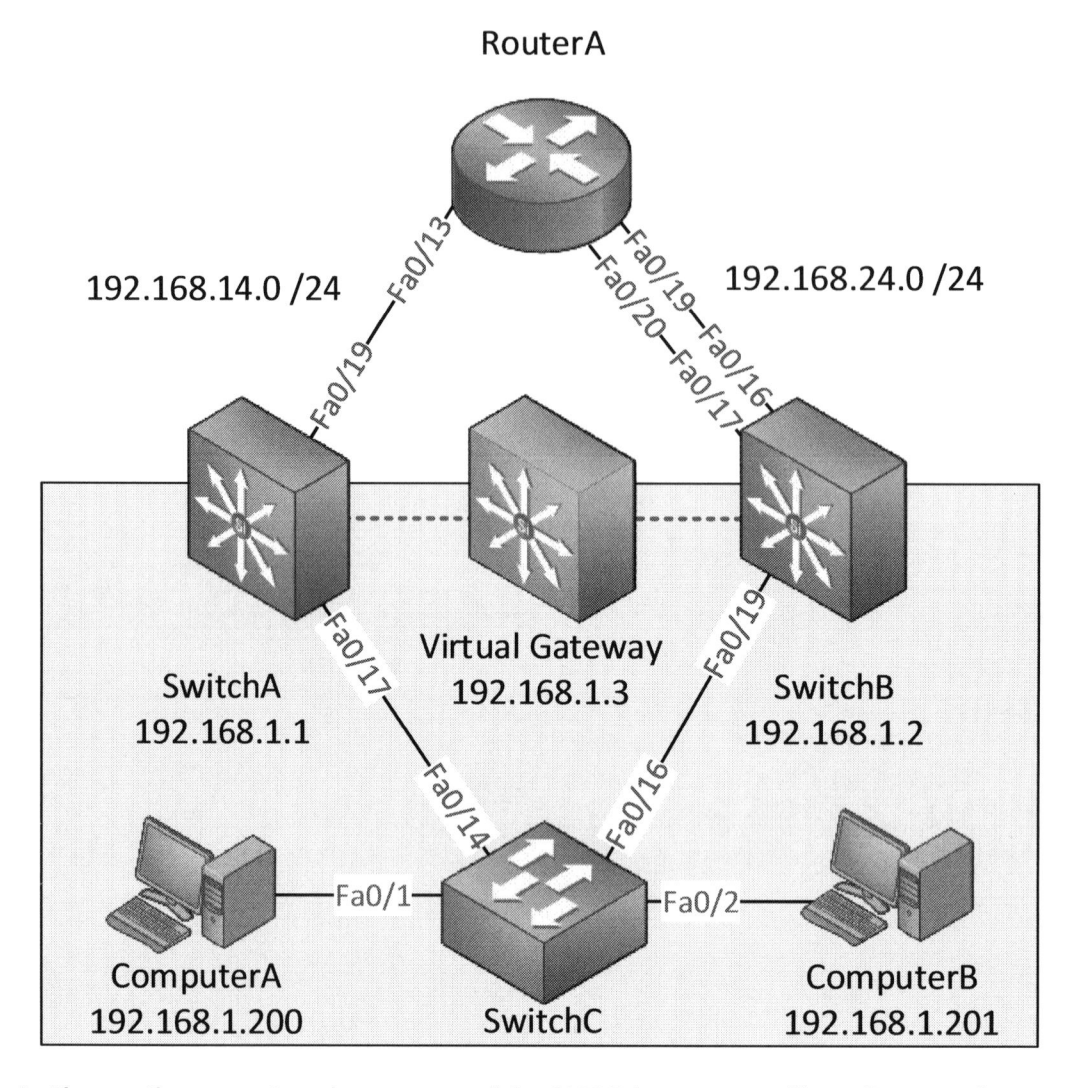

ComputerB
192.168.1.201

Let's use the same topology we used for HSRP but now we'll configure it for VRRP.

```
SwitchA(config)#interface fa0/17
SwitchA(config-if)#no standby 1 ip 192.168.1.3
```

```
SwitchB(config)#interface fa0/19
SwitchB(config-if)#no standby 1 ip 192.168.1.3
```

We'll start by getting rid of HSRP. This is the quick and dirty way of disabling it. It's better to remove all the "standby" commands on the interface so your config stays clean.

15. Gateway Redundancy (VRRP, GLBP, HSRP)

```
SwitchA(config)#interface fa0/17
SwitchA(config-if)#vrrp 1 ip 192.168.1.3
SwitchA(config-if)#vrrp 1 priority 150
SwitchA(config-if)#vrrp 1 authentication md5 key-string mykey
```

```
SwitchB(config-if)#interface fa0/19
SwitchB(config-if)#vrrp 1 ip 192.168.1.3
SwitchB(config-if)#vrrp 1 authentication md5 key-string mykey
```

Here's an example how to configure VRRP. You can see the commands are pretty much the same but I didn't type "standby" but **vrrp.** I have changed the priority on SwitchA to 150 and I've enabled MD5 authentication on both switches.

```
SwitchA#
%VRRP-6-STATECHANGE: Fa0/17 Grp 1 state Init -> Backup
%VRRP-6-STATECHANGE: Fa0/17 Grp 1 state Backup -> Master
```

```
SwitchB#
%VRRP-6-STATECHANGE: Fa0/19 Grp 1 state Init -> Backup
%VRRP-6-STATECHANGE: Fa0/19 Grp 1 state Backup -> Master
%VRRP-6-STATECHANGE: Fa0/19 Grp 1 state Master -> Backup
```

You will see these messages pop-up in your console. VRRP uses different terminology than HSRP. SwitchA has the best priority and will become the **master router**. SwitchB will become a **standby router**.

```
SwitchA#show vrrp
FastEthernet0/17 - Group 1
  State is Master
  Virtual IP address is 192.168.1.3
    Secondary Virtual IP address is 192.168.1.4
  Virtual MAC address is 0000.5e00.0101
  Advertisement interval is 1.000 sec
  Preemption enabled
  Priority is 150
  Authentication MD5, key-string "mykey"
  Master Router is 192.168.1.1 (local), priority is 150
  Master Advertisement interval is 1.000 sec
  Master Down interval is 3.414 sec
```

```
SwitchB#show vrrp
FastEthernet0/19 - Group 1
  State is Backup
  Virtual IP address is 192.168.1.3
  Virtual MAC address is 0000.5e00.0101
  Advertisement interval is 1.000 sec
  Preemption enabled
  Priority is 100
  Authentication MD5, key-string "mykey"
  Master Router is 192.168.1.1, priority is 150
  Master Advertisement interval is 1.000 sec
  Master Down interval is 3.609 sec (expires in 3.065 sec)
```

Use **show vrrp** to verify your configuration. The output looks similar to HSRP; one of the differences is that VRRP uses **another virtual MAC address**:

0000.5e00.01XX (where X = group number)

```
SwitchA(config)#interface fa0/17
SwitchA(config-if)#shutdown
```

We can shut the interface on SwitchA so we can see that SwitchB will take over.

```
SwitchA#
%VRRP-6-STATECHANGE: Fa0/17 Grp 1 state Master -> Init
```

```
SwitchB#
%VRRP-6-STATECHANGE: Fa0/19 Grp 1 state Backup -> Master
```

Same principle...different terminology!

15. Gateway Redundancy (VRRP, GLBP, HSRP)

RouterA

192.168.14.0 /24   192.168.24.0 /24

Virtual Gateway
192.168.1.3
192.168.1.4

SwitchA
192.168.1.1

SwitchB
192.168.1.2

ComputerA
192.168.1.200

SwitchC

ComputerB
192.168.1.201

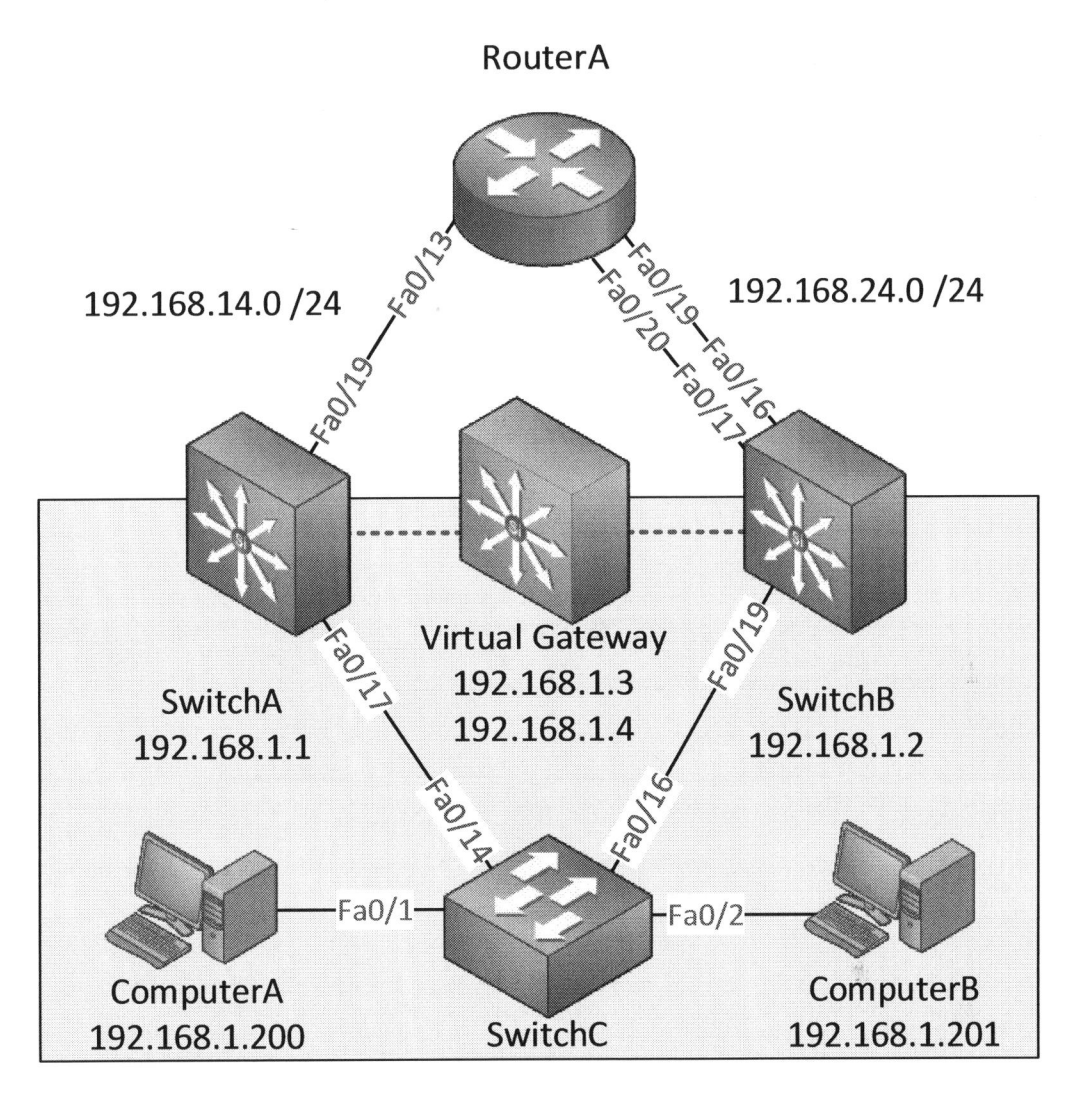

Is it possible to do load balancing when we use HSRP or VRRP? Both protocols elect one device to be the active/master device which will take care of forwarding all the IP packets. It would be a shame not to use SwitchB at all right? In the example above I have added ComputerB and I would like it to use SwitchB as its gateway without losing redundancy. If we pull this off we'll have a 50/50 load share (if both computers would send the same amount of data).

```
SwitchA(config)#interface fa0/17
SwitchA(config-if)#standby 1 ip 192.168.1.3
SwitchA(config-if)#standby 1 priority 150
SwitchA(config-if)#standby 2 ip 192.168.1.4
```

```
SwitchB(config)#interface fa0/19
SwitchB(config-if)#standby 1 ip 192.168.1.3
SwitchB(config-if)#standby 2 ip 192.168.1.4
```

```
SwitchB(config-if)#standby 2 priority 150
```

Here's an example for HSRP. I created two groups so we have two virtual IP addresses:

- 192.168.1.3 and 192.168.1.4 are both virtual IP addresses we can use as a gateway.
- SwitchA has the highest priority (150) for virtual IP address 192.168.1.3.
- SwitchB has the highest priority (150) for virtual IP address 192.168.1.4.
- ComputerA can use 192.168.1.3 as its default gateway.
- ComputerB can use 192.168.1.4 as its default gateway.
- We now have load sharing and SwitchA and SwitchB will be redundant for each other!

```
SwitchA(config)#interface fa0/17
SwitchA(config-if)#vrrp 1 ip 192.168.1.3
SwitchA(config-if)#vrrp 1 priority 150
SwitchA(config-if)#vrrp 2 ip 192.168.1.4
```

```
SwitchB(config-if)#interface fa0/19
SwitchB(config-if)#vrrp 1 ip 192.168.1.3
SwitchB(config-if)#vrrp 2 ip 192.168.1.4
SwitchB(config-if)#vrrp 2 priority 150
```

Here's the same configuration for VRRP.

That's all I have on VRRP. Let's take a look at the last virtual gateway protocol **GLBP.** GLBP stands for **Gateway Load Balancing Protocol** and one of the key differences is that it can do load balancing without the group configuration that HSRP/VRRP use (what's in a name right?).

15. Gateway Redundancy (VRRP, GLBP, HSRP)

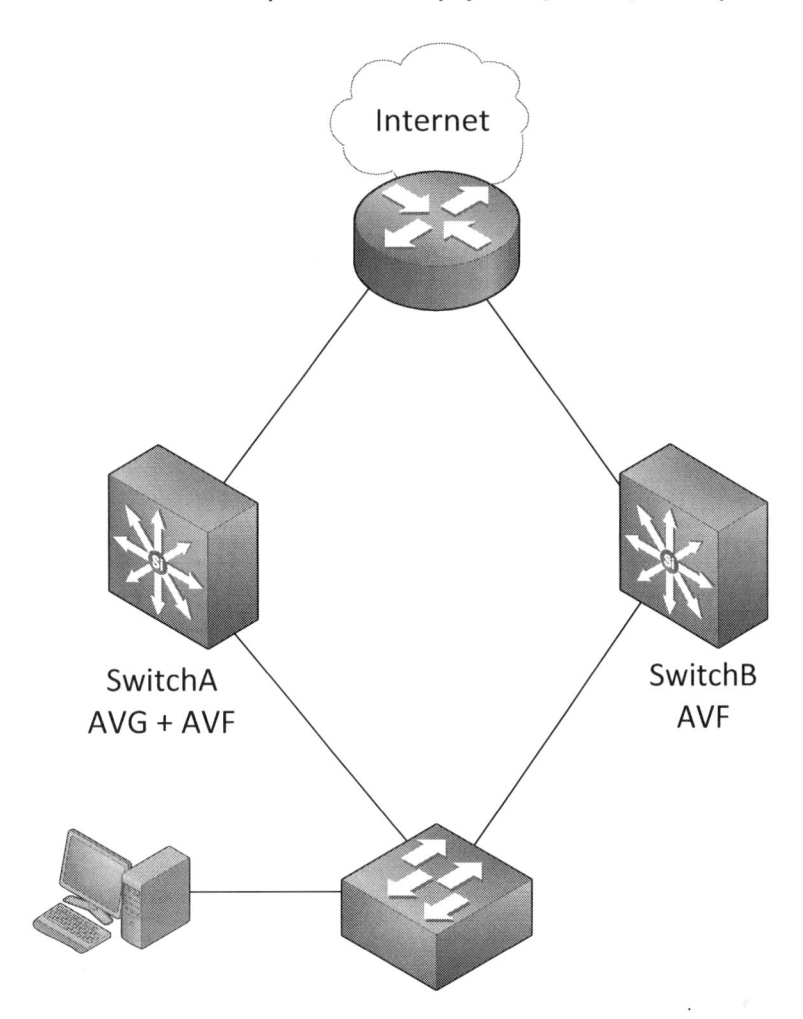

All devices running GLBP will elect an **AVG (Active Virtual Gateway).** There will be only one AVG for a single group running GLBP but other devices can take over this rule if the AVG fails. The role of the AVG is to assign a **virtual MAC address** to all other devices running GLBP. All devices will become an **AVF (Active Virtual Forwarder)** including the AVG. Whenever a computer sends an ARP Request the AVG will respond with one of the virtual MAC addresses of the available AVFs. Because of this mechanism all devices running GLBP will be used to forward IP packets.

There are multiple methods for load balancing:

- **Round-robin:** the AVG will hand out the virtual MAC address of AVF1, then AVF2, AVF3 and gets back to AVF1 etc.
- **Host-dependent**: A host will be able to use the same virtual MAC address of an AVF as long as it is reachable.
- **Weighted**: If you want some AVFs to forward more traffic than others you can assign them a different weight.

RouterA

192.168.14.0 /24   192.168.24.0 /24

SwitchA
192.168.1.1
AVG+AVF

Virtual Gateway
192.168.1.3

SwitchB
192.168.1.2
AVF

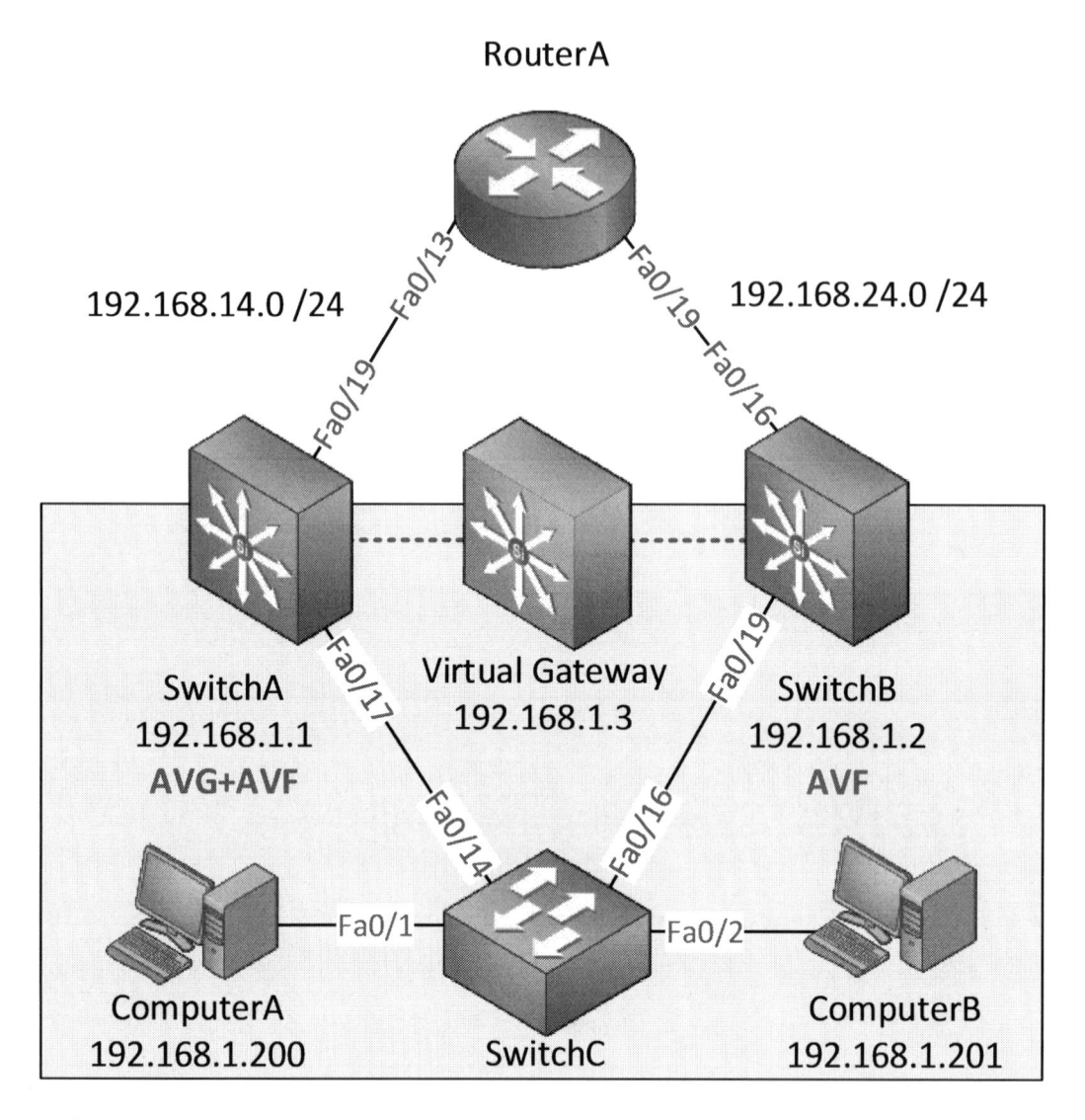

ComputerA — Fa0/1 — SwitchC — Fa0/2 — ComputerB
192.168.1.200   192.168.1.201

Let's configure GLBP with the same topology. Make sure you get rid of all your HSRP or VRRP stuff first.

```
SwitchA(config)#interface f0/17
SwitchA(config-if)#glbp 1 ip 192.168.1.3
SwitchA(config-if)#glbp 1 priority 150
```

```
SwitchB(config-if)#interface f0/19
SwitchB(config-if)#glbp 1 ip 192.168.1.3
```

I'll enable GLBP on SwitchA and SwitchB using the same group number (1). I changed the priority on SwitchA because I want it to be the AVG.

15. Gateway Redundancy (VRRP, GLBP, HSRP)

```
SwitchA#show glbp brief
Interface   Grp  Fwd Pri  State    Address          Active router    Standby router
Fa0/17      1    -   150  Active   192.168.1.3      local            192.168.1.2
Fa0/17      1    1   -    Active   0007.b400.0101   local            -
Fa0/17      1    2   -    Listen   0007.b400.0102   192.168.1.2      -
```

```
SwitchB#show glbp brief
Interface   Grp  Fwd Pri  State    Address          Active router    Standby router
Fa0/19      1    -   100  Standby  192.168.1.3      192.168.1.1      local
Fa0/19      1    1   -    Listen   0007.b400.0101   192.168.1.1      -
Fa0/19      1    2   -    Active   0007.b400.0102   local            -
```

Use the **show glbp brief** command to verify your configuration. There are a couple of things we can see here:

- SwitchA has become the AVG for group 1. SwitchB (192.168.1.2) is standby for the AVG role and will take over in case SwitchA fails.
- Group1 has two AVFs:
    - 1: SwitchA: Virtual MAC address 0007.b400.0101.
    - 2: SwitchB: Virtual MAC address 0007.b400.0102.

The **virtual MAC address that GLBP uses is 0007.b400.XXYY** (where X = GLBP group number and Y = AVF number).

```
C:\Documents and Settings\ComputerA>ipconfig

Windows IP Configuration


Ethernet adapter Local Area Connection:

        IP Address. . . . . . . . . . . . : 192.168.1.200
        Subnet Mask . . . . . . . . . . . : 255.255.255.0
        Default Gateway . . . . . . . . . : 192.168.1.3
```

```
C:\Documents and Settings\ComputerB>ipconfig

Windows IP Configuration


Ethernet adapter Local Area Connection:

        IP Address. . . . . . . . . . . . : 192.168.1.201
        Subnet Mask . . . . . . . . . . . : 255.255.255.0
        Default Gateway . . . . . . . . . : 192.168.1.3
```

We can use our computers to check which virtual MAC address they use for their gateway. Make sure both use the same gateway IP address (192.168.1.3).

```
C:\Documents and Settings\ComputerA>arp -a

Interface: 192.168.1.200--- 0x2
  Internet Address      Physical Address      Type
  192.168.1.3           00-07-b4-00-01-01     dynamic
```

```
C:\Documents and Settings\ComputerB>arp -a

Interface: 192.168.1.201--- 0x2
  Internet Address      Physical Address      Type
  192.168.1.3           00-07-b4-00-01-02     dynamic
```

You can see ComputerA uses the virtual MAC address of SwitchA (00-07-b4-00-01-01) while ComputerB uses the virtual MAC address of SwitchB (00-07-b4-00-01-02) for the same IP address (192.168.1.3). This is how GLBP will load balance traffic from hosts.

```
SwitchA(config)#interface fa0/17
SwitchA(config-if)#glbp 1 preempt
SwitchA(config-if)#glbp 1 authentication md5 key-string mypass
```

```
SwitchB(config)#interface fa0/19
SwitchB(config-if)#glbp 1 preempt
SwitchB(config-if)#glbp 1 authentication md5 key-string mypass
```

15. Gateway Redundancy (VRRP, GLBP, HSRP)

If you want you can configure things like preemption and authentication just like HSRP or VRRP. The configuration is the same but now you use the "glbp" command.

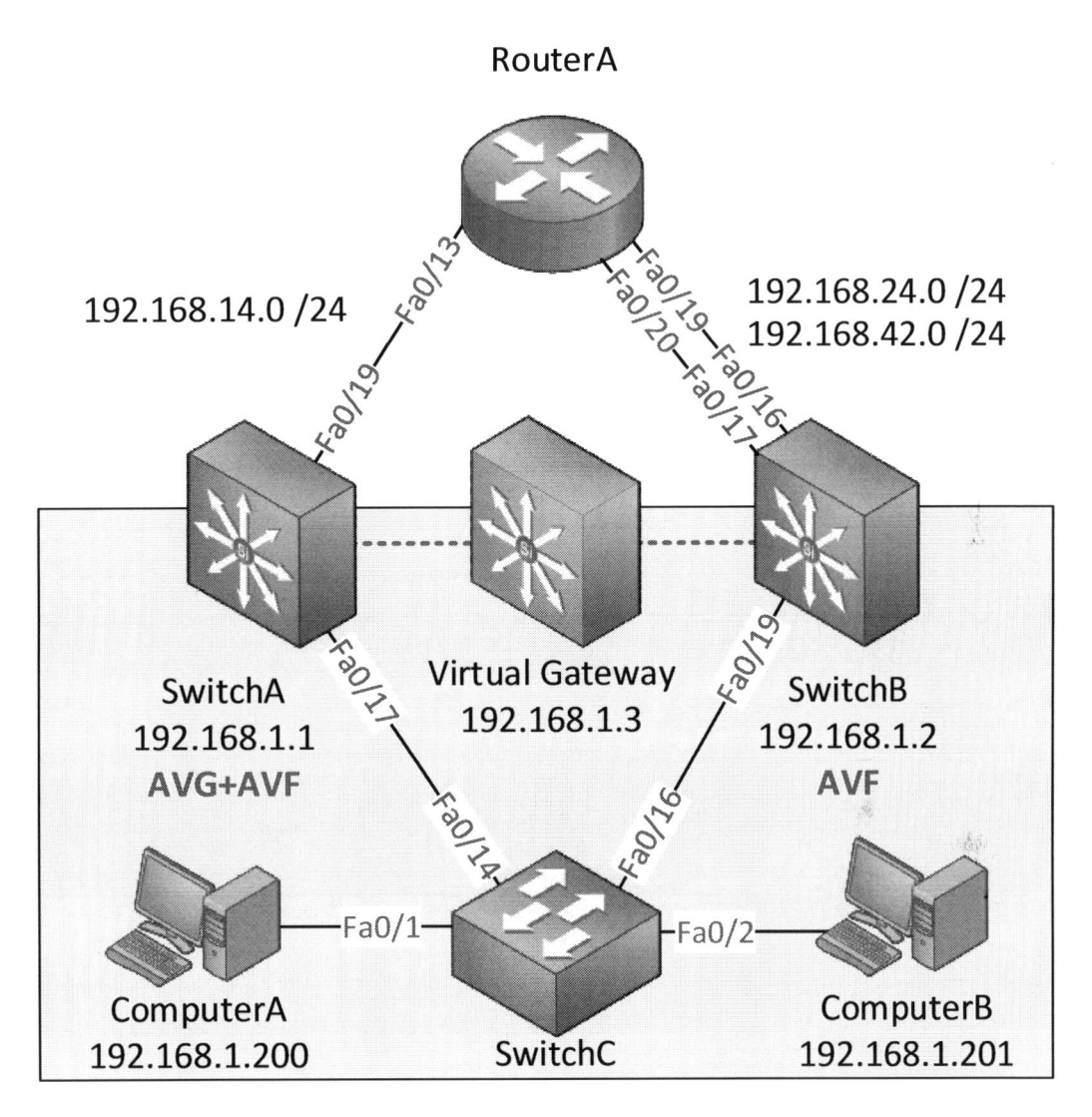

Interface tracking works differently for GLBP compared to HSRP or VRRP. HSRP/VRRP use a single threshold to determine which router is active/master. If you priority decreases and becomes lower than another device you'll lose the active/master state and someone else takes over. GLBP works differently and has a **weighting** mechanism. Weighting will be used to determine if a device can be AVF or not.

In the picture above I have added another interface between RouterA and SwitchB. Here's what I want to do:

331

- When one of the links fails it there is no problem so SwitchB can remain as an AVF.
- When both links fails we have a problem and SwitchB shouldn't be an AVF anymore.
- I only want SwitchB to become an AVF again once **both links** are operational again.

This is something we can do with GLBP, let me show you how:

```
SwitchB#show glbp | include Weighting
  Weighting 100 (default 100)
```

This is the default weighting of SwitchB (100).

```
SwitchB(config)#track 16 interface fastEthernet 0/16 line-protocol
SwitchB(config)#track 17 interface fastEthernet 0/17 line-protocol
```

First I will configure object tracking for interface FastEthernet 0/16 and 0/17.

```
SwitchB(config)#interface fa0/19
SwitchB(config-if)#glbp 1 weighting track 16 decrement 20
SwitchB(config-if)#glbp 1 weighting track 17 decrement 20
```

Here's how I configure tracking for GLBP. Whenever interface fa0/16 or fa0/17 goes down it should decrement the weight by 20.

```
SwitchB(config-if)#glbp 1 weighting 100 lower 70 upper 90
```

This is how we configure weighting; this is what it will do:

- The default weighting has a value of 100.
- Once we fall below a weighting value of 70 SwitchB will no longer be an AVF.
- Once the weighting gets above 90 we will become an AVF once again.

Let's see it in action!

```
SwitchB#show glbp | include Weighting
  Weighting 100 (configured 100), thresholds: lower 70, upper 90
```

Here are the values I just configured.

```
SwitchB(config)#interface fa0/16
SwitchB(config-if)#shutdown
```

Let's shut the fa0/16 interface.

15. Gateway Redundancy (VRRP, GLBP, HSRP)

```
SwitchB#show glbp | include Weighting
  Weighting 80 (configured 100), thresholds: lower 70, upper 90
```

Our weighting is now down to 80 but still nothing has changed, we need to get below 70 before anything happens.

```
SwitchB(config)#interface fa0/17
SwitchB(config-if)#shutdown
```

This will decrement our weighting once more with 20 which should get our weighting to a value of 60.

```
SwitchB#
%GLBP-6-FWDSTATECHANGE: FastEthernet0/19 Grp 1 Fwd 2 state
Active -> Listen
```

```
SwitchB#show glbp | include Weighting
  Weighting 60, low (configured 100), thresholds: lower 70,
upper 90
```

Our weighting is now 60 which lower than the "lower" value that we configured at 70. SwitchB is no longer an AVF.

```
SwitchB(config)#interface fa0/16
SwitchB(config-if)#no shutdown
```

Let's bring one of the interfaces back to the land of the living...

```
SwitchB#show glbp | include Weighting
  Weighting 80, low (configured 100), thresholds: lower 70,
upper 90
```

Nothing will change at this moment. Our weighting is 80 but we need to climb **above** the "upper" value of 90.

```
SwitchB(config)#interface fa0/17
SwitchB(config-if)#no shutdown
```

```
SwitchB#show glbp | include Weighting
  Weighting 100, low (configured 100), thresholds: lower 70,
upper 90
```

Now our weighting is back to 100 and we exceeded the upper value of 90. We are back in the game!

```
SwitchB#
```

333

```
%GLBP-6-FWDSTATECHANGE: FastEthernet0/19 Grp 1 Fwd 2 state
Listen -> Active
```

You can see on the console that SwitchB is once again an AVF.

This is everything I wanted to show you about GLBP and this is also the end of this chapter. You have now seen how HSRP, VRRP and GLBP operate and ready to bring redundancy to your gateways.

If you want to practice the configuration of these protocols I highly recommend you to use GNS3. Some of the IOS versions on switches only support HSRP and not VRRP or GLBP. The configuration of these protocols is exactly the same on routers as on switches. You can take a look at some of the pre-built labs I created for all three protocols:

http://gns3vault.com/Network-Services/hot-standby-routing-protocol.html

http://gns3vault.com/Network-Services/vrrp-virtual-router-redundancy-protocol.html

http://gns3vault.com/Network-Services/glbp-gateway-load-balancing-protocol.html

15. Gateway Redundancy (VRRP, GLBP, HSRP)

16. Switch Security

At this moment you should have a pretty solid understanding of how switches operate. You've seen VLANs, trunks, spanning-tree and more. In this chapter we are going to take a look at a number of things that could possibly go wrong with switches...it's time for security!

> *"The only real security that a man can have in this world is a reserve of knowledge, experience and ability."*
> *~Henry Ford*

Most security solutions focus on the "outside" of our network. The Internet is the wild west and a bad place while our LANs is where we feel happy and secure.

Most products you can buy focus on "defending" the outside of your network....firewalls, packet inspection, intrusion prevention systems and such.

What if someone would just walk into your office and plugs a laptop into an empty RJ45 wall socket?

The first attack we will look at is **MAC flooding.** This is a very simple (but sometimes effective) attack.

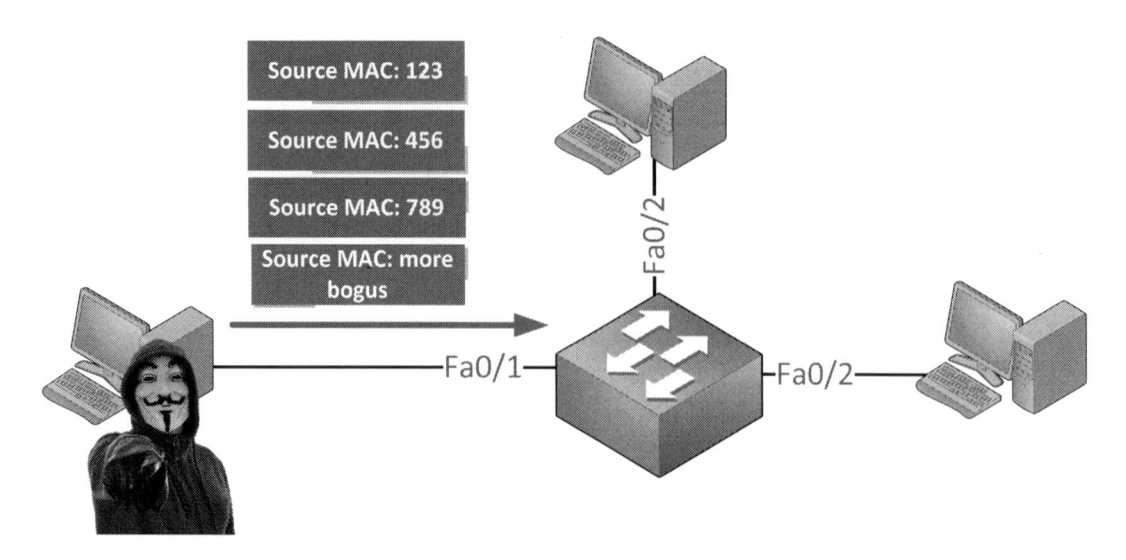

The idea behind MAC flooding is to **overflow the MAC address table** of the switch (also known as CAM table). There are tools that will generate Ethernet frames with bogus source MAC addresses and these will be sent on the interface. The switch will learn these MAC addresses and only has a limited capability to store MAC addresses. Once it's full it won't learn any new MAC addresses and as a result it will **flood traffic.** The attacker can run wireshark and try to capture some of the traffic of legitimate devices that is being flooded.

The solution to MAC flooding is quite easy and if you studied CCNA you have seen it before. It's called **port security** and you can use it to limit the number of MAC addresses per interface.

```
SwitchA(config)#interface fa0/1
SwitchA(config-if)#switchport mode access
SwitchA(config-if)#switchport port-security
SwitchA(config-if)#switchport port-security maximum 1
```

You can enable port security on interfaces in access mode. Use the **switchport port-security** command to enable it. I have configured the interface so only one MAC address is allowed. Normally on access interfaces you will only learn one MAC address (computer, server or laptop). The only exception is when you use VoIP phones because you'll connect the phone to the switch and the computer to the phone, in this case you'll learn two MAC addresses on the interface. Once the switch sees another MAC address on the interface it will be in **violation** and something will happen. I'll show you what happens in a bit...

```
SwitchA(config)#interface fa0/1
SwitchA(config-if)#switchport port-security mac-address
aaaa.bbbb.cccc
```

Besides setting a maximum on the number of MAC addresses we can also use port security to **filter** MAC addresses. In the example above I configured port security so it only allows MAC address aaaa.bbbb.cccc. This is not the MAC address of my computer so it's perfect to demonstrate a violation.

```
C:\Documents and Settings\ComputerA>ping 1.2.3.4
```

Make sure to generate some traffic from the Computer so we can cause a violation. I'm pinging to some bogus IP address...

```
SwitchA#
%PM-4-ERR_DISABLE: psecure-violation error detected on Fa0/1,
putting Fa0/1 in err-disable state
%PORT_SECURITY-2-PSECURE_VIOLATION: Security violation occurred,
caused by MAC address 0090.cc0e.5023 on port FastEthernet0/1.
%LINEPROTO-5-UPDOWN: Line protocol on Interface FastEthernet0/1,
changed state to down
%LINK-3-UPDOWN: Interface FastEthernet0/1, changed state to down
```

Banzai! We have a security violation and as a result the port goes in **err-disable state**. As you can see it is now down.

```
SwitchA#show port-security interface fa0/1
Port Security               : Enabled
Port Status                 : Secure-shutdown
Violation Mode              : Shutdown
Aging Time                  : 0 mins
Aging Type                  : Absolute
SecureStatic Address Aging  : Disabled
Maximum MAC Addresses       : 1
Total MAC Addresses         : 1
Configured MAC Addresses    : 1
Sticky MAC Addresses        : 0
Last Source Address:Vlan    : 0090.cc0e.5023:1
Security Violation Count    : 1
```

Here is a useful command to check your port security configuration. Use **show port-security interface** to see the port security details per interface. You can see the violation mode is shutdown and that the last violation was caused by MAC address 0090.cc0e.5023 (ComputerA). The **aging time** is 0 mins which means it will stay in err-disable state forever.

```
SwitchA#show interfaces fa0/1
FastEthernet0/1 is down, line protocol is down (err-disabled)
```

Shutting the interface after a security violation is a good idea (security-wise) but the problem is that the interface will **stay in err-disable state**. This probably means another call to the helpdesk and *you* bringing the interface back to the land of the living!

339

```
SwitchA(config)#interface fa0/1
SwitchA(config-if)#shutdown
SwitchA(config-if)#no shutdown
```

To get the interface out of err-disable state you need to type "shutdown" followed by "no shutdown". Only typing "no shutdown" is **not enough**!

```
SwitchA(config)#errdisable recovery cause psecure-violation
SwitchA(config)#interface fa0/1
SwitchA(config-if)#switchport port-security aging time 10
```

You can change the aging time from 0 to whatever value you like with the **switchport port-security aging time** command. After 10 minutes it will automatically recover from err-disable state. Make sure you solve the problem though because otherwise it will just have another violation and end up in err-disable state again. Make sure you don't forget to enable automatic recovery with the **errdisable recovery cause psecure-violation** command.

```
SwitchA(config-if)#no switchport port-security mac-address
aaaa.bbbb.cccc
SwitchA(config-if)#switchport port-security mac-address sticky
```

Instead of typing in MAC addresses yourself you can also use the **sticky** command. Your switch will learn the MAC address on the interface and save this one for port security.

```
SwitchA#show run interface fa0/1
Building configuration...

Current configuration : 228 bytes
!
interface FastEthernet0/1
 switchport mode access
 switchport port-security
 switchport port-security aging time 10
 switchport port-security mac-address sticky
 switchport port-security mac-address sticky 000c.2928.5c6c
```

You can see that it will save the MAC address of ComputerA in the running-configuration by itself.

```
SwitchA(config-if)#switchport port-security violation ?
  protect    Security violation protect mode
  restrict   Security violation restrict mode
  shutdown   Security violation shutdown mode
```

Maybe shutting the interface is a bit too much.

16. Switch Security

There are other options like **protect** and **restrict.**

- **Protect:** Ethernet frames from MAC addresses that are not allowed will be dropped but you won't receive any logging information.
- **Restrict:** Ethernet frames from MAC addresses that are not allowed will be dropped but you will see logging information and a SNMP trap is sent.
- **Shutdown:** Ethernet frames from MAC addresses that are not allowed will cause the interface to go to err-disable state. You will see logging information and a SNMP trap is sent. For recovery you have two options:
    - Manual: The default aging time is 0 mins so you'll have to enable the interface yourself.
    - Automatic: Configure the aging time to another value.

Another security issue that has to do with flooding is called a **broadcast storm**. When we have an excessive amount of broadcast traffic on the network then all devices within the VLAN will suffer. The switch has to flood all broadcast frames to interfaces in the same VLAN while hosts might have to respond (for example to ARP requests).

Too much broadcast traffic could be caused by malicious software but also by a malfunctioning NIC. To protect ourselves against this, Cisco switches offer the **storm-control feature**. We can configure a threshold on interfaces to set a limit to the number of broadcast, multicast or unknown unicast traffic and an action when the threshold is exceeded.

Here's an example how to configure this:

```
SwitchA(config-if)#storm-control ?
  action     Action to take for storm-control
  broadcast  Broadcast address storm control
  multicast  Multicast address storm control
  unicast    Unicast address storm control
```

We can set an action and threshold for broadcast, multicast or unknown unicast traffic. Let's take a look at broadcast traffic:

```
SwitchA(config)#interface FastEthernet0/1
SwitchA(config-if)#storm-control broadcast level ?
  <0.00 - 100.00>  Enter rising threshold
  bps              Enter suppression level in bits per second
  pps              Enter suppression level in packets per second
```

I have a couple of options here...when you use the rising threshold then the value you enter is a percentage of the interface bandwidth. The other two options are BPS (bits per second) or PPS (packets per second). Let's start with a simple example:

```
SwitchA(config-if)#storm-control broadcast level 30
```

Whenever broadcast traffic exceeds 30% of the interface bandwidth, we will take action. I didn't configure any action yet but the default action will **drop exceeding traffic**.

Let's look at an example for multicast:

```
SwitchA(config-if)#storm-control multicast level bps ?
  <0.0 - 10000000000.0>[k|m|g]   Enter rising threshold
```

Now I can select a threshold in BPS. You can use K,M or G to indicate Kbps, Mbps or Gbps. Let's pick something:

```
SwitchA(config-if)#storm-control multicast level bps 10m
```

Once multicast exceeds 10Mbps, it will be dropped. In the previous examples I only configured a **rising threshold**. This means that once we exceed the threshold, the traffic will be dropped. Once we are below this threshold it will be permitted. We can also use a **falling threshold**:

```
SwitchA(config-if)#storm-control unicast level pps 30m 20m
```

Here's an example for unknown unicast traffic and PPS. The rising threshold is 30Mbps, once we get above this then the traffic will be dropped. The falling threshold is 20Mbps which means that the amount of traffic has to be below 20Mbps before we permit it again.

Last but not least, we can change the action:

```
SwitchA(config-if)#storm-control action ?
  shutdown   Shutdown this interface if a storm occurs
  trap       Send SNMP trap if a storm occurs
```

By default the exceeding traffic is dropped but we can also choose to shutdown the interface or to send a SNMP trap.

```
SwitchA(config-if)#storm-control action trap
```

To verify our work we can use the **show storm-control** command:

```
SwitchA#show storm-control
Interface  Filter State    Upper        Lower        Current
---------  ------------    -----------  -----------  ----------
Fa0/1      Forwarding       30.00%       30.00%       0.00%
```

This only gives us the information for broadcast traffic. If we want to verify our settings for unicast or multicast traffic then we have to add a parameter:

16. Switch Security

```
SwitchA#show storm-control multicast
Interface   Filter State   Upper         Lower         Current
---------   ------------   -----------   -----------   ----------
Fa0/1       Forwarding     10m bps       10m bps       0 bps
```

```
SwitchA#show storm-control unicast
Interface   Filter State   Upper         Lower         Current
---------   ------------   -----------   -----------   ----------
Fa0/1       Forwarding     30m pps       20m pps       0 pps
```

These commands are also useful to see the current traffic levels. These will help to make up a baseline for the thresholds that you want to use.

That's all there is about storm-control. We'll continue with 802.1X authentication, let me show you a picture:

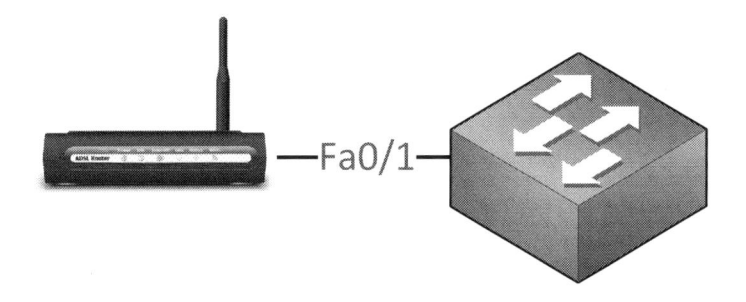

Port security is nice but it can only do so much because:

- MAC addresses are very easy to spoof.
- It doesn't stop someone from bringing their (wireless) router and connecting it to the switch port.

Network users might bring their own wireless router from home and connect it to the switch so they can share wireless internet with all their colleagues. An access point like this is called a **rogue access point** and this is something you DON'T want to see on your network. It's hard to detect because on the switch you'll only see one MAC address. The router is doing NAT so you will only see one IP address.

One way of dealing with issues like this is to use **AAA**.

AAA stands for **Authentication, Authorization** and **Accounting**:
- **Authentication**: Verify the identity of the user, who are you?
- **Authorization**: What is the user allowed to do? what resources can he/she access?

343

- **Accounting**: Used for billing and auditing.

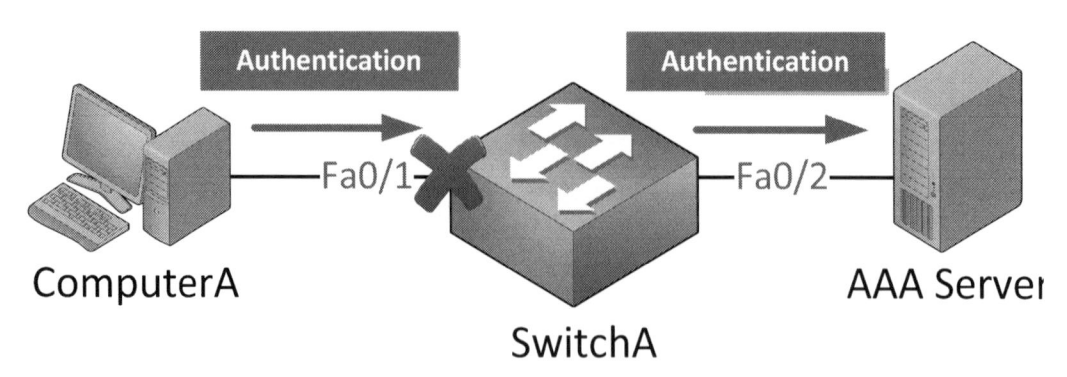

The idea behind AAA is that a user has to authenticate before getting access to the network. The fa0/1 interface on SwitchA will be blocked and you are not even getting an IP address. The only thing the user is allowed to do is send his/her credentials which will be forwarded to the AAA server. If your credentials are OK the port will be unblocked and you will be granted access to the network.

Before 802.1X Authentication   After 802.1X Authentication

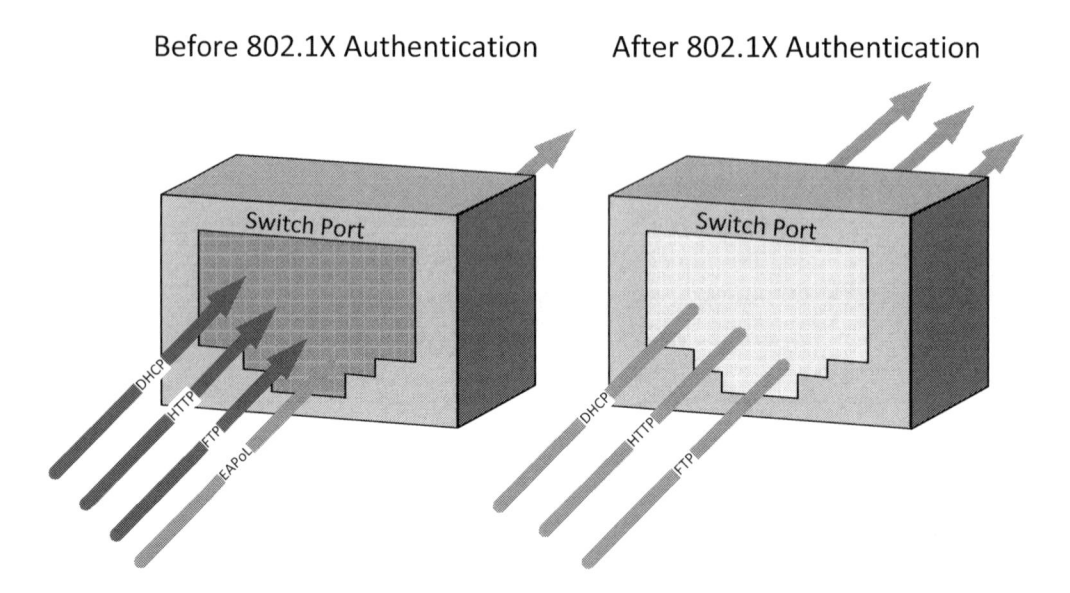

802.1X is the mechanism that will **block** or **unblock** the interface. It's called **port-based control.** In the picture above an unknown user plugged in a cable to the switch. All traffic is being dropped with the exception of **EAPoL** (**Extensible Authentication Protocol over LAN).** EAP is what we use to exchange authentication information. Once the user (Alice) has authenticated and everything is OK she is granted access to the network.

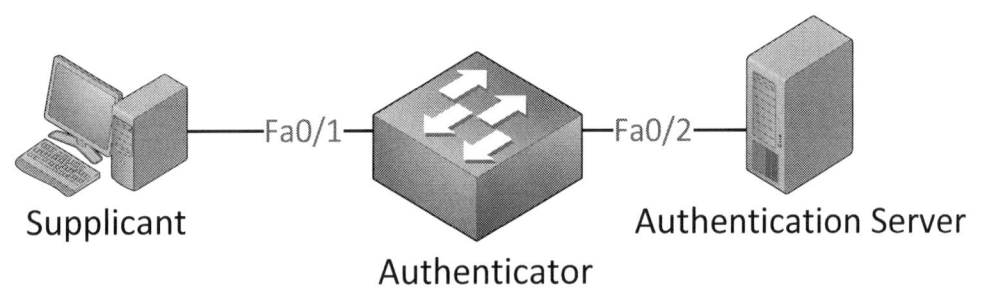

16. Switch Security

Supplicant — Fa0/1 — Authenticator — Fa0/2 — Authentication Server

In the picture above you see the terminology that 802.1X uses. The user device is called the **supplicant**; it "supplies" authentication information. The switch is called the **authenticator** because it accepts the authentication information and passes it along to the **authentication server**. User information is stored on the authentication server.

There are two types of authentication servers:
- **RADIUS**
- **TACACS+**

The most common authentication server is RADIUS (Remote Authentication Dial In User Service). It's a protocol that has been standardized by the IETF. TACACS+ (Terminal Access Controller Access-Control System) does a similar job but its Cisco proprietary.

There are many different RADIUS servers you can use, for example:

- Cisco ACS (Cisco's RADIUS and TACACS+ server software)
- Microsoft IAS (you can install it on Windows server 2003 or 2008).
- Freeradius (very powerful and free)
- Integrated in network devices (Cisco's Wireless LAN controller have RADIUS server software for example).

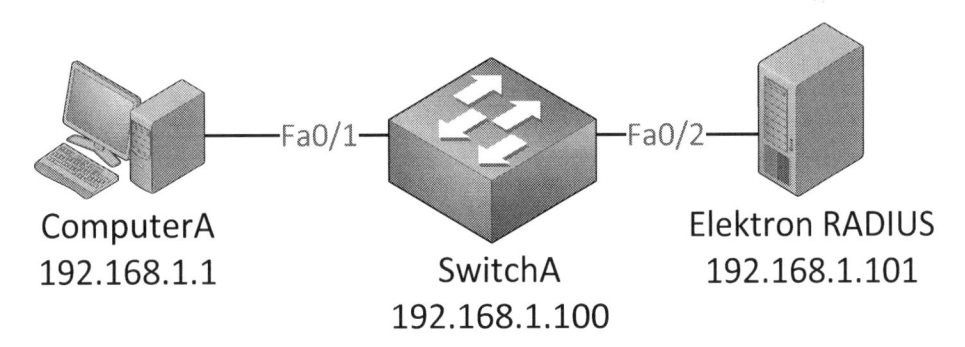

ComputerA 192.168.1.1 — Fa0/1 — SwitchA 192.168.1.100 — Fa0/2 — Elektron RADIUS 192.168.1.101

I will show you an example of 802.1X with a RADIUS server. I am going to use Elektron RADIUS server as the authentication server because it's easy to install and has a nice GUI. If you want to try it you can download it here:

https://www.dropbox.com/s/boif6jpziesf5vk/ElektronSetup-2.1.2376.exe

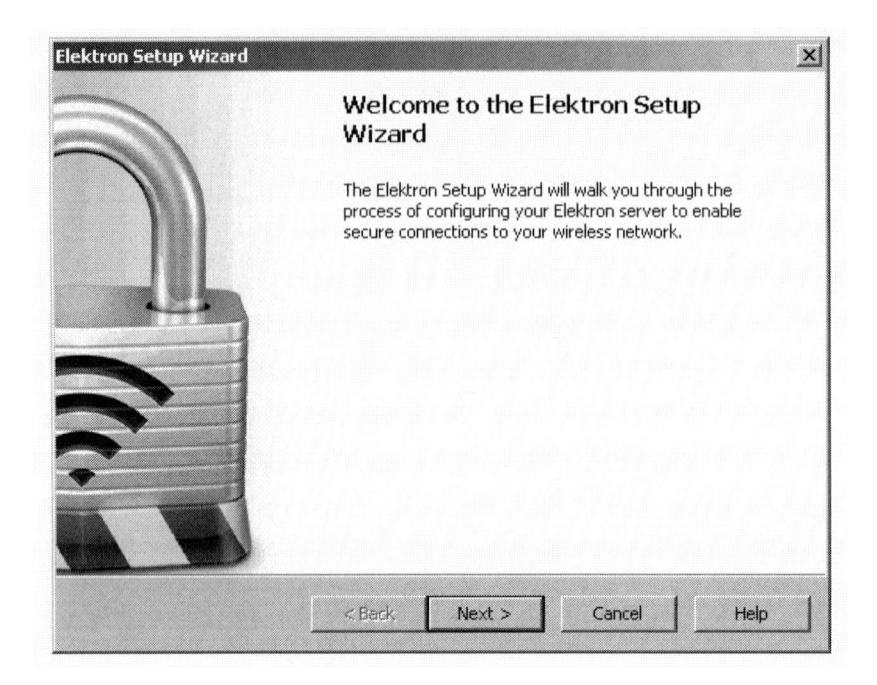

This makes me feel like I'm writing a Microsoft Windows book :) Using a RADIUS server like Elektron will save you the time of hassling with installing Windows Server, configuring Active Directory and checking many checkboxes...

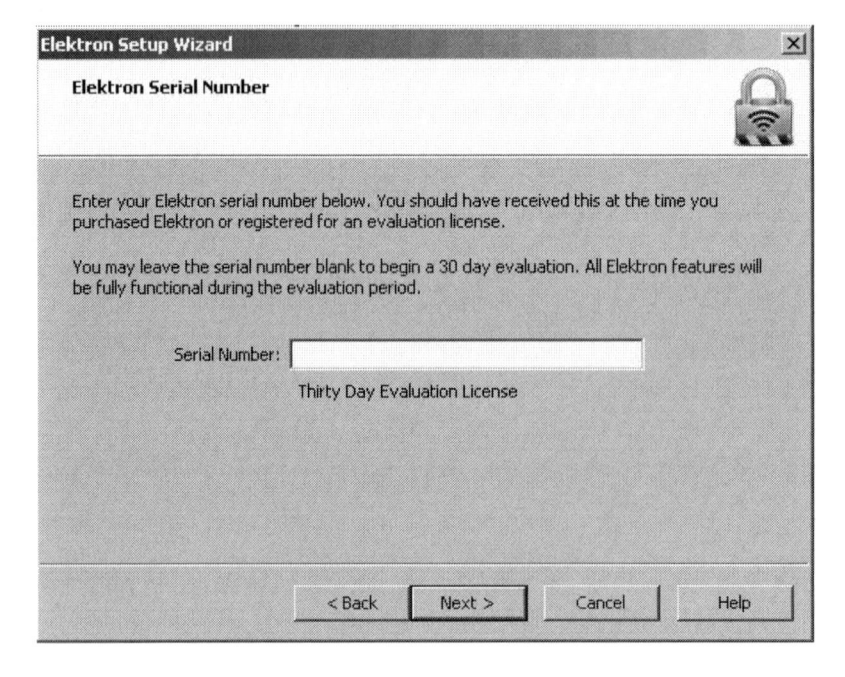

Don't type in a serial number so you can use the 30 day trial.

16. Switch Security

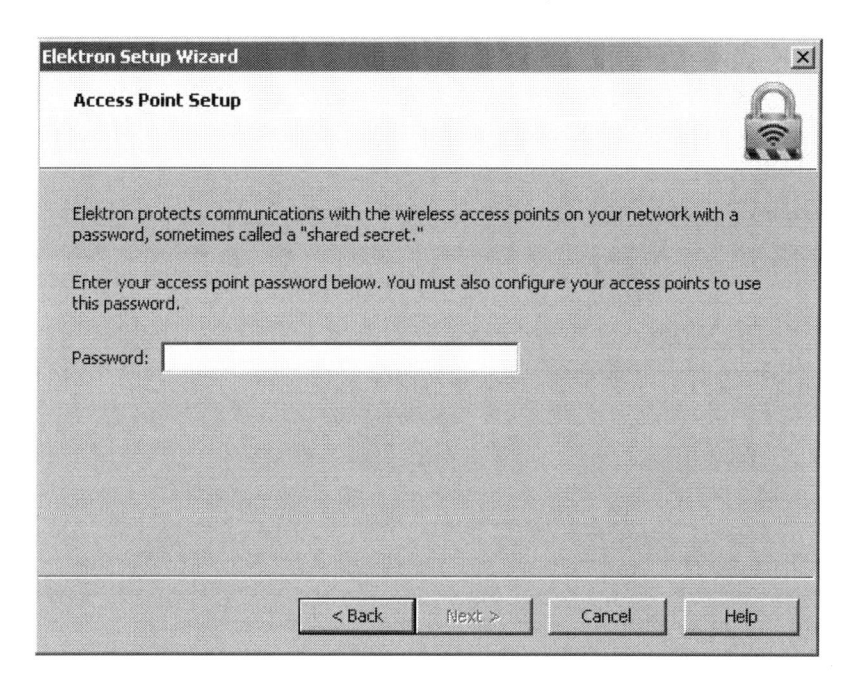

On the authenticator (SwitchA) and the authentication server (Elektron) we need to use a shared secret. I'm going to use "radiuspass".

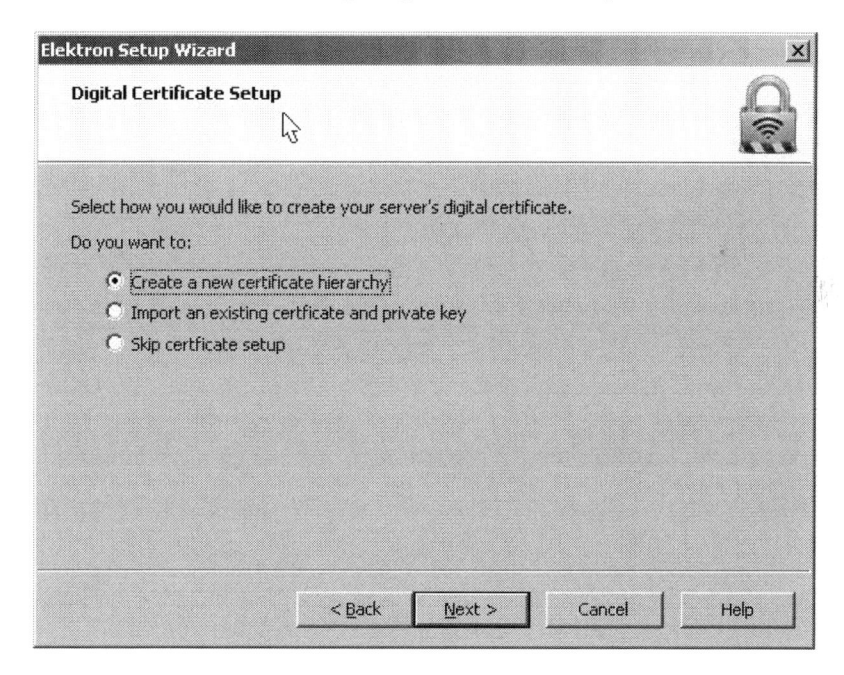

There are different methods for authentication, for example:

- Only username and password.
- Username, password and a digital certificate on the server.
- Username, password, digital certificate on the server AND on the clients.

In a production network you might already have a certificate authority within your network. I don't care about certificates for this demonstration but we'll generate them anyway in case you want to play with them sometime in the future.

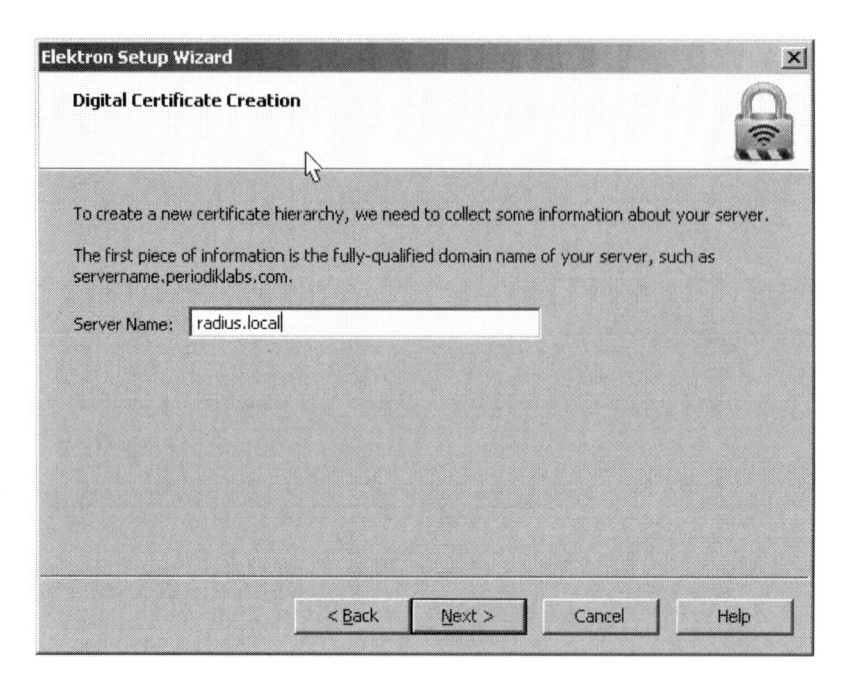

Pick a name for your server; I'm going to call mine "radius.local".

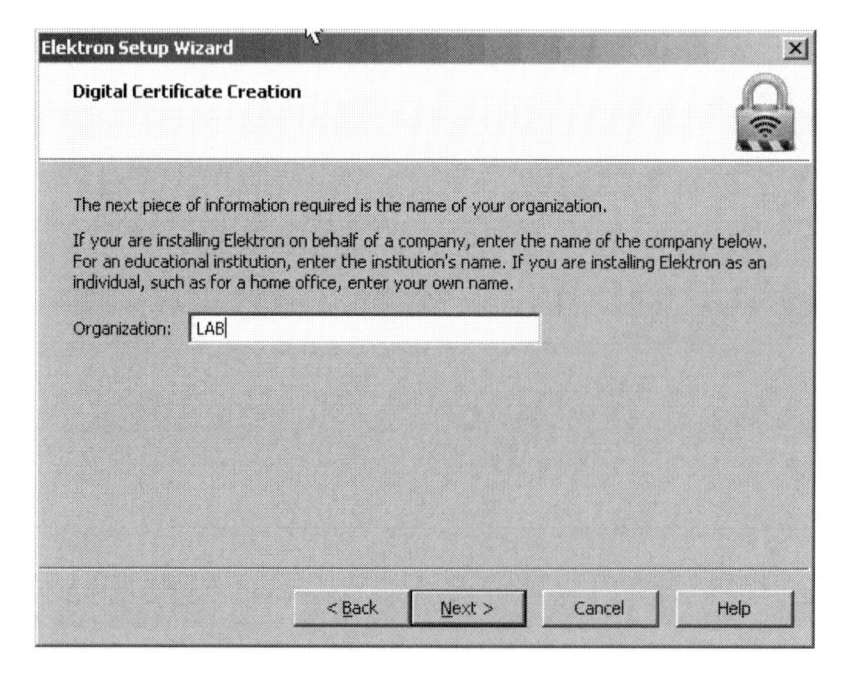

Pick any name you like, I'm just going to call my organization "LAB".

16. Switch Security

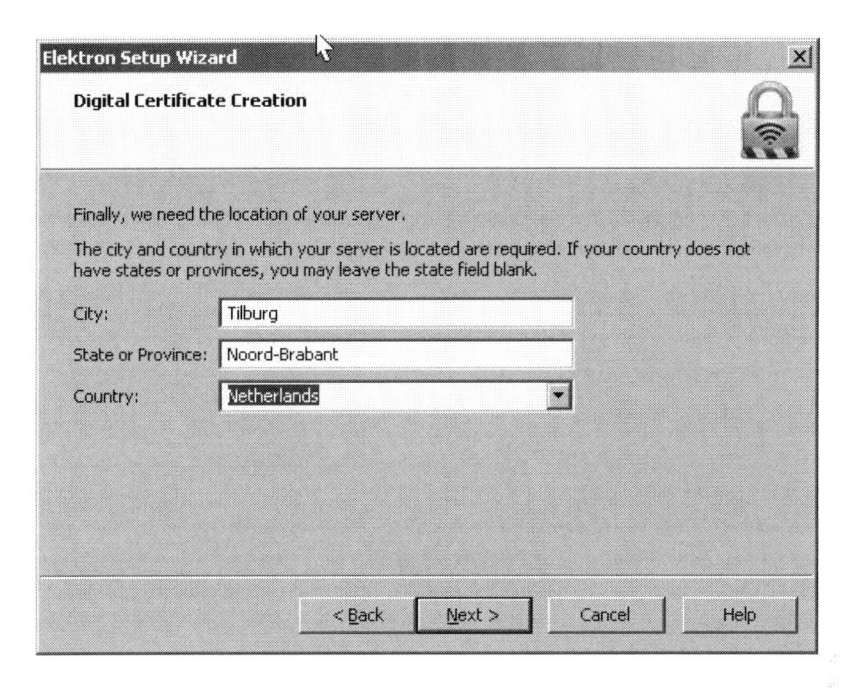

Last step is to fill in a city, state/province and country in order to generate a certificate. Fill in whatever you like here.

Press finish and you are good to go!

349

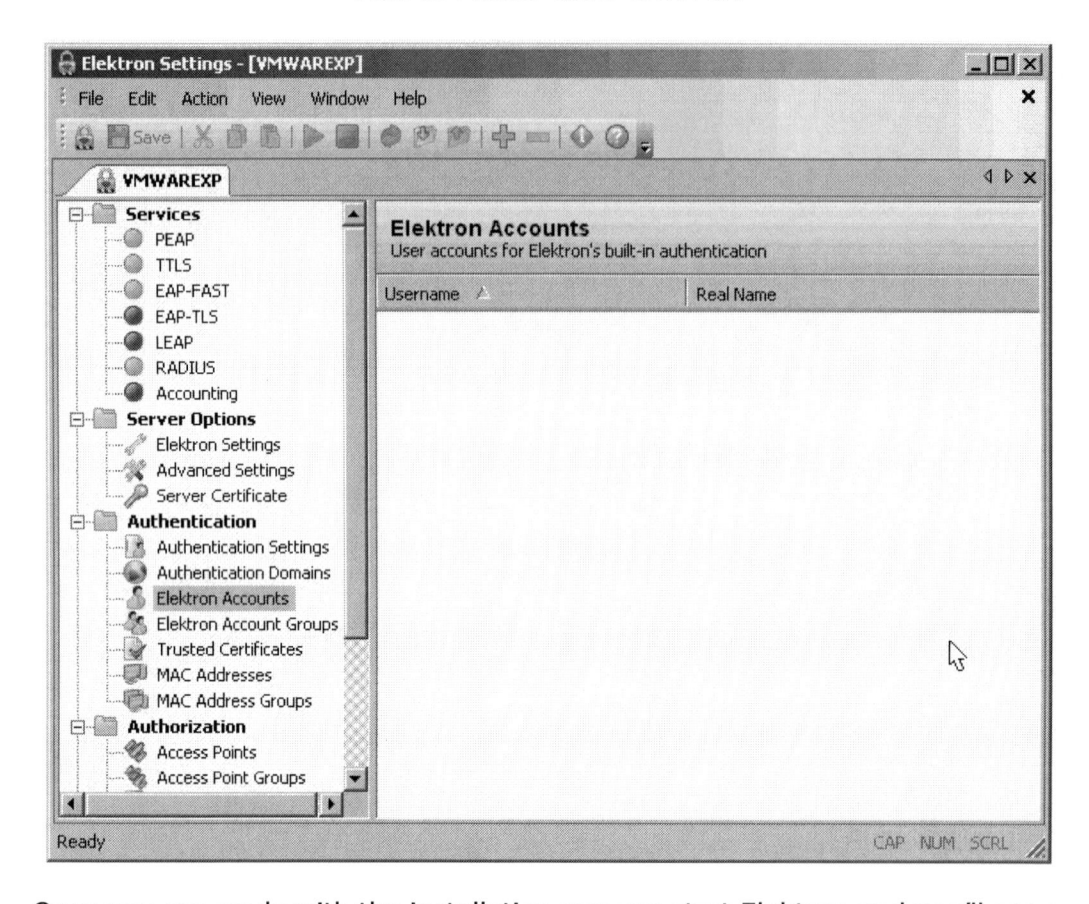

Once you are ready with the installation you can start Elektron and you'll see a nice GUI with all the different options. By default everything should work out of the box so we don't have to touch anything.

16. Switch Security

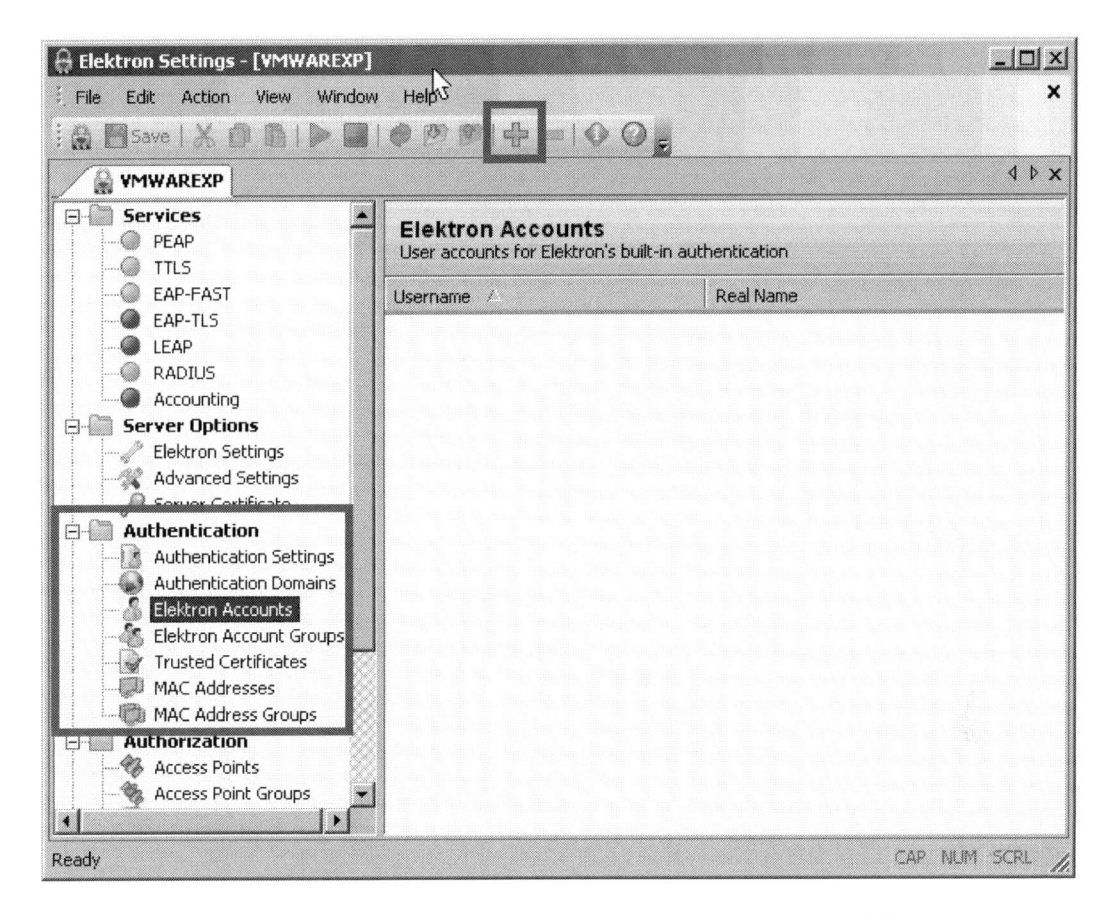

I want to create a new user account. Click on authentication, Elektron accounts and then on the big green plus symbol in the menu.

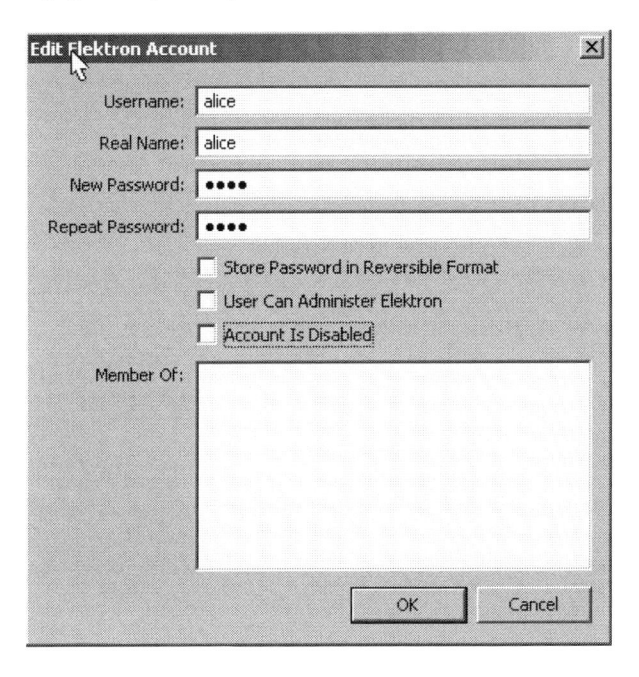

351

My new user account will be for Alice. My password will be "safe" and I don't need her to be member of any groups. Click on OK.

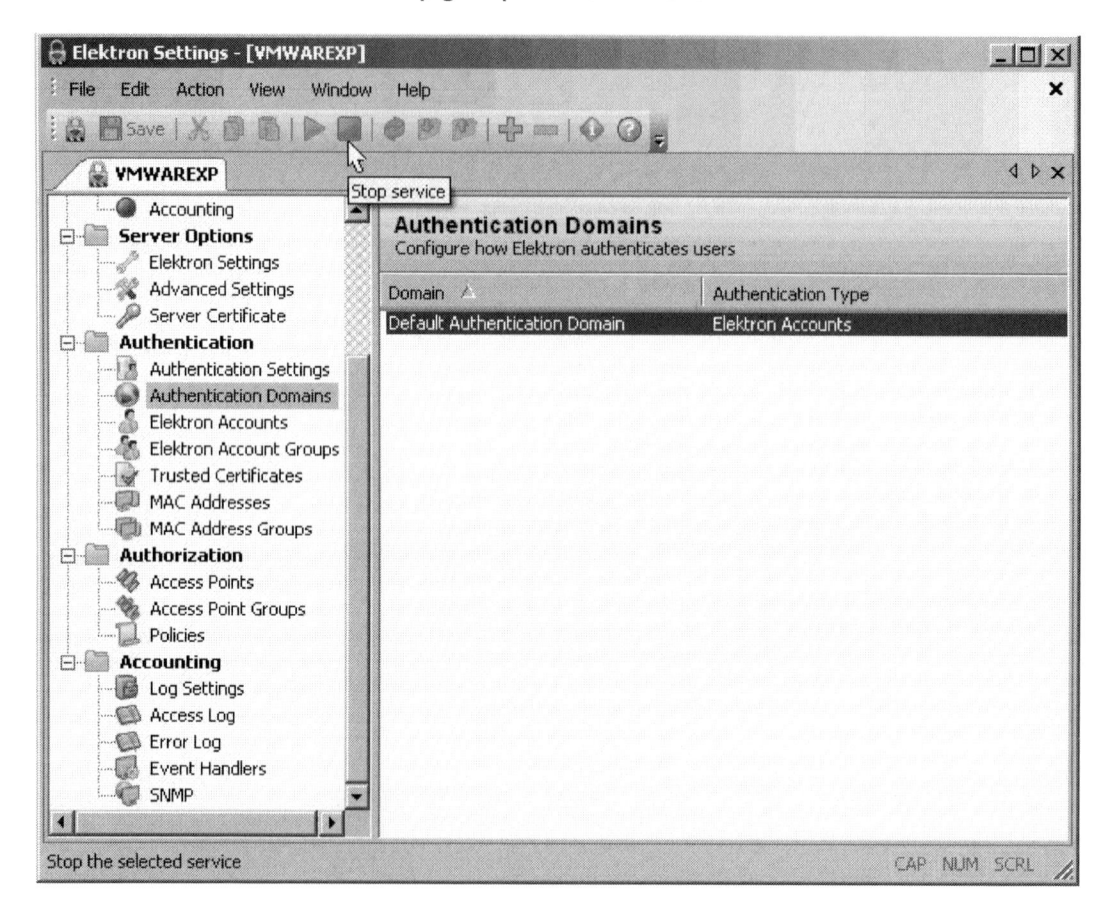

By default Elektron will check Windows usernames instead of its own database. We need to configure it so the local database is used. Click on "Authentication Domains" and then on "Default Authentication Domain".

16. Switch Security

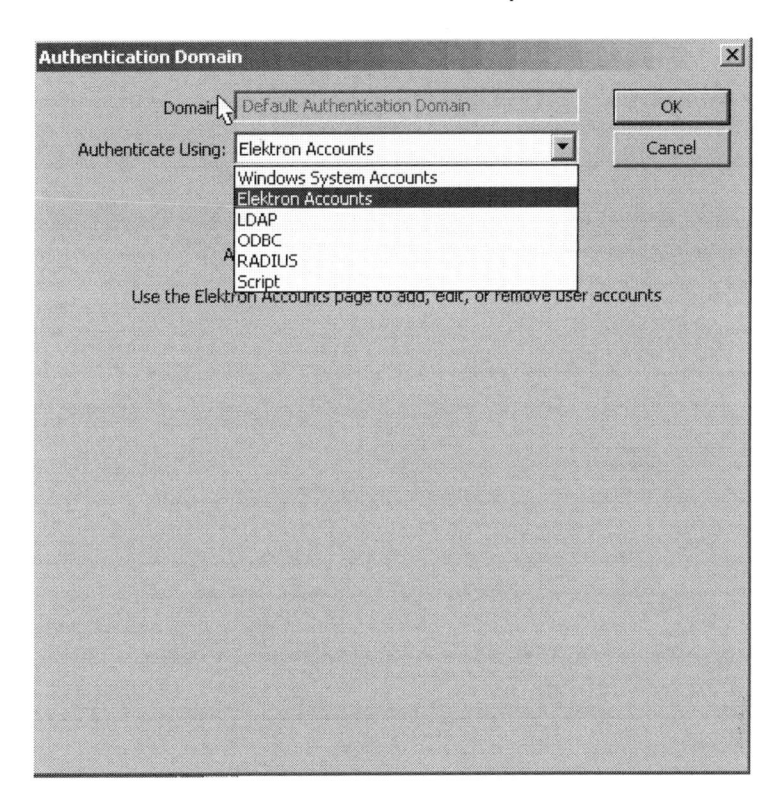

![Authentication Domain dialog showing Domain field with "Default Authentication Domain" and Authenticate Using dropdown with options: Windows System Accounts, Elektron Accounts (highlighted), LDAP, ODBC, RADIUS, Script. Text below reads: "Use the Elektron Accounts page to add, edit, or remove user accounts"]

Change it to "Elektron Accounts" and click on OK. That's all you have to do on the Elektron RADIUS server, we'll look at the switch now!

```
SwitchA(config)#interface vlan 1
SwitchA(config-if)#ip address 192.168.1.100 255.255.255.0
```

First I need to make sure SwitchA and the Elektron RADIUS server can reach each other. We'll use the management interface (VLAN 1) and configure an IP address on it.

```
SwitchA(config)#aaa new-model
```

This is an important command. Use **aaa new-model** to unlock all the different AAA commands that we need.

```
SwitchA(config)# radius-server host 192.168.1.101 auth-port 1812 acct-port 1646 key radiuspass
```

We configure SwitchA with the IP address of the Elektron RADIUS server. I also have to specify the shared secret "radiuspass" that I configured previously here. Make sure to use the correct port number.

```
SwitchA(config)#aaa authentication dot1x default group radius
```

353

This is how we configure SwitchA to use the RADIUS server for authentication for 802.1X enabled interfaces. You can create multiple groups with RADIUS servers if you want.

```
SwitchA(config)#aaa authentication ?
  arap              Set authentication lists for arap.
  attempts          Set the maximum number of authentication attempts
  banner            Message to use when starting login/authentication.
  dot1x             Set authentication lists for IEEE 802.1x.
  enable            Set authentication list for enable.
  eou               Set authentication lists for EAPoUDP
  fail-message      Message to use for failed login/authentication.
  login             Set authentication lists for logins.
  nasi              Set authentication lists for NASI.
  password-prompt   Text to use when prompting for a password
  ppp               Set authentication lists for ppp.
  sgbp              Set authentication lists for sgbp.
  username-prompt   Text to use when prompting for a username
```

Besides 802.1X you can use AAA for many other things, for example:

- Privileged mode (enable): Instead of using a enable password/secret on your device your credentials will be checked at the authentication server.
- Login: You can also check credentials for telnet or SSH access.

```
SwitchA(config)#dot1x system-auth-control
SwitchA(config)#interface fa0/1
SwitchA(config-if)#dot1x port-control auto
```

Last step is to enable 802.1X on the fa0/1 interface that connects to ComputerA. We need to use the **dot1x system-auth-control** command globally before 802.1X works. On the interface level we need to use the **dot1x port-control auto** command.

```
SwitchA#
%LINEPROTO-5-UPDOWN: Line protocol on Interface FastEthernet0/1, changed state to down
```

After typing in those 802.1X commands you'll see that the interface to ComputerA will go down. It's time for some authentication! I will use Windows XP as an example for the client.

16. Switch Security

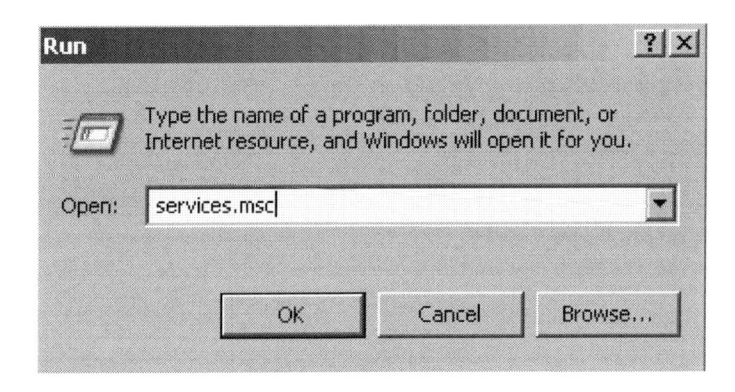

802.1X doesn't always work out of the box so we need to check if a certain service is running. Press "start", click on "run" and type "services.msc".

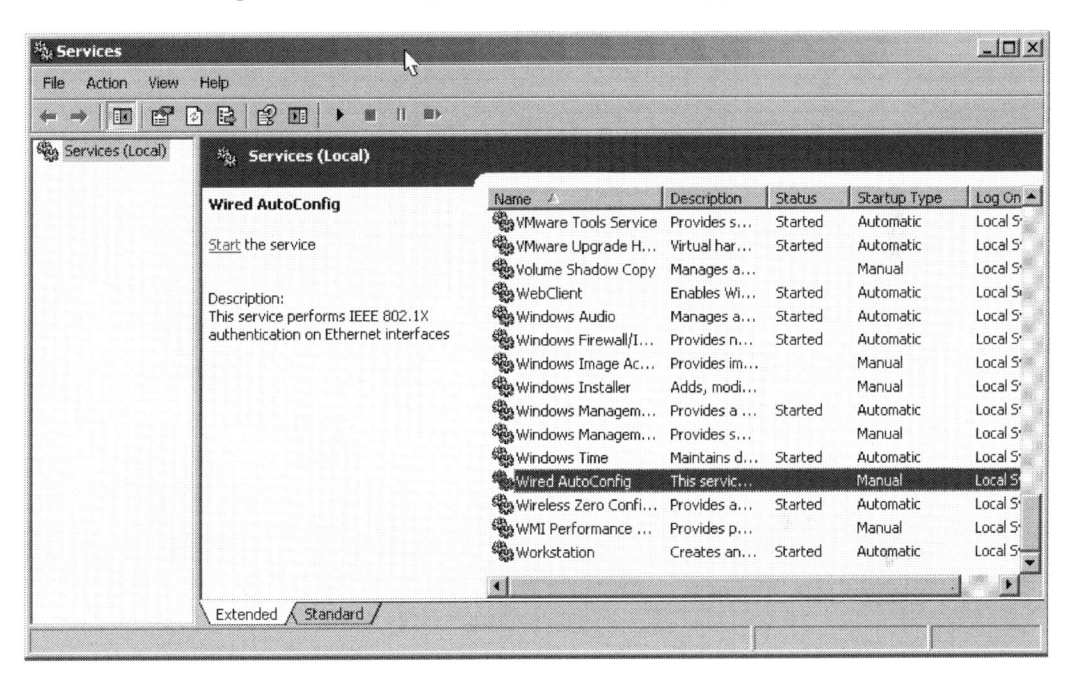

Look for the "Wired Autoconfig" service and start it if it's not running.

How to Master CCNP SWITCH

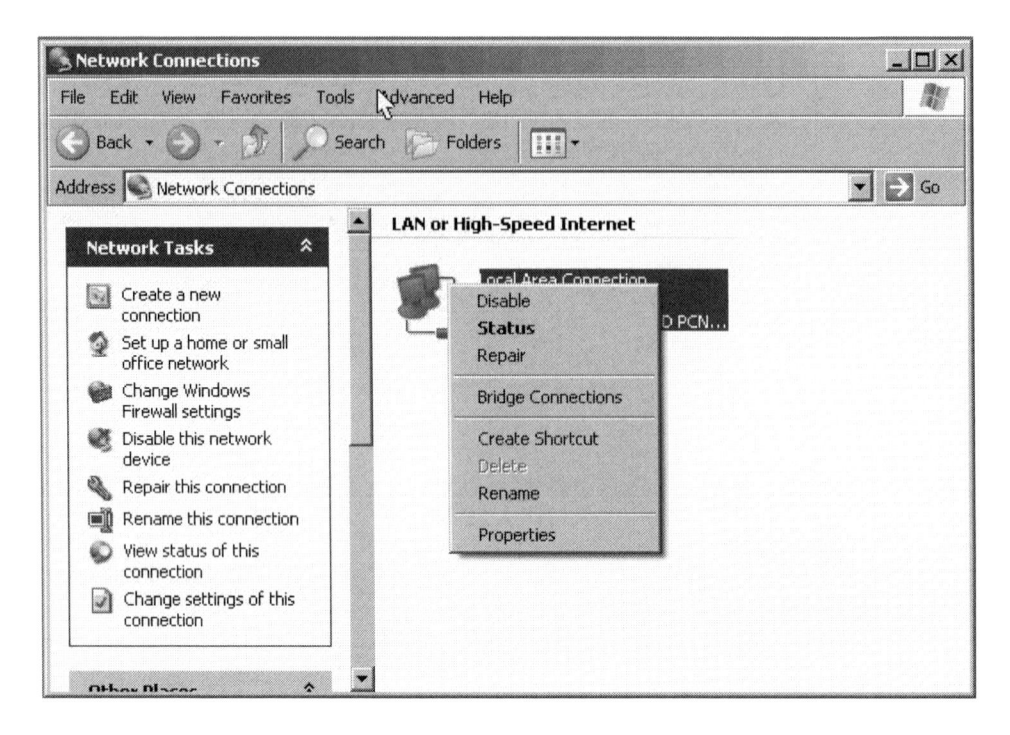

Now go to Network connections and open the properties of your network card.

16. Switch Security

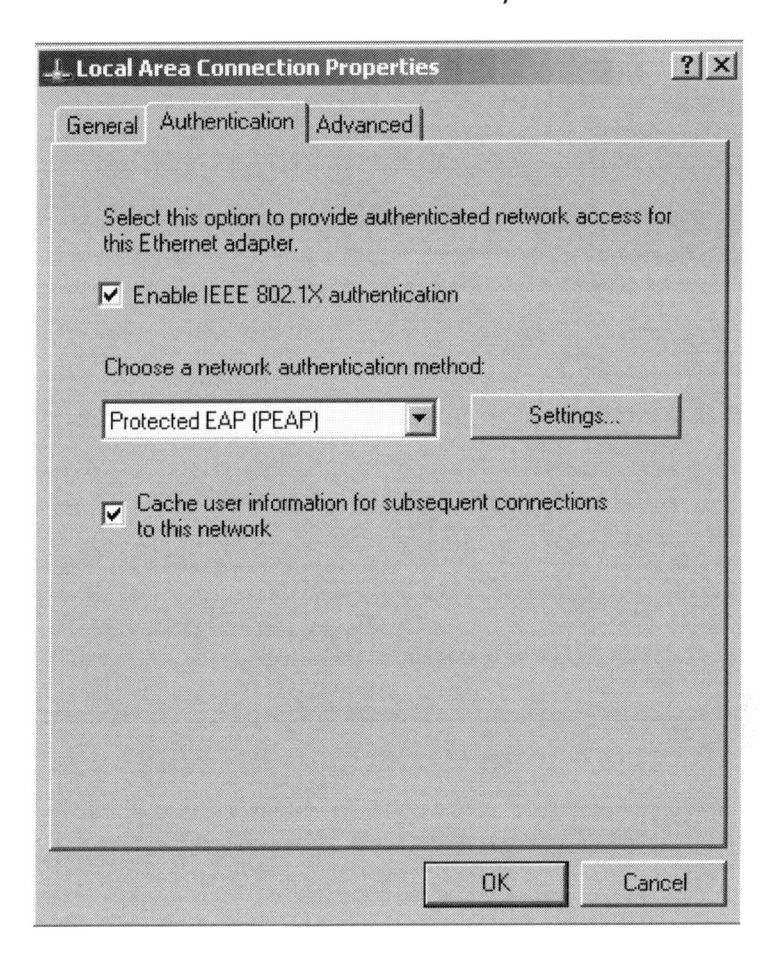

By default it will have 802.1X authentication enabled and PEAP is selected. Press "Settings" to continue.

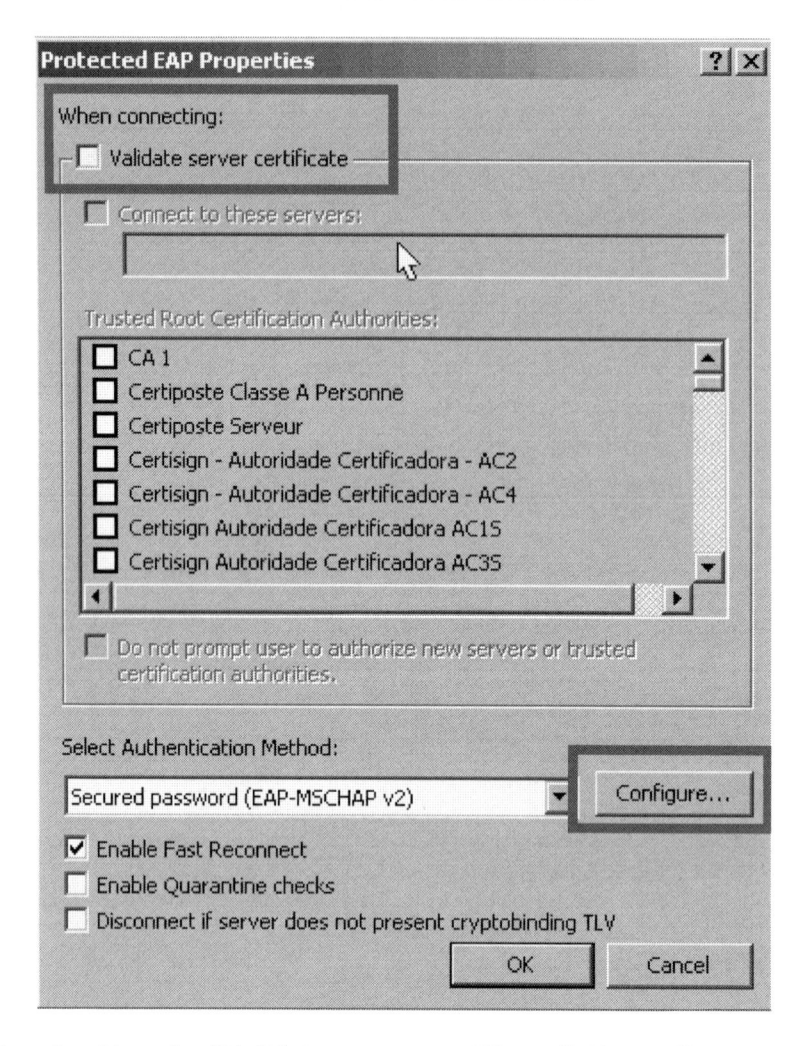

Disable the checkbox for "Validate server certificate". Normally you can use this so the client can check the authenticity of the RADIUS server. Click on the "Configure" button to continue.

Disable the checkbox here or it will use your Windows credentials by default to authenticate. Click on OK on all windows until they all disappear.

16. Switch Security

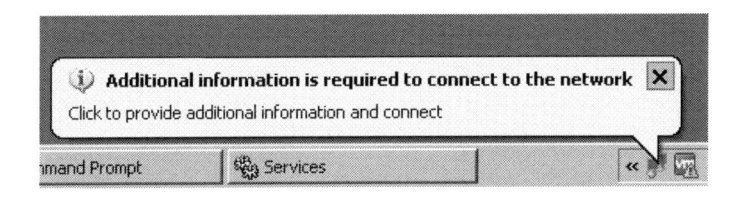

You should now see this pop-up in the notification screen. If not just unplug the network cable or disable/enable your network card.

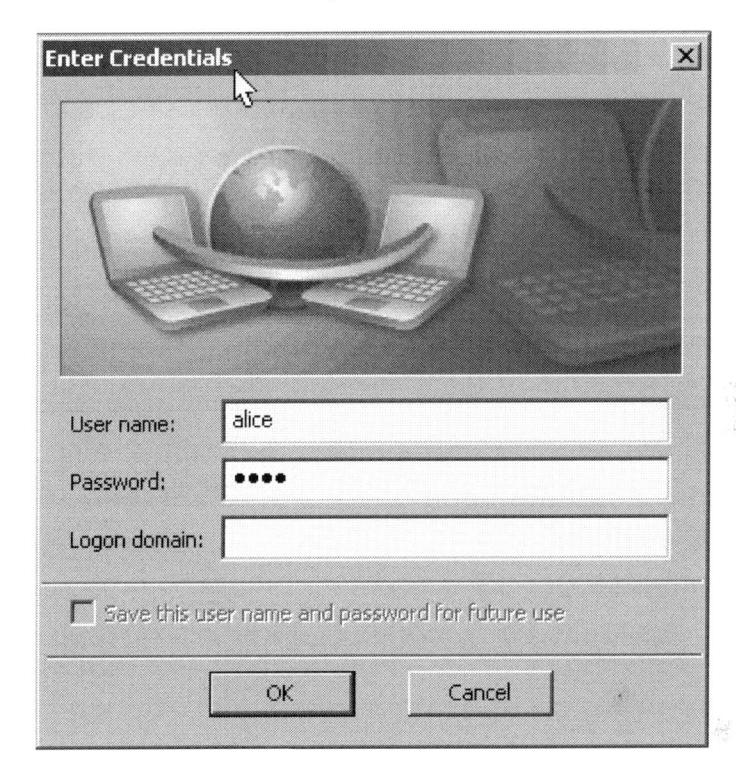

Click on the pop-up and you'll be asked for your credentials. Type in the username and password that you configured in Elektron RADIUS server and press OK.

359

If everything went OK you should now be connected!

```
C:\Documents and Settings\ComputerA>ping 192.168.1.100

Pinging 192.168.1.100 with 32 bytes of data:

Reply from 192.168.1.100: bytes=32 time=3ms TTL=255
Reply from 192.168.1.100: bytes=32 time<1ms TTL=255
Reply from 192.168.1.100: bytes=32 time<1ms TTL=255
Reply from 192.168.1.100: bytes=32 time=1ms TTL=255

Ping statistics for 192.168.1.100:
    Packets: Sent = 4, Received = 4, Lost = 0 (0% loss),
Approximate round trip times in milli-seconds:
    Minimum = 0ms, Maximum = 3ms, Average = 1ms
```

As you can see I can ping SwitchA from ComputerA. I haven't configured a DHCP server so I had to configure the IP address manually.

That's how you configure 802.1X for clients with a RADIUS server. This is a very secure solution because we now have user authentication on the interface level. The downside of this solution is that you need to do so some (minor) configuration on the client devices like I Just did on my Windows XP machine.

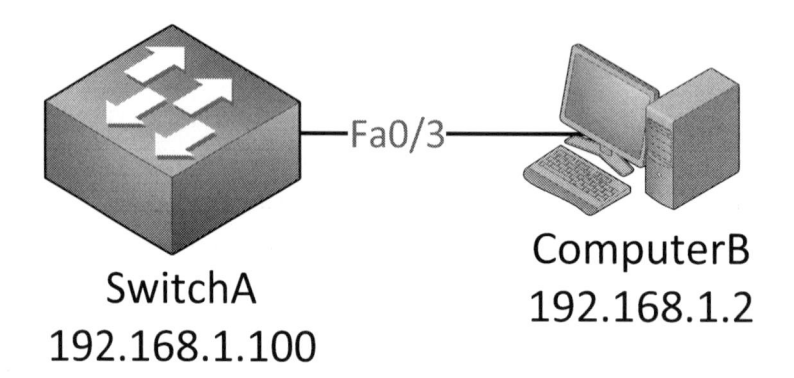

SwitchA — Fa0/3 — ComputerB
192.168.1.100   192.168.1.2

One more example I want to show you. We can use AAA to authenticate users trying to gain access through telnet to the switch. I have added ComputerB which is connected to SwitchA. The interface is up and running and the devices can reach each other.

```
SwitchA(config)#aaa new-model
SwitchA(config)#radius-server host 192.168.1.101 auth-port 1812
key sharedpass
```

Enable AAA globally and configure a RADIUS server. In my topology picture I don't have a RADIUS server because I want to show you the fallback feature of AAA.

16. Switch Security

```
SwitchA(config)#aaa authentication login default group radius local
```

Pay attention to the command above. I'm configuring my switch so it has to use AAA for **login** and to use the default group of RADIUS servers. When the RADIUS servers are unavailable it should switch to **local authentication.**

```
SwitchA(config)#username john password mypass
```

Whenever the RADIUS server is unavailable it will check the local database for credentials. Make sure you create a user account with the **username** command.

```
SwitchA(config)#line vty 0 4
SwitchA(config-line)#login authentication default
```

Configure the VTY lines so it uses the AAA information for authentication.

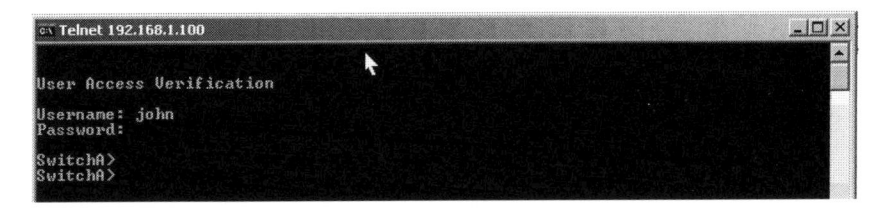

```
Telnet 192.168.1.100

User Access Verification

Username: john
Password:
SwitchA>
SwitchA>
```

If you try to telnet to the switch it will ask for your credentials. It will take a while because SwitchA first tries to reach the RADIUS server which isn't available. It will then check for the local usernames and grant you access.

Once you enable AAA it will use AAA default group authentication for all lines **including the console line!** This means you'll have to enter credentials when you try to access the console port (blue cisco cable). If you don't want this to happen we have to add something to our configuration:

```
SwitchA(config)#aaa authentication login NOAUTH none
```

First I'll create an AAA group called NOAUTH that requires no authentication.

```
SwitchA(config)#line con 0
SwitchA(config-line)#login authentication NOAUTH
```

Tell SwitchA to use the NOAUTH AAA group on the console so it will never ask for credentials. This is everything I want to show you on AAA and 802.1X. Let's continue to the next security issue.

361

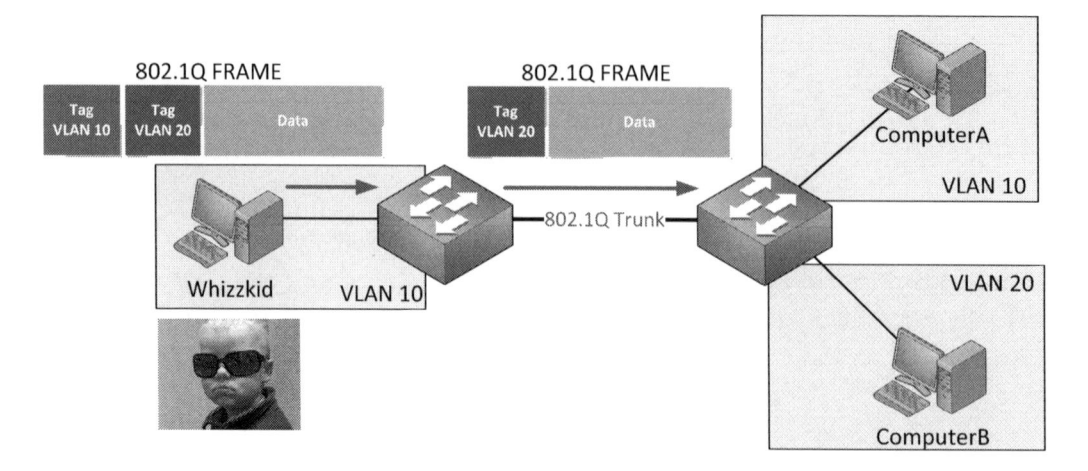

VLAN hopping is an attack where the attacker will send Ethernet Frames with two 802.1Q tags on it. In my picture above the whizzkid is sending an Ethernet frame that has been tagged for VLAN 10 and VLAN 20.

The switch on the left side will strip the VLAN 10 tag and forward the frame to the switch on the right side. The frame still has a tag for VLAN 20 when it arrives at the switch on the right side. The tag will be removed and the Ethernet frame will be forwarded to ComputerB in VLAN 20. The attacker has successfully "hopped" from VLAN 10 to VLAN 20.

In order to stop this you should do a couple of things that I showed you in the "VLANs and Trunks" chapter:

- Disable DTP (Dynamic Trunking Protocol). You don't want interfaces that connect to computers or clients to dynamically become trunk ports.
- Don't allow all VLANs on trunk ports. If you don't need them...prune them!
- Place interfaces that are not in use in a separate VLAN, don't leave them in VLAN 1 which is the default.
- Shut interfaces that are not in use.

16. Switch Security

SwitchA

VLAN 10

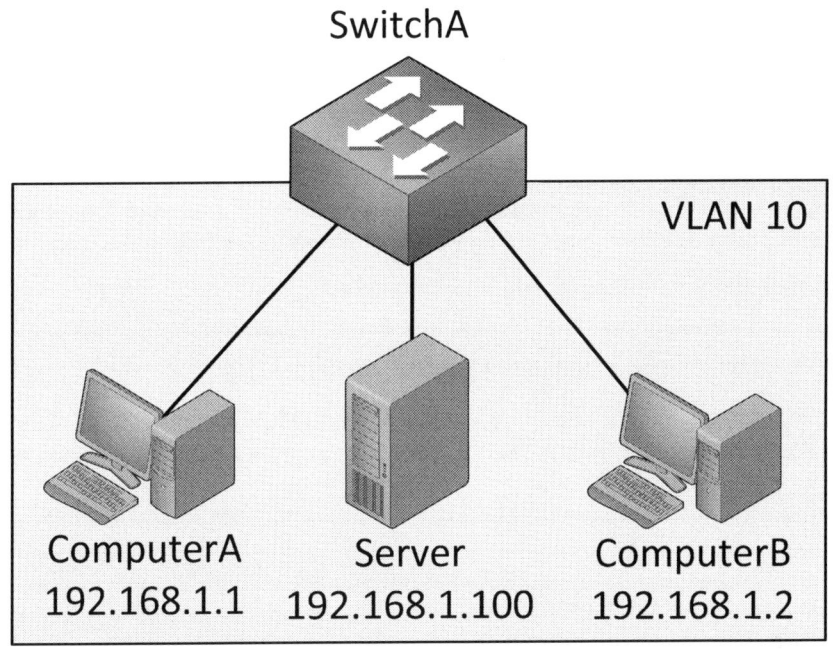

ComputerA: 192.168.1.1
Server: 192.168.1.100
ComputerB: 192.168.1.2

What if I have devices within the same VLAN and I want to enhance security? You saw port security before but it can only filter on MAC addresses. There are three kinds of access-lists we can use for filtering:

- **Routed ACL**: This is a standard or extended access-list applies to a layer 3 (router) interface.
- **Port ACL (PACL):** This is a standard or extended access-list applies to a layer 2 (switchport) interface.
- **VLAN ACL (VACL):** This one is new; a VACL will apply to **ALL** traffic within a VLAN.

Let's create a VACL for the example above. I'll show you how to create a VACL so ComputerA and ComputerB are unable to reach the server.

```
SwitchA(config)#access-list 100 permit ip any host 192.168.1.100
```

First step is to create an extended access-list. Traffic from any source to destination IP address 192.168.1.100 should match my access-list. This might look confusing to you because your gut will tell you to use "deny" in this statement...don't do it though, use the permit statement!

```
SwitchA(config)#vlan access-map NOT-TO-SERVER 10
SwitchA(config-access-map)#match ip address 100
SwitchA(config-access-map)#action drop
SwitchA(config-access-map)#vlan access-map NOT-TO-SERVER 20
SwitchA(config-access-map)#action forward
```

Next step is to create the VACL. Mine is called "NOT-TO-SERVER".

- Sequence number 10 will look for traffic that matches access-list 100. All traffic that is permitted in access-list 100 will match here. The action is to drop this traffic.
- Sequence number 20 doesn't have a match statement so everything will match, the action is to forward traffic.

As a result all traffic from any host to destination IP address 192.168.1.100 will be dropped, everything else will be forwarded.

```
SwitchA(config)#vlan filter NOT-TO-SERVER vlan-list 10
```

Last step is to apply the VACL to the VLANs you want. I apply mine to VLAN 10.

```
C:\Documents and Settings\ComputerA>ping 192.168.1.100

Pinging 192.168.4.4 with 32 bytes of data:

Request timed out.
Request timed out.
Request timed out.
Request timed out.

Ping statistics for 192.168.4.4:
    Packets: Sent = 4, Received = 0, Lost = 4 (100% loss),
```

ComputerA is no longer able to reach the server.

You can use VACLs to do some cool stuff, maybe you want to block IPv6 traffic for all hosts within a VLAN:

```
SwitchA(config)#mac access-list extended NO-IPV6
SwitchA(config-ext-macl)#permit any any 0x86DD 0x000
```

First I'll create a MAC access-list that filters on ethertypes. 0x86DD is the ethertype for IPv6 traffic.

```
SwitchA(config)#vlan access-map BLOCK-IPV6 10
SwitchA(config-access-map)#match mac address NO-IPV6
SwitchA(config-access-map)#action drop
SwitchA(config-access-map)#vlan access-map BLOCK-IPV6 20
SwitchA(config-access-map)#action forward
```

- Sequence number 10 will match traffic that is defined in MAC access-list "NO-IPV6". It will match on Ethernet frames with ethertype 0x86DD as defined in the MAC access-list. The action is to drop traffic.
- Sequence number 20 does not have a match statement so everything will match. The action is to forward traffic.

16. Switch Security

As a result IPv6 traffic will be dropped and all other traffic will be forwarded.

```
SwitchA(config)#vlan filter NOT-TO-SERVER vlan-list 20
```

Don't forget to enable it on an interface. I'll activate it on VLAN 20 this time.

That's all you need to know about VACLs. There are three more security issues I want to share with you that have to do with spoofing:

- **DHCP spoofing**
- **ARP spoofing**
- **IP spoofing**

Let's start with DHCP spoofing!

DHCP Server

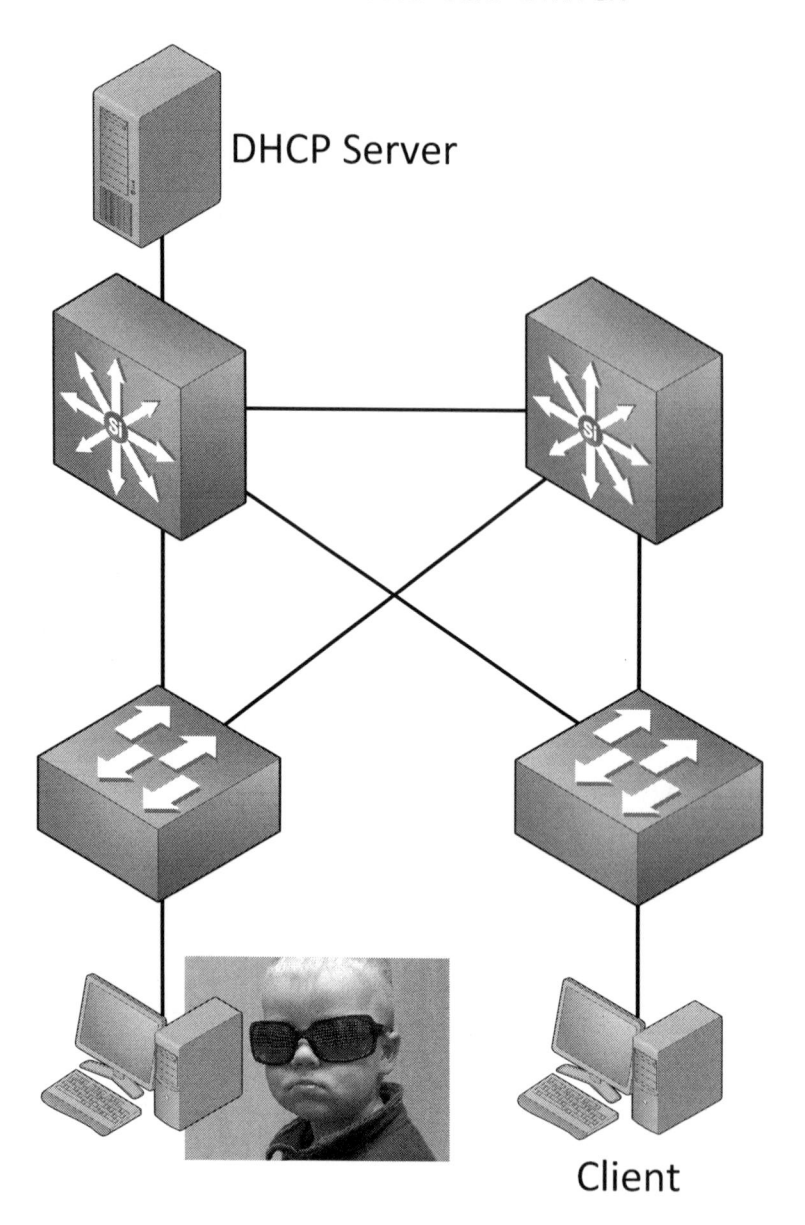

Client

In the picture above I have a DHCP server connected to the switch on the top left. At the bottom right you see a legitimate client that would like to get an IP address. What if ~~the l33t hacker~~ script kiddy on the left would run DHCP server software on his computer? Who do you think will respond first to the DHCP discover message? The legitimate DHCP server or the script kiddy's DHCP server software?

On larger networks you will probably find a central DHCP server somewhere in the server farm. If an attacker runs a DHCP server in the same subnet he will probably respond faster to the DHCP discover message of the client. If this succeeds he might assign the client with its own IP address as the default gateway for a man-in-the-middle attack. Another option would be to send your

16. Switch Security

own IP address as the DNS server so you can spoof websites etc.

The attacker could also send DHCP discover messages to the DHCP server and try to deplete its DHCP pool.

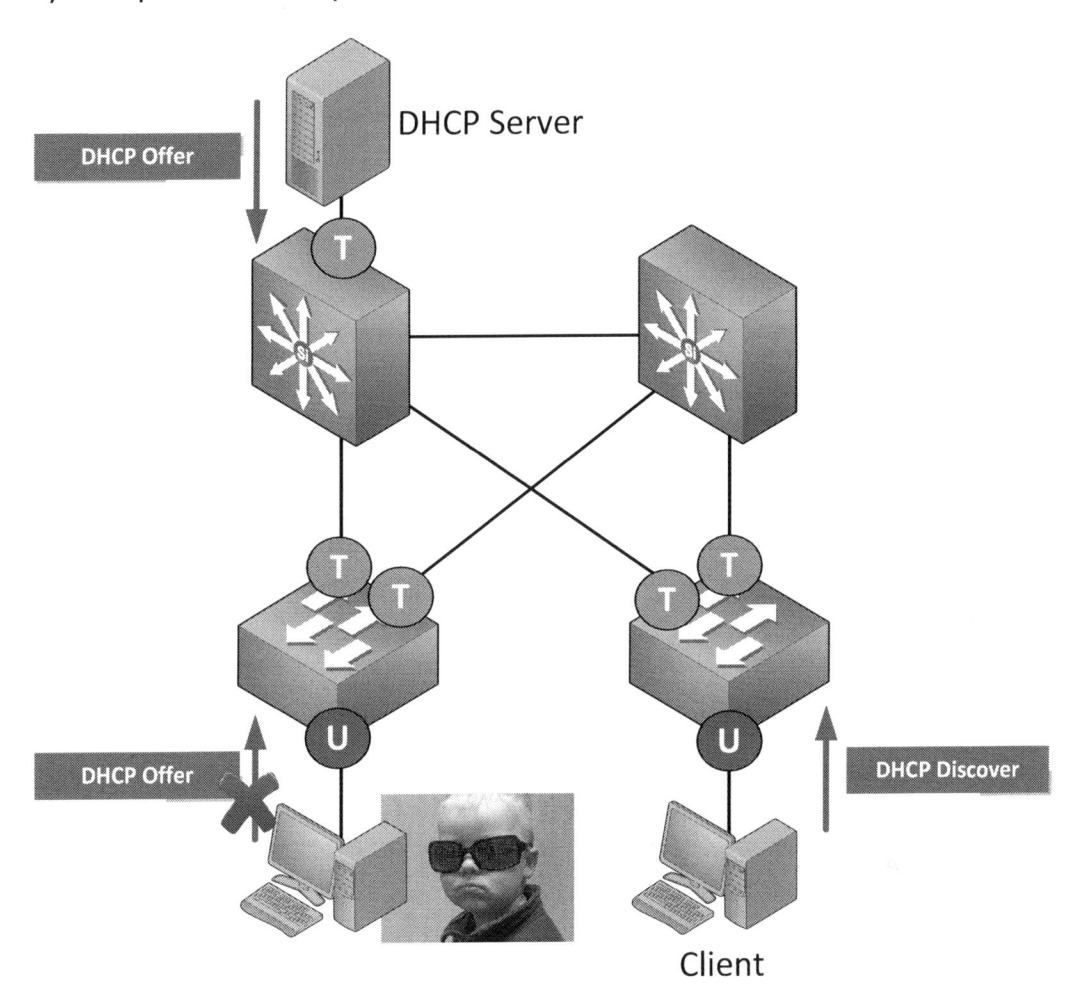

So what can we do to stop this madness? **DHCP snooping** to the rescue! We can configure our switches so they track the **DHCP discover** and **DHCP offer** messages. Interfaces that connect to clients should never be allowed to send a DHCP offer message. We can enforce this by making them **untrusted.** An interface that is untrusted will **block DHCP offer** messages. Only an interface that has been configured as **trusted** is **allowed** to forward DHCP offer messages. We can also **rate-limit** interfaces to they can't send an unlimited amount of DHCP discover messages, this will prevent attacks from depleting the DHCP pool.

Attacker DHCP Server

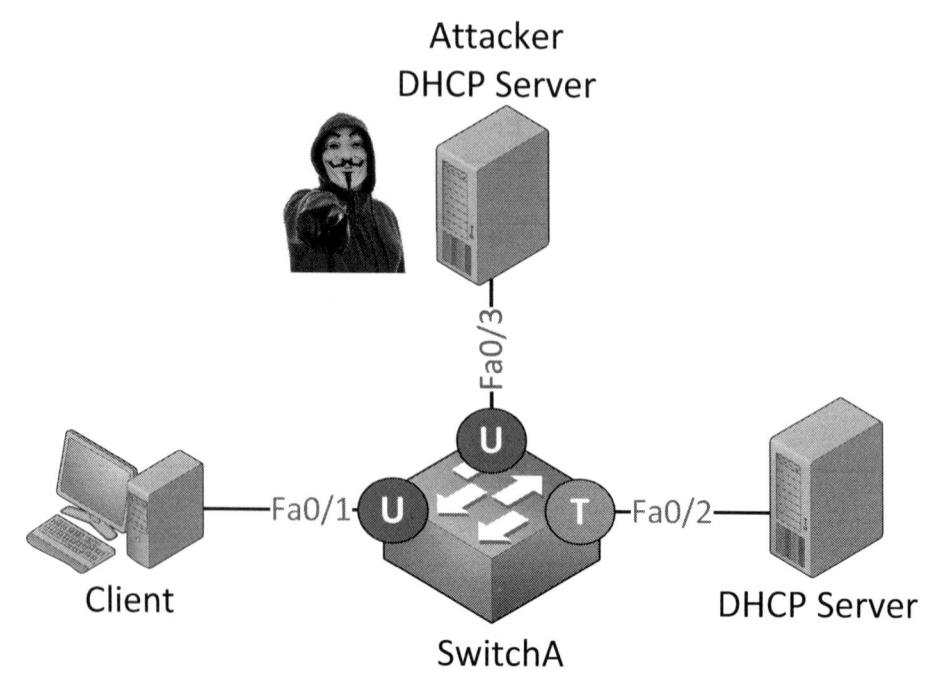

[Diagram: Attacker DHCP Server connected via Fa0/3 (U) to SwitchA. Client connected via Fa0/1 (U). DHCP Server connected via Fa0/2 (T).]

Client — Fa0/1 — SwitchA — Fa0/2 — DHCP Server

I'm going to show you how to configure DHCP snooping. Interface fa0/1 is connected to a client that would like to get an IP address from the DHCP server connected to interface fa0/2. There's an attacker connected to fa0/3 that is running DHCP server software. Let's see if we can stop him...

```
SwitchA(config)#ip dhcp snooping
```

First you need to enable DHCP snooping globally.

```
SwitchA(config)#no ip dhcp snooping information option
```

By default the switch will add option 82 to the DHCP discover message before passing it along to the DHCP server. Some DHCP servers don't like this and will drop the packet. If you client doesn't get an IP address anymore after enabling DHCP snooping globally you should use this command.

```
SwitchA(config)#ip dhcp snooping vlan 1
```

Select the VLANs for which you want to use DHCP snooping.

```
SwitchA(config)#interface fa0/2
SwitchA(config-if)#ip dhcp snooping trust
```

Once you enable DHCP snooping all interfaces by default are **untrusted.** Make sure interfaces that lead to the DHCP server are trusted.

16. Switch Security

```
SwitchA(config)#interface fa0/1
SwitchA(config-if)#ip dhcp snooping limit rate 10
```

Optionally you can rate-limit the number of DHCP packets that the interface can receive. I've set the fa0/1 interface so it can't receive more than 10 DHCP packets per second.

```
SwitchA#show ip dhcp snooping
Switch DHCP snooping is enabled
DHCP snooping is configured on following VLANs:
1
DHCP snooping is operational on following VLANs:
1
DHCP snooping is configured on the following L3 Interfaces:

Insertion of option 82 is enabled
   circuit-id format: vlan-mod-port
   remote-id format: MAC
Option 82 on untrusted port is not allowed
Verification of hwaddr field is enabled
Verification of giaddr field is enabled
DHCP snooping trust/rate is configured on the following
Interfaces:

Interface                    Trusted    Rate limit (pps)
------------------------     -------    ----------------
FastEthernet0/1              no         10
FastEthernet0/2              yes        unlimited
```

Use the show ip dhcp snooping command to verify your configuration.

```
SwitchA#show ip dhcp snooping binding
MacAddress         IpAddress         Lease(sec)     Type              VLAN
Interface
------------------ ---------------   ----------     --------------    ---- -
------------------
00:0C:29:28:5C:6C  192.168.1.1       85655          dhcp-snooping     1
FastEthernet0/1
```

Once your client receives an IP address from the legit DHCP server you can see SwitchA keeps track of the MAC to IP binding. DHCP offer messages from the DHCP server on the untrusted interface will be dropped.

> *If you are labbing this up keep in mind you can also use a multilayer switch or router as a DHCP server. A routed interface (layer 3) can be configured to use DHCP to configure an IP address with the "ip address dhcp" command.*

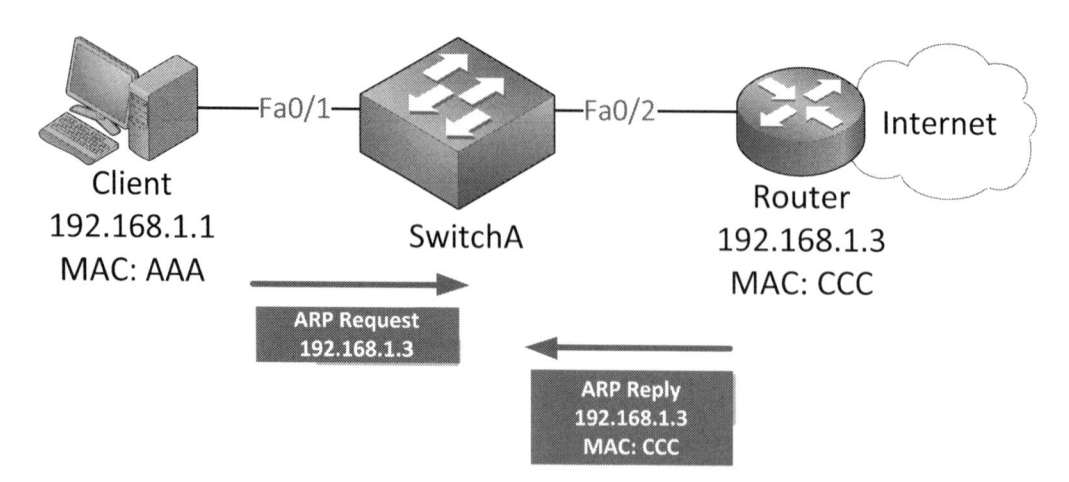

Besides DHCP snooping we also have to deal with **ARP poisoning**. In the example above I have a small network. The client on the left side is looking for the MAC address of the router on the right side. It will send an ARP request. The router will respond with a ARP reply and sends its MAC address towards the client. So far life is good...

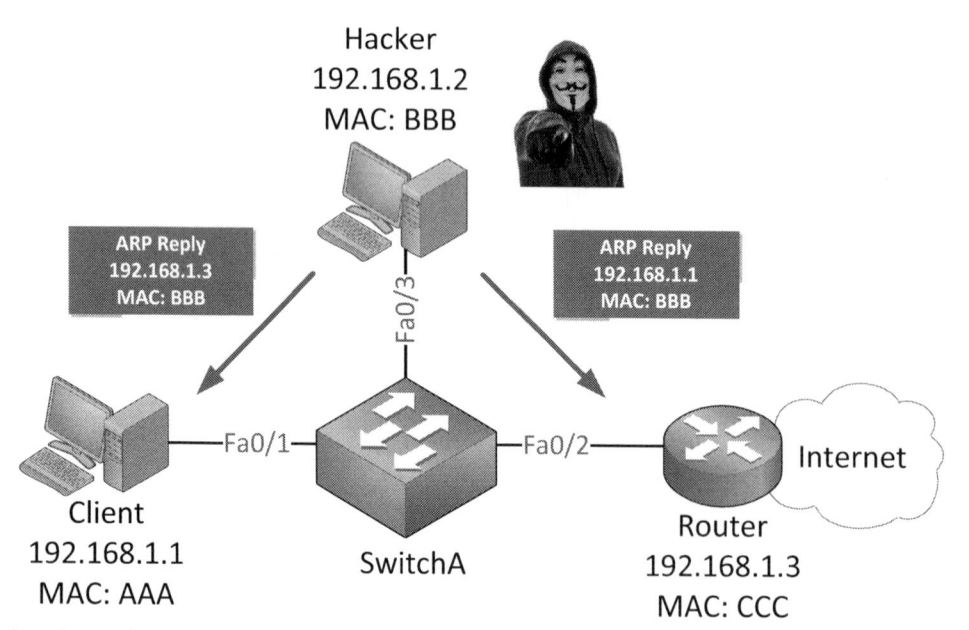

Here's when things can go wrong. A hacker is connected to the switch and sends **gratuitous ARPs** to our client and router. Basically what it does is send an ARP reply to the client claiming that 192.168.1.3 belongs to MAC address BBB. To the router it will send an ARP reply claiming that 192.168.1.1 belongs to MAC address BBB.
The client and router will update their ARP tables and send traffic meant for each other to the hacker's computer. We now have a man-in-the-middle attack.

16. Switch Security

ARP doesn't have any authentication so it's very easy to perform an ARP poisoning attack.

```
SwitchA#show ip dhcp snooping binding
MacAddress          IpAddress        Lease(sec)   Type              VLAN
Interface
------------------  ---------------  ----------   --------------    ----
------------------
00:0C:29:28:5C:6C   192.168.1.1      85655        dhcp-snooping     1
FastEthernet0/1
```

In the previous example we configured DHCP snooping and as a result the switch started saving the binding between MAC address and IP address. This information can be used to defend against ARP poisoning. This solution is called **DAI (Dynamic ARP Inspection)** and we can only use it if we have DHCP snooping up and running.

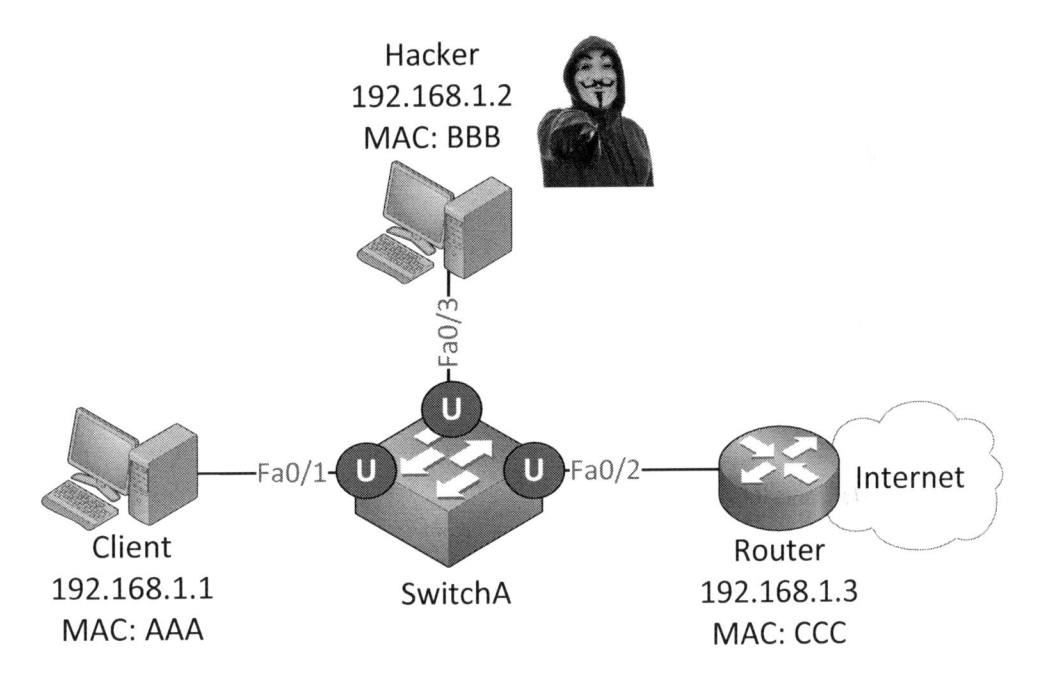

Hacker
192.168.1.2
MAC: BBB

Client
192.168.1.1
MAC: AAA

SwitchA

Router
192.168.1.3
MAC: CCC

Internet

Let's use this example to configure DAI.

```
SwitchA(config)#ip dhcp snooping
SwitchA(config)#ip dhcp snooping vlan 1
```

DHCP snooping is a prerequisite so make sure you enable it. I'm activating it only for VLAN 1.

```
SwitchA(config)#ip arp inspection vlan 1
```

DAI needs to be enabled per VLAN. Use the **ip arp inspection** command to do so. I've enabled it for VLAN 1 only. This is all you have to do to enable DAI.

371

```
SwitchA(config)#interface fa0/1
SwitchA(config-if)#ip arp inspection limit rate 10
```

Optionally you can set a limit to the number of ARP packets per second, as an example I've set mine to 10.

```
SwitchA#show ip arp inspection statistics

Vlan        Forwarded           Dropped         DHCP Drops          ACL
Drops
----        ---------           -------         ----------          ---------
-
   1            0                  0                0
0

Vlan      DHCP Permits      ACL Permits    Probe Permits      Source MAC
Failures
----      ------------      -----------    -------------      ----------
---------
   1            0                  0                0
0

Vlan      Dest MAC Failures     IP Validation Failures       Invalid
Protocol Data
----      -----------------     ----------------------       -------
----------
   1            0                         0
0
```

You can see the number of dropped ARP packets with the **show ip arp inspection statistics** command.

If you want to try an actual ARP poisoning attack you can take a look at the windows application "Cain & Abel". ARP poisoning is one of the many attacks this application can do. NEVER try this on a production network...only do this in a LAB environment. I'm not responsible for any possible damage or loss caused by applications like this one.

Anything else you need to know about security? There are two protocols left...

16. Switch Security

If you studied CCNA you probably know about CDP (Cisco Discovery Protocol). CDP can be very useful but it also has a security risk.

```
SwitchA#show cdp neighbors detail
-------------------------
Device ID: SwitchB
Entry address(es):
Platform: cisco WS-C3560-24PS,  Capabilities: Switch IGMP
Interface: FastEthernet0/15,  Port ID (outgoing port):
FastEthernet0/15
Holdtime : 136 sec

Version :
Cisco IOS Software, C3560 Software (C3560-ADVIPSERVICESK9-M),
Version 12.2(44)SE1, RELEASE SOFTWARE (fc1)
Copyright (c) 1986-2008 by Cisco Systems, Inc.
Compiled Fri 07-Mar-08 00:10 by weiliu

advertisement version: 2
Protocol Hello:  OUI=0x00000C, Protocol ID=0x0112; payload
len=27,
value=00000000FFFFFFFF010220FF000000000000019569D5700FF0000
VTP Management Domain: ''
Native VLAN: 1
Duplex: full
Management address(es): 2.2.2.2
```

As you can see CDP is giving away quite some information:

- IP address
- Model
- IOS Version

```
SwitchA(config)#no cdp run
```

Because of security reasons you might want to disable CDP. You can use the **no cdp run** command to disable it globally. CDP is **enabled by default.**

```
SwitchA(config)#interface fa0/1
SwitchA(config-if)#no cdp enable
```

You can also disable it on an interface level. I would recommend disabling CDP if you don't need it. You might require it for some devices like the Cisco phones.

373

CDP is **Cisco proprietary** and there's also another similar protocol that is a standard, it's called **LLDP (Link Layer Discovery Protocol).**

```
SwitchA(config)#lldp run
```

```
SwitchB(config)#lldp run
```

LLDP is **disabled by default** so you need to turn it on.

```
SwitchA#show lldp neighbors detail

Chassis id: 0019.569d.570f
Port id: Fa0/13
Port Description: FastEthernet0/13
System Name: SwitchB.cisco.com

System Description:
Cisco IOS Software, C3560 Software (C3560-ADVIPSERVICESK9-M),
Version 12.2(44)SE1, RELEASE SOFTWARE (fc1)
Copyright (c) 1986-2008 by Cisco Systems, Inc.
Compiled Fri 07-Mar-08 00:10 by weiliu

Time remaining: 118 seconds
System Capabilities: B,R
Enabled Capabilities: B
Management Addresses:
    IP: 2.2.2.2
Auto Negotiation - supported, enabled
Physical media capabilities:
    10base-T(HD)
    10base-T(FD)
    100base-TX(HD)
    100base-TX(FD)
Media Attachment Unit type: 16
```

You can see it looks similar to CDP. It has similar features like CDP.

```
SwitchA(config)#no lldp run
```

If you don't need it it's better to keep it disabled.

```
SwitchA(config)#interface fa0/1
SwitchA(config-if)#no lldp enable
```

Or if you need it you can disable it on certain interfaces.

That's all I have for you on switch security. You can see there's quite some stuff that possibly could go wrong. Does this mean you should enable everything we just looked at? Maybe but it really depends on the security required for your organization. If you want your users to authenticate

16. Switch Security

themselves with a fingerprint scan, iris scan, 60-character complex passwords and a one-time-password (token) you will increase security but it might not do much good to productivity. I'm exaggerating a bit but I think you get the message. It will also place a burden on network staff because they have to take care of more stuff.

The only thing I have left for you are a couple of labs, I would highly recommend taking a look at them:

http://gns3vault.com/Switching/vacl-vlan-access-list.html

http://gns3vault.com/Switching/dhcp-snooping.html

17. Final Thoughts

Here we are, you worked your way through all the different chapters that showed you how you can master the CCNP SWITCH exam. There is only one thing left for you to do and that's *labs, labs and even more labs!* The CCNP exam is very hands-on minded so you need to lab a lot to gain practical experience! If you want labs just visit http://gns3vault.com where I have about everything on CCNP SWITCH level. If you feel there is something missing drop me a message/mail/PM/twitter and I'll make sure to add a new lab.

One last word of advice: If you do a Cisco exam you always do the tutorial before you start the exam which takes 15 minutes. These 15 minutes are not taken from your exam time so this is valuable time you can spend creating your own cheat sheet or anything else you would like to dump from your brain onto paper.

I hope you enjoyed reading my book and truly learned something! If you have any questions or comments how you feel I could improve the book please let me know by sending an e-mail to info@renemolenaar.nl or drop a message at my website: http://gns3vault.com.

I wish you good luck practicing and mastering that CCNP exam!

Appendix A – How to create mindmaps

A mindmap is a diagram which consists of text, images or relationships between different items. Everything is ordered in a tree-like structure. In the middle of the mindmap you write down your subject. All the topics that have to do with your subject can be written down as a branch of your main subject. Each branch can have multiple branches where the pieces of information are leaves. Mindmaps are great because they show the relationship between different items where notes are just lists...

You can create mindmaps by drawing them yourself or use your computer. I prefer the second method because I can save / print them but also because I'm a faster at typing than writing.

You can download Xmind over here, it's free:

http://xmind.net

Once you have installed it and started a new project you can add some items.

Here's an example I created for CCNP SWITCH with some of the items, just to give you an impression:

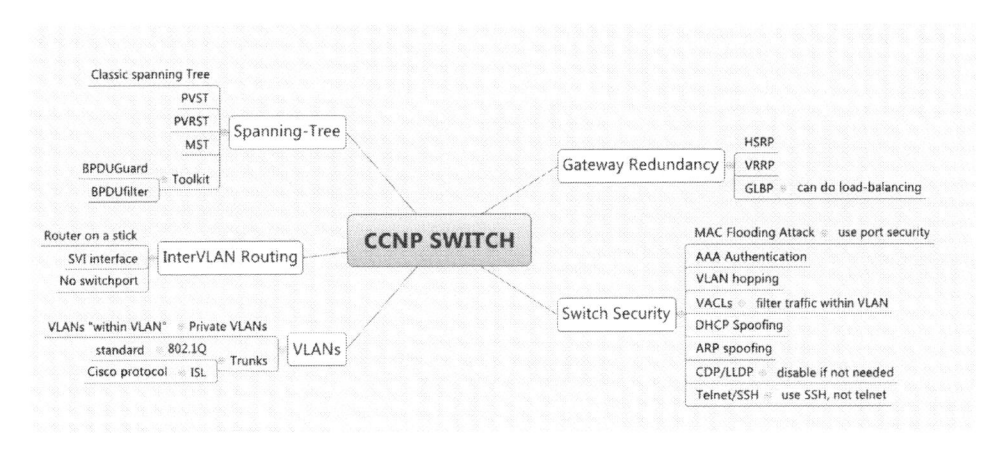

Just add all the items and build your own mind-map using your own words. Now you have a nice overview with all the stuff you need to remember but also the relationship between items. Give it a shot and see if you like it!

Printed in Great Britain
by Amazon